Evelyn Martinego-Cesaresco

The Liberation of Italy

1815-1870

Evelyn Martinego-Cesaresco

The Liberation of Italy
1815-1870

ISBN/EAN: 9783337229900

Printed in Europe, USA, Canada, Australia, Japan

Cover: Foto ©ninafisch / pixelio.de

More available books at **www.hansebooks.com**

THE

LIBERATION OF ITALY

1815-1870

BY THE
COUNTESS EVELYN MARTINENGO-CESARESCO
AUTHOR OF
'ITALIAN CHARACTERS IN THE EPOCH OF UNIFICATION' (*Patriotti Italiani*), ETC.

WITH PORTRAITS

LONDON
SEELEY AND CO. LIMITED
ESSEX STREET, STRAND
1895

PREFACE

THE old figure of speech 'in the fulness of time' embodies a truth too often forgotten. History knows nothing of spontaneous generation; the chain of cause and effect is unbroken, and however modest be the scale on which an historical work is cast, the reader has a right to ask that it should give him some idea, not only of what happened, but of why it happened. A catalogue of dates and names is as meaningless as the photograph of a crowd. In the following retrospect, I have attempted to trace the principal factors that worked towards Italian unity. The Liberation of Italy is a cycle waiting to be turned into an epic.

In other words, it presents the appearance of a series of detached episodes, but the parts have an intimate connection with the whole, which, as time wears on, will constantly emerge into plainer light. Every year brings with it the issue of documents, letters, memoirs, that help to unravel the tangled threads in which this subject has been enveloped, and which have made it less generally understood than the two other great struggles of the century, the American fight for the Union, and the unification of Germany.

I cannot too strongly state my indebtedness to the voluminous literature which has grown up in Italy round the *Risorgimento* since its completion; yet it must not be supposed that the witness of contemporaries published from hour to hour, in every European tongue, while the events were going on, has become or will ever become valueless. I have had access to a collection of these older writings, formed with much care between the years 1850-1870, and some authorities that were wanting, I found in the library of Sir James Hudson, given by him to Count Giuseppe Martinengo Cesaresco after he left the British legation at Turin.

There are, of course, many books in which the affairs of Italy figure only incidentally, which ought to be consulted by anyone who wishes to study the inner working of the Italian movement. Of such are Lord Castlereagh's *Despatches and Correspondence*, and the autobiographies of Prince Metternich and Count Beust.

Perhaps I have been helped in describing the events clearly, by the fact that I am familiar with almost all the places where they occurred, from the heights of Calatafimi to the unhappy rock of Lissa. Wherever the language of the *Si* sounds, we tread upon the history of the Revolution that achieved what a great English orator once called, 'the noblest work ever undertaken by man.'

The supreme interest of the re-casting of Italy arises from the new spectacle of a nation made one not by conquest but by consent. Above and beyond the other causes that contributed to the conclusion must always be reckoned the gathering of an emotional wave, only comparable to the phenomena displayed by the mediæval religious revivals. Sentiment, it is said, is what makes the real historical miracles. A writer on Italian Liberation would be indeed misleading who failed to take account of the passionate longing which stirred and swayed even the most outwardly cold of those who took part in it, and nerved an entire people to heroic effort.

Salò, Lago di Garda.

CONTENTS

CHAPTER I
RESURGAM
Italy from the Battle of Lodi to the Congress of Vienna, . page 1

CHAPTER II
THE WORK OF THE CARBONARI
Revolutions in the Kingdom of Naples and in Piedmont—The Conspiracy against Charles Albert, ... 21

CHAPTER III
PRISON AND SCAFFOLD
Political Trials in Venetia and Lombardy—Risings in the South and Centre—Ciro Menotti, ... 40

CHAPTER IV
YOUNG ITALY
Accession of Charles Albert—Mazzini's Unitarian Propaganda—The Brothers Bandiera, ... 56

CHAPTER V
THE POPE LIBERATOR
Events leading to the Election of Pius IX.—The Petty Princes—Charles Albert, Leopold and Ferdinand, . . . 71

CHAPTER VI
THE YEAR OF REVOLUTION

Insurrection in Sicily—The Austrians expelled from Milan and Venice—Charles Albert takes the Field—Withdrawal of the Pope and King of Naples—Piedmont defeated—The Retreat, . . . page 91

CHAPTER VII
THE DOWNFALL OF THRONES

Garibaldi arrives—Venice under Manin—The Dissolution of the Temporal Power—Republics at Rome and Florence, . . . 120

CHAPTER VIII
AT BAY

Novara—Abdication of Charles Albert—Brescia crushed—French Intervention—The Fall of Rome—The Fall of Venice, ... 137

CHAPTER IX
'J'ATTENDS MON ASTRE'

The House of Savoy—A King who Keeps his Word—Sufferings of the Lombards—Charles Albert's death, ... 165

CHAPTER X
THE REVIVAL OF PEIDMONT

Restoration of the Pope and Grand-Duke of Tuscany—Misrule at Naples—The Struggle with the Church in Piedmont—The Crimean War, 183

CHAPTER XI
PREMONITIONS OF THE STORM

Pisacane's Landing—Orsini's Attempt—The Compact of Plombières—Cavour's Triumph, ... 208

CHAPTER XII

THE WAR FOR LOMBARDY

Austria declares War — Montebello — Garibaldi's Campaign — Palestro — Magenta — The Allies enter Milan — Ricasoli saves Italian Unity — Accession of Francis II. — Solferino — The Armistice of Villafranca,   page 227

CHAPTER XIII

WHAT UNITY COST

Napoleon III. and Cavour — The Cession of Savoy and Nice — Annexations in Central Italy, ... 251

CHAPTER XIV

THE MARCH OF THE THOUSAND

Origin of the Expedition — Garibaldi at Marsala — Calatafimi — The Taking of Palermo — Milazzo — The Bourbons evacuate Sicily, . . 266

CHAPTER XV

THE MEETING OF THE WATERS

Garibaldi's March on Naples — The Piedmontese in Umbria and the Marches — The Volturno. Victor Emmanuel enters Naples, . 298

CHAPTER XVI

BEGINNINGS OF THE ITALIAN KINGDOM

The Fall of Gaeta — Political Brigandage — The Proclamation of the Italian Kingdom — Cavour's Death, ... 326

CHAPTER XVII

'ROME OR DEATH!'

Cavour's Successors — Aspromonte — The September Convention — Garibaldi's Visit to England, ... 340

CHAPTER XVIII
THE WAR FOR VENICE

The Prussian Alliance—Custoza—Lissa—The Volunteers—Acquisition of Venetia, ... page 356

CHAPTER XIX
THE LAST CRUSADE

The French leave Rome—Garibaldi's Arrest and Escape—The Second French Intervention—Monte Rotondo—Mentana, . . . 381

CHAPTER XX
ROME THE CAPITAL

M. Rouher's 'Never!'—Papal Infallibility—Sédan—The Breach in Porta Pia—The King of Italy in Rome, ... 397

LIST OF ILLUSTRATIONS

	PAGE
GIUSEPPE GARIBALDI,	*Frontispiece*
GIUSEPPE MAZZINI,	60
KING VICTOR EMMANUEL,	166
COUNT CAVOUR,	192

xii

The Liberation of Italy

CHAPTER I

RESURGAM

Italy from the Battle of Lodi to the Congress of Vienna.

THE unity of Italy, which the statesmen of Europe and all save a small number of the Italians themselves still regarded as an utopia when it was on the verge of accomplishment, was, nevertheless, desired and foreseen by the two greatest intellects produced by the Italian race. Dante conceived an Italy united under the Empire, which returning from a shameful because self-imposed exile would assume its natural seat in Rome. To him it was a point of secondary interest that the Imperial Lord happened to be bred beyond the Alps, that he was of Teutonic, not of Latin blood. If the Emperor brought the talisman of his authority to the banks of the Tiber, Italy would overcome the factions which rent her, and would not only rule herself, but lead mankind. Vast as the vision was, Dante cannot be called presumptuous for having entertained it. The Rome of the Cæsars, the Rome of the Popes, had each transformed the world: Italy was transforming it for a third time at that moment by the spiritual awakening which, beginning with the Renaissance, led by inevitable steps to the Reformation. The great Florentine poet had the right to dream that his country was invested with a providential mission, that his people was a chosen people, which, by its own fault and by the fault of others, had lost its way, but would find it again. Such was Dante's so-called Ghibelline programme—less Ghibelline than intensely and magnificently Italian. His was a mind too mighty to be caged within the limits of partisan ambitions. The same may be said of Machiavelli. He also imagined, or rather discerned in the future, a regenerate Italy under a single head, and this, not the advancement of any particular man, was the grand event he endeavoured to hasten. With the impatience of a heart consumed by the single passion of patriotism, he conjured his fellow-countrymen to seize the first chance that presented itself, promising or unpromising, of reaching the goal. The concluding passage in the *Principe* was meant as an exhortation; it reads as a prophecy. 'We ought not therefore,' writes Machiavelli, 'to let this occasion pass whereby, after so long waiting, Italy may behold the coming of a saviour. Nor can I express with what love he would be received in all those provinces which have suffered from the foreign inundations; with what thirst of vengeance, with what obstinate faith, with what worship, with what tears! What doors would be closed against him? What people would deny him obedience? What jealousy would oppose him? What Italian would not do him honour? The barbarous dominion of the stranger stinks in the nostrils of all.'

Another man of genius, an Italian whom a fortuitous circumstance made the citizen and the master of a country not his own, grasped both the vital necessity of unity from an Italian point of view, and the certainty of its ultimate achievement. Napoleon's notes on the subject, written at

St Helena, sum up the whole question without rhetoric but with unanswerable logic:—'Italy is surrounded by the Alps and the sea. Her natural limits are defined with as much exactitude as if she were an island. Italy is only united to the Continent by 150 leagues of frontier, and these 150 leagues are fortified by the highest barrier that can be opposed to man. Italy, isolated between her natural limits, is destined to form a great and powerful nation. Italy is one nation; unity of customs, language and literature must, within a period more or less distant, unite her inhabitants under one sole government. And Rome will, without the slightest doubt, be chosen by the Italians as their capital.'

Unlike Dante and Machiavelli, who could only sow the seed, not gather the fruit, the man who wrote these lines might have made them a reality. Had Napoleon wished to unite Italy—had he had the greatness of mind to proclaim Rome the capital of a free and independent state instead of turning it into the chief town of a French department—there was a time when he could plainly have done it. Whether redemption too easily won would have proved a gain or a loss in the long run to the populations welded together, not after their own long and laborious efforts, but by the sudden exercise of the will of a conqueror, is, of course, a different matter. The experiment was not tried. Napoleon, whom the simple splendour of such a scheme ought to have fascinated, did a very poor thing instead of a very great one: he divided Italy among his relations, keeping the lion's share for himself.

Napoleon's policy in Italy was permanently compromised by the abominable sale of Venice, with her two thousand years of freedom, to the empire which, as no one knew better than he did, was the pivot of European despotism. After that transaction he could never again come before the Italians with clean hands; they might for a season make him their idol, carried away by the intoxication of his fame; they could never trust him in their inmost conscience. The ruinous consequences of the Treaty of Campo Formio only ceased in 1866. The Venetians have been severely blamed, most of all by Italian historians, for making Campo Formio possible by opening the door to the French six months before. Napoleon could not have bartered away Venice if it had not belonged to him. The reason that it belonged to him was that, on the 12th of May 1797, the Grand Council committed political suicide by dissolving the old aristocratic form of government, in compliance with a mere rumour, conveyed to them through the ignoble medium of a petty shopkeeper, that such was the wish of General Buonaparte. In extenuation of their fatal supineness, it may be urged that they felt the inherent weakness of an oligarchy out of date; and in the second place, that the victor of Lodi, the deliverer of Lombardy, then in the first flush of his scarcely tarnished glory, was a dazzling figure, calculated indeed to turn men's heads. But, after all, the only really valid excuse for them would have been that Venice lacked the means of defence, and this was not the case. She had 14,000 regular troops, 8000 marines, a good stock of guns—how well she might have resisted the French, had they, which was probable, attacked her, was to be proved in 1849. Her people, moreover, that *basso popolo* which nowhere in the world is more free from crime, more patient in suffering, more intelligent and public-spirited than in Venice, was anxious and ready to resist; when the nobles offered themselves a sacrifice on the Gallic altar by welcoming the proposed democratic institutions, the populace, neither hoodwinked nor scared into hysterics, rose to the old cry of San Marco, and attempted a righteous reaction, which was only smothered when the treacherous introduction of French troops by night on board Venetian vessels settled the doom of Venice's independence.

'Under all circumstances,' Napoleon wrote to the Venetian Municipality, 'I shall do what lies in my power to prove to you my desire to see your liberty consolidated, and miserable Italy assume, at last, a glorious place, free and independent of strangers.' On the 10th of the following October he made over Venice to Austria, sending as a parting word the cynical message to the Venetians 'that they were little fitted for liberty: if they were capable of appreciating it, and had the virtue necessary for acquiring it well and good; existing circumstances gave them an excellent opportunity of proving it. At the time, the act of betrayal was generally regarded as part of a well-considered plot laid by the French Directory, but it seems certain that it was not made known to that body before it was carried out, and that with Napoleon himself it was a sort of after-thought, sprung from the desire to patch up an immediate peace with Austria on account of the appointment of Hoche to the chief command of the army in Germany. The god to which he immolated Venice was the selfish fear lest another general should reap his German laurels.

Venice remained for eight years under the Austrians, who thereby obtained what, in flagrant perversion of the principles on which the Congress of Vienna professed to act, was accepted in 1815 as their title-deeds to its possession. Meanwhile, after the battle of Austerlitz, the city of the sea was tossed back to Napoleon, who incorporated it in the newly-created kingdom of Italy, which no more corresponded to its name than did the Gothic kingdom of which he arrogated to himself the heirship, when, placing the Iron Crown of Theodolinda upon his brow, he uttered the celebrated phrase: 'Dieu me l'a donnée, gare à qui la touche.'

This is not the place to write a history of French supremacy in Italy, but several points connected with it must be glanced at, because, without bearing them in mind, it is impossible to understand the events which followed. The viceroyalty of Eugène Beauharnais in North Italy, and the government of Joseph Buonaparte, and afterwards of Joachim Murat, in the South, brought much that was an improvement on what had gone before: there were better laws, a better administration, a quickening of intelligence. 'The French have done much for the regeneration of Italy,' wrote an English observer in 1810; 'they have destroyed the prejudices of the inhabitants of the small states of Upper Italy by uniting them; they have done away with the Pope; they have made them soldiers.' But there was the reverse side of the medal: the absence everywhere of the national spirit which alone could have consolidated the new *régime* on a firm basis; the danger which the language ran of losing its purity by the introduction of Gallicisms; the shameless robbery of pictures, statues, and national heirlooms of every kind for the replenishment of French museums; the bad impression left in the country districts by the abuses committed by the French soldiery on their first descent, and kept alive by the blood-tax levied in the persons of thousands of Italian conscripts sent to die, nobody knew where or why; the fields untilled, and Rachel weeping for her children: all these elements combined in rendering it difficult for the governments established under French auspices to survive the downfall of the man to whose sword they owed their existence.

Their dissolution was precipitated, however, by the discordant action of Murat and Eugène Beauharnais. Had these two pulled together, whatever the issue was it would have differed in much from what actually happened. Murat was jealous of Eugène, and did not love his brother-in-law, who had annoyed and thwarted him through his whole reign; he was uneasy about his Neapolitan throne, and, in all likelihood, was already dreaming of acquiring the crown of an independent Italy. Throwing off his allegiance to Napoleon, he imagined the vain thing that he might gain his object by taking sides with the Austrians. It must be remembered that there was a time when the Allied Powers had distinctly contemplated Italian independence as a dyke to France, and there were people foolish enough to think that Austria, now she felt herself as strong as she had then felt weak, would consent to such a plan. Liberators, self-called, were absolutely swarming in Italy; Lord William Bentinck was promising entire emancipation from Leghorn; the Austrian and English allies in Romagna ransacked the dictionary for expressions in praise of liberty; an English officer was made the mouthpiece for the lying assurance of the Austrian Emperor Francis, that he had no intention of re-asserting any claims to the possession of Lombardy or Venetia.

In 1814, Napoleon empowered Prince Eugène to adopt whatever attitude he thought best fitted to make head against Austria; for himself, he resigned the Iron Crown, and his Italian soldiers were freed from their oaths. It was not, therefore, Eugène's loyal scruples which prevented him from throwing down a grand stake when he led his 60,000 men to the attack. It was want of genius, or of what would have done instead, a flash of genuine enthusiasm for the Italian idea. In place of appealing to all Italians to unite in winning a country, he appealed to one sentiment only, fidelity to Napoleon, which no longer woke any echo in the hearts of a population that had grown more and more to associate the name of the Emperor with exactions which never came to an end, and with wars which had not now even the merit of being successful. It is estimated that although the Italian troops amply proved the truth of Alfieri's maxim, that 'the plant man is more vigorous in Italy than elsewhere,' by bearing the hardships and resisting the cold in Russia better than the soldiers of any other nationality, nevertheless 26,000 Italians were lost in the retreat from Moscow. That happened a year ago. Exhausted patience got the better of judgment; in April 1814, the Milanese committed the irremediable error of revolting against their Viceroy, who commanded the only army which could still save Italy: the pent-up passions of a long period broke loose, the peasants from the country, who had always hated the French, flooded the streets of Milan, and allying themselves unimpeded with the dregs of the townsfolk, they murdered with great brutality General Prina, the Minister of Finance, whose remarkable abilities had been devoted towards raising funds for the Imperial Exchequer. Personally incorruptible, Prina was looked upon as the general representative of French voracity; he met his death with the utmost calmness, only praying that he might be the last victim. No one else was, in fact, killed, and next day quiet was resumed, but the affair had another victim—Italy. You cannot change horses when you are crossing a stream. Prince Eugène was in Mantua with a fine army, practically intact, though it had suffered some slight reverses; the fortress was believed to be impregnable; by merely waiting, Eugène might, if nothing else, have exacted favourable terms. But the news of Prina's murder, and the blow dealt at his own authority in Milan, caused him to give over the fortress and the army to the Austrians without more ado; an act which looked like revenge, but it was most likely prompted by moral cowardice. The capitulation signed with Field-Marshal Bellegarde on the 23rd of April, so exasperated the army that the officers in command of the garrison decided to arrest Eugène, but it was found that he was already on his way to Germany, taking with him his treasure, in accordance with a secret agreement entered into with the Austrian Field-Marshal. Such was the end to the Italian career of Eugène Beauharnais.

For the *Beau Sabreur* another ending was in store. Back on Napoleon's side in 1815, his Austrian allies having given him plenty of reason for suspecting their sincerity, he issued from Rimini, on the 30th of March, the proclamation of an independent Italy from the Alps to Sicily. There was no popular reply to his call. Italy, prostrate and impoverished, was unequal to a great resolve. The Napoleonic legend was not only dead, but buried; Napoleon had literally no friends left in Italy except those of his old soldiers who had managed to get back to their homes, many of them deprived of an arm or a leg, but so toughened that they lived to great ages. These cherished to their last hour the worship of their Captain, which it was his highest gift to be able to inspire. 'I have that feeling for him still, that if he were to rise from the dead I should go to him, if I could, wherever he was,' said the old conscript Emmanuele Gaminara of Genoa, who died at nearly a hundred in a Norfolk village in 1892: the last, perhaps, of the Italian veterans, and the type of them all.

But a few scattered invalids do not make a nation, and the Italian nation in 1815 had not the least wish to support any one who came in the name of Napoleon. So Murat failed without even raising a strong current of sympathy. Beaten by the Austrians at Tolentino on the 3rd of May, he retreated with his shattered army. In the last desperate moment, he issued the constitution which he ought to have granted years before. Nothing could be of any avail now; his admirable Queen, the best of all the House of Buonaparte, surrendered Naples to the English admiral; and Murat, harried by a crushing Austrian force, renounced his kingdom on the 30th of May. After Waterloo, when a price was set on his head in France, he meditated one more forlorn hope; but, deserted by the treachery of his few followers, and driven out of his course by the violence of the waves, he was thrown on the coast of Calabria with only twenty-six men, and was shot by order of Ferdinand of Naples, who especially directed that he should be only allowed half-an-hour for his religious duties after sentence had been delivered by the mock court-martial. His dauntless courage did not desert him: he died like a soldier. It was a better end for an Italian prince than escaping with money-bags to Germany. Great as were Murat's faults, an Italian should remember that it was he who first took up arms to the cry which was later to redeem Italy: independence from Alps to sea; and if he stand on the ill-omened shore of Pizzo, he need not refuse to uncover his head in silence.

When Mantua surrendered, the Milanese sent a deputation to Paris with a view of securing for Lombardy the position of an independent kingdom under an Austrian prince. They hoped to obtain the first by acquiescing in the second. They were aroused from their unheroic illusions with startling rapidity. Lord Castlereagh, to whom they went first (for they fancied that the English were interested in liberty), referred them 'to their master, the Austrian Emperor.' The Emperor Francis replied to their memorial that Lombardy was his by right of conquest; they would hear soon enough at Milan what orders he had to give them. Even after that, the distracted Lombards hoped that the English at Genoa would befriend them. All uncertainty ceased on the 23rd of May 1814, when Field-Marshal Bellegarde formally took possession of Lombardy on behalf of his Sovereign, dissolved the Electoral Colleges, and proclaimed himself Regent. There was no question of reviving the conditions under which Austria ruled Lombardy while there was still a German Empire: conditions which, though despotic in theory, were comparatively easy-going in practice, and did not exclude the native element from the administration. Henceforth the despotism was pure and simple; for Italians to even think of politics was an act of high treason.

It is not generally known that a British army ultimately sent to Spain was intended for Italy,* but its destination was changed because the Italians showed so little disposition to rise against Napoleon. The English Government was continually advised by its agents in Italy to make Sicily, which was wholly in its power, the *point d'appui* for a really great intervention in the destinies of the peninsula. 'The grand end of all the operations in the Mediterranean,' wrote one of Lord Castlereagh's correspondents, 'is the emancipation of Italy, and its union in one great state.' Lord William Bentinck urged that if Sicily were reunited to Naples under the Bourbons, liberty, established there by

* See *Memoirs of Lord Castlereagh*, 1848, Vol. i. p. 34.

his own incredible efforts, would be crushed, and the King would wreck vengeance on the Constitution and its supporters. Universal terror, he said, was felt at 'the unforgiving temper of their Majesties.' He strongly supported a course proposed for her own reasons by Queen Caroline: the purchase of Sicily by the English Government which could make it 'not only the model but the instrument of Italian independence.'

This way of talking was not confined to private despatches, and it was no wonder if the Italians were disappointed when they found that England declined to plead their cause with the Allies in Paris, and afterwards at Vienna. When charged directly with breach of faith before the House of Commons, Lord Castlereagh said that Austria, being 'in truth the great hinge on which the fate of mankind must ultimately depend,' had to be paid (this was exactly the sense, though not the form, of his defence) by letting her do what she liked with Italy. There is a certain brutal straightforwardness in the line of argument. Lord Castlereagh did not say that independence was not a good thing. He had tried to obtain it for Poland and had failed; he had not tried to obtain it for Italy, because he was afraid of offending Austria. At least he had the courage to tell the truth, and did not prate about the felicity of being subjects of the Austrian Emperor, as many English partisans of Austria prated in days to come.

The political map of Italy in the summer of 1814 showed the Pope (Pius VII.) reinstated in Rome, Victor Emmanuel I. at Turin, Ferdinand III. of Hapsburg-Lorraine in Tuscany, the Genoese Republic for the moment restored by the English, Parma and Piacenza assigned to the Empress Marie-Louise, and Modena to the Austrian Archduke Francis, who was heir through the female line to the last of the Estes. Murat was still at Naples, Ferdinand IV. in Sicily, Austria acknowledged supreme in Lombardy and Venetia, and the island of Elba ironically handed over to Napoleon. These were the chief features, so far as Italy was concerned, of the Treaty of Paris, signed on the 30th of May 1814. Next year the Congress of Vienna modified the arrangement by providing that the Spanish Infanta Maria Louisa, on whom had been bestowed the ex-republic of Lucca, should have the reversion of Parma and Piacenza, while Lucca was to go in the end to Tuscany. Murat having been destroyed, the Neapolitan Bourbons recovered all their old possessions. San Marino and Monaco were graciously recognised as independent, which brought the number of Italian states up to ten. The Sardinian monarchy received back the part of Savoy which by the Treaty of Paris had been reserved to France. It was also offered a splendid and unexpected gift—Genoa.

Lord William Bentinck entered Genoa by a convention concluded with the authorities on the 18th of April 1814. A naval demonstration following an ably-conducted operation, by which Bentinck's hybrid force of Greeks and Calabrese, with a handful of English, became master of the two principal forts, hastened this conclusion, but the Genoese had no reluctance to open their gates to the English commander, who inspired them with the fullest confidence. He came invested with the halo of a constitution-maker-under-difficulties; it was known that he had stopped at nothing in carrying out his mission in Sicily; not even at getting rid of the Queen, who found in Bentinck the Nemesis for having led a greater Englishman to stain his fame in the roads of Naples. Driven rather than persuaded to leave Sicily, Marie Antoinette's sister encountered so frightful a sea voyage that she died soon after joining her relations at Vienna. Lord William had acquired the art of writing the finest appeals to the love of freedom; a collection of his manifestoes would serve as handy-book to anyone instructed to stir up an oppressed nationality. He immediately gave the Genoese some specimens of his skill as a writer, and by granting them at once a provisional constitution, he dispelled all doubts about the future recognition of their republic. What was not, therefore, their dismay, when they were suddenly informed of the decision of the Holy Alliance to make a present of them to the people whom, of all others, they probably disliked the most. Italians had not ceased yet from reserving their best aversion for their nearest neighbours.

Bentinck did not mean to deceive; perhaps he thought that by going beyond the letter of his instructions he should draw his government after him. That he did, in effect, deceive, cannot be denied; even Lord Castlereagh, while necessarily refusing to admit that definite promises had been made, yet allowed that, 'Of course he would have been glad if the proclamation issued to the Genoese had been more precisely worded.' The motive of the determination to sacrifice the republic was, he said, 'a sincere conviction of the necessity of a barrier between France and Italy, which ought to be made effectual on the side of Piedmont. The object was to commit the defence of the Alps and of the great road leading round them by the Gulf of Genoa, between France and Italy, to the same power to which it had formerly been entrusted. On that principle, the question relating to Genoa had been entertained and decided upon by the allied sovereigns. It was not resolved upon because any particular state had unworthy or sordid views, or from any interest or feeling in favour of the King of Sardinia, but solely to make him, as far as was necessary, the instrument of the general policy of Europe.'

A better defence might have been made. Piedmont was destined to serve as a bulwark, not so much against France, which for the time was not to be feared, as against Austria, absolute except for the subalpine kingdom in all Italy. But this belongs to the shaping of rough-hewn ends, which is in higher hands than those of English ministers. The ends then looked very rough-hewn.

Piedmont was a hotbed of reaction and bigotry. True, she had a history differing vastly from that of the other Italian states, but the facts of the hour presented her in a most unattractive light. The Genoese felt the keenest heart-burnings in submitting to a decision in which they had no voice, and which came to them as a mandate of political extinction from the same powers that confirmed the sentence of death on Genoa's ancient and glorious rival. The seeds were laid of disaffection, always smouldering among the Genoese, till Piedmont's king became King of Italy. It might almost be said that the reconciliation was not consummated till the day when the heir and namesake of Humbert of the White Hands received the squadrons of Europe in the harbour of Genoa, and the proud republican city showed what a welcome she had prepared for her sovereign of the Savoy race.

After the Congress of Vienna finished its labours, there were, as has been remarked, ten states in Italy, but out of Sardinia (whose subjugation Prince Metternich esteemed a mere matter of time) there was one master. The authority of the Emperor Francis was practically as undisputed from Venice to the Bay of Naples as it was in the Grand Duchy of Austria. The

Austrians garrisoned Piacenza, Ferrara and Commacchio; Austrian princes reigned in Tuscany, Parma, Modena and Lucca; the King of Naples, who paid Austria twenty-six million francs for getting back his throne, thankfully agreed to support a German army to protect him against his subjects. In the secret treaty concluded between himself and the Emperor of Austria, it was stipulated that the King of the Two Sicilies should not introduce into his government any principles irreconcilable with those adopted by His Imperial Majesty in the government of his Italian provinces. As for the Roman States, Austria reckoned on her influence in always securing the election of a Pope who would give her no trouble. Seeing herself without rivals and all-powerful, she deemed her position unassailable. She forgot that, by giving Italy an unity of misery, she was preparing the way for another unity. Common hatred engendered common love; common sufferings led on to a common effort. If some prejudices passed away under the Napoleonic rule, many more still remained, and possibly, to eradicate so old an evil, no cure less drastic than universal servitude would have sufficed. Italians felt for the first time what before only the greatest among them had felt—that they were brothers in one household, children of one mother whom they were bound to redeem. Jealousies and millennial feuds died out; the intense municipal spirit which, imperfect as it was, had yet in it precious political germs, widened into patriotism. Italy was re-born.

Black, however, was the present outlook. Total commercial stagnation and famine increased the sentiment of unmitigated hopelessness which spread through the land. The poet Monti, who, alas! sang for bread the festival songs of the Austrians as he had sung those of Napoleon, said in private to an Englishman who asked him why he did not give his voice to the liberties of his country which he desired, though he did not expect to see them: 'It would be *vox clamantis in deserto;* besides, how can the grievances of Italy be made known? No one dares to write—scarcely to think—politics; if truth is to be told, it must be told by the English; England is the only tribunal yet open to the complaints of Europe.' A greater poet and nobler man, Ugo Foscolo, had but lately uttered a wail still more despondent: 'Italy will soon be nothing but a lifeless carcass, and her generous sons should only weep in silence without the impotent complaints and mutual recriminations of slaves.' That as patriotic a heart as ever beat should have been afflicted to this point by the canker of despair tells of the quagmire—not only political but spiritual—into which Italy was sunk. The first thing needful was to restore the people to consciousness, to animation of some sort, it did not matter what, so it were a sign of life. Foscolo himself, who impressed on what he wrote his own proud and scornful temperament, almost savage in its independence, fired his countrymen to better things than the despairing inertia which he preached. Few works have had more effect than his *Letters of Jacobo Ortis*. As often happens with books which strongly move contemporaries, the reader may wonder now what was the secret of its power, but if the form and sentiment of the Italian *Werther* strike us as antiquated, the intense, though melancholy patriotism that pervades it explains the excitement it caused when patriotism was a statutory offence. Such mutilated copies as were allowed to pass by the censor were eagerly sought; the young read it, women read it—who so rarely read—the mothers of the fighters of to-morrow. Foscolo's life gave force to his words: when all were flattering Napoleon, he had reminded him that no man can be rightly praised till he is dead, and that his one sure way of winning the praise of posterity was to establish the independence of Italy. The warning was contained in a 'discourse' which Foscolo afterwards printed with the motto from Sophocles: 'My soul groans for my country, for myself and for thee.' Sooner than live under the Austrians, he went into voluntary exile, and finally took refuge in England, where he was the *fêted* lion of a season, and then forgotten, and left almost without the necessaries of life. No one was much to blame; Foscolo was born to misunderstand and to be misunderstood; he hid himself to hide his poverty, which, had it been known, might have been alleviated. His individual tragedy seemed a part of the universal tragedy.

With Foscolo, his literary predecessor Alfieri must be mentioned as having helped in rekindling the embers of patriotic feeling, because, though dead, he spoke; and his plays, one of which was prophetically dedicated *al libero Popolo Italiano*, had never been so much read. The *Misogallo*, published for the first time after the fall of Napoleon, though aimed at the French, served equally well as an onslaught on every foreign dominion, or even moral or intellectual influence. 'Shall *we* learn liberty of the Gauls, *we* who taught every lofty thing to others?' was a healthy remonstrance to a race that had lost faith in itself; and the Austrians were wise in discountenancing the sale of a work that contained the line which gave a watchword to the future:—

Schiavi or siam si; ma schiavi almen frementi.

Like Foscolo's, Alfieri's life was a lesson in independence: angry at the scant measure of freedom in Piedmont, he could never be induced to go near his sovereign till Charles Emmanuel was staying at Florence as a proscript. Then the poet went to pay his respects to him, and was received with the good-humoured banter: 'Well, Signor Conte, here am I, a king, in the condition you would like to see them all.'

Against the classical, not to say pagan, leanings of these two poets, a reaction set in with Alessandro Manzoni, the founder of Italian Romanticism, to which he gave an aspect differing from that which the same movement wore in France, because he was an ardent Catholic at a time when Christianity had almost the charm of novelty. His religious outpourings combine the fervour of the Middle Ages with modern expansion, and he freed the Italian language from pedantic restrictions without impairing its dignity. It was once the fashion to inveigh against Manzoni for, as it was said, inculcating resignation; but he did nothing of the kind. As a young man he had sung of the Italians as 'Figli tutti d'un solo Riscatto,' and though he was not of those who fight either with the sword or the pen, yet that 'Riscatto' was the dream of his youth and manhood, and the joy of his old age. His gentleness was never contaminated by servility, and the love for his country, profound if placid, which appears in every line of his writings, appealed to a class that could not be reached by fiery turbulence of thought.

In an age when newspapers have taken the place of books, it may seem strange to ascribe any serious effect to the works of poets and romancists; but in the Italy of that date there were no newspapers to speak of; the ordinary channels of opinion were blocked up. Books were still not only read, but discussed and thought over, and every slight allusion to the times was instantly applied. In the prevailing listlessness, the mere fact of increased mental activity was of importance. A spark of genius does much to raise a nation. It is in itself the incontrovertible proof that the race lives: a dead people does not produce men of genius. Whatever awakes one part of the intelligence reacts on all its parts. You cannot lift, any more than you can degrade, the heart of man piecemeal. In this sense not literature only but also music helped, who can say how effectually, to bring Italy back to life. The land was refreshed by a flood of purely national song, full of the laughter and the tears of Italian character, of the sunshine and the storms of Italian nature. Music, the only art uncageable as the human soul, descended as a gift from heaven upon the people whose articulate utterance was stifled. And

> . . . No speech may evince
> Feeling like music.

CHAPTER II

THE WORK OF THE CARBONARI
1815-1821

Revolutions in the Kingdom of Naples and in Piedmont—The Conspiracy against Charles Albert.

CONSIDERING what the state of the country was after 1815, and how apparently inexhaustible were the resources of the Empire of which the petty princes of the peninsula were but puppets, it is remarkable that political agitation, with a view to reversing the decisions of Vienna, should have begun so soon, and on so large a scale. Not that the nation, as a whole, was yet prepared to move; every revolution, till 1848, was partial in the sense that the mass of the people stood aloof, because unconvinced of the possibility of loosening their chains. But, during that long succession of years, the number of Italians ready to embark on enterprises of the most desperate character, accounting as nothing the smallness of the chance of success, seems enormous when the risks they ran and the difficulties they faced are fully recognised. Among the means which were effective in first rousing Italy from her lethargy, and in fostering the will to acquire her independence at all costs, the secret society of the Carbonari undoubtedly occupies the front rank. The Carbonari acted in two ways; by what they did and by what they caused to be done by others who were outside their society, and perhaps unfavourable to it, but who were none the less sensible of the pressure it exercised. The origin of Carbonarism has been sought in vain; as a specimen of the childish fables that once passed for its history may be noticed the legend that Francis I. of France once stumbled on a charcoal burner's hut when hunting 'on the frontiers of his kingdom next to Scotland,' and was initiated into the rites similar to those in use among the sectaries of the nineteenth century. Those rites referred to vengeance which was to be taken on the wolf that slew the lamb; the wolf standing for tyrants and oppressors, and the lamb for Jesus Christ, the sinless victim, by whom all the oppressed were represented. The Carbonari themselves generally believed that they were heirs to an organisation started in Germany before the eleventh century, under the name of the Faith of the Kohlen-Brenners, of which Theobald de Brie, who was afterwards canonised, was a member. Theobald was adopted as patron saint of the modern society, and his fancied portrait figured in all the lodges. That any weight should have been attached to these pretensions to antiquity may appear strange to us, as it certainly did not matter whether an association bent on the liberation of Italy had or had not existed in German forests eight hundred years before; age and mystery, however, have a great popular attraction, the first as an object of reverence, the second as food for curiosity with the profane, and a bond of union among the initiated. The religious symbolism of the Carbonari, their oaths and ceremonies, and the axes, blocks and other furniture of the initiatory chamber, were well calculated to impress the poorer and more ignorant and excitable of the brethren. The Vatican affected to believe that Carbonarism was an offshoot of Freemasonry, but, in spite of sundry points of resemblance, such as the engagements of mutual help assumed by members, there seems to have been no real connection between the two. Political Freemasonry remained somewhat of an exotic in Italy, and was inclined to regard France as its centre. As far as can be ascertained, it gave a general support to Napoleon, while Carbonarism rejected every foreign yoke. The practical aims of the Carbonari may be summed up in two words: freedom and independence. From the first they had the penetration to grasp the fact that independence, even if obtained, could not be preserved without freedom; but though their predilections were theoretically republican, they did not make a particular form of government a matter of principle. Nor were they agreed in a definite advocacy of the unity of Italy.

A Genoese of the name of Malghella, who was Murat's Minister of Police, was the first person to give a powerful impetus to Carbonarism, of which he has even been called the inventor, but the inference goes too far. Malghella ended miserably; after the fall of Murat he was arrested by the Austrians, who consigned him as a new subject to the Sardinian Government, which immediately put him in prison. His name is hardly known, but no Italian of his time worked more assiduously, or in some respects more intelligently, for the emancipation of Italy. Whatever was truly Italian in Murat's policy must be mainly attributed to him. As early as 1813 he urged the King to declare himself frankly for independence, and to grant a constitution to his Neapolitan subjects. But Malghella did not find the destined saviour of Italy in Murat; his one lasting work was to establish Carbonarism on so strong a basis that, when the Bourbons returned, there were thousands, if not hundreds of thousands, of Carbonari in all parts of the realm. The discovery was not a pleasant one to the restored rulers, and the Prince of Canosa, the new Minister of Police, thought to counteract the evil done by his predecessor by setting up an abominable secret society called the Calderai del Contrapeso (Braziers of the Counterpoise), principally recruited from the refuse of the people, lazzaroni, bandits and let-out convicts, who were provided by Government with 20,000 muskets, and were sworn to exterminate all enemies of the Church of Rome, whether Jansenists, Freemasons or Carbonari. This association committed some horrible excesses, but otherwise it had no results. The Carbonari closed in their ranks, and learnt to observe more strictly their rules of secrecy. From the kingdom of Naples, Carbonarism spread to the Roman states, and found a congenial soil in Romagna, which became the focus whence it spread over the rest of Italy. It was natural that it should take the colour, more or less, of the places where it grew. In Romagna, where political assassination is in the blood of the people, a dagger was substituted for the symbolical woodman's axe in the initiatory rites. It was probably only in Romagna that the conventional threat against informers was often carried out. The Romagnols invested Carbonarism with the wild intensity of their own temperament, resolute even to crime, but capable of supreme impersonal enthusiasm. The ferment of expectancy that prevailed in Romagna is reflected in the Letters and Journals of Lord Byron, whom young Count Pietro Gamba made a Carbonaro, and who looked forward to seeing the Italians send the barbarians of all nations back to their own dens, as to the most interesting spectacle and moment in existence. His lower apartments, he writes, were full of the bayonets, fusils and cartridges of his Carbonari cronies; 'I suppose that they consider me as a dépôt, to be sacrificed in case of accidents. It is no great matter, supposing that Italy could be liberated, who or what is sacrificed. It is a grand object—the very poetry of politics. Only think—a free Italy!!! Why, there has been nothing like it since the days of Augustus.'

The movement on which such great hopes were set was to begin in the kingdom of Naples in the spring of 1820. The concession of the hard-won Spanish Constitution in the month of March encouraged the Neapolitans to believe that they might get a like boon from their own King if they directed all the forces at their command to this single end. To avoid being compromised, they sought rather to dissociate themselves from the patriots of other parts of Italy than to co-operate with them in an united effort. The Carbonari of the Neapolitan kingdom, who were the entire authors of the revolution, which, after many unfortunate delays, broke out on the 1st of July, had good cause for thinking that they were in a position to dictate terms; the mistake they made was to suppose that a charter conceded by a Bourbon of Naples could ever be worth the paper on which it was written. Not only among the people, but in the army the Carbonari had thousands of followers on whom they could rely, and several whole regiments were only waiting their orders to rise in open revolt. The scheme was to take possession of the persons of the King and the royal family, and retain them as hostages till the Constitution was granted. Such extreme measures were not necessary. The standard of rebellion was raised at Monteforte by two officers named Morelli and Silvati, who had brought over a troop of cavalry from Nola, and by the priest Menechini. In all Neapolitan insurrections there was sure to be a priest; the Neapolitan Church, much though there is to be laid to its account, must be admitted to have frequently shown sympathy with the popular side. Menechini enjoyed an immense, if brief, popularity which he used to allay the anger of the mob and to procure the safety of obnoxious persons. The King sent two generals and a body of troops against the Chartists, but when the Carbonari symbols were recognised on the insurgent flags, the troops showed such clear signs of wishing to go over to the enemy that they were quietly taken back to Naples. The cry of 'God, the King, and the Constitution,' was taken up through the land; General Pepe, who had long been a Carbonaro in secret, was enthusiastically hailed as commander of the Chartist forces, which practically comprised the whole army. The King was powerless; besides which, when pushed up into any corner people who do not mind breaking their word have a facility for hard swearing. On the 13th of July, Ferdinand standing at the altar of the royal chapel, with his hand on the Bible, swore to defend and maintain the Constitution which he had just granted. If he failed to do so, he called upon his subjects to disobey him, and God to call him to account. These words he read from a written form; as if they were not enough, he added, with his eyes on the cross, and his face turned towards heaven: 'Omnipotent God, who with Thine infinite power canst read the soul of man and the future, do Thou, if I speak falsely, or intend to break my oath, at this moment direct the thunder of Thy vengeance on my head.'

The Neapolitans had got their liberties, but they soon found themselves face to face with perplexities which would have taxed the powers of men both wiser and more experienced in free government than they were. In the first place, although a revolution may be made by a sect, a government cannot be carried on by one.

The Carbonari who had won the day were blind to this self-evident truth; and, to make matters worse, there was a split in their party, some of them being disposed to throw off the Bourbon yoke altogether; a natural desire, but as it was only felt by a minority, it added to the general confusion. Then came, as it was sure to come, the cry for separation from Sicily. The Sicilians wanted back the violated constitution obtained for them by the English in 1812, and would have nothing to do with that offered them from Naples. In every one of the struggles between Sicily and Naples, it is impossible to refuse sympathy to the islanders, who, in the pride of their splendid independent history, deemed themselves the victims of an inferior race; but it is equally impossible to ignore that, politically, they were in the wrong. In union, and in union alone, lay the only chance of resisting the international plot to keep the South Italian populations in perpetual bondage. The Sicilian revolt was put down at first mildly, and finally, as mildness had no effect, with the usual violence by the Neapolitan Constitutional Government, which could not avoid losing credit and popularity in the operation. Meanwhile, the three persons who traded under the name of Europe met at Troppau, and came readily to the conclusion that 'the sovereigns of the Holy Alliance exercised an incontestable right in taking common measures of security against states which the overthrow of authority by revolt placed in a hostile attitude towards every legitimate government.' The assumption was too broadly stated, even for Lord Castlereagh's acceptance; but he was contented to make a gentle protest, which he further nullified by allowing that, in the present case, intervention was very likely justified. France expressed no disapproval. Only the Netherlands, Switzerland, Sweden and Spain gave the Constitutional *régime* tacit support by recognising it. The Emperor of Russia was very anxious to take part in the business, and would have sent off an army instantly had not his royal brother of Prussia hesitated to consent to the inconvenience of a Cossack march through his territory. The work was left, therefore, to the Emperor of Austria. Before entering upon it, it occurred to these three to invite the King of Naples to meet them at Laybach. They knew his character.

Ferdinand assured his Parliament that he was going to Laybach solely to induce the Holy Alliance to think better of its opposition, and to agree, at least, to all the principal features of the new state of things. Most foolishly the Parliament, which, according to the Constitution, might have vetoed his leaving the country, let him go. Before starting he wrote an open letter to his dear son, the Duke of Calabria, who was appointed Regent, in which he said: 'I shall defend the events of the past July before the Congress. I firmly desire the Spanish Constitution for my kingdom; and although I rely on the justice of the assembled sovereigns, and on their old friendship, still it is well to tell you that, in whatever circumstance it may please God to place me, my course will be what I have manifested on this sheet, strong and unchangeable either by force or by the flattery of others.'

Brave words! News came in due time of the sequel. On the 9th of February 1821, the Regent received a letter from the King, in which he gave the one piece of advice that the people should submit to their fate quietly. He was coming back with 50,000 Austrians, and a Russian army was ready to start if wanted. Nevertheless, to prevent a sudden outbreak before the foreign troops arrived, the Regent carried on a game of duplicity to the last, and pretended to second, whilst he really baulked, the preparations for resistance decreed by Parliament. Baron Poerio, the father of two patriot martyrs of the future, sustained the national dignity by urging Parliament to yield only to force, and to defy the barbarous horde which was bearing down on the country. The closing scene is soon told. On the 7th of March, in the mountains near Rieti, General Guglielmo Pepe, with 8000 regular troops and a handful of militia, encountered an overwhelmingly superior force of Austrians. The Neapolitans stood out well for six hours, but on the Austrian reserves coming up, they were completely routed, and obliged to fly in all directions.

'Order reigned' in the kingdom of Naples. In Sicily, a gallant attempt at insurrection was begun, but there was not the spirit to go on with it, and General Rossaroll, its initiator, had to fly to Spain. The afterpiece is what might have been expected; an insensate desire for vengeance got hold of Ferdinand, and the last years of his life were spent in hunting down his enemies, real or imaginary. Morelli and Silvati were hung, the fugitives, Pepe and Rossaroll, were condemned to death, but this was only the beginning. The Austrian commander counselled mercy, but in this respect the King showed an independent mind. A court-martial was instituted to examine the conduct of ecclesiastics, public functionaries and soldiers, from the year 1793 downwards. No one was safe who had expressed a dislike of absolutism within the last thirty years. A blameless gentleman who was a Carbonaro, was conducted through Naples on the back of an ass, and beaten with a whip, to which nails were attached. Eight hundred persons are said to have perished at the hands of the state in one year. Ferdinand himself expired on the 3rd of January 1825, after misgoverning for sixty-five years.

The Neapolitan revolution had just collapsed, when another broke out in Piedmont, which, though short in duration, was to have far-reaching consequences.

At that time, the King of Sardinia was Victor Emmanuel I., who succeeded his brother Charles Emmanuel in 1802, when the latter abdicated and retired to Rome, where he joined the Society of Jesus. Victor Emmanuel's only son was dead, and the throne would devolve on his youngest brother, Charles Felix, Duke of Genoa, whom reasons of state led to abandon the wish to become a monk, which he had formed as a boy of eleven, on being taken to visit a convent near Turin. But Charles Felix, though married, was without children, and the legitimate heir-presumptive was Charles Albert, Prince of Carignano, who represented the younger branch of the family, which divided from the main line in the early part of the seventeenth century. Charles Albert's father was the luckless Prince Charles of Carignano, who, alone of his house, came to terms with Napoleon, who promised him a pension, which was not paid. His mother, a Saxon Princess, paraded the streets of Turin, dressed in the last republican fashion, with her infant son in her arms. Afterwards, she gave him a miscellaneous education, that included a large dose of Rousseau from a Swiss professor. The boy was shifted from place to place, happier when his mother forgot him, than when, in temporary recollection of his existence, she called him to her. Once when he was travelling with the Princess and her second husband, M. de Montléart, Charles Albert was made to sit on the box of the carriage, in a temperature many degrees below zero.

His uncles (as the King and Charles Felix called themselves, though they were his cousins) heard with natural horror of the vagaries of the Princess of Carignano, and they extended their antipathy from the mother to the son, even when he was a child. In Victor Emmanuel, this antipathy was moderated by the easy good-nature of his character; in Charles Felix, it degenerated into an intense hatred.

It is a singular thing that Prince Metternich, from the very first, had an instinctive feeling that the unfortunate boy, who seemed the most hopeless and helpless of human creatures, would prove the evil genius of the Austrian power. He therefore set to work to deprive him of his eventual rights. He was confident of success, as fortune had arranged matters in a manner that offered a readymade plan for carrying out the design. Victor Emmanuel had four daughters, precluded from reigning by the Salic law, which was in force in Piedmont. His wife, the Queen Maria Teresa, a woman of great beauty and insatiable ambition, was sister to the Austrian Archduke Francis d'Este, Duke of Modena. Francis had never married, having been robbed of his intended bride, the Archduchess Marie-Louise, by her betrothal to Napoleon. What simpler than to marry the eldest of the Sardinian princesses to her uncle, abrogate the Salic law, and calmly await the desired consummation of an Austrian prince, by right of his wife, occupying the Sardinian throne?

The first step was soon taken; princesses came into the world to be sacrificed. The plot ran on for some time, the Queen, who was in the habit of calling Charles Albert 'that little vagrant,' giving it her indefatigable support. Victor Emmanuel was weak, and stood in considerable awe of his wife, who had obtained a great ascendancy over him in the miserable days of their residence in the island of Sardinia. His nephew, who was almost or wholly unknown to him, partook of the nature of a disagreeable myth. Nevertheless he had a sense of justice, as well as Savoy blood, in his veins—he resisted; but the day came when his surrender seemed probable. Just at that moment, however, the Duke of Modena prematurely revealed the project by asking through his representative at the Congress of Vienna for the port of Spezia, in order that he might conveniently connect his own state with his prospective possession, the island of Sardinia. Prince Talleyrand was alarmed by the vision of Austria supreme in the Mediterranean, and through his opposition the conspiracy, for the time, was upset, and the rights of Charles Albert were recognised.

Curiously enough, Prince Metternich had insisted on the young Prince, then seventeen, visiting the headquarters of the Allies. Charles Felix (who was unconnected with the Modena scheme) wrote a letter to the King on this subject, in which he stated it as his belief that the Austrian plan was to get Charles Albert accidentally killed, or to plunge him in vice, or to make him contract a discreditable marriage. This was why they had invited him to their camp. He adds the characteristic remark that their nephew would be in no less danger at the headquarters of the Duke of Wellington 'à cause de la religion.' Have him home and have him married, is his advice. 'We are well treated, because there is the expectation of soon devouring our remains by extinguishing the House of Savoy. It is the habit of the cabinet of Vienna; it was thus they made an end of the House of Este.'

These counsels were the more likely to impress Victor Emmanuel from his knowledge that they were inspired by no shadow of personal interest in 'the little vagrant,' but by the race-feeling alone. The Queen contrived to prevent the immediate recall of the Prince of Carignano, but she was obliged to give way, and he was definitely established in Piedmont. In 1818 he was married at Florence to the Archduchess Maria Teresa of Tuscany, who, on the 14th of March 1820, gave birth to the child that was to become the first King of Italy.

Very soon after his return to his country, the hopes of the Liberal party began to centre in the young Prince, whom some of their more ardent spirits already saluted as the rising sun. Those who made his acquaintance were fascinated by the charm of manner which he could always exert when he chose, and were confirmed in their hopes by his evident susceptibility to the magnetism of new ideas and fatalistic ambitions. What they did not perceive was, that in his nature lay that ingrained tendency to drift before the wind, which is the most dangerous thing in politics. In the mid-sea of events he might change his course without conscious insincerity, but with the self-abandonment of a mind which, under pressure, loses the sense of personal responsibility.

In Piedmont, Carbonarism had made great way among the upper classes and among the younger officers; the flower of the country was enrolled in its ranks, and the impatience to take some action towards procuring free institutions for themselves, and doing something for their Lombard brothers, had reached fever heat in the spring of 1821, when the affairs of Naples were creating much excitement. The principal conspirators, noble young men, full of unselfish ardour, were the chosen friends and companions of the Prince of Carignano. It was formerly the opinion that they made him the confidant of their plans from the first, that he was one of them, in short—a Carbonaro bound by all the oaths and obligations of the society. The judgment of his conduct afterwards is, of course, much affected by this point; were the assumption correct, the invectives launched against him, not by any means only by republican writers, would hardly seem excessive. But by the light of documents issued in recent times, it appears more just as well as more charitable to suppose that Charles Albert's complicity was of a much less precise character. A little encouragement from a prince goes a long way.

According to his own account, he was taken by surprise when, on the 2nd or 3rd of March, his friends Carail, Collegno, Santa Rosa and Lisio came to tell him in secret that they belonged to societies which had been long working for the independence of Italy, and that they reckoned on him, knowing well his affection for his country, to aid them in obtaining from the King some few first concessions, which would be the prelude of a glorious future. It is clear that he ought either to have broken with them altogether from that moment or to have cast his lot with them for good or evil. He tried a middle course. He induced the conspirators to put off the revolution by which they intended to enforce their demands, and he conveyed to the King information of what had happened, asking at the same time that no measures should be taken against incriminated persons.

In fact, no precautions of any kind seem to have been taken. Victor Emmanuel, frightened at first, was soon reassured. The revolution, which was to have begun on the 8th, actually broke out on the 10th of March at Alessandria, where the counter orders issued at Charles Albert's request, after the interview just described, were not obeyed. The garrison 'pronounced' in favour of the Spanish Constitution. It was now impossible to draw back. From Alessandria the revolution spread to the capital. The bulk of the army sympathised with the movement, and relied on the support of the people.

The greatest ladies mixed with the crowds which gathered under the Carbonaro flag—black, blue and red. On the other hand, there were a few devoted servants of the House of Savoy who beheld these novelties with the sensations of a quiet person who sees from his window the breaking loose of a menagerie. Invincibly ignorant of all that was really inspiring in this first breath of freedom, they saw nothing in it but an unwarrantable attack on the authority of their amiable, if weak, old King, for whom they would gladly have shed every drop of their blood—not from the rational esteem which the people of Italy, like the people of England, now feel for their sovereign, but from the pure passion of loyalty which made the cavalier stand blindly by his prince, whether he was good or bad, in the right or in the wrong. Men of their type watched the evolution of Piedmont into Italy from first to last with the same presentiment of evil, the same moral incapacity of appreciation. A handful of these loyal servitors hurried to Victor Emmanuel to offer their assistance. They marshalled their troop in battle-array in the courtyard of the palace. Their arms were antiquated pistols and rapiers, and they themselves were veterans, some of them of eighty years, mounted on steeds as ancient. The King thanked them, but declined their services; nor would he give *carte blanche* to Captain Raimondi, who assured him that with his one company he could suppress the insurrection if invested with full powers. Soon after this refusal, a firing of guns announced that the citadel was in the hands of the insurgents. The troops within and without fraternised; it was a fine moment for those who knew history and who were bent in their hearts on driving the foreigner out of Italy. Here at the citadel of Turin, during the siege of 1706, occurred the memorable deed of Pietro Micca, the peasant-soldier, who, when he heard the enemy thundering at the door of the gallery, thought life and the welcome of wife and child and the happy return to his village of less account than duty, and fired the mine which sent him and three companies of French Grenadiers to their final reckoning.

After vacillating for two or three days, Victor Emmanuel abdicated on the 13th of March. The Queen desired to be appointed regent, but, to her intense vexation, the appointment was given to Charles Albert. A more unenviable honour never fell to the lot of man.

Deserted by the ministers of the crown, who resigned in a body, alone in the midst of a triumphant revolution, appealed to in the name of those sentiments of patriotism which he could never hear invoked unmoved, the young Prince uttered the words which were as good as a surrender: 'I, too, am an Italian!' That evening he allowed the Spanish Constitution to be proclaimed subject to the arrival of the orders of the new King.

The new King! No one remembered that there existed such a person. Nor had anyone recollected that the Spanish Constitution abrogated the Salic law, and that hence, instead of a new King, they had a new Queen—the wife of the Duke of Modena! An eminent Turinese jurisconsulist, who was probably the only possessor of a copy of the charter in the town which was screaming itself hoarse for it, divulged this awkward discovery. Several hours were spent in anxious discussion, when the brilliant suggestion was made that the article should be cancelled. The article was cancelled.

But Charles Felix could not be disposed of so easily. The news of the late events reached him at Modena of all places in the world, the rallying-point of the Prince of Carignano's bitterest foes. He was not long in sending his orders. He repudiated everything that had been done, and commanded Charles Albert, 'if he had a drop of our royal blood left in his veins,' to leave the capital instantly for Novara, where he was to await his further instructions.

Charles Albert obeyed. He was accompanied on his journey—or, as it may be called, his flight—by such of the troops as remained loyal. At Novara he found a sentence of exile, in a fresh order, to quit Piedmontese territory. Tuscany was indicated as the state where he was to reside.

The Austrians crossed the frontier with the consent of the King. Charles Felix's opinion of Austria has been already given; another time he said: 'Austria is a sort of bird-lime which, if you get it on your fingers, you can never rub off.' If anything was needed to increase his loathing for the revolution, it was the necessity in which it placed him, as he thought, of calling in this unloved ally. But Charles Felix was not the man to hesitate. Not caring a straw for the privilege of wearing a crown himself, his belief in the divine right of kings, and the obligation to defend it, amounted to monomania. The Austrian offer was therefore accepted. On her part Austria declined the obliging proposal of the Czar of a loan of 100,000 men. She felt that she could do the work unaided, nor was she mistaken.

On the 8th of April the Constitutionalist troops which marched towards Novara, sanguine that the loyal regiments there quartered would end by joining them, were met by an armed resistance, in which the newly-arrived Austrians assisted. Their defeat was complete, and it was the signal of the downfall of the revolution. The leaders retired from Turin to Alessandria, and thence to Genoa, that had risen last and was last to submit. Thus most of them escaped by sea, which was fortunate, as Charles Felix had the will to establish a White Terror, and was only prevented by the circumstance that nearly all the proposed victims were outside his kingdom. Capital sentences were sent after them by the folio: there was hardly a noble family which had not one of its members condemned to death. When his brother, Victor Emmanuel, recommended mercy, he told him that he was entirely ready to give him back the crown, but that, while he reigned, he should reign after his own ideas. He seems to have had thoughts of hanging the Prince of Carignano, and for a long time he seriously meant to devise the kingdom to his son, the infant Prince Victor. Thus a new set of obstacles arose between Charles Albert and the throne.

Of the personal friends of that ill-starred Prince all escaped. One of them, the noble-minded Count Santorre di Santa Rosa, died fighting for liberty in Greece. In the miseries of exile and poverty he had never lost faith in his country, but fearlessly maintained that 'the emancipation of Italy was an event of the nineteenth century.' To another, Giacinta di Collegno, it was reserved to receive the dying breath of Charles Albert, when as an exiled and crownless king he found rest, at last, at Oporto.

There were deeper reasons than any which appear on the surface for the failure of the revolutionary movements of this period. North and south, though the populations exhibited a childish delight at the overthrow of the old, despotic form of government, their effervescence ended as rapidly as it began. They did not really understand what was going on. 'By-the-bye, what *is* this same constitution they are making such a noise about?' asked a lazzarone who had been shouting 'Viva la Costituzione' all the day. Within a few weeks of the breakdown at Novara, Count Confalonieri wrote wisely to Gino Capponi that revolutions are not made by high intelligences, but by the masses which are moved by enthusiasm, and for a possibility of success, the word Constitution, the least magical of words, should have been replaced by the more comprehensible and stirring call: 'War to the stranger.' But this, instead of sounding from every housetop, was purposely stifled at Naples, and kept a mysterious secret in Piedmont.

CHAPTER III

PRISON AND SCAFFOLD

1821-1831

Political Trials in Venetia and Lombardy—Risings in the South and Centre—Ciro Menotti.

THE Austrians fully expected a rising in Lombardy in the middle of March, and that they were not without serious fears as to its consequences is proved by the preparations which they quietly made to abandon Milan, if necessary. The Court travelling-carriages were got ready, and the younger princes were sent away. Carbonarism had been introduced into Lombardy the year before by two Romagnols, Count Laderchi and Pietro Maroncelli. It was their propaganda that put the Austrian Government on the alert, and was the cause of the Imperial decree which denounced the society as a subversive conspiracy, aiming at the destruction of all constituted authority, and pointed to death and confiscation of property as the penalty for joining it. There was the additional clause, destined to bear terrible fruit, which declared accomplices, punishable with life-imprisonment, all who knew of the existence of lodges (*Vendite*, as they were called) or the names of associates, without informing the police. In the autumn of 1820, Maroncelli and many others, including Silvio Pellico, the young Piedmontese poet, were arrested as Carbonari, while the arrest of the so-called accomplices began with Count Giovanni Arrivabene of Mantua, who had no connection with the society, but was charged with having heard from Pellico that he was a member. Pellico and his companions were still lying untried in the horrible Venetian prisons, called, from their leaden roofs, the 'Piombi,' when the events of 1821 gave rise to a wholesale batch of new arrests. As soon as they knew of a movement in Piedmont, the Lombard patriots prepared to co-operate in it; that they were actually able to do nothing, was because it broke out prematurely, and also, to some extent, because their head, Count Confalonieri, was incapacitated by severe illness. But though their activity profited not at all to the cause, it was fatal to themselves. The Austrian Government had, as has been stated, a correct general notion of what was going on, but at the beginning it almost entirely lacked proofs which could inculpate individuals. In the matter of arrests, however, there was one sovereign rule which all the despotic Governments in Italy could and did follow in every emergency: it was to lay hands on the most intelligent, distinguished and upright members of the community. This plan never failed; these were the patriots, the conspirators of those days. The second thing which the Austrians made a rule of doing, was to extort from the prisoners some incautious word, some shadow of an assent or admission which would place them on the track of other compromised persons, and furnish them with such scraps of evidence as they deemed sufficient, in order to proceed against those already in their power. In their secret examination of prisoners, they had reduced the system of provocative interrogation to a science. They made use of every subterfuge, and, above all, of fabricated confessions fathered on friends of the prisoner, to extract the exclamation, the nod of the head, the confused answer, which served their purpose. The prisoners, men of good faith, and inexperienced in the arts of deception, were but children in their hands, and scarcely one of them was not doomed to be the involuntary cause of some other person's ruin—generally that of a dear and intimate friend.

The first to be arrested was Gaetano De-Castillia, who went with the Marquis Giorgio Pallavicini on a mission to Piedmont while the revolution there was at its height. They even had an interview with the Prince of Carignano, 'a pale and tall young man, with a charming expression' (so Pallavicini describes him), but had obtained from him no assurance, except the characteristic parting word: 'Let us hope in the future.' When De-Castillia was arrested, Pallavicini, then a youth of twenty, and full of noble sentiments, rushed to the director of the police with the avowal: 'It was I who induced De-Castillia to go to Piedmont; if the journey was a crime, the fault is mine; punish me!' No error could have proved more calamitous; till that moment the Austrians were in ignorance of the Piedmontese mission; De-Castillia was arrested on some far more trifling charge. Pallavicini's generous folly was rewarded by fourteen years' imprisonment, and its first consequence was the arrest of Count Confalonieri, at whose instance the visit to Turin had been made. For months the Austrians had desired to have a clue against him; the opportunity was come at last.

Federico Confalonieri, brilliant, handsome, persuasive, of great wealth and ancient lineage, innately aristocratic, but in the best sense, was morally at the head of Lombardy, by the selection of the fittest, which at certain junctures makes one man pre-appointed leader while he is still untried. When in England, the Duke of Sussex prevailed upon him to become a Freemason, but he was not a Carbonaro in the technical sense, though both friends and foes believed him to be one. He knew, however, more about this and the other secret societies then existing in Italy—even those of the reactionary party—than did most of the initiated. In an amusing passage in his memoirs he relates how, when once forcibly detained in a miserable hostelry in the Calabrian Mountains, a den of brigands, of whom the chief was the landlord, he guessed that this man was a Calderaio, and it occurred to him to make the sign of that bloodthirsty sect. Things changed in a second; the brigand innkeeper was at his feet, the complete household was set in motion to serve him. In 1821, he founded at Milan, not a secret society, but an association in which all the best patriots were enrolled, and of which the sole engagement was the formula, repeated on entering its ranks: 'I swear to God, and on my honour, to exert myself to the utmost of my power, and even at the sacrifice of my life, to redeem Italy from foreign dominion.'

Knowing to what extent he was a marked man, Confalonieri would have only exercised common prudence in leaving the country, but he could not reconcile himself to the idea of flight. Anonymous warnings rained upon him: most likely they all came from the same quarter, from Count Bubna, the Austrian Field-Marshal, with whom Confalonieri was personally on friendly terms. On the 12th of December the Countess Bubna made a last effort to save him; her carriage was ready, she implored him to take it and escape across the frontier. He refused, and next day he was arrested.

Austrian legal procedure was slow; the trial of the first Carbonari, Silvio Pellico and his companions, did not take place till 1822. On the 22nd of February the sentence of death was read to Silvio Pellico in his Venetian prison, to be commuted to one of fifteen years' imprisonment at Spielberg, a fortress converted into a convict prison in a bleak position in Moravia. To that rock of sorrow, consecrated for ever by the sufferings of some of the purest of men, Silvio Pellico and Pietro Maroncelli, with nine or ten companions, condemned at the same time, were the first Italians to take the road. Here they remained for the eight years described by the author of *Francesca da Rimini*, in *Le Mie Prigioni*, a book that served the Italian cause throughout the world. Even now some Italians are indignant at the spirit of saintly resignation which breathes upon Silvio Pellico's pages, at the veil which is drawn over many shocking features in the treatment of the prisoners; they do not know the tremendous force which such reticence gave his narrative. *Le Mie Prigioni* has the reserve strength of a Greek tragedy.

Maroncelli contracted a disease of the leg through the hardships endured; amputation became necessary, but could not be performed till permission was received from Vienna—a detail showing the red-tapism which governed all branches of the Austrian administration. This patriot went, after his release, to America, where he died, poor, blind and mad. Pellico, crushed in soul, devoted his latter years entirely to religion. Only men of iron fibre could come out as they went in. The Spielberg prisoners wore chains, and their food was so bad and scanty that they suffered from continual hunger, with its attendant diseases. Unlike the thieves and assassins confined in the same fortress, the State prisoners were given no news of their families. Such was Spielberg, 'a sepulchre without the peace of the dead.'

The State trials of the Lombard patriots in 1823 resulted in seven capital sentences on the Milanese, thirteen on the Brescians, and four on the Mantuans. The fate of the other prisoners depended on that of Count Confalonieri. If the sentence on him were not carried out, the lives at least of the others might be regarded as safe, since he was looked upon as the head. It is certain that the authorities, and the Emperor himself, had the most firm intention of having him executed; the more merciful decision was solely due to the Countess Confalonieri's journey to Vienna. Accompanied by the prisoner's aged father, this beautiful and heroic woman, a daughter of the noble Milanese house of Casati, went to Vienna before the conclusion of the trial, to be ready for any eventuality. When the sentence of death was passed, it was announced by the Emperor to old Count Confalonieri, whom he advised to return with the Countess Teresa as fast as possible if they wished to see the condemned man alive. Undaunted by the news, the brave wife sought an interview with the Empress, in whom she found a warm advocate, but who was obliged to own, after several attempts to obtain a reprieve, that she despaired of success. Teresa Confalonieri hurried back to Milan through the bitter winter weather, in doubt whether she should arrive before the execution had taken place. But the unceasing efforts of the Empress won the day. The respite was granted on the 13th of January; life-imprisonment was substituted for death. The countess sent her husband the pillow which she had bathed with her tears during her terrible journey; needless to say that it was not given to him. She died broken-hearted with waiting before he was set at liberty in the year 1836.

When Count Confalonieri reached Vienna on his way to Spielberg, he was surprised to find himself installed in a luxurious apartment, with three servants to wait upon him. Though too ill to touch solid food, a sumptuous breakfast and dinner were daily set before him; and but for the constant jingle of his chains, he would have thought himself in a first-class hotel on a journey of pleasure. The object of these attentions was clear when one evening Prince Metternich came to see him, and stayed for three hours, endeavouring by every exquisite flattery, by every promise and persuasion, to worm out of him the secrets of which he alone was believed to be the depositary. The Austrian Government had spent £60,000 on the Milan Commission, and, practically, they were no wiser than when it began. Would Confalonieri enlighten them? Whatever scruples he might have felt during the trial could be now laid aside; there was no question of new arrests. It was from pure, abstract love of knowledge that the Government, or, rather, the Emperor, desired to get at the truth. If he preferred to open his mind to the Emperor in person, His Majesty would grant him a secret audience. Above all, what was the real truth about the Prince of Carignano?

All the rest was a blind; it was the wish to have some damnatory evidence against Charles Albert, such as would for ever exclude him from the throne, that had induced the Emperor and his astute minister to make this final attempt.

'Confalonieri need never go to Spielberg,' said the Prince; 'let him think of his family, of his adored wife, of his own talents, of his future career, which was on the brink of being blotted out as completely as if he were dead!' Confalonieri was worthy of his race, of his class, of himself; he stood firm, and next morning, almost with a sense of relief, he started for the living grave.

'The struggle was decided,' Prince Metternich had said in the course of the interview, 'and decided not only for our own, but for many generations. Those who still hoped to the contrary were madmen.'

Some years of outward quiet doubtless confirmed him in the first opinion, while the second was not likely to be shaken by the next attempt that was made to take up arms for freedom. On the 28th of June 1828, several villages in the province of Salerno rose in obedience to the harangues of two patriotic ecclesiastics, Canon de Luca and Carlo da Celle, superior of a capuchin convent. This was meant to develop into a general insurrection, but it was nowhere followed up, and the sword of vengeance fell speedily on the wretched villagers. Surrounded by the royal troops, they were forced into submission, many were shot on the spot, others were dragged in chains to Salerno, not even a drop of water being allowed them during the journey under the scorching sun. The village of Bosco was rased to the ground. The priest, the monk, and twenty-two insurgents were shot after the repression. The heads of the victims were cut off and placed in iron cages where their wives or mothers were likely to see them. A woman went to Naples to beg for the pardon of her two grandsons, by name Diego and Emilio. The King, with barbarous clemency, told her to choose one. In vain she entreated that if both could not be saved the choice should be left to chance, or decided by someone else. But no; unless she chose they would both be shot. At last she chose Diego. Afterwards she went mad, and was constantly heard wailing: 'I have killed my grandson Emilio.' This anecdote gives a fair notion of Francis I., whose short reign was, however, less signalised by acts of cruelty, though there were enough of these, than by a venality never surpassed. The grooms-in-waiting and ladies-of-the-bedchamber sold the public offices in the daylight; and the King, who was aware of it, thought it a subject for vulgar jokes with his intimates. Francis died in 1830 of bad humour at the Paris revolution, and was succeeded by Ferdinand II., to be known hereafter as Bomba — then a clownish youth, one of whose first kingly cares was to create St Ignatius Loyola a Field-Marshal.

The revolution which upset the throne of Charles X., and ushered in the eighteen years' reign of the Citizen King, seemed likely to have momentous consequences for Italy. The principle of non-intervention proclaimed by French politicians would, if logically enforced, sound the death-knell of the Austrian power in Italy. Dupin, the Minister of War, enlarged on the theme in a speech which appeared to remove all doubt as to the real intentions of the Government. 'One phrase,' he remarked, 'has made a general impression; it expresses the true position of a loyal and generous Government. Not only has the President of the Council laid down the principle that France should abstain from intervention; he has declared that she would not tolerate intervention on the part of others. France might have shut herself up in a cold egotism, and simply said that she would not intervene; this would have been contemptible, but the proclamation of not suffering the interventions of others is the noblest attitude a strong and magnanimous people can assume; it amounts to saying: Not only will I not attack or disturb other nations, but I, France, whose voice is respected by Europe and by the whole world, will never permit others to do so. This is the language held by the ministry and by the ambassadors of Louis Philippe; and it is this which the army, the National Guard, France entire, is ready to maintain.'

Truly language was invented to travesty the truth,

and when French politicians say they are going to the right it is an almost sure sign that they are going to the left; nevertheless, is it possible to blame the Italians who read in these assurances a positive promise affecting their own case?

The same assurances were repeated again and again through the winter of 1830-31; they were repeated authoritatively as late as March in the latter year. Well may a French writer inquire: 'Was it insanity or treachery?'

The good tidings were published by the Italian exiles, who, living close to the great centres of European politics, were the first to intoxicate themselves with the great delusion. From London, Gabriele Rossetti sent the exultant summons:

> Cingi l'elmo, la mitra deponi,
>   O vetusta Signora del mondo:
> Sorgi, sorgi dal sonno profondo,
>   Io son l'alba del nuovo tuo dì.
>
> Saran rotte le vostre catene,
>   O Fratelli che in ceppi-languite;
> O Fratelli che il giogo soffrite
>   Calcherete quel giogo col piè.

The child beside whose cradle the ode was written, was to grow to manhood while Italy still remained 'the weeping, desolate mother.' The cry of the poet was not, however, without an echo. In 1831, Romagna, Parma and Modena rose in rebellion.

Things had been going, without much variation, from bad to worse in the Roman states, ever since 1815. Pius VII. (Chiaramonti), who died in 1823, was succeeded by Leo XII. (Genga), an old man who was in such enfeebled health that his death was expected at the time of his election, but, like a more famous pontiff, he made a sudden recovery, which was attributed to the act of a prelate, who, in prayer, offered his own life for the Pope's, and who died a few days after resolving on the sacrifice. During this Pope's reign, the smallpox was rife in Rome, in consequence of the suppression of public vaccination. The next conclave, held in 1829, resulted in the election of Pius VIII. (Castiglioni da Cingoli), who died on the 30th of November 1830, and was followed by Gregory XVI. (Cappellari). In each conclave, Austria had secured the choice of a 'Zealot,' as the party afterwards called Ultramontane was then designated. The last traces of reforms introduced by the French disappeared; criminal justice was again administered in secret; the police were arbitrary and irresponsible. All over the Roman states, but especially in Romagna, the secret society of the Sanfedesti flourished exceedingly; whether, as is probable, an offshoot of the Calderai or of indigenous growth, its aims were the same. The affiliated swore to spill the last drop of the blood of the Liberals, without regard to sex or rank, and to spare neither children nor old men. Many Romagnols had left their country after the abortive agitation of 1821, and amongst these were the Gambas. Count Pietro died in Greece, where he had gone on the service of freedom. Had he lived, this young man would have been sure to win a fair name in the annals of Italian patriotism; he should not, as it is, be quite forgotten, as it was chiefly due to him that Byron's life took the redeeming direction which led to Missolonghi.

In February 1831, Romagna and the Marches of Ancona threw off the Papal Government with an ease which must have surprised the most sanguine. The white, red and green tricolor was hoisted at Bologna, where, as far as is known, this combination of colours first became a political badge. Thirty-six years before Luigi Zamboni and Gian Battista De Rolandis of Bologna had distributed rosettes of white, red and green ribbon; Zamboni was arrested, and strangled himself, afraid of betraying his friends; De Rolandis was hung on the 23rd of April 1796. Such was the origin of the flag, but, until 1831, the Carbonaro red, blue and black was the common standard of the revolution. From that year forth, the destinies of Italy were accomplished under the colours of better augury, so fit to recall her fiery volcanoes, her wooded Apennines, her snow-crowned Alps; colours which in one sense she receives from Dante, who clothes in them the vision of the glorified Beatrice.

The rising at Parma requires but little comment. The Empress Marie-Louise neither hated her subjects, nor was hated by them, but her engagements with Austria prevented her from granting the demanded concessions, and she abandoned her state, to return to it, indeed, under Austrian protection, but without the odious corollary of vindictive measures which was generally meant by a restoration.

Much more important is the history of the Modenese revolution. Apologists have been found for the Bourbons of Naples, but, if anyone ever said a good word for Francesco d'Este, it has escaped the notice of the present writer. Under a despotism without laws (for the edicts of the Prince daily overrode the Este statute book which was supposed to be in force), Modena was far more in the power of the priests, or rather of the Jesuits, than any portion of the states of the Church. Squint-eyed, crooked in mind and bloodthirsty, Francis was as ideal a bogey-tyrant as can be discovered outside fiction. In 1822, he hung the priest Giuseppe Andreoli on the charge of

Carbonarism; and his theory of justice is amusingly illustrated by the story of his sending in a bill to Sir Anthony Panizzi—who had escaped to England—for the expenses of hanging him in effigy.

Francis felt deeply annoyed by the narrow limits of his dominions, and his annoyance did not decrease with the decreasing chances of his ousting the Prince of Carignano from the Sardinian throne. He was intensely ambitious, and one of his subjects, a man, in other respects, of high intelligence, thought that his ambition could be turned to account for Italy. It was the mistake over again that Machiavelli had made with Cesare Borgia.

Ciro Menotti, who conceived the plan of uniting Italy under the Duke of Modena, was a Modenese landed proprietor who had exerted himself to promote the industry of straw-plaiting, and the other branches of commerce likely to be of advantage to an agricultural population. He was known as a sound philanthropist, an excellent husband and father, a model member of society. Francis professed to take an interest in industrial matters; Menotti, therefore, easily gained access to his person. In all the negotiations that followed, the Modenese patriot was supported and encouraged by a certain Dr Misley, who was of English extraction, with whom the Duke seems to have been on familiar terms. It appears not doubtful that Menotti was led to believe that his political views were regarded with favour, and that he also received the royal promise that, whatever happened, his life would be safe. This promise was given because he had the opportunity of saving the Duke from some great peril—probably from assassination, though the particulars were never divulged.

Misley went to Paris to concert with the Italian committee which had its seat there; the movement in Modena was fixed for the first days of February. But spies got information of the preparations, and on the evening of the 3rd, before anything had been done, Menotti's house was surrounded by troops, and after defending it, with the help of his friends, for two hours, he was wounded and captured. Next day the Duke despatched the following note to the Governor of Reggio-Emilia: 'A terrible conspiracy against me has broken out. The conspirators are in my hands. Send me the hangman. —Francis.'

Not all, however, of the conspirators were in his hands; the movement matured, in spite of the seizure of Menotti, and Francis, 'the first captain in the world,' as he made his troops call him, was so overcome with fright that on the 5th of February he left Modena with his family, under a strong military escort, dragging after him Ciro Menotti, who, when Mantua was reached, was consigned to an Austrian fortress.

Meanwhile, the revolution triumphed. Modena chose one of her citizens as dictator, Biagio Nardi, who issued a proclamation in which the words 'Italy is one; the Italian nation is one sole nation,' testified that the great lesson which Menotti had sought to teach had not fallen on unfruitful ground. Wild as were the methods by which, for a moment, he sought to gain his end, his insistance on unity nevertheless gives Menotti the right to be considered the true precursor of Mazzini in the Italian Revolution.

Now that the testing-time was come, France threw to the winds the principle announced in her name with such solemn emphasis. 'Precious French blood should never be shed except on behalf of French interests,' said Casimir Périer, the new President of the Council. A month after the flight of the Duke of Modena, the inevitable Austrians marched into his state to win it back for him. The hastily-organised little army of the new government was commanded by General Zucchi, an old general of Napoleon, who, when Lombardy passed to Austria, had entered the Austrian service. He now offered his sword to the Dictator of Modena, who accepted it, but there was little to be done save to retire with honour before the 6000 Austrians. Zucchi capitulated at Ancona to Cardinal Benvenuti, the Papal delegate. Those of the volunteers who desired it were furnished with regular passports, and authorised to take ship for any foreign port. The most compromised availed themselves of this arrangement, but the vessel which was to bear Zucchi and 103 others to Marseilles, was captured by the Austrian Admiral Bandiera, by whom its passengers were kidnapped and thrown into Venetian prisons, where they were kept till the end of May 1832. This act of piracy was chiefly performed with a view to getting possession of General Zucchi, who was tried as a deserter, and condemned to twenty years' imprisonment. Among the prisoners was the young wife of Captain Silvestro Castiglioni of Modena. 'Go, do your duty as a citizen,' she had said, when her husband left her to join the insurrection. 'Do not betray it for me, as perhaps it would make me love you less.' She shared his imprisonment, but just at the moment of the release, she died from the hardships endured.

By the end of the month of March, the Austrians had restored Romagna to the Pope, and Modena to Francis IV. In Romagna the amnesty published by Cardinal Benvenuti was revoked, but there were no executions; this was not the case in Modena. The Duke brought back Ciro Menotti attached to his triumphal car, and when he felt that all danger was past, and that the presence of the Austrians was a guarantee against a popular expression of anger, he had him hung.

' When my children are grown up, let them know how well I loved my country,' Menotti wrote to his wife on the morning of his execution. The letter was intercepted, and only delivered to his family in 1848. The revolutionists found it in the archives of Modena. On the scaffold he recalled how he was once the means of saving the Duke's life, and added that he pardoned his murderer, and prayed that his blood might not fall upon his head.

During the insurrection in Romagna, an event occurred which was not without importance to Europe, though it passed almost unnoticed at the time. The eldest son of Queen Hortense died in her arms at Forlì, of a neglected attack of measles; some said of poison, but the report was unfounded. He and his brother Louis, who had been closely mixed up with Italian conspiracies for more than a year, went to Romagna to offer their services as volunteers in the national army. By the death of the elder of the two, Louis Napoleon became heir to what seemed then the shadowy sovereignty of the Buonapartes.

No sooner had the Austrians retired from the Legations in July 1831, than the revolution broke out again. Many things had been promised, nothing performed; disaffection was universal, anarchy became chronic, and was increased by the indiscipline of the Papal troops that were sent to put it down. The Austrians returned and the French occupied Ancona, much to the Pope's displeasure, and not one whit to the advantage of the Liberals. This dual foreign occupation of the Papal states lasted till the winter of 1838.

CHAPTER IV

'YOUNG ITALY'

1831-1844

Accession of Charles Albert—Mazzini's Unitarian Propaganda
—The Brothers Bandiera.

ON 27th April 1831, Charles Albert came to the throne he had so nearly lost. His reconciliation with his uncle, Charles Felix, had been effected after long and melancholy preliminaries. To wash off the Liberal sins of his youth, or possibly with a vague hope of finding an escape from his false position in a soldier's death, he joined the Duc d'Angoulême's expedition against the Spanish Constitutionalists. His extraordinary daring in the assault of the Trocadero caused him to be the hero of the hour when he returned with the army to Paris; but the King of Sardinia still refused to receive him with favour—a sufficiently icy favour when it was granted—until he signed an engagement, which remained secret, to preserve intact during his reign the laws and principles of government which he found in force at his accession. If there had been an Order of the Millstone, Charles Felix would doubtless have conferred it upon his dutiful nephew; failing that, he presented to him for signature this wonderful document, the invention of which he owed to Prince Metternich. At the Congress of Verona in 1822, Charles Albert's claims to the succession were recognised, thanks chiefly to the Duke of Wellington, who represented England in place of Lord Londonderry (Castlereagh), that statesman having committed suicide just as he was starting for Verona. Prince Metternich then proposed that the Prince of Carignano should be called upon to enter into an agreement identical with the compact he was brought to sign a couple of years later. In communicating the proposal to Canning, the Duke of Wellington wrote that he had demonstrated to Prince Metternich 'the fatality of such an arrangement,' but that he did not think that he had made the slightest impression on him. So the event proved; baffled for the moment, the Prince managed to put his plan in execution through a surer channel.

With the accession of Charles Albert appears upon the political scene a great actor in the Liberation of Italy, Giuseppe Mazzini. Young and unknown, except for a vague reputation for restlessness and for talent which caused the government of Charles Felix to imprison him for six or seven months at Savona, Mazzini proposed to the new King the terms on which he might keep his throne, as calmly as Metternich had proposed to him the terms on which he might ascend it. The contrast is striking; on the one side the statesman, who still commanded the armed force of three-fourths of Europe, doing battle for the holy alliance of autocrats, for the international law of repression, for all the traditions of the old diplomacy; on the other, the young student with little money and few friends, already an exile, having no allies but his brain and his pen, who set himself, certain of success, to dissolve that mighty array of power and pomp. All his life Charles Albert was a Faust for the possession of whose soul two irreconcilable forces contended; the struggle was never more dramatically represented than at this moment in the person of these two champions.

Mazzini's letter to Charles Albert, which was read by

the King, and widely, though secretly, circulated in Piedmont, began by telling him that his fellow-countrymen were ready to believe his line of conduct in 1821 to have been forced on him by circumstances, and that there was not a heart in Italy that did not quicken at his accession, nor an eye in Europe that was not turned to watch his first steps in the career that now unfolded before him. Then he went on to show, with the logical strength in developing an argument which, joined to a novel and eloquent style, caused his writings to attract notice from the first, that the King could take no middle course. He would be one of the first of men, or the last of Italian tyrants; let him choose. Had he never looked upon Italy, radiant with the smile of nature, crowned with twenty centuries of sublime memories, the mother of genius, possessing infinite means, to which only union was lacking, girt round with such defences that a strong will and a few courageous breasts would suffice to defend her? Had it never struck him that she was created for a glorious destiny? Did he not contemplate her people, splendid still, in spite of the shadow of servitude, the vigour of whose intellect, the energy of whose passions, even when turned to evil, showed that the making of a nation was there? Did not the thought come to him: 'Draw a world out of these dispersed elements like a god from chaos; unite into one whole the scattered members, and pronounce the words, "It is mine, and it is happy"?'

Mazzini in 1831 was twenty-six years of age. His father was a Genoese physician, his mother a native of Chiavari. She was a superior woman, and devoted more than a mother's care to the excitable and delicate child, who seemed to her (mothers have sometimes the gift of prophecy) to be meant for an uncommon lot. One of the few personal reminiscences that Mazzini left recorded, relates to the time and manner in which the idea first came to him of the possibility of Italians doing something for their country. He was walking with his mother in the Strada Nuova at Genoa one Sunday in April 1821, when a tall, black-bearded man with a fiery glance held towards them a white handkerchief, saying: 'For the refugees of Italy.' Mazzini's mother gave him some money, and he passed on. In the streets were many unfamiliar faces; the fugitives from Turin and Alessandria were gathered at Genoa before they departed by sea into exile. The impression which that scene made on the mind of the boy of sixteen was never effaced.

Owing to his delicate health, Mazzini's early education was carried on at home, where the social atmosphere was that of one of those little centres in a provincial capital which are composed of a few people, mostly kindred, of similar tastes, who lead useful and refined lives, content with moderate ease. The real exclusiveness of such centres exceeds any that exists in the most aristocratic sphere in the world. The Mazzinis were, moreover, Genoese to the core; and this was another reason for exclusiveness, and for holding aloof from the governing class. Mazzini was born a few days after Napoleon entered Genoa as its lord. He had not, therefore, breathed the air of the ancient Republic; but there was the unadulterated republicanism of a thousand years in his veins.

When he grew to manhood his appearance was striking. The black, flowing hair, the pale, olive complexion, the finely-cut features and lofty brow, the deep-set eyes, which could smile as only Italian eyes can smile, but which could also flash astral infinitudes of scorn, the fragile figure, even the long, delicate, tapering fingers, marked him for a man apart—though whether a poet or an apostle, a seer or a saint, it was not easy to decide. Yet this could be said at once : if this man concentrated all his being on a single point, he would wield the power, call it what we will, which in every age has worked miracles and moved mountains.

Mazzini became a Carbonaro, though the want of clear, guiding principles in Carbonarism made him misdoubt its efficacy, and its hierarchical mysteries and initiatory ordeals repelled him by their childishness. Then followed his arrest, and his detention in the fortress of Savona, which was the turning-point in his mental life. Before that date he learnt, after it he taught. From his high-perched cell he saw the sea and the sky —with the Alps, the sublimest things in Nature. The voices of the fishermen reached his ears, though he could not see them. A tame goldfinch was his companion. Here, in a solitude and peace which he remembered with regret in the stormy and sorrowful years that were to come, he conceived his message and the mission, in which he believed to the last day of his life.

He resolved to found a new association on broader and simpler lines than the secret societies of the past, which should aim not only at the material freeing of Italy from her present bondage, but at her moral and religious regeneration. To aim at material progress of any kind, without at the same time aiming at a higher moral progress, seemed to Mazzini absurd ; to attempt to pull down without attempting to build up seemed to him criminal. Thus he accused the Socialists of substituting the progress of humanity's kitchen for the progress of humanity. He believed that Italy, united and redeemed, was destined to shed through the world the

Giuseppe Mazzini.

light of a new moral unity, which should end the reign of Scepticism, triumphant among discordant creeds. Mazzini's religious belief was the motor of his whole being. The Catholicism in which he was outwardly brought up never seems to have touched his inner nature; he went through no spiritual wrench in leaving a faith that was never a reality to him. The same is true of innumerable young Italians, who, when they begin to read and study, drift out of their childhood's religion without a struggle or a regret. But thought and study brought Mazzini what it rarely brings to these young men—the necessity to find something in which he could believe. He had not long to seek for a basis to his creed, because he was one of the men from the prophets of old to Spinoza, from Spinoza to Gordon, to whom the existence of God is a matter of experience rather than an object of faith. Starting from this point, he formed his religion out of what he regarded as its inevitable deductions. If God existed, his creatures must be intended for perfection; if this were the Divine scheme, man's one business was to carry it out. He considered the idea of duty separated from the idea of God to be illogical. Either the development of human things depended on a providential law, or it was left to chance and passing circumstance, and to the dexterity of the man who turned these to most account. God was the sole source of duty; duty the sole law of life. Mazzini did not denounce Catholicism or any other religion as false. He saw in it a stepping-stone to purer comprehension, which would be reached when man's intellect was sufficiently developed for him to be able to do without symbols.

The conscience of humanity is the last tribunal. Ideas, as well as institutions, change and expand, but

—certain fundamental principles are fixed. The family would always exist; property would always exist. The first, 'the heart's fatherland,' was the source of the only true happiness, the only joys untainted by grief, which were given to man. Those who wished to abolish the second were like the savage who cut down the tree in order to gather the fruit. In the future, free association would be the great agent of moral and material progress. The authority which once rested in popes and emperors now devolved on the people. Instead of 'God and the King,' Mazzini proposed the new formula 'God and the People.' By the people he understood no caste or class, whether high or low, but the universality of men composing the nation. The nation is the sole sovereign; its will, expressed by delegates, must be law to all its citizens.

By degrees certain words acquired more and more a mystical significance in Mazzini's mind; the very name of Rome, for instance, had for him a sort of talismanic fascination, not unlike that possessed by Jerusalem for the mediæval Christian. When he spoke of the people or the republic he frequently used those terms in an ideal and visionary sense (as theologians use the Church) rather than in one strictly corresponding with the case of any existing nation, or any hitherto tried form of government. This does not alter the fact that his theories, which have been briefly summarised, are not hard to comprehend, as has been said by those who did not know in what they consisted, nor, taken one by one, are they novel. What was new in the nineteenth century was the appearance of a revolutionary leader, who was before all things a religious and ethical teacher. And though Mazzini never founded the Church of Precursors, of which he dreamt, his influence was as surely due to his belief in his religious mission, as was the influence of Savonarola. The Italians are not a mystical people, but they have always followed mystical leaders. The less men are prone to ideal enthusiasm the more attracted are they by it; Don Quixote, as Heine remarked, always draws Sancho Panza after him.

Mazzini had a natural capacity for organisation, and the Association of Young Italy which he founded at Marseilles, the first nucleus being a group of young, penniless refugees, soon obtained an astonishing development. Up to the time of his 'Letter to Charles Albert,' his exile had been so far voluntary that he might have remained in Piedmont had he agreed to live in one of the smaller towns under the watchful care of the police, but he declined the terms, and the first effect of the 'Letter' was a stringent order to arrest him if he recrossed the frontier. He was not surprised at that result. Mazzini's attitude towards the Sardinian monarchy was perfectly well defined. Republican himself, even to fanaticism, he placed the question of unity, which for him meant national existence, above the question of the republic. He did not believe that the House of Savoy would unite Italy, but if unity could only be had under what he looked upon as the inauspicious form of monarchy, he would not reject it. He was like the real mother in the judgment of Solomon, who, because she loved her child, was ready to give it up sooner than see it cut in two.

Apart from personal hereditary instincts and predilections, Mazzini thought that he saw in the glorious memories of the Italian republics a clear indication that the commonwealth was the form of government which ought and would be adopted by the Italy of the future. But, unlike most politicians, he laid down the principle that, after all, when free, the nation must decide for itself. 'To what purpose,' he asks, 'do we constantly speak of the sovereignty of the people, and of our reverence for the national will, if we are to disregard it as soon as it pronounces in contradiction to our wishes?'

He did not succeed in making the majority of his countrymen republicans, but he contributed more than any other man towards inspiring the whole country with the desire for unity. Herein lies his great work. Without Mazzini, when would the Italians have got beyond the fallacies of federal republics, leagues of princes, provincial autonomy, insular home-rule, and all the other dreams of independence reft of its only safeguard which possessed the minds of patriots of every party in Italy and of nearly every well-wisher to Italian freedom abroad?

In 1831, most educated Italians did not even wish for unity, and this is still truer of the republicans than of the monarchists. Some, like Manzoni, did wish for it, but, like him, said nothing about it, for fear of being thought madmen. A flash of the true light illuminated the mind of Ciro Menotti, but that was extinguished on the scaffold. Then it was that Mazzini came forward with the news that Italy could *only* be made free and independent by being united; unity was the ruling tendency of the century, and, as far as Italy went, no Utopia, but a certain conclusion. This was repeated over and over again, wherever there were Italians, over the inhabited globe. By means of sailors, 'Young Italy' spread like lightning. Giuseppe Garibaldi was made a member by a sailor on the shores of the Black Sea.

With the masses, unity proved the wonder-working word which Confalonieri had said was the one thing needful—a word yet fitter to work wonders than 'War to the Stranger.' Among the cultivated classes, it was much slower in gaining ground, and particularly among statesmen and diplomatists. But in the end it was to convert them all.

'"Young Italy,"' writes Mazzini, 'closed the period of political sects, and initiated that of educational associations.' 'Great revolutions,' he says again, 'are the work of principles rather than of bayonets.' It was by the diffusion of ideas that 'Young Italy' became a commanding factor in the events of the next thirty years. The insurrectional attempts planned under its guidance did not succeed, nor was it likely that they should succeed. Devised by exiles, at a distance, they lacked the first elements of success. The earliest of these attempts aimed at an invasion of Savoy; it was hoped that the Sardinian army and people would join the little band of exiles in a movement for the liberation of Lombardy. The revolution of 1821 had evidently suggested this plan to Mazzini, but it was foredoomed to misfortune. The Piedmontese authorities got wind of it, and a hunt followed for the members of 'Young Italy'; most severe measures were taken; there were eleven executions, and numberless sentences to long terms of imprisonment. Jacobo Ruffini, the younger brother of the author of *Dr Antonio*, and Mazzini's most beloved friend, committed suicide in prison, fearing to reveal the names of his associates. The apologists for Charles Albert say that if he had not shown the will and ability to deal severely with the conspirators, Austria would have insisted on a military occupation. Whatever were his motives, this is the saddest page of his unhappy reign.

Checked in 1833, the descent on Savoy was actually attempted in 1834, with Mazzini's consent, though not by his wish. An officer who had won some celebrity in the Polish revolution, General Ramorino, a Savoyard by origin, was given the command. Ramorino was a gambler, who could not be trusted with money, but Mazzini's suspicion that on this occasion he played the part of traitor is not proved. However that may be, the expedition ended almost as soon as it began. Ramorino crossed the frontier of Savoy at the head of the column, but when he heard that a Polish reinforcement had been stopped on the Lake of Geneva, he retreated into Switzerland, and advised the band to follow him.

After these events, Mazzini could no longer carry on his propaganda in France. He took refuge in England, where a great part of his life was to be passed, and of which he spoke, to the last, as his second country. The first period of his residence in England was darkened by the deep distress and discouragement into which the recent events had plunged him; but his faith in the future prevailed, and he went on with his work. His endeavours to help his fellow-exiles reduced him to the last stage of poverty; the day came when he was obliged to pawn a coat and an old pair of boots. These money difficulties did not afflict him, and by degrees his writings in English periodicals brought some addition to the small quarterly allowance which he received from his mother. It seems strange, though it is easily explained, that it was in London that he first got to know the Italian working classes. He was surprised and gladdened by the abundance of good elements which he found in them. No country, indeed, has more reason to hope in her working men than the land whose sons have tunnelled the Alps, cut the most arduous railway lines in America and India, brought up English ships from the deep, laid the caissons (a task of extreme danger) which support the great structure of the Bridge of the Firth of Forth, and left their bones to whiten at Panama. 'It is the universal testimony,' writes a high American authority, 'that no more faithful men have come among us.' What was the cause of the slaughter of the Aigues Mortes? That the Italians worked too well.

Mazzini wrote for his humble friends the treatise on *The Duties of Man*, in which he told them that he loved them too well to flatter them. Another work that occupied him and consoled him was the rescue and moral improvement of the children employed by organ-grinders, and he was the first to call attention to the white slavery to which many of them were subjected. He opened a school in Hatton Garden, in which he taught, and which he mainly supported for the seven years from 1841 to 1848.

The enterprise of the Brothers Bandiera belongs to the history of 'Young Italy,' though Mazzini himself had tried to prevent it, believing that it could only end in the sacrifice of all concerned. Nor, at the last, did the actors in it expect anything else. They had hoped for better things; for a general movement in the South of Italy, or at least for an undertaking on a larger and less irrational basis. But promises failed, money was not forthcoming, and it was a choice between doing nothing or a piece of heroic folly. Contrary to Mazzini's entreaties, they chose the second alternative.

Attilio and Emilio Bandiera were sons of the Austrian admiral who, in 1831, arrested Italian fugitives at sea. Placed by their father in the Austrian navy, they renounced every prospect of a brilliant career to enter the service of their down-trodden country. When they deserted, strong efforts were made by the Archduke

Rainieri, through their mother, to win them back, but neither the offers of pardon nor the poor woman's tears and reproaches turned them from their purpose. Another deserter was with them, Lieutenant Domenico Moro, a youth of great charm of person and disposition, who had been employed with a mixed force of Englishmen and Austrians in the Lebanon, where he formed a warm friendship with Lieutenant, now Admiral, Sir George Wellesley, who still preserves an affectionate remembrance of him. Nicola Ricciotti, a Roman subject who had devoted all his life to Italy, and Anacarsi Nardi, son of the dictator of Modena, were also of the band, which counted about twenty.

The Bandieras and their companions sailed from Corfu for the coast of Calabria on the 11th of June 1844. 'If we fall,' they wrote to Mazzini, 'tell our countrymen to imitate our example, for life was given to us to be nobly and usefully employed, and the cause for which we shall have fought and died is the purest and holiest that ever warmed the heart of man.' It was their last letter. After they landed in Calabria one of their number disappeared; there is every reason to suppose that he went to betray them. They wandered for a few days in the mountains, looking for the insurgent band which they had been falsely told was waiting for them, and then fell into an ambush prepared by the Neapolitan troops. Some died fighting; nine were shot at Cosenza, including the Bandieras, Mori, Ricciotti and Nardi. Boccheciampi the Corsican, whom they suspected of treason, was brought up to be confronted with them during the trial; when asked if he knew who he was, Nardi replied: 'I know no word in my divine Italian language that can fitly describe that man.' Boccheciampi was condemned to a nominal imprisonment; when he came out of prison he wrote to a Greek girl of Corfu, to whom he was engaged, to join him at Naples, that they might be married. The girl had been deeply in love with him, and had already given him part of her dowry, but she answered: 'A traitor cannot wed a Greek maiden; I bear with me the blessing of my parents; upon you rests the curse of God.'

The martyrdom of the Bandieras made a great impression, especially in England, where the circumstance came to light that their correspondence with Mazzini had been tampered with in the English Post Office, and that information as to their plans had reached the Austrian and Neapolitan Governments through the British Foreign Office. The affair was brought before the House of Commons by Thomas Duncombe. The Home Secretary repeated a calumny which had appeared many years before in a French newspaper, to the effect that the murder of an Italian in Rodez by two of his fellow-countrymen was the result of an order from the Association of Young Italy. Sir James Graham had to apologise afterwards for 'the injury inflicted on Mr Mazzini' by this statement, which he was obliged to admit was supported by no evidence, and was contrary to the opinion of the Judge who tried the case.

The *Times* having observed in a leading article that the gravity of the fact in question, the violation of private correspondence in the Post Office, was not affected by the merits or demerits of Mr Mazzini, of whom it professed to 'know nothing,' Thomas Carlyle wrote next day a letter containing words which may be quoted as some of the best and truest ever written about the great Italian: 'I have had the honour to know Mr Mazzini for a series of years, and, whatever I may think of his practical insight and skill in worldly affairs, I can with great freedom testify that he, if I have ever seen one such, is a man of genius and virtue, one of those rare men, numerable unfortunately but as units in this world, who are worthy to be called martyr souls; who in silence, piously in their daily life, understand and practise what is meant by that.' [1]

[1] It is now Carlyle's turn to be aspersed. Let Mazzini speak for him from the grave: 'I do not know if I told you,' he wrote to the Marchesa Eleonora Curlo Ruffini, in a letter published a few months ago, 'that I have met upon my path, deserted enough, I hope, by choice, a Scotchman of mind and things, the first person here, up till now, with whom I sympathise and who sympathises with me. We differ in nearly all opinions, but his are so sincere and disinterested that I respect them. He is good, good, good; he has been, and I think he is still, unhappy in spite of the fame which surrounds him; he has a wife with talent and feeling; always ailing; no children. They live out of town, and I go to see them every now and then. They have no insular or other prejudices that jar upon me. I have grown more intimate with this man in consequence, I think, of an article I wrote here, after knowing him, against an historical work of his; perhaps, accustomed as he is to common-place praise, to which he is indifferent, my frankness pleased him. For the rest I shall see him rarely, and I can only give him esteem and the warmest sympathy—not friendship, which I can henceforth give to no one.' (22nd March 1840.)

CHAPTER V

THE POPE LIBERATOR
1844-1847

*Events leading to the Election of Pius IX.—The Petty Princes—
Charles Albert, Leopold and Ferdinand.*

THE day is drawing near when the century which witnessed the liberation of Italy will have passed away. Already a generation has grown up which can but faintly realise the passionate hopes and fears with which the steps that led through defeat to the ultimate victory were watched, not only by Italians, but by thousands who had never set foot in Italy. Never did a series of political events evoke a sympathy so wide and so disinterested, and it may be foretold with confidence that it never will again. Italy rising from the grave was the living romance of myriads of young hearts that were lifted from the common level of trivial interests and selfish ends, from the routine of work or pleasure, both deadening without some diviner spark, by a sustained enthusiasm that can hardly be imagined now. There were, indeed, some who asked what was all this to them? What were the 'extraneous Austrian Emperor,' or the 'old chimera of a Pope' (Carlyle's designations) to the British taxpayer? Some there were in England who were deeply attached still to the 'Great Hinge on which Europe depended,' and even to the most clement Spanish Bourbons of Naples, about whom strangely beautiful things are to be read in old numbers of the *Quarterly Review*. But on the whole, English men and women—in mind half Italian, whether they will it or not, from the day they begin to read their own literature from Chaucer to Shakespeare, from Shakespeare to Shelley, from Shelley to Rossetti and Swinburne—were united at that time in warmth of feeling towards struggling Italy as they have been united in no political sentiment relating to another nation, and in few concerning their own country.

It would be vain to expect that the record of Italian vicissitudes during the years when the fate of Italy hung in the balance can awake or renew the spellbound interest caused by the events themselves. The reader of recent history is like the novel reader who begins at the last chapter — he is too familiar with how it all ended to be keenly affected by the development of the plot. Yet it is plain that we are in a better position to appreciate the process of development than was the case when the issue remained uncertain. We can estimate more accurately the difficulties which stood in the way, and judge more impartially the means that were taken to remove them. One outcome of this fuller knowledge is the conviction that patriotism was the monopoly of no single Italian party. The leaders, and still more their henchmen, were in the habit of saying very hard things about each other. It was natural and unavoidable; but there is no excuse now for failing to recognise that there were pure and devoted patriots on the one side as well as on the other—men whose only desire was the salvation of Italy, to effect which no sacrifice seemed too great. Nor were their labours unfruitful, for there was work for all of them to do; and the very diversity of opinion, though unfortunate under some aspects, was not so under all. If no one had raised the question of unity before all things, Italy might be still a geographical expression. If no one had tried to wring concessions from the old governments, their inherent and irremediable vices would never have been proved; and though they might have been overturned, they would have left behind a lasting possibility of ignorant reaction.

The Great Powers had presented to the Court of Rome in 1831 a memorandum, in which various moderate reforms and improvements were proposed as urgently necessary to put an end to the intolerable abuses which were rife in the states of the Church, and, most of all, in Romagna. The abolition of the tribunal of the Holy Office, the institution of a Council of State, lay education, and the secularisation of the administration were among the measures recommended. In 1845 a certain Pietro Renzi collected a body of spirited young men at San Marino, and made a dash on Rimini, where he disarmed the small garrison. The other towns were not prepared, and Renzi and his companions were obliged to retire into Tuscany; but the revolution, partial as it had been, raised discussion in consequence of the manifesto issued by its promoters, in which a demand was made for the identical reforms vainly advocated by European diplomacy fourteen years before. If these were granted, the insurgents engaged to lay down their arms. The manifesto was written by Luigi Carlo Farini, who was destined to play a large part in future affairs. It proved to Europe that even the most conservative elements in the nation were driven to revolution by the sheer hopelessness of the dead-lock which the Italian rulers sought by every means to prolong. Massimo d'Azeglio, who was then known only as a painter of talent and a writer of historical novels, first made his mark as a politician by the pamphlet entitled *Gli ultimi casi di Romagna*, in which his arguments derived force from the fact that, when travelling in the district, he had done all in his power to induce the Liberals to keep within the bounds of legality. But he confessed that, when someone says: 'I suffer too much,' it is an unsatisfactory answer to retort: 'You have not suffered enough.' Massimo d'Azeglio had lived for many years an artist's life in Rome and the country round, where his aristocratic birth and handsome face made him popular with all classes. The transparent integrity of his nature overcame the diffidence usually inspired by strangers among a somewhat suspicious people, and he got to know more thoroughly than any other North Italian the real aspirations of the Pope's subjects. He listened to their complaints and their plans, and if they asked his advice, he invariably replied: 'Let us speak clearly. What is it that you wish and I with you? You wish to have done with priestly rule, and to send the Teutons out of Italy? If you invite them to decamp, they will probably say, "No, thank you!" Therefore you must use force; and where is it to be had? If you have not got it, you must find somebody who has. In Italy who has it, or, to speak more precisely, who has a little of it? Piedmont, because it, at least, enjoys an independent life, and possesses an army and a surplus in the treasury.' His friends answered: 'What of Charles Albert, of 1821, of 1832?' Now, there was no one who felt less trust in Charles Albert than Massimo d'Azeglio; he admitted it with something like remorse in later years. But he believed in his ambition, and he thought it madness to throw away what he regarded as the sole chance of freeing Italy on account of private doubts of the King of Sardinia's sincerity.

Charles Albert had reigned for fourteen years, and still the mystery which surrounded his character formed as impenetrable a veil as ever. The popular nickname of *Re Tentenna* (King Waverer) seemed, in a sense, accepted by him when he said to the Duke d'Aumale in 1843: 'I am between the dagger of the Carbonari and the chocolate of the Jesuits.' He chose, as bride for his eldest son, an Austrian princess, who, however, had known no country but Italy. His internal policy was not simply stationary, it was retrograde. If his consent was obtained to some progressive measure, he withdrew it at the last moment, or insisted on the introduction of modifications which nullified the whole. His want of stability drove one of his ministers to jump out of a window. In spite of the candid reference to the Jesuit's cup of chocolate, he allowed the Society of Jesus to dictate its will in Piedmont. Victor Amadeus, the first King of Sardinia, took public education out of the hands of the Jesuits, after receiving the following deathbed communication from one of the Order who was his own confessor: 'Deeply sensible of your many favours, I can only show my gratitude by a final piece of advice, but of such importance that perhaps it may suffice to discharge my debt. Never have a Jesuit for confessor. Do not ask me the grounds of this advice, I should not be at liberty to tell them to you.' The lesson was forgotten now. Charles Albert was not content to wear a hair-shirt himself; he would have liked to see all his subjects furnished with the same garment. The result was, that Piedmont was not a comfortable place for Liberals to live in, nor a lively place for anyone. Yet there is hardly anything more certain than that all this time the King was constantly dreaming of turning the Austrians out of Italy. His government kept its attention fixed on two points: the improvement of the army, and the accumulation of a reserve fund to be available in case of war. Drill and thrift, which made the German Empire out of Prussia, if they did not lead straight to equally splendid results

south of the Alps, were still what rendered it possible for
Piedmont to defy Austria when the time came. In 1840,
Charles Albert wrote to his Minister of War: 'It is a
fine thing to win twenty battles; as for me, I should be
content to win ten on behalf of a cause I know of, and
to fall in the tenth—then, indeed, I would die blessing
the Lord.' A year or two later, he unearthed and re-
assumed the ancient motto of the House of Savoy:
'J'attends mon astre.' Nevertheless, to the outward
world his intentions remained enigmatical, and it was
therefore with extreme surprise that Massimo d'Azeglio
(who, on his return from the Roman states, asked permission to inform the King of the impressions made on
him by his travels) received the injunction to tell his
Liberal friends 'that when the occasion presented itself,
his life, the life of his sons, his treasure, and his army
would all be spent for the Italian cause.'

The fifteen years' pontificate of Gregory XVI. ended
on the 1st June of 1846. In spite of the care taken by those
around him to keep the aged pontiff in a fool's paradise
with regard to the real state of his dominions, a copy
of *The Late Events in Romagna* fell into his hands,
and considerably disturbed his peace of mind. He sent
two prelates to look into the condition of the congested
provinces, and their tour, though it resulted in nothing
else, called forth new protests and supplications from the
inhabitants, of which the most noteworthy was an address
written by Count Aurelio Saffi, who was destined to pass
many honourable years of exile in England. This address
attacked the root of the evil in a passage which exposed
the unbearable vexations of a government based on
espionage. The acknowledged power of an irresponsible
police was backed by the secret force of an army of
private spies and informers. The sentiment of legality

was being stamped out of the public conscience, and with it religion and morality. 'Bishops have been heard to preach civil war—a crusade against the Liberals; priests seem to mix themselves in wretched party strife, egging on the mob to vent its worst passions. There is not a Catholic country in which the really Christian priest is so rarely found as in the States of the Church.'

If Gregory XVI. was not without reasons for disquietude in his last hours, he could take comfort in the fact that he had succeeded in keeping railways out of all parts of his dominions. Gas and suspension bridges were also classed as works of the Evil One, and vigorously tabooed. Among the Pope's subjects there was a young prelate who had never been able to make out what there was subversive to theology in a steam-engine, or why the safety of the Papal government should depend on its opposing every form of material improvement, although in discussing these subjects he generally ended by saying: 'After all I am no politician, and I may be mistaken.' This prelate was Cardinal Mastai-Ferretti, Bishop of Imola. Born in 1792 at Sinigaglia, of a good though rather needy family, Count Giovanni Maria Mastai was piously brought up by his mother, who dedicated him at an early age to the Virgin, to whom she believed that she owed his recovery from an illness which had been pronounced fatal. Roman Catholic writers connect the promulgation of the dogma of the Immaculate Conception with this incident of childhood. After entering the priesthood, young Mastai devoted most of his energies to active charity, and remained, as he said, 'no politician,' being singularly ignorant of the world and of public affairs, though full of amiable wishes that everyone should be happy. Some years spent in missionary work in South America failed to enlarge his practical knowledge, the limits of which he was the first to recognise—a fact that tended to make him all his life the instrument, not of his own will, but of the wills of men whom he honestly thought cleverer and more experienced than himself. His chief friends in his Romagnol diocese, friends on the intimate basis of social equality and common provincial interests, were sound patriots, though not revolutionists, and the future Pio Nono involuntarily adopted their ideas and sympathies. He saw with his eyes certain abuses so glaring that they admitted of no two opinions, and these helped to convince him of the truth of his friends' arguments in favour of a completely new order of things. One such abuse was the encouragement given by government to the Society of the Centurioni, the latest evolution of the Calderai; the Centurions, recruited among roughs and peasants, were set upon the respectable middle classes, over which they tyrannised by secret accusations or open violence: it was well understood that anyone called a Liberal, or Freemason, or Carbonaro could be beaten or killed without inquiries being made.

The Bishop of Imola was frequently in the house of the Count and Countess Pasolini, who kept their friend well supplied with the new books on Italian affairs; thus he read not only D'Azeglio's *Casi di Romagna*, but also Cesare Balbo's *Le Speranze d'Italia*, which propounded a plan for an Italian federation, and Gioberti's *Primato morale e civile degli Italiani*, in which this plan was elaborately developed. Gioberti indicated the Supreme Pontiff as the natural head of the Italian Union, and the King of Sardinia as Italy's natural deliverer from foreign domination. The eternal fitness of things, and the history of many centuries, proved the Pope to be the proper paramount civil authority in Italy, 'which is the capital of Europe, because Rome is the religious metropolis of the world.' An ex-member of 'Young Italy,' a Piedmontese by birth, a priest by ordination, Gioberti's profession of faith was derived from these three sources, and it attracted thousands of Italians by its apparent reconciliation of the interests of the papacy, and of the Sardinian monarchy, with the most advanced views of the newest school. History, to which Gioberti appealed, might have told him that a reversal of the law of gravity was as likely to happen as the performance by the papacy of the mission he proposed to it; but men believe what they wish to believe, and his work found, as has been said, thousands of admirers, among whom none was more sincere than Cardinal Mastai. The day on which Count Pasolini gave him a copy of *Il Primato* he created that great, and under some aspects pathetic illusion, the reforming Pope.

The Conclave opened on the 14th of June 1846. During the Bishop of Imola's journey to Rome a white pigeon had perched several times on his carriage. The story became known; people said the same thing had occurred to a coming Pope on former occasions, and the augury was accepted with joy and satisfaction. He was, in fact, elected after the Conclave had lasted only two days, while the Conclave which elected his predecessor lasted sixty-four. The brevity of that to which Pius IX. owed the tiara was looked upon by the populace as something miraculous, but it was the result of the well-considered determination of the Italian Cardinals not to allow time for Austrian intrigues to obtain the election of a Pope who would be ruled from Vienna. When the new Pope appeared on the balcony of the Quirinal to give his first benediction, the people, carried away by his youthful yet majestic bearing, and by the hopes which already centred in him, broke into frantic cries of: 'We have a Pope! He loves us! He is our Father!' If they had cried: 'We have a new heaven and a new earth,' they would but have expressed the delirium which, starting from Rome, spread throughout Italy.

On the night of the 6th of December 1846, the whole line of the Apennines from Liguria to Calabria was illuminated. A hundred years before, a stone thrown by the child Balilla had given the signal for the expulsion of the Austrians from Genoa: this was the memory flashed from height to height by countless beacons, but while celebrating the past, they were the fiery heralds of a greater revolution.

The upheaval of Europe did not become a fact, however, for another year. Meantime, the Roman States attracted more attention than any other part of the peninsula, from the curiosity awakened by the progress of the experiment of which they were the scene. It is not doubtful that at the first moment Pius IX. was under the impression that the problem he had taken in hand was eminently simple. A little goodwill on the part of everybody, an amnesty to heal old sores, and a few administrative reforms, ought, he thought, to set everything right. Such was not the opinion of intelligent onlookers who were students of politics—especially if they were foreigners, and could therefore keep their heads moderately cool in the prevailing excitement. The wave of a wand may seem to effect marvels, but long and silent causes prepare the way for each event. Now what had been going on for years in the Roman States was not the process of gradual growth, but the process of rapid disintegration. The Temporal Power of the Popes had died without anyone noticing it, and there was nothing left but a body in the course of dissolution. Every foreigner in Rome during the reign of Gregory XVI. bore witness that his government depended for its existence absolutely on the Swiss Guards. In 1845, Count Rossi told Guizot that without the Swiss regiments the government in the Legations and the Marches 'would be overthrown in the twinkling of an eye.' The British agent in Rome, writing during the Conclave, bore this out by the statement, which applied not to one portion of the Roman states, but to all, that 'the government could not stand without the protection of Austria and the immediate presence of the Swiss.' On the accession of Pius IX., the props, such as they were, which had prevented an earlier collapse of the Temporal Power, were either removed or rendered useless. The Swiss might as well have been disbanded at once as retained merely to be a bone of contention between the new government and the people, since it was understood that a vigorous use of their services would never be resorted to; while Austrian protection was transferred from the Pope to the disaffected party in the Church, which consisted in a large proportion of the cardinals and of the inferior clergy who were afraid that, with the reform of abuses, they would lose their influence over the lower class of their flocks. The English diplomatic agents in Italy also firmly believed that Austria coupled with her support of the ultramontane malcontents the direct encouragement of the disorderly elements of the population. To resist all these contrary forces, Pius IX. had only a popularity which, though for the time immense, was founded almost completely on imagination. 'It was,' said Mr Petre, 'the name and known views of Pius, rather than his acts, which aroused so much interest.' If for 'known views' be substituted

F

'supposed views,' the remark exactly describes the situation.

Popularity is very well, but a government cannot long subsist on the single fact of the popularity of the sovereign. When the Roman mob began to cry: 'Viva Pio Nono *solo*,' the fate of the experiment was sealed. Real control slipped from the hands that nominally wielded it. 'The influence,' Mr Petre wrote to Sir George Hamilton, 'of one individual of the lower class, Angelo Brunetti, hardly known but by his nickname of Ciceruacchio, has for the last month kept the peace of the city more than any power possessed by the authorities, from the command which he exerts over the populace.' It was Ciceruacchio who preserved order when in July 1847 the air was full of rumours of a vast reactionary plot, which aimed at carrying off the Pope, and putting things back as they were under Gregory. That such a plot was ever conceived, or, at anyrate, that it received the sanction of the high personages whose names were mentioned in connection with it, is generally doubted now; but it was believed in by many of the representatives of foreign Powers then in Italy. The public mind in Rome was violently disturbed. Austria made the excitement the excuse for occupying the town of Ferrara, where, by the accepted interpretation of the Treaty of Vienna, she had only the right to garrison the fortress. This aggression called forth a strong remonstrance from the Pope's Secretary of State, Cardinal Ferretti; and though a compromise was arrived at through the mediation of Lord Palmerston, the feeling against Austria grew more and more exasperated in the Roman states, and the Pope consented, not, it seemed, much against the grain, to preparations being taken in hand with a view to the possible eventuality of war.

At this date the Italian question was better apprehended at Vienna than in any other part of Europe. A man of Prince Metternich's talents does not devote a long life to statecraft without learning to distinguish the real drift of political currents. While Lord Palmerston still felt sure that reforms, and nothing but reforms, were what Italy wanted, Prince Metternich saw that two real forces were at work from the Alps to the Straits of Messina, and two only: desire for union, hatred of Austria. Nor was it his fault if the English Cabinet or the rest of the world remained unenlightened. Besides enlarging on this truth in frequent diplomatic communications, he caused it to be continually dwelt upon in the Vienna *Observer*, the organ of the Austrian Government, which printed illustrative quotations from the writings of Mazzini, of whom it said that 'he has the one merit of despising hypocrisy, and proceeding firmly and directly to his true end. Persons who are versed in history will know that this is exactly the same end as that at which Arnold of Brescia and Cola di Rienzi formerly aimed. The only difference is, that the revolutionary dream has in the course of centuries gained in self-reliance and confidence.' It may truly be affirmed after this that Metternich 'had the one merit of despising hypocrisy.' Exactly the same end as Arnold of Brescia and Cola di Rienzi—who better could have described the scheme of Italian redemption?

In the course of the summer of 1847, the Prince said more than once to the British Ambassador: 'The Emperor is determined not to lose his Italian dominions.' It was no idle boast, the speaker felt confident, that the troops in Lombardy and Venetia could keep those provinces from taking an active part in the 'revolution' which he declared to be already complete over all central

Italy, though the word revolution had never yet been mentioned. Nor was it only in the Austrian army that he trusted; Metternich was persuaded that neither in Lombardy nor in Venetia was there any fear of a really popular and, therefore, formidable movement. He believed that Austria's only enemy was the aristocracy. He even threw out hints that if the Austrian Government condescended to do so, it could raise a social or peasants' war of the country people against their masters. This is the policy which has been elaborately followed by the Russians in Poland. The Austrians pointed to their virtue in not resorting to it; but some tentative experiments in such a direction had not given results of a kind to encourage them to go on. The Italian peasant, though ignorant, had a far quicker innate intelligence than his unfortunate Polish brother. He did not dislike his masters, who treated him at least with easy familiarity, and he detested foreigners—those foreigners, no matter of what nation, who for two thousand years had brought the everlasting curse of war upon his fields. The conscription, which carried off his sons for eight years into distant lands, of which he could not pronounce the name, was alone enough to alienate him from the Austrian Government. In hoping to find a friend in the Italian peasant, Metternich reckoned without his host. On the other hand, he was strictly correct in his estimate of the patriotism of the aristocracy. The fact always seemed to the Prince a violation of eternal laws. According to him, the foreordained disaffected in every country were drawn from the middle classes. What business had noblemen with ancient names and fine estates to prefer Spielberg to their beautiful palaces and fairy-like villas on the Lombard lakes? Was it on purpose to spite the best of governments, and the one most favourable to the aristocratic principle, which had always held out paternal hands to them? Could anything be imagined more aggravating?

This feature in Italian liberation has been kept mostly in the background. Democratic chroniclers were satisfied to ignore it, and to the men themselves their enormous sacrifices seemed so natural that they were very willing to let them pass out of mind. It is in the works of those who, while sympathising with Italy, are not Italians, that the best record of it is to be found; nowhere better than in a recent book by a French writer, M. Paul Bourget, in which occurs the following just and eloquent tribute: 'We must say in praise of the aristocracy on this side of the Alps that the best soldiers of independence were nobles. If Italy owes the final success to the superior capabilities of Victor Emmanuel and Cavour, and to the agitating power of the General of the Thousand, it is well not to forget the struggles sustained for years by gentlemen whose example did so much to raise partisans among the humble. These aristocrats, passionate for liberty, have (like our own of the eighteenth century) done more for the people than the people itself. The veritable history of this *Risorgimento* would be in great part that of the Italian nobility in which the heroic blood of feudal chiefs revolted against the oppressions and, above all, the perpetual humiliation, born of the presence of the stranger.'

When Prince Metternich looked beyond the borders of those provinces which he said that his Sovereign did not intend to lose, he saw sooner than most people that a ball was set rolling which would not stop half way down the hill. The one element in the situation which came as a surprise to him, was that introduced by Pius IX. 'A liberal Pope is an impossible being!' he exclaimed

Nevertheless this impossible being was a reality which had to be dealt with. He hoped all along, however, that Pius would fall a victim to the Frankenstein he had called into existence, and his only real anxiety lay where it had always lain—on the side of Piedmont. 'Charles Albert ought to let us know,' he wrote to the Austrian Minister at Turin, 'whether his reign has been only a mask under which was hidden the Prince of Carignano, who ascended the throne through the order of succession re-established in his favour by the Emperor Francis.' Considering all things, the endeavour to make it appear that the King was indebted for his crown to Austria was somewhat venturesome. Charles Albert, Metternich went on to say, had to choose between two systems, the system now in force, or 'the crassest revolution.' He wrote again: 'The King is sliding back upon the path which he enters for the second time in his life, *and which he will never really quit.*' Words of a bitter enemy, but juster than the 'Esecrato o Carignano,' hurled for a quarter of a century at Charles Albert by those who only saw in him a traitor.

The constant invocation of the revolutionary spectre by the Austrian statesman convinced the King that the wish was father to the thought, and, afraid of introducing the thin end of the wedge, he showed himself more than ever averse to reforming the antiquated machinery of the Sardinian Government. Instead of being the first of Italian princes to yield to popular demands, he was almost the last. He believed that the question of nationality, of independence, could be separated from the question of free institutions. Of all the chimerical ideas then afloat, this was the most chimerical. Even the example of the Pope, for whom Charles Albert felt a romantic devotion, was not enough to induce him to open the road to reforms. The person who seems first to have impressed him with their absolute necessity was Lord Minto, whose visit to Turin, in October 1847, coincided with the dismissal of Count della Margherita, the minister most closely associated with the absolutist and Jesuitical *régime*. Lord Minto was sent to Italy to encourage in the ways of political virtue those Italian princes who were not entirely incorrigible. His mission excited exaggerated hopes on the part of the Liberals, and exaggerated wrath in the retrograde party—both failing to understand its limitations. The hopes died a natural death, but long afterwards, reactionary writers attributed all the 'troubles' in Italy to this estimable British diplomatist. What is not doubtful is, that, accustomed as they were to being lectured and bullied by foreign courts, the Italians derived the greatest encouragement from the openly expressed sympathy of well-known English visitors, whether they came in an official capacity like Lord Minto, or unofficially like Mr Cobden, who travelled as a missionary of Free Trade, and was received with rapture—with which, it is to be feared, Free Trade had little to do—by the leading Liberals in Italy: Massimo d'Azeglio at Genoa, Mancini at Naples Cavour and Scialoja at Turin, Minghetti at Bologna, Ridolfi at Florence, and Manin and Tommaseo at Venice.

Towards the end of 1847, there was a curious shuffling of the cards in the small states of Lucca and Parma, resulting in much irritation, which, in an atmosphere so charged with revolutionary electricity, was not without importance. The dissolute Bourbon prince who reigned in Lucca, Charles Ludovico, had but one desire, which was to increase his civil list. He hit upon an English jockey named Ward, who came to Italy in the service of a German count, and this person he made his Chancellor of the Exchequer. By various luminous strokes, Ward furthered his Sovereign's object without much increasing the taxation, and when matters began to grow complicated, and here, too, a cry was raised for a Constitution (which had been solemnly guaranteed to the people of Lucca at the Congress of Vienna, but had never been heard of since), he proposed the sale of the Duchy offhand to Tuscany, with which it would, in any case, be united, when, on the death of the ex-Empress Marie-Louise, the Duchy of Parma devolved on the Duke of Lucca. At the same time, by a prior agreement, a district of Tuscany called the Lunigiana was consigned, one-half to the Duchess of Parma, and the other to the Duke of Modena. The indignation of the population, which was made, by force, subject to the Duke of Modena, was intense, and the whole transaction of handing about Italians to suit the pleasure of princes, or to obey the articles of forgotten treaties, reminded the least sensitive of the everyday opprobrium of their lot.

The bargain with Tuscany had been struck only eight days when Marie-Louise died—unlamented, since the latter years of her reign formed a sad contrast to the earlier. Marie-Louise had not a bad disposition, but she always let her husband of the hour govern as he chose; of the four or five of these husbands, the last two, and particularly the hated Count de Bombelles, undid all the good done by their more humane predecessors. The Parmese petitioned their new Duke to send the man away, and to grant them some measure of freedom. The answer he gave was the confirmation of Bombelles in all his honours, and the conclusion of a treaty with Austria, securing the assistance of her arms. A military force had been sent to Parma to escort the body of the late Duchess to Vienna; but on the principle that the living are of more consequence than the dead, it remained there to protect the new Duke from his subjects. Marie-Louise and her lovers, Charles Ludovico and his jockey-minister, are instructive illustrations of the scandalous point things had reached in the small states of Italy.

There was, indeed, one state in which, though the dynasty was Austrian, the government was conducted without ferocity and without scandal. This was Tuscany. The branch of the Hapsburg-Lorraine family established in Tuscany produced a series of rulers who, if they exhibited no magnificent qualities, were respectable as individuals, and mild as rulers. Giusti dubbed Leopold II. 'the Tuscan Morpheus, crowned with poppies and lettuce leaves,' and the clear intelligence of Ricasoli was angered by the languid, let-be policy of the Grand-Ducal government, but, compared with the other populations of Italy, the Tuscans might well deem themselves fortunate. Only on one occasion had the Grand Duke given up a fugitive from the more favoured provinces, and the presence of distinguished exiles lent brilliancy to his capital. Leopold II. hesitated between the desire to please his subjects and the fear of his Viennese relations, who sent him through Metternich the ominous reminder, 'that the Italian Governments had only subsisted for the last ten years by the support they received from Austria' —an assertion at which Charles Albert took umbrage, but he was curtly told that he was not intended. In spite of his fears, however, the Grand Duke instituted a National Guard on the 4th of September, which was correctly judged the augury of further concessions. In August, the Austrian Minister had distinctly threatened to occupy Tuscany, or any other of the Italian duchies where a National Guard was granted; its institution was therefore interpreted as a decisive act of rebellion against the Imperial dictatorship. The red, white and green tricolor, not yet permitted in Piedmont, floated already from all the towers of the city on the Arno.

Where there were no signs of improvement was in the government of the Two Sicilies. King Ferdinand undertook a journey through several parts of the country, but as Lord Napier, the British Minister, expressed it: 'Exactly where the grace of the royal countenance was principally conferred, the rebels sprung up most thickly.' A revolution was planned to break out in all the cities of the kingdom, but the project only took effect at Messina and at Reggio, and in both places the movement was stifled with prompt and barbarous severity. When the leader of the Calabrian attempt, Domenico Romeo, a landed proprietor, was caught on the heights of Aspromonte, his captors, after cutting off his head, carried it to his young nephew, whom they ordered to take it to Reggio with the cry of 'Long live the King.' The youth refused, and was immediately killed. In the capital, Carlo Poerio and many patriots were thrown into prison on suspicion. Settembrini had just time to escape to Malta.

The year 1847 closed amid outward appearances of quiet.

CHAPTER VI

THE YEAR OF REVOLUTION
1848

Insurrection in Sicily—The Austrians expelled from Milan and Venice —Charles Albert takes the Field—Withdrawal of the Pope and King of Naples—Piedmont defeated—The Retreat.

ON the 12th of January, the birthday of the King of the Two Sicilies, another insurrection broke out in Sicily; this time it was serious indeed. The City of the Vespers lit the torch which set Europe on fire.

So began the year of revolution which was to see the kings of the earth flying, with or without umbrellas, and the principle of monarchy more shaken by the royal see-saw of submission and vengeance than ever it was by the block of Whitehall or the guillotine of the Place Louis XV.

In Italy, the errors and follies of that year were not confined to princes and governments, but it will remain memorable as the time when the Italian nation, not a dreamer here or there, or a handful of heroic madmen, or an isolated city, but the nation as a whole, with an unanimity new in history, asserted its right and its resolve to exist.

King Ferdinand sent 5000 soldiers to 'make a garden,' as he described it, of Palermo, if the offers sent at the same time failed to pacify the inhabitants. These offers were refused with the comment: 'Too late,' and the Palermitans prepared to resist to the death under the guidance of the veteran patriot Ruggiero Settimo, Prince of Fitalia. 'Separation,' they said, 'or our English Constitution of 1812.' Increased irritation was awakened by the discovery in the head office of the police at Palermo of a secret room full of skeletons, which were supposed to belong to persons privately murdered. The Neapolitans were compelled to withdraw with a loss of 3000 men, but before they went, the general in command let out 4000 convicts, who had been kept without food for forty-eight hours. The convicts, however, did not fulfil the intentions of their liberator, and did but little mischief. Not so the Neapolitan troops, who committed horrors on the peasantry as they retreated, which provoked acts of retaliation almost as barbarous. In a short time all Sicily was in its own hands except the citadel of Messina.

It is not possible to follow the Sicilians in their long struggle for their autonomy. They stood out for some fourteen months. An English Blue-book is full of the interminable negotiations conducted by Lord Napier and the Earl of Minto in the hope of bringing the strife to an end. When the parliament summoned by the revolutionary government declared the downfall of the House of Bourbon, all the stray princes in Europe, including Louis Napoleon, were reviewed as candidates for the throne. The choice fell on the Duke of Genoa; it was well received in England, and the British men-of-war were immediately ordered to salute the Sicilian flag. But the Duke's reign never became a reality. After an heroic struggle, the islanders were subjugated in the spring of 1849.

So stout a fight for independence must win admiration, if not approval. The political reasons against the course taken by the Sicilians have been suggested in a former chapter. In separating their lot from that of Naples, in rejecting even freedom unless it was accompanied by disruption, they hastened the ruin of the Neapolitans and of themselves, and surely played into the hands of the crafty tyrant who desired nothing better than to fish in the troubled waters of his subjects' dissensions.

In the gathering storm of January 1848, the first idea that occurred to Ferdinand II. was the good old plan of calling in Austrian assistance. But the Austrians were told by Pius IX. that he would not allow their troops to pass through his territory. Had they attempted to pass in spite of his warning, events would have taken a different turn, as the Pope would have been driven into a war with Austria then and there; perhaps he would have been glad, as weak people commonly are, of the compulsion to do what he dared not do without compulsion. The Austrian Government was too wise to force a quarrel; it was easy to lock up Austrian subjects for crying 'Viva Pio Nono,' but the enormous importance of keeping the Head of the Church, if possible, in a neutral attitude could not be overlooked. All thoughts of going to Ferdinand's help were politely abandoned, and he, seeing himself in a defenceless position, and pondering deeply on the upsetting of Louis Philippe's throne, which was just then the latest news, decided on that device, dear to all political conjurors, which is known as taking the wind out of your enemy's sails. The Pope, the Grand Duke of Tuscany and the King of Sardinia, had worried him for six months with admonitions. 'Very well,' he now said; 'they urge me forward, I will precipitate them.' Constitution, representative government, unbridled liberty of the press, a civic guard, the expulsion of the Jesuits; what mattered a trifle more or less when everything could be revoked at the small expense of perjury? Ferdinand posed to perfection in the character of Citizen King. He reassured those who ventured to show the least signs of apprehension by saying: 'If I had not intended to carry out the Statute, I should not have granted it.'

Not many days later, the Grand Duke of Tuscany and the King of Sardinia each promulgated a Charter. In the case of Charles Albert, it had been formally promised on the 8th of February, after sleepless nights, severe fasts, much searching of the heart—contrasting strangely with the gay transformation scene at Naples; but promises have a more serious meaning to some persons than to others. Nor did Charles Albert take any pleasure in the shouts of a grateful people. 'Born in revolution,' he once wrote, 'I have traversed all its phases, and I know well enough what popularity is worth—*viva* to-day, *morte* to-morrow.'

In the Lombardo-Venetian provinces all seemed still quiet, but the brooding discontent of the masses increased with the increasing aggressiveness of the Austrian soldiers, while the refusal to grant the studiously moderate demands of men like Nazari of Bergamo and Manin and Tommaseo of Venice, who were engaged in a campaign of legal agitation, brought conviction to the most cautious that no measure of political liberty was obtainable under Austrian rule.

At the Scala Theatre some of the audience had raised cries of 'Viva Pio Nono' during a performance of *I Lom-*

bardi.* This was the excuse for prohibiting every direct or indirect public reference to the reigning Pontiff. Nevertheless, a few young men were caught singing the Pope's hymn, upon which the military charged the crowd. On the 3rd of January the soldiers fell on the people in the Piazza San Carlo, killing six and wounding fifty-three. The parish priest of the Duomo said that he had seen Russians, French and Austrians enter Milan as invaders; but a scene like that of the 3rd of January he had never witnessed; 'they simply murdered in the streets.'

The *Judicium Statuarium*, equivalent to martial law, was proclaimed in February; but the Viennese revolution of the 8th of March, and Prince Metternich's flight to England, were followed by promises to abolish the censure, and to convoke the central congregations of the Lombardo-Venetian kingdom. The utmost privilege of these assemblies was consultative. In 1815 they were invested with the right to 'make known grievances,' but they had only once managed to perform this modest function. It was hardly worth while to talk about them on the 18th of March 1848.

On the morning of that day, Count O'Donnel, the Vice-Governor of Milan, announced the Emperor's concessions. Before night he was the hostage of the revolution, signing whatever decrees were demanded of him till in a few hours even his signature was dispensed with. The Milanese had begun their historic struggle.

* On the production of Verdi's opera, *I Lombardi alla prima Crociata*, the Austrian Archbishop of Milan wished the Commissary of Police to prohibit the performance because it treated of sacred subjects. When it was recognised as one of the accelerating causes of the revolution, he drily remarked that they would have done better to take his advice. The grand chorus, 'O Signore dal tetto natìo,' in which the censor had only seen a pious chant, became the morning-song of national resurrection.

Taking refuge in the Citadel, Radetsky wrote to the Podestà, Count Gabrio Casati (brother of Teresa Confalonieri), that he acknowledged no authority at Milan except his own and that of his soldiers. Those who resisted would be guilty of high treason. If arguments did not avail, he would make use of all the means placed in his hands by an army of 100,000 men to bring the rebel city to obedience. Unhappily for Radetsky, there were not any such 100,000 men in Italy, though long before this he had told Metternich that he could not guarantee the safety of Lombardy with less than 150,000. In spite of partial reinforcements, the number did not amount to more than from 72,000 to 75,000, while at Milan it stood at between 15,000 and 20,000. But if we take the lower estimate, 15,000 regular troops under such a commander, who, most rare in similar emergencies, knew his own mind, and had no thought except the recovery of the town for his Sovereign, constituted a formidable force against a civilian population, which began the fight with only a few hundred fowling-pieces. The odds on the side of Austria were tremendous.

If the Milan revolt had been one of the customary revolutions, arranged with the help of pen and paper, its first day would have been certainly its last. But even more than the Sicilian Vespers, it was the unpremeditated, irresistible act of a people sick of being slaves. At the beginning Casati tried to restrain it; so, with equal or still stronger endeavours, did the republican Carlo Cattaneo, whose influence was great. 'You have no arms,' he said again and again. Not a single man of weight took upon himself the awful responsibility of urging the unarmed masses upon so desperate an enterprise; but when the die was cast none held back. Initiated by the populace, the revolt was led to its victorious close by the nerve and ability of the influential men who directed its course.

Towards nightfall on the 18th, during which day there had been only scuffles between the soldiers and the people, Radetsky took the Broletto, where the Municipality sat, after a two hours' siege, and sent forthwith a special messenger to the Emperor with the news that the revolution was on a fair way to being completely crushed. Meanwhile, he massed his troops at all the entrances to the city, so that at dawn he might strangle the insurrection by a concentric movement, as in a noose. The plan was good ; but to-morrow does not belong even to the most experienced of Field-Marshals.

In all quarters of the city barricades sprang up like mushrooms. Everything went, freely given, to their construction ; the benches of the Scala, the beds of the young seminarists, the court carriages, found hidden in a disused church, building materials of the half-finished Palazzo d'Adda, grand pianofortes, valuable pieces of artistic furniture, and the old kitchen table of the artisan. Before the end of the fight the barricades numbered 1523. Young nobles, dressed in the velvet suits then in vogue, cooks in their white aprons, even women and children, rushed to the defence of the improvised fortifications. Luciano Manara and other heroes, who afterwards fell at Rome, were there to lead. In the first straits for want of arms the museums of the Uboldi and Poldi-Pozzoli families were emptied of their rare treasures by permission of the owners ; the crowd brandished priceless old swords and specimens of early firearms. More serviceable weapons were obtained by degrees from the Austrian killed and wounded, and from the public offices which fell into their hands. Bolza, long the hated agent of the Austrian police, was discovered by the people, but they did not harm him. Throughout the five days, the Milanese showed a forbearance which was the more admirable, because there can be no doubt that when the Austrians found they were getting the worst of it, they vented their rage in deplorable outrages on non-combatants. That Radetsky was personally to blame for these excesses has never been alleged, and it was perhaps beyond the power of the officers to keep discipline among soldiers who, towards the end, were wild with panic.

'The very foundations of the city were torn up,' wrote the Field-Marshal in his official report; 'not hundreds, but thousands of barricades crossed the streets. Such circumspection and audacity were displayed that it was evident military leaders were at the head of the people. The character of the Milanese had become quite changed. Fanaticism had seized every rank and age and both sexes.'

As always happens with street-fighting, the number of the slain has never been really known; the loss of the citizens was small compared with that of the Austrians, who, according to some authorities, lost 5000, between killed and wounded.

Radetsky ordered the evacuation of the town and citadel on the night of Wednesday, the 22nd of March. The Milanese had won much more than freedom—they had won the right to it. And what they had done they had done alone. When the news that the capital was up in arms spread through Lombardy, there was but one gallant impulse, to fly to its aid. But the earliest to arrive, Giuseppe Martinengo Cesaresco, with his troop of Brescian peasants, found when he reached Milan that they were a few hours too late to share in the last shots fired upon the retreating Austrians.

Nowhere, except in Milan, did the revolution meet

with a Radetsky. The Austrian authorities became convinced that their position was untenable, and they desired to avoid a useless sacrifice of life. This, rather than cowardly fears, was the motive which induced Count Palffy and Count Zichy, the civil and military governors of Venice, to yield the city without deluging it in blood. The latter had been guilty of negligence in leaving the Venetian arsenal in charge of troops so untrustworthy that Manin could take it on the 22nd of March by a simple display of his own courage, and without striking a blow, but after this first success on the side of the revolution, which supplied the people with an unlimited stock of arms and ammunition, the Austrians did well to give way even from their own point of view. At seven o'clock on the evening of the 22nd of March, the famous capitulation was signed. Manin's prediction of the previous day, 'To-morrow the city will be in my power, or I shall be dead,' had been realised in the first alternative.

Daniel Manin, who was now forty-four years of age, was by profession a lawyer, by race a Jew. His father became a Christian, and, according to custom, took the surname of his godfather, who belonged to the family of the last Doge of Venice. Manin and the Dalmatian scholar, Niccolò Tommaseo, had been engaged in patiently adducing proof after proof that Austria did not even abide by her own laws when the expression of political opinion was concerned. At the beginning of the revolution they were in prison, and Palffy's first act of surrender was to set them free. Henceforth Manin was undisputed lord of the city. It is strange how, all at once, a man who was only slightly known to the world should have been chosen as spokesman and ruler. It did not, however, happen by chance. The people in Italy are observant; the Venetians had observed Manin, and they trusted him. The power of inspiring trust was what gave this Jewish lawyer his ascendancy, not the talents which usually appeal to the masses. He had not the advantage of an imposing presence, for he was short, slight, with blue eyes and bushy hair; in all things he was the opposite to a demagogue; he never beguiled, or flattered, or told others what he did not believe himself. But, on his side, he *knew* the people, whom most revolutionary leaders know not at all. 'That is my sole merit,' he used to say. It was that which enabled him to cleanse Venice from the stain of having bartered her freedom for the smile of a conqueror, and give her back the name and inheritance of 'eldest child of liberty.'

It was a matter of course that emancipated Venice should assume a republican form of government. Here the republic was a restoration. At Milan the case was different; there were two parties, that of Cattaneo, which was strongly republican, that of Casati, which was strongly monarchical. There was a third party, which thought of nothing except of never again seeing a soldier with a white coat. By mutual agreement, the Provisional Government declared that the decision as to the form of government should be left to calmer days. For a time this compromise produced satisfactory results.

The revolution gained ground. Francis of Modena executed a rapid flight, and the Duke of Parma presently followed him. By the end of March, Lombardy and Venetia were free, saving the fortresses of the Quadrilateral. The exception was of far greater moment than, in the enchantment of the hour, anyone dreamt of confessing. Mantua, Legnano, Peschiera and Verona were so many cities of refuge to the flying Austrian troops, where they could rest in safety and nurse their strength.

Still, the results achieved were great, almost incredible; with the expectation that Rome, Naples, Tuscany and Piedmont would send their armies to consolidate the work already done, it was natural to think that, whatever else might happen, Austrian dominion was a thing of the past. Alessandro Bixio (brother of the General), who was a naturalised Frenchman, wrote to the French Government on the 7th of April from Turin: 'In the ministries, in meetings, in the streets, you only see and hear people to whom the question of Italian independence seems to be one of those historical questions about which the time is past for talking. According to the general opinion, Austria is nothing but a phantom, and the army of Radetsky a shadow.' Such were the hopes that prevailed. They were vain, but they did not appear so then.

Pius IX. seemed to throw in his lot definitely with the revolution when, on the 19th of March, he too granted a Constitution, having previously formed a lay ministry, which included Marco Minghetti and Count Pasolini, under the presidency of Cardinal Antonelli, who thus makes his first appearance as Liberal Premier. That the Roman Constitution was an unworkable attempt to reconcile lay and ecclesiastical pretensions, that the proposed Chamber of Deputies, which was not to make laws affecting education, religious corporations, the registration of births and marriages; or to confer civil rights on non-catholics, or to touch the privileges and immunities of the clergy, might have suited Cloud-cuckoo-town, but would not suit the solid earth, were facts easy to recognise, but no one had time to pause and consider. It was sufficient to hear Pius proclaim that in the wind which was uprooting oaks and cedars might be clearly distinguished the Voice of the Lord. Such utterances, mingled with blessings on Italy, brought balm to patriotic souls. The Liberals had no fear that the Pope would veto the participation of his troops in the national war, for they were blind to the complications with which a fighting Pope would find himself embarrassed in the middle of the nineteenth century. But the other party discerned these complications from the first, and knew what use to make of them.

The powers of reaction had only to catch hold of a perfectly modern sentiment, the doctrine that ecclesiastics should be men of peace, in order to dissipate the myth of a Pope liberator. It was beside the question that, from the moment he accepted such a doctrine, the Pope condemned the institution of prince-bishoprics, of which he represented the last survival. Nor was it material that, if he adopted it, consistency should have made him carry it to its logical consequence of non-resistance. By aid of this theory of a peaceful Pontiff, with the threat, in reserve, of a schism, Austria felt confident that she could avoid the enormous moral inconvenience of a Pope in arms against her.

Either, however, the full force of the influence which caused Pius IX. to draw back was not brought to bear till somewhat late in the day, or the part acted by him during the months of March and April can be hardly acquitted of dissimulation. War preparations were continued, with the warm co-operation of the Cardinal President of the Council, and when General Durando started for the frontier with 17,000 men, he would have been a bold man who had said openly in Rome that they were intended not to fight.

While the Pope was still supposed to favour the war, Ferdinand of Naples did not dare to oppose the enthusiasm of his subjects, and the demand that a Neapolitan contingent should be sent to Lombardy. The first relay of troops actually started, but the generals had secret orders to take the longest route, and to lose as much time as possible.

Tuscany had a very small army, but such assistance as she could give was both promised and given. The fate of the Tuscan corps of 6000 men will be related hereafter. The Grand Duke Leopold identified himself with the Italian cause with more sincerity than was to be found at Rome or Naples; still, the material aid that he could offer counted as next to nothing.

There remained Piedmont and Charles Albert. Now was the time for the army which he had created (for Charles Felix left no army worthy of the name) to assert upon the Lombard fields the reason of its existence. War with Austria was declared on the 23rd of March. It was midnight; a vast crowd waited in silence in Piazza Castello. At last the windows of the palace were opened, a sudden flood of light from within illuminating the scene. Charles Albert stepped upon the balcony between his two sons. He was even paler than usual, but a smile such as no one had seen before was on his lips. He waved the long proscribed tricolor slowly over the heads of the people.

The King said in his proclamation that 'God had placed Italy in a position to provide for herself' ('in grado di fare da sè'). Hence the often repeated phrase: 'L'Italia farà da sè.' He told the Lombard delegates, who met him at Pavia that he would not enter their capital, which had shown such signal valour, till after he had won a victory. He declared to all that his only aim was to complete the splendid work of liberation so happily begun; questions of government would be reserved for the conclusion of the war. Joy was the order of the day, but the fatal mistakes of the campaign had already commenced; there had been inexcusable <u>delay in declaring war</u>; if it was pardonable to wait for the Milanese initiative, it was as inexpedient as it seemed ungenerous to wait till the issue of the struggle at Milan was decided. Then, <u>after the declaration of war</u>, considering that the Sardinian Government must have seen its imminence for weeks, and indeed for months, there was <u>more time lost</u> than ought to have been the case in getting the troops under weigh. Still, at the opening of the campaign, two grand possibilities were left. The first was obviously to cut Radetsky off in his painful retreat, largely performed along country by-roads, as he had to avoid the principal cities which were already free. Had Charles Albert caught him up while he was far from the Quadrilateral, the decisive blow would have been struck, and the only man who could save Austria in Italy would have been taken prisoner. Radetsky chose the route of Lodi and the lower Brescian plains to Montechiaro, where the encampments were ready for the Austrian spring manœuvres: from this point an easy march carried him under the walls of Verona. Here he met General d'Aspre, who had just arrived with the garrison of Padua. D'Aspre, by skill and resolution, had brought his men from Padua without losing one, having refused the Paduans arms for a national guard, though ordered from Milan to grant them. 'You come to tell me all is lost,' said the Field-Marshal when they met. 'No,' rejoined the younger general, 'I come to tell you all is saved.'

This great chance missed, there was another which could have been seized. Mantua, extraordinary to relate, was defended by only three hundred artillerymen and a handful of hussars. It would have fallen into the hands of its own citizens but for the presence of mind of its commandant, the Polish General Gorzhowsky, who told them that to no one on earth would he deliver the keys of the fortress except to his Emperor, and that the moment he could no longer defend it he would blow it into the air, with himself and half Mantua. He showed them the flint and the steel with which he intended to do the deed. Enemy though he was, that incident ought to be recorded in letters of gold on the gates of Mantua, as a perpetual lesson of that most difficult thing for a country founded in revolution to learn: the meaning of a soldier's duty.

It is easy to see that, if Charles Albert had made an immediate dash on Mantua, the fortress, or its ruins, would have been his, to the enormous detriment of the Austrian position. But this chance too was missed. On the 31st of March, the 9000 men sent with all speed by Radetsky to the defenceless fortress arrived, and henceforth Mantua was safe. Charles Albert only got within fifteen or sixteen miles of it five days later, to find that all hope of its capture was gone.

The campaign began with political as well as with military mistakes. At the same time that the King of Sardinia was declaring in the Proclamation addressed to the Lombards that, full of admiration of the glorious feats performed in their capital, he came to their aid as brother to brother, friend to friend, his ambassadors were trying to persuade the foreign Powers, and especially Austria, Prussia and Russia, that the only object of the war was to avoid a revolution in Piedmont, and to prevent the establishment of a republic in Lombardy. No one was convinced or placated by these assurances; far better as policy than so ignominious an attempt at hedging would have been the acknowledgment to all the world of the noble crime of patriotism. But, as Massimo d'Azeglio once observed, Charles Albert had the incurable defect of thinking himself cunning. It was, moreover, only too true that, although in these diplomatic communications the King allowed the case against him to be stated with glaring exaggeration, yet they contained an element of fact. He *was* afraid of revolution at home; he *was* afraid of a Lombard republic; these were not the only, nor were they the strongest, motives which drove him into the war, but they were motives which, associated with deeper causes, contributed to the disasters of the future.

The Piedmontese force was composed of two *corps d'armée*, the first under General Bava and the second under General Sonnaz: each amounted to 24,000 men. The reserves, under the Duke of Savoy, numbered 12,000. Radetsky, at first (after strengthening the garrisons in the fortresses), could not put into the field more than 40,000 men. As has been stated, the King assumed the supreme command, which led to a constant wavering between the original plan of General Bava, a capable officer, and the criticisms and suggestions of the staff. The greatest mistake of all, that of never bringing into the field at once more than about half the army, was not without connection with the supposed necessity, based on political reasons, of garrisoning places in the rear which might have been safely left to the care of their national guards.

Besides the royal army, there were in the field 17,000 Romans, 3000 Modenese and Parmese, and 6000 Tuscans. There were also several companies of Lombard volunteers, Free Corps, as they were called, which might have been increased to almost any extent had they not been discouraged by the King, who was believed to look coldly on all these extraneous allies, either from doubt of their efficiency, or from the wish to keep the whole glory of the campaign for his Piedmontese army.

The first engagements were on the line of the Mincio. On the 8th of April the Sardinians carried the bridge of Goito after a fight of four hours. The burning of the village of Castelnuovo on the 12th, as a punishment for its having received Manara's band of volunteers, excited great exasperation; many of the unfortunate villagers perished in the flames, and this and other incidents of the same kind did much towards awakening a more vivid hatred of the Austrians among the peasants.

After easily gaining possession of the left (Venetian) bank of the Mincio, Charles Albert employed himself in losing time over chimerical operations with a view to taking the fortresses of Peschiera and Mantua, now strongly garrisoned, and impregnable while their provisions lasted. This object governed the conduct of the campaign, and caused the waste of precious months during every day of which General Nugent, with his 30,000 men, was approaching one step nearer from the mountains of Friuli, and General Welden, with his 10,000, down the passes of Tyrol. If, instead of playing at sieges, Charles Albert had cut off these reinforcements, Radetsky would have been rendered powerless, and the campaign would have had another termination. Never was there a war in which the adoption of Napoleon's system of crushing his opponents one by one, when he could not outnumber them if united, was more clearly indicated.

General Durando crossed the Po on the 21st of April with 17,000 men, partly Pontifical troops and partly volunteers, to which weak corps fell the task of opposing Nugent's advance in Venetia. The colours of the Pontifical troops were solemnly blessed before they left

Rome, but as the order was only given to go to the frontier, and nothing was said, though everything was understood, about crossing it, the Pope was technically able to assert that the war was none of his making. His ministry ventured to suggest to him that the situation was peculiar. Now it was that Catholic Austria and Russia, herself schismatic, flourished in the face of the Pope the portentous scare of a new schism. It is said that the Pope's confessor, a firm Liberal, died just at this time, not without suspicion of poison. Thoroughly alarmed in his spiritual capacity, the Pope issued his Encyclical Letter of the 29th of April—when his ministers and the whole country still hoped from day to day that he would formally declare war—in which he protested that his sacred office obliged him to embrace all nations in an equal paternal love. If his subjects, he added, followed the example of the other Italians, he could not help it: a half-hearted admission which could not mitigate the indignation which the document called forth. With regard to Durando's corps, the Pope did what was the best thing under the altered circumstances; he sent L. C. Farini as envoy to the King of Sardinia, with the request that he would take the Roman troops under his supreme command, the Papal Government agreeing to continue the pay of such of them as belonged to the regular army. Pius IX. made one last effort to help his fellow-countrymen which people hardly noticed, so futile did it appear, but which was probably made in profound seriousness. He wrote a letter to the Emperor of Austria begging him to make all things right and pleasant by voluntarily withdrawing from his Italian dominions. Popes had dictated to sovereigns before now; was there not Canossa? Besides, if a miracle was sought, why should not a miracle happen? Pope and Emperor shaking hands over a free Italy and a world reconciled — how delightful the prospect! Who can doubt that when the Pope wrote that letter all the beautiful dreams of Cardinal Mastai carried him once more away (it was the last time) in an ecstasy of blissful hopes? 'Let not your Majesty take offence,' ran the appeal, 'if we turn to your pity and religion, exhorting you with fatherly affection to desist from a war which, powerless to re-conquer the hearts of the Lombards and Venetians, can only lead to a dark series of calamities. Nor let the generous Germanic nation take offence if we invite it to abandon old hatreds, and convert into useful relations of friendly neighbourhood a dominion which can be neither noble nor happy if it depend only on the sword. Thus we trust in the nation itself, honestly proud of its own nationality, to no longer make a point of honour of sanguinary attempts against the Italian nation, but rather to perceive that its true honour lies in recognising Italy as a sister.'

The Emperor received the bearer of the letter with coldness, and referred him to his ministers, who simply called his attention to the fact that the Pope owed the Temporal Power to the same treaties as those which gave Austria the possession of Lombardy and Venetia.

The day after the publication of the Encyclical, that is to say, the 30th of April, the Piedmontese obtained their first important success in the battle of Pastrengo, near Peschiera. Fighting from daybreak to sundown, they drove the enemy back into Verona, with a loss of 1200 killed and wounded. The Austrians were in rather inferior numbers; but the victory was highly creditable to the hitherto untried army of Piedmont, and showed that it contained excellent fighting material. It was not followed up, and might nearly as well have never been fought.

The Neapolitan troops, of whom 41,000 were promised, 17,000 being on the way already, were intended to reinforce Durando's corps in Venetia. With the two or three battalions which Manin could spare from the little army of Venice, the Italian forces opposed to Nugent's advance would have been brought up to 60,000 men; in which case not even Charles Albert's 'masterly inactivity' could have given Austria the victory.

The Neapolitan Parliament convoked under the new Constitution was to meet on the 15th of May. A dispute had been going on for several days between the Sovereign and the deputies about the form of the parliamentary oath, the deputies wishing that the Chambers should be left free to amend or alter the Statute, while the King desired that they should be bound by oath to maintain it as it was presented to them. It was unwise to provoke a disagreement which was sure to irritate the King. However, late on the 14th, he appeared to yield, and consented that the wording of the oath should be referred to the discussion of Parliament itself. It seems that, at the same time, he ordered the troops of the garrison to take up certain positions in the city. A colonel of the National Guard raised the cry of royal treason, calling upon the people to rise, which a portion of them did, and barricades were constructed in the Toledo and other of the principal streets. A more insane and culpable thing than this attempt at revolution was never put in practice. It was worse even than that 20th of May at Milan, which threw Eugène into the arms of Austria. Its consequences were those which everyone could have foreseen—a two days' massacre in the streets of Naples, begun by the troops and continued by the lazzaroni, who were allowed to pillage to their hearts' content; the deputies dispersed with threats of violence, Parliament dissolved before it had sat, the original Statute torn up, and (by far the most important) the Neapolitan troops, now at Bologna, recalled to Naples. This was the pretty work of the few hundred reckless rioters on the 15th of May.

Had not Pius IX. by this time repudiated all part in the war, the King of the Two Sicilies would have thought twice before he recalled his contingent, though the counsels of neutrality which he received from another quarter—from Lord Palmerston in the name of the English Government—strengthened his hand not a little in carrying out a defection which was the direct ruin of the Italian cause. When the order to return reached Bologna, the veteran patriot, General Pepe, who had been summoned from exile to take the chief command, resolved to disobey, and invited the rest to follow him. Nearly the whole of the troops were, however, faithful to their military oath. The situation was horrible. The choice lay between the country in danger and the King, who, false and perjured though he might be, was still the head of the State, to whom each soldier had sworn obedience. One gallant officer escaped from the dilemma by shooting himself. Pepe, with a single battalion of the line, a company of engineers, and two battalions of volunteers, went to Venice, where they fought like heroes to the end.

On the 27th of May, Radetsky, taking the offensive with about 40,000 men, marched towards Mantua, near which was stationed the small Tuscan corps, whose commander only received when too late General Bava's order to retire from an untenable position. On the 29th the Austrians, in overwhelming numbers, bore down upon the 6000 Tuscans at Montanara and Curtatone, and defeated them after a resistance of six hours. The Tuscan professor, Giuseppe Montanelli, fell severely wounded while holding the dead body of his favourite pupil, but he recovered to show less discretion in politics than he had shown valour in the field.

Peschiera, where the supplies were exhausted, capitulated on the 30th, and the day after found 22,000 Piedmontese ready to give Radetsky battle at Goito, whence, after a severe contest, they drove him back to Mantua. The Austrians lost 3000 out of 25,000 men. The honours of the day fell to the Savoy brigade, which was worthy of its own fame and of the future King of Italy, who was slightly wounded while leading it. Outwardly this seemed the most fortunate period of the war for Charles Albert, but that had already happened which was to cause the turning of the tide. Nugent, with his 30,000 men, had joined Radetsky. His march across Venetia was harassed by the inhabitants, who left him no peace, especially in the mountain districts, but the poor little force of Romans and volunteers under Durando and Ferrari was unable to seriously check his progress in the open country, though he failed in the attempt to take the towns of Treviso and Vicenza in his passage. The repulse of the Austrians, 18,000 strong, from Vicenza on the 23rd of May, did great credit to Durando, who only had 10,000 men, most of them *Crociati*, as the volunteers were called, whose ideas about fighting were original. It is hard to see how this General could have done more than he did with the materials at his disposal, or in what way he merited the abuse which was heaped upon him. The case would have been very different if his hybrid force had been supported by the Neapolitan army.

Nugent was ordered by Radetsky to let the intermediate places alone, and to come on to him as fast as circumstances would admit. The junction of their troops was, the Field-Marshal saw, of vital necessity, but when this was achieved, and when Welden had also brought his 15,000 fresh men from Tyrol, he turned his attention to Vicenza, since, as long as that town remained in Durando's hands, Venetia would still be free. He conceived the bold plan of making an excursion to Vicenza with his complete army, while Charles Albert enjoyed the pleasant illusion that the Austrians were in full retreat owing to his success at Goito. The result of Radetsky's attack was not doubtful, but the defence of the town on the 10th of June could not have been more gallant; the 3500 Swiss, the Pontifical Carabineers, and the few other troops belonging to the regular army of the Pope did wonders. Cialdini, the future general, and Massimo d'Azeglio, the future prime minister, fought in this action, and the latter was severely wounded. After several hours' resistance there was nothing to be done but to hoist the white flag; Radetsky's object was accomplished, the Venetian *terra firma* was practically once more in the power of Austria. On the 14th he was back again at Verona without the least harm having happened in his absence.

Only military genius of the first order could now have saved the Piedmontese, and what prevailed was the usual infatuation. Charles Albert's lines were extended across forty miles of country, from Peschiera to Goito. On the 23rd of July the Austrians fell upon their weakest point, and obliged Sonnaz' division to cross over to the right bank of the Mincio. On the 24th, the King succeeded in dislodging the Austrians from Custozza after four hours' struggle; but next day, which was spent entirely in fighting, Radetsky retook Custozza, and obliged the King to fall back on Villafranca. Now began the terrible retreat on Milan, performed under the ceaseless fire of the pursuers, who attacked and defeated the retreating army for the last time, close to Milan, on the 4th of August. Radetsky had with him 45,000 men; Charles Albert's forces were reduced to 25,000. He had lost 5000 since he recrossed the Mincio. He begged for a truce, and, defeated and undone, he entered the city which he had vowed should only receive him victorious.

To suppose that anything could have been gained by subjecting Milan to the horrors of a siege seems at this date the veriest madness; whatever Charles Albert's sins were, the capitulation of Milan was not among them. The members of a wild faction, however, demanded resistance to the death, or the death of the King if he refused. It is their severest censure to say that their pitiless fury is not excused even by the tragic fate of a population which, having gained freedom unaided less than six months before, saw itself given back to its ancestral foe by the man in whom it had hoped as a saviour. They saw crimes where there were only blunders, which had brought the King to a pass only one degree less wretched than their own. Crushed, humiliated, his army half destroyed, his personal ambition—to rate no higher the motive of his actions—trodden in the dust; and now the name of traitor was hissed in his ears by those for whom he had made these sacrifices.

Stung to the heart, the King instructed General Bava to tell the Milanese that if they were ready to bury themselves under the ruins of the city, he and his sons were ready to do the same. But the Municipality, convinced of the desperateness of the situation, had already entered into negotiations with Radetsky, by which the capitulation was ratified. On this becoming known, the Palazzo Greppi, where Charles Albert lodged, was the object of a new display of rage; an attempt was even made to set it on fire. During the night, the King succeeded in leaving the palace on foot, guarded by a company of Bersaglieri and accompanied by his son, the Duke of Genoa, who, on hearing of his father's critical position, disobeyed the order to stay with his regiment, and came into the city to share his danger.

The next day, the 6th of August, the Austrians re-entered Milan. They themselves said that the Milanese seemed distraught. The Municipality was to blame for having concealed from the people the real state of things, by publishing reports of imaginary victories. Had the unthinking fury of the mob ended, as it so nearly ended, in an irreparable crime, the authors of these falsehoods would have been, more than anyone else, responsible for the catastrophe.

The campaign of 1848 was finished. From the frontier, Charles Albert issued a proclamation to his people, calling upon the Piedmontese to render the common misfortunes less difficult to bear by giving his army a brotherly reception. 'In its ranks,' he concluded, 'are my sons and I, ready, as we all are, for new sacrifices, new hardships, or for death itself for our beloved fatherland.'

The political and diplomatic transactions connected with the war in Lombardy were the subject after it closed of much discussion, and of some violent recriminations. Even from the short account given in these pages, it ought to be apparent that the supreme cause of disaster was simply bad generalship. Contemporaries, however, judged otherwise; if they were monarchists, they attributed the failure to the want of whole-hearted co-operation of the Provisional Governments of Lombardy with the liberating King; if they were republicans, they attributed it to the King's want of trust in the popular element, and anxiety lest, instead of receiving an increase of territory, he should find himself confronted with a new republic at his door. Both parties were so far correct that the strain of double purposes, or, at least, of incompatible aspirations which ran through the conduct of affairs, militated against a fortunate ending. The Piedmontese Government, even had it wished, would have found it difficult to adhere strictly to the programme of eaving all political matters for discussion after the war. What actually happened was that the union, under the not altogether attractive form of Fusion with Piedmont (instead of in the shape of the formation of an Italian kingdom), was effected at the end of June and beginning of July over the whole of Lombardy and Venetia, including Venice, where, perhaps alone, the feeling against it was not that of a party, but of the bulk of the population. Manin shared that feeling, but his true patriotism induced him to push on the Fusion in order to avoid the risk of civil war. He retired into private life the day it was accomplished, only to become again by acclamation Head of the State when the reverses of Sardinia obliged the King's Government to renounce the whole of his scarcely-acquired possessions, not excepting Modena, which had been the first, by a spontaneous plebiscite, to elect him Sovereign.

The diplomatic history of the war is chiefly the history of the efforts of the English Cabinet to pull up a runaway horse. Lord Minto had been sent to urge the Italian princes to grant those concessions which Austria always said (and she was perfectly right) would lead to a general attack upon her power, but when the attack began, the British Government strained every nerve to limit its extension and diminish its force. That Lord Palmerston in his own mind disliked Austria, and would have been glad to see North Italy free, does not alter the fact that he played the Austrian game, and played it with success. He strongly advised every Italian prince to abstain from the conflict, and it is further as certain as anything can well be, that his influence, exercised through Lord Normanby, alone averted French intervention in August 1848, when the desperate state of things made the Italians willing to accept foreign aid. What would have happened if the French had intervened it is interesting to speculate, but impossible to decide. Their help was not desired, except as a last resource, by any party in Italy, nor by any man of note except Manin. The republicans wished Italy to owe her liberation to herself; Charles Albert wished her to owe it to him. The King also feared a republican propaganda, and was uneasy, not without reason, about Savoy and Nice. Lamartine would probably have been satisfied with the former, but it is doubtful if Charles Albert, though capable of giving up his crown for Italy, would have been capable of renouncing the cradle of his race. When Lamartine was succeeded by Cavaignac, perhaps Nice would have been demanded as well as Savoy. That both the King and Mazzini were right in mistrusting the sentiments of the French Government, is amply testified by a letter written by Jules Bastide to the French representative at Turin, in which the Minister of Foreign Affairs speaks of the danger to France of the formation of a strong monarchy at the foot of the Alps, that would tend to assimilate the rest of Italy, adding the significant words: 'We could admit the unity of Italy on the principle and in the form of a federation of independent states, each balancing the other, but never a unity which placed the whole of Italy under the dominion of one of these states.'

Whether, in spite of all this, a political mistake was not made in not accepting French aid when it was first offered (in the spring of 1848) must remain an open question. When the French came eleven years later, they were actuated by no purer motives, but who would say that Cavour, instead of seeking, should have refused the French alliance?

One other point has still to be noticed: the proposal made by Austria in the month of May to give up Lombardy unconditionally if she might keep Venetia, which was promised a separate administration and a national army. Nothing shows the state of mind then prevailing in a more distinct light than the scorn with which this offer was everywhere treated. Lord Palmerston declined to mediate on such a basis 'because there was no chance of the proposal being entertained,' which proved correct, as when it was submitted to the Provisional Government of Milan, it was not even thought worth taking into consideration. No one would contemplate the sacrifice of Venice by a new Campo Formio.

Far, indeed, was Austria the victorious in August from Austria the humiliated in May. On the 9th of August, Hess and Salasco signed the armistice between the lately contending Powers. The next day the Emperor Ferdinand returned to his capital, from which he had been chased in the spring. He might well congratulate himself upon the marvellous recovery of his empire; but the revolution in Hungary was yet to be quelled, and another rising at Vienna in October tried his nerves, which were never of the strongest. On the 2nd of December he abdicated in favour of his young nephew, the Archduke Francis Joseph, who had been brought face to face more than once on the Mincio with the Duke of Savoy, whom he rivalled in personal courage.

On the 10th of December, another event occurred which placed a new piece on the European chess-board: Louis Napoleon was elected to the Presidency of the French Republic.

CHAPTER VII

THE DOWNFALL OF THRONES

1848-1849

Garibaldi Arrives—Venice under Manin—The Dissolution of the Temporal Power—Republics at Rome and Florence.

WHILE the remnant of the Piedmontese army recrossed the bridge over the Ticino at Pavia, crushed, though not through want of valour, outraged in the person of its King, surely the saddest vanquished host that ever retraced in sorrow the path it had traced in the wildest joy, a few thousand volunteers in Lombardy still refused to lay down their arms or to recognise that, after the capitulation of Milan, all was lost. Valueless as a fact, their defiance of Austria had value as a prophecy, and its prophetic aspect comes more clearly into view when it is seen that the leader of the little band was Garibaldi, while its standard-bearer was Mazzini. These two had lately met for the first time since 1833, when Garibaldi, or 'Borel,' as he was called in the ranks of 'Young Italy,' went to Marseilles to make the acquaintance of the head and brain of the society which he had joined, as has been mentioned, on the banks of the Black Sea.

'When I was young and had only aspirations,' said Garibaldi in London in April 1864, ' I sought out a man who could give me counsel and guide my youthful years; I sought him as the thirsty man seeks water. This man I found; he alone kept alive the sacred fire, he alone watched while all the world slept; he has always remained my friend, full of love for his country, full of devotion for the cause of freedom: this man is Joseph Mazzini.'

The words spoken then—when the younger patriot was the chosen hero of the greatest of free nations, while the elder, still misunderstood by almost all, was shunned and calumniated, and even called 'the worst enemy of Italy'—gave one fresh proof, had one been wanting, that, though there have been more flawless characters than Garibaldi, never in a human breast beat a more generous heart. Politically, there was nearly as much divergence between Mazzini and Garibaldi as between Mazzini and Cavour; the master thought the pupil lacked ideality, the pupil thought the master lacked practicalness; but they were at one in the love of their land and in the desire to serve her.

On parting with Mazzini in 1833, Garibaldi, then captain of a sailing vessel, went to Genoa and enrolled himself as a common sailor in the Royal Piedmontese Navy. The step, strange in appearance, was certainly taken on Mazzini's advice, and the immediate purpose was doubtless to make converts for 'Young Italy' among the marines. Had Garibaldi been caught when the ruthless persecution of all connected with 'Young Italy' set in, he would have been shot offhand, as were all those who were found dabbling with politics in the army and navy. He escaped just in time, and sailed for South America.

The *Gazzetta Piemontese* of the 17th of June 1834 published the sentence of death passed upon him, with the rider which declared him exposed to public vengeance 'as an enemy of the State, and liable to all the penalties of a brigand of the first category.' He saw the paper; and it was the first time that he or anyone else had seen the name of Giuseppe Garibaldi in print; a name of which Victor Emmanuel would one day say that 'it filled the furthest ends of the earth.'

Profitable to Italy, over nearly every page of whose recent history might be written 'out of evil cometh forth good,' was the banishment which threw Garibaldi into his romantic career of the next twelve years between the Amazon and the Plata. Soldier of fortune who did not seek to enrich himself; soldier of freedom who never aimed at power, he always meant to turn to account for his own country the experience gained in the art of war in that distant land, where he rapidly became the centre of a legend, almost the origin of a myth. Antique in simplicity, singleness, superabundance of life, and in a sort of naturalism which is not of to-day; unselfconscious, trustful in others, forgiving, incapable of fear, abounding in compassion, Garibaldi's true place is not in the aggregation of facts which we call history, but in the apotheosis of character which we call the *Iliad*, the *Mahabharata*, the *Edda*, the cycles of Arthur and of Roland, and the *Romancero del Cid*.

In childhood he rescued a drowning washerwoman; in youth he nursed men dying of cholera; as a veteran soldier he passed the night among the rocks of Caprera hunting for a lamb that was lost. No amount of habit could remove the repugnance he felt at uttering the word 'fire.' Yet this gentle warrior, when his career was closed and he lay chained to his bed of pain, endorsed his memoirs with the Spanish motto: 'La guerra es la verdadera vida del hombre.' War was the veritable life of Garibaldi; war, not conspiracy; war, not politics; war, not, alas! model farming, for which the old chief fancied in his later years that he had discovered in himself a vocation.

Riding the wild horses and chasing the wild cattle of the Pampas, his eyes covering the immense spaces untrodden by man, this corsair of five-and-twenty drank deep of the innocent pleasures of untamed nature, when not occupied in fighting by land or sea, with equal fortune; or rather, perhaps, with greater fortune and greater proof of inborn genius as commander of the naval campaign of the Paraná than as defender of Monte Video. No adventures were wanting to him; he was even imprisoned and tortured. In South America he found the one woman worthy to bear his name, the lion-hearted Anita, whom he carried off, she consenting, from her father and the man to whom her father had betrothed her. Garibaldi in after years expressed such deep contrition for the act which bore Anita away from the quiet life in store for her, and plunged her into hardships which only ended when she died, that, misinterpreting his remorse, many supposed the man from whom he took her to have been already her husband. It was not so. Shortly before the Church of San Francisco at Monte Video was burnt down (some twenty years ago), the marriage register of Garibaldi and Anita was found in its archives, and a legal copy was made. In it she is described as 'Doña Ana Maria de Jesus, unmarried daughter of Don Benito Rivevio de Silva, of Laguna, in Brazil.' The bridegroom, who during all his American career had scarcely clothes to cover him, parted with his only possession, an old silver watch, to pay the priest's fees. Head of the Italian Legion, he only took the rations of a common soldier, and as candles were not included in the rations, he sat in the dark. Someone reported this to the Government, who sent him a present of £20, half of which he gave to a poor widow.

When the first rumours that something was preparing

in Italy reached Monte Video, Garibaldi wrote a letter offering his services to the Pope, still hailed as Champion of Freedom, and soon embarked himself for the Old World, with eighty-five of his best soldiers, among whom was his beloved friend, Francesco Anzani. Giacomo Medici had been despatched a little in advance to confer with Mazzini. At starting, the Legion knew nothing of the revolution in Milan and Venice, or of Charles Albert having taken the field. Great was their wonder, therefore, on reaching Gibraltar, to see hoisted on a Sardinian ship a perfectly new flag, never beheld by them out of dreams—the Italian tricolor.

So Garibaldi returned at forty-one years of age to the country where the sentence of death passed upon him had never been revoked. Before the law he was still 'a brigand of the first category.' Nor was he quite sure that he would not be arrested, and, as a precaution, when he cast anchor in the harbour of his native Nice, he ran up the Monte Videan colours. It was needless. Throngs of people crowded the quays to welcome home the Ligurian captain, who had done great things over sea. Anita was there; she had preceded him to Europe with their three children, Teresita, Menotti and Ricciotti. There, also, was his old mother, who never ceased to be beautiful, the 'Signora Rosa,' as the Nizzards called her. She was almost a woman of the people, but the simple dignity of her life made all treat her as a superior being. To her prayers, while she lived, Garibaldi believed that he owed his safety in so many perils, and after her death the soldiers used to say that on the eve of battles he walked apart communing with her spirit.

From Nice, Garibaldi went to Genoa, where he took a last leave of his friend Anzani, who returned from exile not to fight, as he had hoped, but to die. The day before he expired, Medici arrived at Genoa; he was very angry with the Chief, in consequence of some disagreement as to the place of landing. Anzani said to him entreatingly: 'Do not be hard, Medici, on Garibaldi; he is a predestined man: a great part of the future of Italy is in his hands.' The counsel from dying lips sank deep into Medici's heart; he often disagreed with Garibaldi, but to his last day he never quarrelled with him again. Long years after, if friction arose between Garibaldi and his King, it was Medici's part to throw oil on the waters.

Garibaldi sought an interview with Charles Albert, and offered him his arms and the arms of his Legion, 'not unused to war.' Pope or prince, little it mattered to him who the saviour of Italy should be. But Charles Albert, though he was polite, merely referred his visitor to his ministers, and the inestimable sword of the hero went begging for a month or more, till the Provisional Government of Milan gave him the command of the few thousand volunteers with whom we saw him at the conclusion of the campaign. The war was over before he had a chance of striking a blow. His indignant cry of defiance could not be long sustained, for Garibaldi never drove men to certain and useless slaughter; when the real position of things became known to him, he led his band over the Swiss confines, and bid them wait for a better and not distant day.

Under Manin's wise rule, which was directed solely to the preservation of peace within the city, and resistance to the enemy at its gates, Venice remained undaunted by the catastrophes in Lombardy, after all the Venetian *terra firma* had been restored to Austria. (Even the heroic little mountain fort of Osopo in the Friuli was compelled to capitulate on the 12th of October.) The blockade of the city on the lagunes did not prevent

Venice from acting not only on the defensive but on the offensive; in the sortie of the 27th of October, 2500 Venetians drove the Austrians from Mestre with severe losses, carrying back six captured guns, which the people dragged in triumph to the Doge's palace. A cabin-boy named Zorzi was borne on the shoulders of the soldiers enveloped in the Italian flag; his story was this: the national colours, floating from the mast of the pinnace on which he served, were detached by a ball and dropped into the water; the child sprang in after them, and with a shout of *Viva l'Italia*, fixed them again at the masthead under a sharp fire. Zorzi was, of course, the small hero of the hour, especially among the women. General Pepe commanded the sortie, with Ulloa, Fontana and Cosenz as his lieutenants; Ugo Bassi, the patriot monk of Bologna, marched at the head of a battalion with the crucifix, the only arms he ever carried, in his hand. The success cost Italy dear, as Alessandro Poerio, poet and patriot, the brother of Baron Carlo Poerio of Naples, lost his life by a wound received at Mestre. But the confidence of Venice in her little army was increased a hundredfold.

The most important event of the autumn of 1848 was the gradual but continuous break-up of the Papal authority in Rome. The meeting of the new Parliament only served to accentuate the want of harmony between the Pope and his ministers; assassinations were frequent; what law there was was administered by the political clubs. In Count Terenzio Mamiani, Pius IX. found a Prime Minister who, for eloquence and patriotism, could hardly be rivalled, but hampered as he was by the opposition he encountered from the Sovereign, and by the absence of any real or solid moderate constitutional party in the Chamber of Deputies, Mamiani could carry out very few of the improvements he desired to effect, and in August he retired from an impracticable task, to be replaced by men of less note and talent than himself.

Wishing to create fresh complications for the Pope, the Austrians invaded the Legations, regardless of his protests, and after the fall of Milan, General Welden advanced on Bologna, where, however, his forces were so furiously attacked by the inhabitants and the few carabineers who were all the troops in the town, that they were dislodged from the strong position they had taken up on the Montagnola, the hill which forms the public park, and obliged to fly beyond the city walls. Radetsky disapproved of Welden's movements on Bologna, and ordered him not to return to the assault.

Had the Austrians returned and massacred half the population of Bologna, the Pope might have been saved. When Rome heard that the stormy capital of Romagna was up in arms, once more, for a moment, there were united counsels. 'His Holiness,' ran the official proclamation, 'was firmly resolved to repel the Austrian invasion with all the means which his State and the well-regulated enthusiasm of his people could supply.' The Chamber confirmed the ministerial proposal to demand French help against Austria. But all this brave show of energy vanished with the pressing danger, and Bologna, which, by its manly courage, had galvanised the whole bloodless body-politic, now hastened the hour of dissolution by lapsing into a state of deplorable anarchy, the populace using the arms with which they had driven out the Austrians, to establish a reign of murder and pillage. L. C. Farini restored something like order, but the general weakness of the power of government became every day more apparent.

The Pope made a last endeavour to avert the catastrophe by calling to his counsels Count Pellegrino Rossi, a man of unyielding will, who was as much opposed to demagogic as to theocratic government. Rossi, having been compromised when very young in Murat's enterprises, lived long abroad, and attained the highest offices under Louis Philippe, who sent him to Rome to arrange with the Pope the delicate question of the expulsion of the Jesuits from France, which he conducted to an amicable settlement, though one not pleasing to the great Society. Not being one of those who change masters as they change their boots according to the state of the roads, the ambassador retired from the French service when Louis Philippe was dethroned. As minister to the Pope, he made his influence instantly felt; measures were taken to restore order in the finances, discipline in the army, public security in the streets, and method and activity in the Government offices. The tax on ecclesiastical property was enforced; fomenters of anarchy, even though they wore the garb of patriots, and perhaps honestly believed themselves to be such, were vigorously dealt with. If anyone could have given the Temporal Power a new lease of life, it would have been a man so gifted and so devoted as Pellegrino Rossi, but the entire forces, both of subversion and of reaction, were against him, and most of all was against him the fatality of dates. Not at human bidding do the dead arise and walk. The most deeply to be regretted event that happened in the course of the Italian revolution gave his inevitable failure the appearance of a fortuitous accident.

Parliament, which had been prorogued on the 26th of August, was to open on the 15th of November. Anarchy, black and red, was in the air. Though disorders were expected, Rossi made no provision for keeping the space clear round the palace where Parliament met; knots of men, with sinister faces, gathered in all parts of the square. Rossi was warned in the morning that an attempt would be made to assassinate him; he was entreated not to go to the Chamber, to which he replied that it was his duty to be present, and that if people wanted his blood they would have it sooner or later, whether he took precautions or not. Two policemen to keep the passage free when he reached the Chamber would, nevertheless, have saved his life. As he walked from his carriage to the stairs, an unknown individual pushed against him on the right side, and when he turned to see who it was, the assassin plunged a dagger in his throat. He fell, bathed in blood, to expire without uttering a word.

In the Chamber, the deputies proceeded to business; not one raised an indignant protest against a crime which violated the independence of the representatives of the nation. The mere understanding of what liberty means is absolutely wanting in most populations when they first emerge from servitude.

After the craven conduct of the deputies, it is no wonder if the dregs of the people went further, and paraded the streets singing songs in praise of the assassin. The Pope summoned the Presidents of the two Chambers and Marco Minghetti, whom he requested to form a new ministry. But the time for regular proceeding was past; the city was in the hands of the mob, which imposed on the Pope the acceptance of a ministry of nonentities nominated by it. The Swiss Guard fired on the crowd which attempted to gain access to the Quirinal; the crowd, reinforced by the Civic Guard, returned to the attack and fired against the walls, a stray shot killing

Monsignor Palma, who was in one of the rooms. The Pope decided on flight. He left Rome in disguise during the evening of the 25th of November. After gaining the Neapolitan frontier, he took the road to Gaeta. The illusion of the Pope Liberator ended with the Encyclical; the illusion of the Constitutional Pope ended with the flight to Gaeta. Pius IX. was only in a limited degree responsible for his want of success, because the task he had set before him was the quadrature of the circle in politics.

The weight of a less qualified responsibility rests upon him for his subsequent actions. On the 3rd of December Parliament voted a proposal to send a deputation to the Pope, praying him to return to his States. To give the deputation greater authority, the Municipality of Rome proposed that the Syndic, the octogenarian Prince Corsini, should accompany it. It also comprised two ecclesiastics, and thus constituted, it left Rome for Gaeta on the 5th of December. On the borders of the Neapolitan kingdom its passage was barred by the police, and it was obliged to retrace its steps to Terracina. Here the deputation drew up a letter to Cardinal Antonelli (no longer the patriotic minister of the spring), in which an audience with the Sovereign Pontiff was respectfully requested. The answer came that the Pope would not receive the deputation. It was an answer that he was at liberty to make, but it should have meant abdication. If, called back by the will of the Parliament of his own making, the Sovereign deigned not even to receive the bearers of the invitation, in what way did he contemplate resuming the throne? It was only too easy to guess. The Head of Christendom had become a convert of King Ferdinand of Naples, otherwise Bomba. By a path strewn with the sinister flowers of war did Pius IX. meditate returning to his subjects—by that path and no other.

The Galetti-Sterbini ministry, appointed by the Pope under popular pressure a few days before his departure, remained in charge of affairs, somewhat strengthened by the adhesion of Terenzio Mamiani as Minister of Foreign Affairs. Mamiani at first declined to form part of the ministry, but joined it afterwards with self-sacrificing patriotism, in the hope of saving things from going to complete rack and ruin during the interregnum caused by the withdrawal of the Head of the State. He only retired from the ungrateful office when he saw the imminence of a radical change in the form of government, which was not desired by him any more than it had been by Rossi.

The mass of the population of the Roman States had desired such a change ever since the days of Gregory; the temporary enthusiasm for Pius, if it arrested the flow of the stream, did not prevent the waters from accumulating beyond the dyke. One day the dyke would burst, and the waters sweep all before them.

A Constituent Assembly was convoked for the 5th of February 1849. The elections, which took place on the 21st of January, were on this basis: every citizen of more than twenty-one years was allowed to vote; every citizen over twenty-five could become a deputy; the number of deputies was fixed at two hundred; a candidate who received less than 500 votes would not be elected. On the 9th of February, the Constituent Assembly voted the downfall of the Temporal Power (free exercise of his spiritual functions being, at the same time, assured to the Supreme Pontiff), and the establishment of a republican form of government. The Roman Republic was proclaimed from the Capitol.

Ten votes were given against the republic. No government ever came into existence in a more strictly legal manner. Had it not represented the true will of the people, the last Roman Commonwealth could not have left behind so glorious, albeit brief, a record.

A youthful poet, descendant of the Doges of Genoa, Goffredo Mameli, whose 'Fratelli d'Italia' was the battle-hymn to which Italy marched, wrote these three words to Mazzini: 'Roma, Repubblica, Venite.' So Mazzini came to Rome, which confided her destinies to him, as she had once confided them to the Brescian Arnold and to Cola di Rienzi. Not Arnold—not Rienzi in his nobler days—dreamed a more sublime dream of Roman liberty than did Giuseppe Mazzini, or more nearly wrote down that dream in facts.

Originally the executive power was delegated to a committee, but this was changed to a Triumvirate, the Triumvirs being Armellini, Saffi and Mazzini. Mazzini's mind and will directed the whole.

On the 18th of February, Cardinal Antonelli demanded in the Pope's name the armed intervention of France, Austria, Spain and Naples, 'as in this way alone can order be restored in the States of the Church, and the Holy Father re-established in the exercise of his supreme authority, in compliance with the imperious exigencies of his august and sacred character, the interests of the universal Church, and the peace of nations. In this way he will be enabled to retain the patrimony which he received at his accession, and transmit it in its integrity to his successors.'

The Pope, who could not bring himself to stain his white robes with the blood of the enemies of Italy, called in four armies to shoot down his subjects, because in no other way could he recover his lost throne.

Pius IX. was the twenty-sixth Pontiff who called the foreigner into Italy.

The final conquest of the Pope by the party of

universal reaction could only be effected by his isolation from all but one set of influences; this is precisely what happened at Gaeta. There are reasons for thinking that his choice of the hospitality of the King of the Two Sicilies, rather than that of France or Spain or Sardinia, was the result of an intrigue in which Count Spaur, the Bavarian minister who represented the interests of Austria in Rome after that power withdrew her ambassador, played a principal part. Even after Pius arrived at Gaeta, it is said that he talked of it as the first stage of a longer journey. He had never shown any liking for the Neapolitan Bourbons, and the willingness which he expressed to Gioberti to crown Charles Albert King of Italy if his arms were successful, was probably duly appreciated by Ferdinand II. To save the Pope from absorption by the retrograde party, and to avoid the certainty of a foreign invasion, Gioberti, who became Prime Minister of Piedmont in November 1848, was anxious to occupy the Roman states with Sardinian troops immediately after the Pope's flight, when his subjects still recognised his sovereignty. Gioberti resigned because this policy was opposed by Rattazzi and other of his colleagues in the ministry. It would have been a difficult *rôle* to play; Sardinia, while endeavouring to checkmate the reaction, might have become its instrument. The failure of Gioberti's plan cannot be regretted, but his forecast of what would happen if it were not attempted proved to be correct.

Soon after the arrival of his exalted guest, King Ferdinand with his family, a great number of priests, and a strong escort, moved his residence from the capital to Gaeta. The modified Constitution, substituted for the first charter after the events of the 15th of May, was still nominally in force; Parliament had met during the summer, but the King solved the riddle of governing through his ministers, on purely retrograde principles, without paying more heed to the representatives of the nations than to the benches on which they sat. Prorogued on the 5th of September, Parliament was to have met on the 30th of November, but when that date approached, it was prorogued again to the 1st of February. 'Our misery has reached such a climax,' wrote Baron Carlo Poerio, 'that it is enough to drive us mad. Every faculty of the soul revolts against the ferocious reactionary movement, the more disgraceful from its execrable hypocrisy. We are governed by an oligarchy; the only article maintained is that respecting the taxes. The laws have ceased to exist; the Statute is buried; a licentious soldiery rules over everything, and the press is constantly employed to asperse honest men. The lives of the deputies are menaced. Another night of St Bartholomew is threatened to all who will not sell body and soul.' Ferdinand only waited till he had recovered substantial hold over Sicily to do away with even the fiction of parliamentary government. Messina had fallen in September, though not till half the city was in flames, the barbarous cruelties practised on the inhabitants after the surrender exciting the indignation of the English and French admirals who witnessed the bombardment. This was the first step to the subjection of Sicily, but not till after Syracuse and Catania fell did the King feel that there was no further cause for anxiety—the taking of the capital becoming a mere question of time. He was so much pleased at the fall of Catania that he had a mock representation of the siege performed at Gaeta in presence of the Pope and of half the sacred college.

On the 13th of March Prince Torelli handed the President of the Neapolitan Chamber of Deputies a sealed packet which contained a royal decree dissolving Parliament. Naples was once more under an irresponsible despotism. The lazzaroni of both the lower and higher classes, if by lazzaroni may be understood the born allies of ignorance, idleness and bigotry, rejoiced and were glad. Nor were they few. Unlike the Austrians in the north, Ferdinand had his party; the 'fidelity of his subjects' of which he boasted, was not purely mythical. Whether, considering its basis, it was much to boast of, need not be discussed.

In March, the happy family at Gaeta was increased by a new arrival. Had he been better advised, Leopold, Grand Duke of Tuscany, would have never gone to breathe that malarious atmosphere. He had played no conjuror's tricks with his promises to his people; Austrian though he was, he had really acted the part of an Italian prince, and there was nothing to show that he had not acted it sincerely. But a persistent bad luck attended his efforts. Though the ministers appointed by him included men as distinguished as the Marquis Gino Capponi, Baron Ricasoli and Prince Corsini, they failed in winning a strong popular support. Leghorn, where the population, unlike that of the rest of Tuscany, is by nature turbulent, broke into open revolution. In the last crisis, the Grand Duke entrusted the government to the extreme Liberals, Montanelli the professor, and Guerrazzi the novelist; both were honourable men, and Guerrazzi was thought by many to be a man of genius. The vigorous rhetoric of his *Assedio di Firenze* had warmed the patriotism of many young hearts. But, as statesmen, the only talent they showed was for upsetting any *régime* with which they were connected.

The Grand Duke was asked to convoke a Constituent

Assembly, following the example of Rome. If every part of Italy were to do the same, the constitution and form of government of the whole country could be settled by a convention of the various assemblies. The idea was worthy of respect because it pointed to unity; but in view of the existing situation, Tuscany's solitary adhesion would hardly have helped the nation, while it was accompanied by serious risks to the state. The Grand Duke seemed about to yield to the proposal, but, on receiving a strong protest from the Pope, he refused to do so on the ground that it would expose himself and his subjects to the terrors of ecclesiastical censure. He still remained in Tuscany, near Viareggio, till he was informed that a band of Leghornese had set out with the intention of capturing his person. Then he left for Gaeta on board the English ship *Bull Dog*. The republic had been already proclaimed at Florence, with Montanelli and Guerrazzi as its chief administrators. It succeeded in pleasing no one. Civil war was more than once at the threshhold of Florence, for the peasants rose in armed resistance to the new government. In less than two months the restoration of the Grand Ducal authority was accomplished almost of itself. Unfortunately, the Grand Duke who was to come back was not the same man as he who went away. The air of Gaeta did its work.

CHAPTER VIII

AT BAY

1849

Novara—Abdication of Charles Albert—Brescia crushed—French Intervention—The Fall of Rome—The Fall of Venice.

IN the spring of 1848, a date might be found when every Italian ruler except the Duke of Modena wore the appearance of a friend to freedom and independence. In the spring of 1849 no Italian prince preserved that appearance except the King of Sardinia. Many causes contributed to the elimination, but most of all the logic of events. It was a case of the survival of the fittest. What seemed a calamity was a step in advance.

Early in March, the Marquis Pallavicini, prisoner of Spielberg, had a long interview with Charles Albert. They sat face to face talking over Italian matters, and the King said confidently that the army was now flourishing; if the die were cast anew, they would win. At parting he embraced the Lombard patriot with the words: 'Dear Pallavicini, how glad I am to have seen you again! You and I had always the same thought; the independence of Italy was the first dream of my youth; it is my dream still, it will be till I die.'

Some characters grow small in misfortune, others grow great. The terrible scene at the Palazzo Greppi, the charge of treason, the shouts of 'death,' had left only one trace on Charles Albert's mind : the burning desire to deliver his accusers.

The armistice was denounced on the 12th of March, a truce of eight days being allowed before the recommencement of hostilities. There is such a thing in politics as necessary madness, and it may be doubted if the Sardinian war of 1849 was not this thing. The programme of *fare da sè* had now to be carried out in stern earnest. Sardinia stood alone, neither from south of the Apennines nor from north of the Alps could help be hoped for. France, which was meditating quite another sort of intervention, refused the loan even of a general. 'They were not going to offend Austria to please Piedmont,' said the French Cabinet. Worse than this, the army was not in the flourishing state of which the King had spoken. The miseries of the retreat, but infinitely more, the incidents of Milan, though wiped out by the King from his own memory, were vividly recollected by all ranks. Affection was not the feeling with which the Piedmontese soldiers regarded the 'fratelli Lombardi.' Did anyone beside the King believe that this army, which had lost faith in its cause, in its leaders and in itself, was going to beat Radetsky? The old Field-Marshal might well show the wildest joy when the denunciation of the armistice was communicated to him. And yet the higher expediency demanded that the sacrifice of Piedmont and of her King for Italy should be consummated.

Rattazzi announced the coming campaign to the Chambers on the 14th of March; the news was well received; there was a general feeling that, whatever happened, the present situation could not be prolonged. With regard to the numbers they could put in the field, Austria and Sardinia were evenly balanced, each having about 80,000 disposable men. The request for a French marshal having been refused, the chief command was given to Chrzanowski, a Pole, who did not know Italian, had not studied the theatre of the war, and was so little favoured by nature that, to the impressionable Italians, his appearance seemed ludicrous. This deplorable appointment was made to satisfy the outcry against Piedmontese generalship; as if it was not enough, the other Polish general, Ramorino, accused of treachery by the revolutionists in 1832, but now praised to the skies by the democratic party, was placed in command of the fifth or Lombard division.

Though Radetsky openly gave the word 'To Turin!' Chrzanowski seems to have failed to realise that the Austrians intended to invade Piedmont. He ordered Ramorino, however, with his 8000 Lombards, to occupy the fork formed by the Po and the Ticino, so as to defend the bridge at Pavia, if, by chance, any fraction of the enemy tried to cross it. What Ramorino did was to place his division on the right bank of the Po, and to destroy the bridge of boats at Mezzana Corte *between* himself and the enemy. The Austrians crossed the Ticino in the night of the 20th of April, not with a fraction, but with a complete army. Ramorino was deprived of his command, and was afterwards tried by court-martial and shot. Whether his treason was intentional or involuntary, it is certain that, had he stemmed the Austrian advance even for half a day, the future disasters, if not averted, would not have come so rapidly, because the Piedmontese would have been forewarned. On the evening of the 21st, General D'Aspre, with 15,000 men, took a portion of the Sardinian army unawares near Mortara, and, owing to the scattered distribution of the Piedmontese, who would have outnumbered him had they been concentrated, he succeeded in forcing his way into Mortara by nightfall. The moral effect of this first reverse was bad, but Chrzanowski rashly decided staking the whole fate of the campaign in a field-day, for which purpose he gathered what troops he could collect at La Biccocca, a hill capped with a village about a mile and a half from Novara. Not more than 50,000 men were collected; some had already deserted, and 20,000 were doing nothing on the other side of the Po.

Towards eleven o'clock D'Aspre arrived, and lost no time in beginning the attack. He sent post-haste to Radetsky, Appel and Thurn to bring all the reinforcements in their power as fast as possible. D'Aspre's daring was rewarded by his carrying La Biccocca at about mid-day, but the Duke of Genoa retook the position with the aid of the valorous 'Piemonte' brigade, and by two p.m. D'Aspre's brave soldiers were so thoroughly beaten, that nothing could have saved his division from destruction, as he afterwards admitted, had Chrzanowski joined in the pursuit instead of staying behind with more than half the army, in accordance with a preconceived plan of remaining on the defensive.

At two o'clock on the 23rd of March, the news started on the wings of the wind, and, as great news will do, swiftly reached every part of the waiting country, that the Sardinians were getting the best of it, that the cause was saved. Men who are not very old remember this as the first strong sensation of their lives—this, and its sequel.

Appel and Thurn, and Wratislaw and the old Field-Marshal were on the march, and by four o'clock they were pouring their fresh troops upon the Piedmontese, who had not known how to profit by their success. Heroism such as few battlefields have seen, disorder such as has rarely disgraced a beaten army, were displayed side by side in Charles Albert's ranks. At eight in. the evening, the whole Sardinian army retired into Novara; the Austrians bivouacked on La Biccocca. The Sardinians had lost 4000 in dead and wounded; the losses of the victors were a thousand less.

All the day long the King courted death, pressing forward where the balls fell like hail and the confusion was at its height, with the answer of despair to the devoted officers who sought to hold him back: 'Let me die, this is my last day.' But death shuns the seeker. Men fell close beside him, but no charitable ball struck his breast. In the evening he said to his generals: 'We have still 40,000 men, cannot we fall back on Alessandria and still make an honourable stand?' They told him that it could not be done. Radetsky was asked on what terms he would grant an armistice; he replied: 'The occupation of a large district in Piedmont, and the heir to the throne as a hostage.' Then Charles Albert knew what he must do. 'For eighteen years,' he said, 'I have made every effort for the good of the people; I grieve to see that my hopes have failed, not so much for myself as for the country. I have not found death on the field of battle as I ardently desired; perhaps my person is the only obstacle to obtaining juster terms. I abdicate the crown in favour of my son, Victor Emmanuel.' And turning to the Duke of Savoy he said: 'There is your King.'

In the night he left Novara alone for Nice. As he passed through the Austrian lines, the sentinels were nearly firing upon his carriage; General Thurn, before whom he was brought, asked for some proof that he was in fact the 'Count de Barge' in whose name his passport was made out. A Bersagliere prisoner who recognised the King, at a sign from him gave the required testimony, and he was allowed to pass. At Nice he was received by the governor, a son of Santorre di Santa Rosa, and to him he addressed the last words spoken by him on Italian ground: 'In whatever time, in whatever place, a regular government raises the flag of war with Austria, the Austrians will find me among their enemies as a simple soldier.' Then he continued his journey to Oporto.

The principal side-issue of the campaign of 1849 was the revolution at Brescia. Had the original plan been carried out, which was to throw the Sardinian army into Lombardy (and it is doubtful whether, even after Radetsky's invasion of Piedmont, it would not have been better to adhere to it), a corresponding movement on the part of the inhabitants would have become of the greatest importance. To Brescia, which was the one Lombard town where the Piedmontese had been received in 1848 with real effusion, the Sardinian Minister of War despatched Count Giuseppe Martinengo Cesaresco with arms and ammunition, and orders to reassume the colonelcy of the National Guard which he held in the previous year, and to take the general control of the movement as far as Brescia was concerned. Martinengo succeeded in transporting the arms through the enemy's country from the Piedmontese frontier to Iseo, and thence to his native city. When he reached Brescia, he found that the Austrians had evacuated the town, though they still occupied the castle which frowns down upon it. This was the 23rd of March: Novara was fought and lost, Piedmont was powerless to come to the assistance of the people she had commanded to rise. What was to be done? Plainly common sense suggested an honourable compromise with the Austrian commandant, by which he should be allowed to reoccupy the city on condition that no hair of the citizens' heads was touched. This is what Bergamo and the other towns did, nor are they to be blamed.

Not so Brescia. Here, where love of liberty was an hereditary instinct from the long connection of Brescia with free Venice, where hatred of the stranger, planted by the ruthless soldiery of Gaston de Foix, had but gone on maturing through three centuries, where the historical title of 'Valiant,' coming down from a remote antiquity, was still no fable; here, with a single mind, the inhabitants resolved upon as desperate a resistance as was ever offered by one little town to a great army.

The Austrian bombardment was begun by the Irish General, Nugent-Lavall, who, dying in the midst of it, left all his fortune to the heroic city which he was attacking. The Austrians, flushed with their victory over Charles Albert's army of 80,000, were seized with rage at the sight of their power defied by a town of less than half that number of souls. But with that rage was mingled, even in the mind of Haynau, an admiration not to be repressed.

Haynau who was sent to replace Nugent, was already known at Brescia, where he had been appointed military governor after the resumption of Austrian authority in 1848. In order to punish the 'persistent opposition manifested to the legitimate Imperial and Royal Government,' and as an example to the other towns, he had imposed on the Brescian householders and the landed proprietors of the province a fine of half a million francs.

He now returned, and what he did may be best read in his own report on the operations. 'It was then,' he wrote, 'that began the most murderous fight; a fight prolonged by the insurgents from barricade to barricade, from house to house, with extraordinary obstinacy. I should never have believed that so bad a cause could have been sustained with such perseverance. In spite of this desperate defence, and although the assault could only be effected in part, and with the help of cannons of heavy calibre, our brave troops with heroic courage, but at the cost of great losses, occupied a first line of houses; but as all my columns could not penetrate into the town at the same time, I ordered the suspension of the attack at nightfall, limiting myself to holding the ground conquered. In spite of that, the combat continued late into the night. On the 1st of April, in the earliest morning light, the tocsin was heard ringing with more fury than ever, and the insurgents reopened fire with an entirely new desperation. Considering the gravity of our losses, as well as the obstinacy and fury of the enemy, it was necessary to adopt a most rigorous measure. I ordered that no prisoners should be taken, but that every person seized with arms in his hand should be immediately put to death, and that the houses from which shots came should be burnt. It is thus that conflagrations, partly caused by the troops, partly by the bombardment, broke out in various parts of the town.'

During the ten days' struggle, the citizens did not flinch for a moment. Count Martinengo was the guiding spirit of the defence, and scarcely left the most exposed of the barricades night or day. From the nobles to the poorest of the people, all did their duty. A youth named Tito Speri led and animated the populace. The horrors of the repression make one think of the fall of Khartoum.

At Bay

Not even in Hungary, where he went from Brescia to continue his 'system,' did Haynau so blacken his own and his country's name as here. In a boys' school kept by a certain Guidi, the master's wife, his mother and ten of his pupils were slaughtered. A little hunchback tailor was carried to the barracks to be slowly burnt alive. But stray details do not give the faintest idea of the whole. And for all this, Haynau was in a far higher degree responsible than the actual executants of the vengeance to which he hounded on his ignorant soldiers, maddened with the lust of blood.

Such was General Haynau, 'whose brave devotion to his master's service was the veteran's sole crime,' said the *Quarterly Review* (June 1853), but who was judged otherwise by some in England. Wherefore was he soundly beaten by the brewers in the employment of Messrs Barclay & Perkins; and the nice words of the *Quarterly* could not undo that beating, redress for which Lord Palmerston blandly advised the complainant to seek 'before the common tribunals.' He thought it best to neglect the advice, and to leave the country.

Among the curious taxes levied at Brescia during the six months after its fall was one of £500 for 'the expenses of the hangman.' Count Martinengo escaped after the Austrians were in possession of the town through the courageous assistance given to him by a few young men of the working class. Camozzi's band of Bergamasques, which started for the relief of the sister city, was driven back with loss.

The end was come, but woe to the victors.

Following the Italian flag to where it still floated, we pass from Brescia in the dust to Rome still inviolate, though soon to be assailed by the bearers of another tricolor. A few days after Novara, the Triumvirate

K

issued a proclamation, in which they said : 'The Republic in Rome has to prove to Italy and to Europe that our work is eminently religious, a work of education and of morality; that the accusations of intolerance, anarchy and violent upturning of things are false ; that, thanks to the republican principle, united as one family of good men under the eye of God, and following the impulse of those who are first among us in genius and virtue, we march to the attainment of true order, law and power united.' Englishmen who were in Rome at the time attest how well the pledge was kept. Peace and true freedom prevailed under the republican banner as no man remembered them to have prevailed before in Rome. The bitter provocation of the quadruple attack was not followed by revengeful acts on the parts of the government against those who were politically and religiously associated with him at whose bidding that attack was made. Nothing like a national party was terrorised or kept under by fear of violence. 'That at such a time,' writes Henry Lushington, who was not favourable to Mazzini, 'not one lawless or evil deed was done would have been rather a miracle than a merit, but on much concurrent testimony it is clear that the efforts of the government to preserve order were incessant, and to a remarkable degree successful.' He adds that the streets were far safer for ordinary passengers under the Triumvirs than under the Papacy.

Of great help in quieting the passions of the lower orders was the people's tribune, Ciceruacchio, who had not put on black cloth clothes, or asked for the ministry of war, or of fine arts, according to the usual wont of successful tribunes. Ciceruacchio had the sense of humour of the genuine Roman *popolano*, and it never came into his head to make himself ridiculous. His influence had been first acquired by works of charity in the Tiber floods. Being a strong swimmer, he ventured where no one else would go, and had saved many lives. At first a wine-carrier, he made money by letting out conveyances and dealing in forage, but he gave away most of what he made. He opposed the whole force of his popularity to a war of classes. 'Viva chi c'ia e chi non c'ia quattrini!'* was his favourite cry. Once when a young poet read him a sonnet in his honour he stopped him at the line 'Thou art greater than all patricians,' saying that he would not have that published: 'I respect the nobility, and never dream of being higher than they. I am a poor man of the people, and such I will always remain.'

When the siege came, Ciceruacchio was invaluable in providing the troops with forage, horses, and even victuals, which he procured by making private sorties on his own account during the night; his intimate knowledge of every path enabling him to go unobserved. He planned the earthworks, at which he laboured with his hands, and when fighting was going on, he shouldered a musket and ran with his two sons, one of them a mere child, to wherever the noise of guns directed him. No picture of Rome in 1849 would be complete without the burly figure and jocund face of Angelo Brunetti.

The republican government found Rome with a mere shadow of an army; the efforts to create one had been too spasmodic to do anything but make confusion worse confounded by changes and experiments soon abandoned. Perseverance and intelligence now had a different result, and the little army, called into existence by the republic, proved admirable in discipline, various- and fantastic as were its components.

Towards the end of April, Garibaldi, who had been

* Long live who has money and who has none.'

stationed at Rieti, was ordered to bring his legion to Rome. Those who witnessed the arrival saw one of the strangest scenes ever beheld in the Eternal City. The men wore pointed hats with black, waving plumes; thin and gaunt, their faces dark as copper, with naked legs, long beards and wild dark hair hanging down their backs, they looked like a company of Salvator Rosa's brigands. Beautiful as a statue amidst his extraordinary host rode the Chief, mounted on a white horse, which he sat like a centaur. 'He was quite a show, everyone stopping to look at him,' adds the sculptor Gibson, to whom these details are owed. 'Probably,' writes another Englishman, 'a human face so like a lion, and still retaining the humanity nearest the image of its Maker, was never seen.' Garibaldi wore the historic red shirt, and a small cap ornamented with gold.

The origin of the red shirt might have remained in poetic uncertainty had it not been mentioned a few years ago in a volume of reminiscences published by an English naval officer. The men employed in the Saladéros or great slaughtering and salting establishments for cattle in the Argentine provinces wore scarlet woollen shirts; owing to the blockade of Buenos Ayres, a merchant at Monte Video had a quantity of these on his hands, and as economy was a great object to the government, they bought the lot cheap for their Italian legion, little thinking that they were making the 'Camicia Rossa' immortal in song and story.

The coming to Rome of the 1200 legionaries aroused private fears in the hearts of the more timid inhabitants, but Garibaldi knew how to keep his wild followers in hand, and gallant was the service they rendered to Roman liberty.

That liberty was now on the eve of its peril. The

preliminaries of the French intervention in Rome are tolerably well known; here it suffices to say that every new contribution to a more precise knowledge of the facts only serves to confirm the charge of dissimulation, or, to use a plainer and far better adapted word, of dishonesty, brought against the French government for their part in the matter. White, indeed, do Austria, Spain and Naples appear—the avowed upholders of priestly despotism — beside the ruler of republican France and his ministers, whose plan it was not to fight the Roman republic: fighting was far from their counsels, but to betray it. It is proved that the restoration of the Temporal Power was the aim of the expedition from the first; it is equally proved that the French sought to get inside Rome by distinct disclaimers of any such intention. 'We do not go to Italy,' they said, 'to impose with our arms a system of government, but to assure the rights of liberty, and to preserve a legitimate interference in the affairs of the peninsula.' They adopted a curious method of assuring the rights of liberty.

The Pope would not have anything to do with the affair. 'If you say openly that you are going to give me back my Temporal Power, well and good; if not, I prefer the aid of Austria.' So he replied to the flattering tales whispered in his ear, while tales no less flattering were being whispered in the ear of Mazzini. He declined to give the French any guarantees as to his future mode of governing; it cannot be said, therefore, that they were under the delusion that they were restoring a constitutional sovereign.

Efforts have been made to cast the responsibility of the Roman intervention entirely on Louis Napoleon. Even Mazzini favoured that view, but it is impossible to separate the President of the Republic from the 325 deputies who voted the supplies for the expedition on the 2nd of April. Does anyone pretend that they were hoodwinked any more than Ledru Rollin was hoodwinked, or the minority, which, roused by his vigorous speech, voted against the grant? Louis Napoleon was far less Papal in his sentiments than were most of the assenting deputies; his own opinion was more truly represented by the letter which, as a private citizen, he wrote to the 'Constitutionnel' in December 1848 than by his subsequent course as President. In this letter he declared that a military demonstration would be perilous even to the interests which it was intended to safeguard. He had but one fixed purpose: to please France, so as to get himself made Emperor. France must be held answerable for the means taken to please her.

General Oudinot landed at Civitavecchia on the 25th of April, his friendly assurances having persuaded the local authorities to oppose no resistance, an unfortunate error, but the last. The correct judgment formed by the Roman Government of the designs of the invaders was considerably assisted by a French officer, Colonel Leblanc, who was sent to Rome by Oudinot to come to an agreement with Mazzini for the amicable reception of the French, and who, losing his temper, revealed more than he was meant to reveal. His last words, 'Les Italiens ne se battent pas,' unquestionably expressed the belief of the whole French force, from the general-in-chief to the youngest drummer. They were soon going to have a chance of testing its accuracy.

The Roman Assembly passed a vote that 'force should be repelled by force.' Well-warned, therefore, but with the proverbial *cœur léger*, Oudinot advanced on Rome with 8000 men early on the 30th of April. At eleven o'clock the two columns came in sight of St Peter's, and soon after, the first which moved towards Porta Angelica was attacked by Colonel Masi. Garibaldi attacked the second column a mile out of Porta San Pancrazio. At the first moment the superior numbers of the French told, and the Italians fell back on Villa Pamphilli, but Colonel Galetti arrived with reinforcements, and before long Garibaldi drove the French from the Pamphilli Gardens and had them in full retreat along the Civitavecchia road. Oudinot was beaten, Rome was victorious. 'This does not surprise us Romans; but it will astonish Paris!' ran a manifesto of the hour; the words are a little childish, but men are apt to be childish when they are deeply moved. And as to the astonishment of Paris, all the words in the world would fail to paint its proportions. Paris was indeed astonished.

Garibaldi had not the chief command of the Roman army, or he would have done more; there was nothing to prevent the Italians from driving Oudinot into the sea. The Triumvirate, when appealed to directly by Garibaldi, refused their sanction, either fearing to leave the capital exposed to the Neapolitans who were advancing, or (and this seems to have been the real reason) still hoping that France would repudiate Oudinot and come to terms. Garibaldi was right on this occasion, and Mazzini was wrong. When you are at war, nothing is so ruinous as to be afraid of damaging the enemy.

The French ministers, bombarded with reproaches by friends and foes, and most uneasy lest their troops in Italy should be destroyed before they could send reinforcements, did disown Oudinot's march on Rome, and Ferdinand de Lesseps was despatched nominally 'to arrange matters in a pacific sense,' but actually to gain time.

In a sitting in the French Assembly, a member of the opposition said to the President of the Council: 'You are going to reinstate the Pope!' 'No, no,' ejaculated Odilon Barrot. 'You are going to do the same as Austria,' cried Lamoricière. 'We should be culpable if we did,' was the answer. Lesseps' instructions, very vague, for the rest, were given to him in this spirit. That Lesseps acted in good faith has been generally admitted, and was always believed by Mazzini. It was to the interest of the French Government to choose a tool who did not see how far he was a tool. But if Lesseps had no suspicions, if he had not strong suspicions of the real object of his employers, then he was already at this date an man singularly easy to deceive.

The French envoy was commissioned to treat, not with the Triumvirate, but with the Roman Assembly: a piece of insolence which the former would have done well to reply to by sending him about his business. Lesseps, however, thought that he would gain by speaking in person to Mazzini, and in order that the interview should remain a secret, he decided to go to him alone in the dead of the night and unannounced. Having made the needful inquiries, he proceeded to the palace of the Consulta, the doors of which seem to have been left open all night; there were guards, but they were asleep, and the French diplomatist traversed the long suite of splendid apartments, opening one into the other without corridors. At last he reached the simply-furnished room where, upon an iron bedstead, Mazzini slept. Lesseps watched him sleeping, fascinated by the beauty of his magnificent head as it lay in repose. He still looked very young, though there was hardly a state in Europe where he was not proscribed. When Lesseps had gazed his full, he called 'Mazzini, Mazzini!' The Triumvir awoke, sat up and asked if he had come to assassinate him? Lesseps told him his name, and a long conversation followed. One thing, at least, that Lesseps said in this interview was strictly true, namely, that Mazzini must not count on the French republican soldiers objecting to fire on republicans: 'The French soldier would burn down the cottage of his mother if ordered by his superiors to do so.' The discipline of a great army is proof against politics.

Lesseps was himself in much fear of being assassinated. He believed that his footsteps were dogged by three individuals, one of whom was an ex-French convict. He complained to Mazzini, who said that he could do nothing, which probably shows that he gave no credence to the story. Then Lesseps had recourse to Ciceruacchio, 'a man of the people who had great influence on the population, and who had organised the revolution.' The tribune seems to have quieted his fears and guaranteed his safety.

The French envoy could not help being struck by the tender care taken of his wounded fellow-countrymen by the Princess Belgiojoso and other noble ladies who attended the hospitals. Of prisoners who were not wounded there were none, as they had been sent back scot-free to their general a few days after the 30th of April. He was struck also by the firm resolve of all classes not to restore the Pope. Some liked the existing government, some did not, but all prayed heaven to be henceforth delivered from the rule of an infallible sovereign.

Whatever was the measure of confidence which Mazzini felt in Lesseps, he was firm as iron on the main point—the non-admittance of the 'friendly' French troops into Rome. Lesseps dragged on the negotiations till his government had finished the preparations for sending to Rome a force which should not be much less than twice in number the whole military resources of the republic. Then they recalled him, and, in order not to be bound by anything that he might have said, they set about the rumour that he was mad. Indignant at such treatment, Lesseps left the diplomatic service, and turned his attention to engineering. This was the origin of the Suez Canal.

While all these things were going on, the Austrians moved from Ferrara and Modena towards Bologna, the Spaniards landed at Fiumicino, and 16,000 Neapolitans, commanded by Ferdinand II., encamped near Albano. Garibaldi was attacked on the 9th of May by the Neapolitan vanguard, which he obliged to fall back. On the 18th, he completely defeated King Ferdinand's army near Velletri, and the King ordered a general retreat into his own dominions, which was accomplished in haste and confusion.

By the end of May, Oudinot's forces were increased to over 35,000 men. The defenders of Rome, under the chief command of General Rosselli, were about 20,000, of whom half were volunteers. Colonel Marnara's Lombard Legion of Bersaglieri was, in smartness of appearance and perfect discipline, equal to any regular troops; in its ranks were the sons of the best and richest Lombard families, such as Dandolo, Morosini and many others. Medici's legion was also composed of educated and well-to-do young men. The Bolognese, under the Marquis Melara, had the impetuous daring of their race, and Count Angelo Masina did wonders with his forty lancers. Wherever Garibaldi was—it was always in the hottest places—there were to be seen, at no great distance, the patriot monk, Ugo Bassi, riding upon a fiery horse, and the young poet of Free Italy, Goffredo Mameli, with his slight, boyish figure, and his fair hair floating in the breeze. Nor must we omit from the list of Garibaldi's bodyguard Forbes, the Englishman, and Anghiar, the devoted negro, who followed his master like a dog.

Oudinot formally disavowed all Lesseps' proceedings from first to last, and announced, on the 1st of June, that he had orders to take Rome as soon as possible. Out of regard, however, for the French residents, he would not begin the attack 'till the morning of Monday the 4th.' Now, though no one knew it but the French general, that Monday morning began with Sunday's dawn, when the French attacked Melara's sleeping battalion at the Roman outposts. It was easy for the French to drive back these 300 men, and to occupy the Villa Corsini ('Villa,' in the Roman sense, means a garden) and the position dominating Porta San Pancrazio; but Galetti came up and retook them all, to lose them again by nine o'clock. Then Garibaldi, who was ill, hurried to the scene from his sick-bed, and thrice that day he retook and thrice he lost the contested positions—a brief statement, which represents prodigies of valour, and the oblation of as noble blood as ever watered the earth of Rome. Melara, Masina, Daverio, Dandolo, Mameli: every schoolboy would know these names if they belonged to ancient, not to modern, history. Bright careers, full of promise, cut short; lives renounced, not only voluntarily, but with joy, and to what end? Not for interest or fame—not even in the hope of winning; but that, erect and crowned with the roses of martyrdom, Rome might send her dying salutation to the world.

At sunset the French had established their possession of all the points outside the Gate of San Pancrazio, except the Vascello, a villa which had been seized from their very teeth by Medici, who held it against all comers. Monte Mario was also in their hands.

Mazzini, whose judgment was obscured by his attribution of the Italian policy of France to Louis Napoleon alone, hoped for a revolution in Paris, but Ledru Rollin's attempt at agitation completely failed, and the country applauded its government now that the mask was thrown away. The reasons for revolutions in Paris have always been the same; they have to do with something else than the garrotting of sister-republics.

Oudinot tightened his cordon; on the 12th of June he invited the city to capitulate. The answer was a refusal; so, with the aid of his excellent artillery, he crept on, his passage contested at each step, but not arrested, till, on the 27th, the Villa Savorelli, Garibaldi's headquarters, fell into the hands of the enemy, and, on the night of the 29th, the French were within the city walls. St Peter's day is the great feast of Rome, and this time, as usual, the cupola of St Peter's was illuminated, the Italian flag flying from the highest point. The thunderstorm, which proverbially accompanies the feast, raged during the night; the French shells flew in all directions; the fight raged fiercer than the storm; Medici held out among the crumbling walls of the Vascello, which had been bombarded for a week; the heroic Manara fell fighting at Villa Spada; Garibaldi, descending into the *mêlée*, dealt blows right and left: he seemed possessed by some supernatural power. Those around him say that it is impossible that he would have much longer escaped death, but suddenly a message came summoning him to the Assembly—it saved his life. When he appeared at the door of the Chamber, the deputies rose and burst into wild applause. He seemed puzzled, but, looking down upon himself, he read the explanation; he was covered with blood, his clothes were honeycombed by balls and bayonet thrusts, his sabre was so bent with striking that it would not go more than half into its sheath.

What the Assembly wanted to know was whether the defence could be prolonged; Garibaldi had only to say that it could not. They voted, therefore, the following decree: 'In the name of God and of the People: the Roman Constituent Assembly discontinues a defence which has become impossible, and remains at its post.' At its post it remained till the French soldiers invaded the Capitol, where it sat, when, yielding to brute force, the deputies dispersed.

Mazzini, who would have resisted still, when all resistance was impossible, wandered openly about the city like a man in a dream. He felt as though he were looking on at the funeral of his best-beloved. How it was that he was not killed or arrested is a mystery. At the end of a week his friends induced him to leave Rome with an English passport.

On the 2nd of July, before the French made their official entry, Garibaldi called his soldiers together in the square of the Vatican, and told them that he was going to seek some field where the foreigner could still be fought. Who would might follow him; 'I cannot offer you honours or pay; I offer you hunger, thirst, forced marches, battles, death.'

Three thousand followed him. Beside her husband rode Anita; not even for the sake of the child soon to come would she stay behind in safety. Ugo Bassi was there; Anghiar was dead, Mameli was dying in a hospital, but there was 'the partisan or brigand Forbes,' as he was described in a letter of the Austrian general D'Aspre to the French general Oudinot, with a good handful of Garibaldi's best surviving officers. Ciceruachio came with his two sons, and offered himself as guide. No one knew what the plan was, or if there was one. Like knights of old in search of adventures, they set out in search of their country's foes. It was the last desperate venture of men who did not know how to yield.

After wandering hither and thither, and suffering severe hardships, the column reached the republic of San Marino. The brave hospitality of that Rock of freedom prevented Garibaldi from falling into the clutches of the Austrians, who surrounded the republic. He treated with the Regent for the immunity of his followers, who had laid down their arms; and, in the night, he himself escaped with Anita, Ugo Bassi, Forbes, Ciceruacchio and a few others. They hoped to take their swords to Venice, but a storm arose, and the boats on which they embarked were driven out of their course. Some of them were stranded on the shore which bounds the pine-forest of Ravenna, and here, hope being indeed gone, the Chief separated from his companions. Of these, Ugo Bassi, and an officer named Livraghi, were soon captured by the Austrians, who conveyed them to Bologna, where they were shot. Ciceruacchio and his sons were taken in another place, and shot as soon as taken. The boat which contained Colonel Forbes was caught at sea by an Austrian cruiser: he was kept in Austrian prisons for two months, and was constantly reminded that he would be either shot or hung; but the English Government succeeded in getting him liberated, and he lived to take part in more fortunate fights under Garibaldi's standard.

Meanwhile, Anita was dying in a peasant's cottage, to which Garibaldi carried her when the strong will and dauntless heart could no longer stand in place of the strength that was finished. This was the 4th of August. Scarcely had she breathed her last breath when Garibaldi, broken down with grief as he was, had to fly from the spot. The Austrians were hunting for him in all directions. All the Roman fugitives were proclaimed outlaws, and the population was forbidden to give them even bread or water. Nevertheless—aided in secret by peasants, priests and all whose help he was obliged to seek—Garibaldi made good his flight from the Adriatic to the Mediterranean, the whole route being overrun by Austrians. When once the western coast was reached, he was able, partly by sea and partly by land, to reach the Piedmontese territory, where his life was safe. Not even there, however, could he rest; he was told, politely but firmly, that his presence was embarrassing, and for the second time he left Europe—first for Tunis and then for the United States.

While the French besieged Rome, the Austrians had not been idle. They took Bologna in May, after eight days' resistance; and in June, after twenty days' attack by sea and land, Ancona fell into their hands. In these towns they pursued means of 'pacification' resembling those employed at Brescia. All who possessed what by a fiction could be called arms were summarily slaughtered. At Ancona, a woman of bad character hid a rusty nail in the bed of her husband, whom she wished to get rid of; she then denounced him to the military tribunal, and two hours later an English family, whose house was near the barracks, heard the ring of the volley of musketry which despatched him. Austria had also occupied the Grand Duchy of Tuscany; and when, in July, Leopold II. returned to his state, which had restored him by general consent and without any foreign intervention, he entered Florence between two files of Austrian soldiery, in violation of the article of the Statute to which he had sworn, which stipulated that no foreign occupation should be invited or tolerated. The Grand Duke wrote to the Emperor of Austria, from Gaeta, humbly begging the loan of his arms. Francis Joseph replied with supreme contempt, that it would have been a better thing if Leopold had never forgotten to whose family he belonged, but he granted the prayer. Such was the way in which the House of Hapsburg-Lorraine, that had done much in Tuscany to win respect if not love, destroyed all its rights to the goodwill of the Tuscan people, and removed what might have been a serious obstacle to Italian unity.

Austria, unable alone to cope with Hungary, committed the immeasurable blunder of calling in the 200,000 Russians who made conquest certain, but the price of whose aid she may still have to pay. Venice, and Venice only, continued to defy her power. Since Novara, the first result of which was the withdrawal of the Sardinian Commissioners, who had taken over the government after the Fusion, Venice had been ruled by Manin on the terms which he himself proposed: 'Are you ready,' he asked the Venetian Assembly, 'to invest the Government with unlimited powers in order to direct the defence and maintain order?' He warned them that he should be obliged to impose upon them enormous sacrifices, but they replied by voting the order of the day: 'Venice resists the Austrians at all costs; to this end the President Manin is invested with plenary powers.' All the deputies then raised their right hand, and swore to defend the city to the last extremity. They kept their word.

It is hard to say which was the most admirable: Manin's fidelity to his trust, or the people's fidelity to him. To keep up the spirits, to maintain the decorum of a besieged city even for a few weeks or a few months, is a task not without difficulty; but when the months run into a second year, when the real pinch of privations has been felt by everyone, not as a sudden twinge, but as a long-drawn-out pain, when the bare necessities of life fail, and a horrible disease, cholera, enters as auxiliary under the enemy's black-and-yellow, death-and-pestilence flag; then, indeed, the task becomes one which only a born leader of men could perform.

The financial administration of the republic was a model of order and economy. Generous voluntary assistance was afforded by all classes, from the wealthy patrician and the Jewish merchant to the poorest gondolier. Mazzini once said bitterly that it was easier to get his countrymen to give their blood than their money; here they gave both. The capable manner in which Manin conducted the foreign policy of the republic is also a point that deserves mention, as it won the esteem even of statesmen of the old school, though it was powerless to obtain their help.

The time was gone when France was disposed to do anything for Venice; no one except the Archbishop of Paris, who was afterwards to die by the hand of an assassin, said a word for her.

In the past year, Lord Palmerston, though he tried to localise the war, and to prevent the co-operation of the south, abounded in good advice to Austria. He repeated till he was tired of repeating, that she would do well to retire from her Italian possessions of her own accord. If the French did not come now, he said, they would come some day, and then her friends and allies would give her scanty support. As for Lombardy, it was notorious that a considerable Austrian party was in favour of giving it up, including the Archduke Ranieri, who was strongly attached to Italy, which was the land of his birth. As

L

for Venice, Austria had against her both the principle of nationality, now the rallying cry of Germany, and the principle of ancient prescription which could be energetically invoked against her by a state to which her title went back no farther than the transfer effected by Buonaparte in the treaty of Campo Formio. These were his arguments; but he was convinced, by this time, that arguments unsupported by big battalions might as well be bestowed on the winds as on the Cabinet of Vienna. From the moment that Radetsky recovered Lombardy for his master, the Italian policy of the Austrian Government was entirely inspired by him, and he was determined that while he lived, what Austria had got she should keep. It was thus that, in reply to Manin's appeal to Lord Palmerston, he only received the cold comfort of the recommendation that Venice should come to terms with her enemy.

The Venetian army of 20,000 men was reduced by casualties and sickness to 18,000 or less. It always did its duty. The defence of Fort Malghera, the great fort which commanded the road to Padua and the bridge of the Venice railway, would have done credit to the most experienced troops in the world. The garrison numbered 2500; the besiegers, under Haynau, 30,000. Radetsky, with three archdukes, came to see the siege, but, tired with waiting, they went away before it was ended. The bombardment began on the 4th of May; in the three days and nights ending with the 25th over 60,000 projectiles fell on the fort. During the night of the 25th the Commandant, Ulloa, by order of Government, quietly evacuated the place, and withdrew his troops; only the next morning the Austrians found out that Malghera was abandoned, and proceeded to take possession of the heap of ruins, which was all that remained.

After the beginning of July, an incessant bombardment was directed against the city itself. Women and children lived in the cellars; fever stalked through the place, but the war feeling was as strong as ever—nay, stronger. Moreover, the provisions became daily scarcer, the day came when hunger was already acutely felt, when the time might be reckoned by hours before the famished defenders must let drop their weapons, and Venice, her works of art and her population, must fall a prey to the savage vengeance of the Austrians, who would enter by force and without conditions.

And this is what Manin prevented. The cry was still for resistance; for the first time bitter words were spoken against the man who had served his country so well. But he, who had never sacrificed one iota to popularity, did not swerve. His great influence prevailed. The capitulation was arranged on the 22nd, and signed on the 24th of July. Manin had calculated correctly; on that day there was literally nothing left to eat in Venice.

In the last sad hours that Manin spent in Venice all the love of his people, clouded for an instant, burst forth anew. Not, indeed, in shouts and acclamations, but in tears and sobs; 'Our poor father, how much he has suffered!' they were heard saying. He embarked on a French vessel bound for Marseilles, poor, worn out and exiled for ever from the city which he had guided for eighteen months; if, indeed, no spark of his spirit animated the dust which it was the first care of liberated Venice to welcome home. The Austrians broke up his doorstep on which, according to a Venetian custom, his name was engraved. Another martyr, Ugo Bassi, had kissed the stone, exclaiming:

'Next to God and Italy — before the Pope — Manin!' The people gathered up the broken fragments and kept them as relics, even as in their hearts they kept his memory, till the arrival of that day of redemption which, in the darkest hour, he foretold.

CHAPTER IX

'J'ATTENDS MON ASTRE'
1849-1850

The House of Savoy—A King who keeps his Word—Sufferings of the Lombards—Charles Albert's Death.

CIRCUMSTANCES more gloomy than those under which Victor Emmanuel II. ascended the throne of his ancestors it would be hard to imagine.

An army twice beaten, a bankrupt exchequer, a triumphant invader waiting to dictate terms; this was but the beginning of the inventory of the royal inheritance. The internal condition of the kingdom, even apart from the financial ruin which had succeeded to the handsome surplus of two years before, was full of embarrassments of the gravest kind. There was a party representing the darkest-dyed clericalism and reaction whose machinations had not been absent in the disaster of Novara. Who was it that disseminated among the troops engaged in the battle broadsides printed with the words: 'Soldiers, for whom do you think you are fighting? The King is betrayed; at Turin they have proclaimed the republic'? There were other broadsides in which Austria was called the supporter of thrones and altars. The dreadful indiscipline witnessed towards the end of, and after the conflict was due more to the demoralising doctrines that had been introduced into the army than to the insubordination of panic. There was another party strengthened by the recent misfortunes and recruited by exiles from all parts of Italy, which was democratic to the verge of republicanism in Piedmont and over that verge at Genoa, where a revolution broke out before the new King's reign was a week old. Constitutional government stood between the fires of these two parties, both fanned by Austrian bellows, the first openly, the second in secret.

Victor Emmanuel was not popular. The indifference to danger which he had shown conspicuously during the war would have awakened enthusiasm in most countries, but in Piedmont it was so thoroughly taken for granted that the Princes of the House of Savoy did not know fear, that it was looked on as an ordinary fact. The Austrian origin of the Duchess of Savoy formed a peg on which to hang unfriendly theories. It is impossible not to compassionate the poor young wife who now found herself Queen of a people which hated her race, after having lived since her marriage the most dreary of lives at the dismallest court in Europe. At first, as a bride, she seemed to have a desire to break through the frozen etiquette which surrounded her; it is told how she once begged and prayed her husband to take her for a walk under the Porticoes of Turin, which she had looked at only from the outside. The young couple enjoyed their airing, but when it reached Charles Albert's ears, he ordered his son to be immediately placed under military arrest. The chilling formalism which invaded even the private life of these royal personages, shutting the door to 'good comradeship' even between husband and wife, may have had much to do with driving Victor Emmanuel from the side of the Princess, whom, nevertheless, he loved and venerated, to unworthy pleasures, the habit of indulgence in which is far easier to contract than to cure.

King Victor Emmanuel.

The King's address at this time was not conciliatory, and, indeed, it never lost a bluntness which later harmonised well enough with the reputation he gained for soldierly integrity, but which then passed for aristocratic haughtiness. His personal friends were said to belong to the aristocratic or even the reactionary party. In the perplexities which encompassed him, he could not reckon on the encouragement of any consensus of good opinion or confidence. He was simply an unknown man, against whom there was a good deal of prejudice.

Radetsky did not refuse to treat with Charles Albert, as has been sometimes said, but the intolerably onerous terms first proposed by him showed that he wished to force the abdication which Charles Albert had always contemplated in the event of new reverses of fortune. Radetsky was favourably disposed to the young Duke of Savoy, as far as his personal feeling was concerned, a fact which was made out in certain quarters to be almost a crime to be marked to the account of Victor Emmanuel. The Field-Marshal did not forget that he was the son-in-law of the Austrian Archduke Ranieri; it is probable, if not proved, that he expected to find him pliable; but Radetsky, besides being a politician of the purest blood-and-iron type, was an old soldier with not a bad heart, and some of his sympathy is to be ascribed to a veteran's natural admiration for a daring young officer.

On the 24th of March, Victor Emmanuel, with the manliness that was born with him, decided to go and treat himself for the conditions of the armistice. It was the first act of his reign, and it was an act of abnegation; but of how much less humiliation than that performed by his father twenty-eight years before, when almost on the same day, by order of King Charles Felix, the Prince of Carignano betook himself to the Austrian camp at Novara, to be greeted with the derisive shout of: 'Behold the King of Italy!' Little did Radetsky think that the words, addressed then in scorn to the father, might to-day have been addressed in truthful anticipation to the son.

The Field-Marshal took good care, however, that nothing but respect should be paid to his visitor, whom he received half-way, surrounded by his superb staff, all mounted on fine horses and clad in splendid accoutrements. As soon as the King saw him coming, he sprang from his saddle, and Radetsky would have done the same had not he required, owing to his great age, the aid of two officers to help him to the ground. After he had laboriously dismounted, he made a military salute, and then embraced Victor Emmanuel with the greatest cordiality. The King was accompanied by very few officers, but the presence of one of these was significant, namely, of the Lombard Count Vimercati, whom he particularly pointed out to Radetsky.

While observing the most courteous forms, the Field-Marshal was not long in coming to the point. The negotiations would be greatly facilitated, nay, more, instead of beginning his reign with a large slice of territory occupied by a foreign enemy for an indefinite period, the King might open it with an actual enlargement of his frontier, if he would only give the easy assurance of ruling on the good old system, and of re-hoisting the blue banner of Piedmont instead of the revolutionary tricolor. The moment was opportune; Victor Emmanuel had not yet sworn to maintain the Constitution. But he replied, without hesitation, that though he was ready, if needs be, to accept the full penalties of defeat, he was determined to observe the engagements entered into by his father towards the people over whom he was called to reign.

One person had already received from his lips the same declaration, with another of wider meaning. During the previous night, speaking to the Lombard officer above mentioned, the King said: 'I shall preserve intact the institutions given by my father; I shall uphold the tricolor flag, symbol of Italian nationality, which is vanquished to-day, but which one day will triumph. This triumph will be, henceforth, the aim of all my efforts.' In 1874, on the twenty-fifth anniversary of Novara, Count Vimercati wrote to the King of Italy from Paris to remind him of the words he had then spoken.

When the King started for his capital, Radetsky offered to draw up his troops as a guard of honour over the whole extent of occupied territory between Novara and Turin. The offer was declined, and Victor Emmanuel took a circuitous route to avoid observation. His journey was marked throughout by a complete absence of state. Before he arrived, a trusty hand consigned to him a note written in haste and in much anguish by the Queen, in which she warned him to enter by night, as he was likely to have a very bad reception. On the 27th of March he reviewed the National Guard in the Piazza Castello on the occasion of its taking the oath of allegiance. The ceremony was attended by Queen Maria Adelaide in a carriage with her two little boys, the Princes Umberto and Amedeo. There was no hostile demonstration, but there was a most general and icy coldness.

That evening, the terms of the armistice were communicated to the Chamber. As was natural, they evoked the wildest indignation, a part of which fell undeservedly on the King. Twenty thousand Austrians were to occupy the district between the Po, Sesia and Ticino and half the citadel of Alessandria. The excitement rose to its height when it was announced that the Sardinian Fleet must be recalled from Venetian waters, depriving that struggling city of the last visible sign of support from without. The Chamber sent a deputation to the King, who succeeded in persuading its members that, hard though the terms were, there was no avoiding their acceptance, and that the original stipulations were harder still.

On the 29th, Victor Emmanuel took the oath to observe the Statute, to exercise the royal authority only in virtue of the laws, to cause justice to be fairly and fearlessly administered, and to conduct himself in all things with the sole view to the interest, honour and prosperity of the nation.

A trifling accident occurred which might have been far from trifling; one of the ornaments of the ceiling of the Palazzo Madama, where the Parliament assembled, fell close to the King. As it was of great weight, it would have killed anyone on whom it had fallen. 'Never mind that,' said the King in Piedmontese dialect to Colonel Menabrea, who was near him, 'it will not be the last!'

The ministry which held office under the late King resigned; a new one was formed, in which General Delaunay was President of the Council, and Gioberti minister without a portfolio. The King was advised to dissolve the Chamber, which had been elected as a war parliament, and was ill-constituted to perform the work now required. General La Marmora had orders to quell the insurrection at Genoa, the motive of which was not nominally a change of government, but the continuance of the war at all costs. Its deeper cause lay in the old irreconcilability of republican Genoa with her Piedmontese masters, breaking out now afresh under the strain of patriotic disappointment. Like the 15th of May at Naples, the Genoese revolution was a folly which can hardly be otherwise described than as a crime; it happened, however, that in Piedmont there was a King who had not the slightest intention of turning it into an excuse for a royal hark-back. Austria and France offered Victor Emmanuel their arms to put down the revolution, but, declining the not exactly disinterested attention, he made a wise choice in La Marmora, who accomplished the ungrateful task with expedition and humanity. An amnesty was granted to all but a very few participators in the revolt. On the brief black list when it was submitted to the King was the name of the Marquis Lorenzo Pareto, who at one time had held the Foreign Office under Charles Albert. As Colonel of the Genoese National Guard, his responsibility in joining the insurrection was judged to be particularly heavy; but the King refused to confirm his exclusion from the amnesty. 'I would not have it said,' he objected, 'that I was harsh to one of my father's old ministers.'

The conception of Victor Emmanuel as a bluff, easy-going monarch is mistaken. Very few princes have had a keener sense of the royal dignity, or a more deeply-rooted family pride, or, when he thought fit to resort to it, a more decisive method of preventing people from taking liberties with him. But he knew that, in nearly all cases, pardon is the best of a king's prerogatives.

An instance to the point happened when he came to the throne. Two officers of the royal household had caused him annoyance while he was Duke of Savoy by telling tales of his unconventionality to his easily-scandalised father. To them, perhaps, he owed the condign punishment he had undergone for the famous promenade under the Porticoes. At anyrate, they had procured for the Duke many bad quarters-of-an-hour, but the King, when he became King, chose to be completely oblivious of their conduct, and they remained undisturbed at their posts. To those who pointed to King Leopold of the Belgians, or to any other foreign example of a loyal sovereign who understood the needs of his people as a model for Victor Emmanuel to imitate, he was in the habit of replying: 'I remember the history of my fathers, and it is enough.'

'The Persians,' says the Greek historian, 'taught their children to ride and to speak the truth.' In a land that had seen as much of enthroned effeminacy and mendacity as Italy had seen, a prince fond of manly exercise and observant of his word was more valuable than a heaven-sent genius, and more welcome than a calendar saint. Piedmont only could give such a prince to Italy. Its kings were not Spaniards who, by way of improvement, became lazzaroni, nor were they Austrians condemned by a fatal law to revert to their original type; they were children of the ice and snow, the fellow-countrymen of their subjects. All their traditions told of obstinacy and hardihood. They brought their useful if scarcely amiable moral qualities from Maurienne in the eleventh century. The second Count of Savoy, known as Amadeus with the Tail, son of Humbert of the White Hands, founder of the House, went to the Holy Roman Emperor with such a body of retainers that the guards refused them entrance to the Council Chamber. 'Either I shall go in with my Tail or not at all,' said Humbert, and with his Tail he went in. This was the metal of the race. Even at the time when they were vassals of the Empire, they expected to dictate rather than to obey. They studiously married into all the great royal houses of Europe. Though they persecuted their Vaudois subjects, who were only in 1848 rewarded by emancipation for centuries of unmerited sufferings and splendid fidelity, yet the Princes of Savoy had from the first, from the White-Handed Humbert himself, held their heads high in all transactions with the Holy See, between which and them there was an ever-returning antagonism. Not to the early part of the nineteenth century, when the rebound from revolutionary chaos did not suffice to denationalise the Kings of Sardinia, but sufficed to ally them with reaction, ought we to turn if we would seize the true bearings of the development of the Counts of Maurienne into Kings of Italy. At that moment the mission of Piedmont, though not lost, was obscured. What has rather to be contemplated is the historic tendency, viewed as a whole, of both reigning house and people. No one has pointed out that tendency more clearly than the anonymous author of a pamphlet entitled *Le Testament politique du Chevalier Walpole* (published at Amsterdam in 1769), who was able to draw the horoscope of the House of Savoy with a correctness which seems almost startling. He was not helped by either sympathy or poetic imagination, but simply by political logic. Sardinia, he said, was the best governed state in Europe. Instead of yielding to the indolent apathy in which other reigning families were sunk, its princes sought to improve its laws and develop its resources according to the wants of the population and the exigences of the climate. Finance, police, the administration of justice, military discipline, presented the picture of order. From the nature of the situation, a King of Sardinia must be ambitious, and to satisfy his ambition he had only to bide his time. Placed between two great Powers he could choose for his ally whichever would give him the most, and by playing this mute *rôle*, it was impossible that he would not hereafter be called upon to play one of the most important parts in Europe. Italy was the oyster disputed by Austria and France; might it not happen that the King of Sardinia, becoming judge and party, would devour the oyster and leave the shells to the rival aspirants? It was unlikely, added this far-seeing observer, that the Italian populations should have got so innured to their chains as to prefer the harsh, vexatious government of Austria to the happy lot which Sardinian domination would secure to them, but even if they had become demoralised to this extent, they could not resist the providential advance of a temperate, robust and warlike nation like Piedmont, led by a prince as enlightened as the King (Charles Emmanuel) who then reigned over it.

The metaphor of the oyster recalls another, that of Italy being an artichoke which the House of Savoy was to devour, a leaf at a time. Whether or not a Duke of Savoy really invented this often-quoted comparison, it is certain that power was what the rulers of Piedmont cared for. They were no more a race of scholars and art patrons than their people was a people of artists and poets. There is a story to the effect that one Duke of Savoy could never make out what poetry was, except that it was written in half lines, which caused a great waste of paper. The only poet born in Piedmont found the country unlivable. Recent research among the archives at Turin revealed facts which were thought to be not creditable to certain princely persons, and a gleaning was therefore made of documents to which the historical student will no longer have access. The step was ill advised; what can documents tell us on the subject that we do not know? Did anyone suppose that the Savoy princes were commonly saints? Sainthood has been the privilege of the women of the family, and they have kept it mostly to themselves. But peccable and rough though the members of this royal house may have been, very few of them were without the governing faculty. 'C'est bien le souverain le plus fin que j'ai connu en Europe,' said Thiers of Victor Emmanuel, whose acquaintance he made in 1870, and in whom he found an able politician instead of the common soldier he had expected. The remark might be extended back to all the race. They understood the business of kings. A word not unlike the 'Tu regere imperio populos, Romane, memento' of Virgil was breathed over the cradle at Maurienne. If it did not send forth sons to rule the world, its children were, at least, to be enthroned in the capital of the Cæsars, and to make Italy one for the first time since Augustus.

From April to August 1849, the peace negotiations dragged on. The pretensions of Austria were still exorbitant, and she resisted the demand which Piedmont, weak and reduced though she was, did not fear to make, that she should amnesty her Italian subjects who had taken part in the revolution. Unequal to cope with the difficulties of the situation, the Delaunay ministry fell, and Massimo d'Azeglio was appointed President of the Council. This was a good augury for Piedmont; D'Azeglio's patriotism had received a seal in the wound which he carried away from the defence of Vicenza. Honour was safe in his hands, whatever were the sacrifices to which he might be obliged to consent.

Some pressure having been put on Austria by France and England, she agreed in July to evacuate Alessandria, and to reduce the war indemnity from 230,000,000 francs to 75,000,000, which Piedmont undertook to pay, onerous though the charge was in her deplorable financial condition. But the amnesty question was the last to be settled, and in this Piedmont stood alone. France and

England gave her no support; the other Powers were against her. The Piedmontese special envoy at Milan, Count Pralormo, wrote to Prince Schwarzenberg on the 2nd of July that his Government could not give up this point. It was a conscientious duty so universally and strongly felt, that they were readier to submit to the consequences, whatever they might be, than to dishonour themselves by renouncing it. In other words, they were ready to face a new war, abandoned to their fate by all Europe, to undergo a new invasion, which meant the utter destruction of their country, rather than leave their Lombard and Venetian fellow-countrymen to the revenge of Austria. Count Pralormo added that he was speaking not only in the name of the ministry, but of the King and the whole nation. The risk was no imaginary one; there were many in Austria who desired an excuse for crushing the life out of the small state which was the eternal thorn in the side of that great Empire. Few remember now the sufferings of Piedmont for Italy, or the perils, only too real, which she braved again and again, not from selfish motives—for the Piedmontese of the old, narrow school, who said that their orderly little country had nothing to gain from being merged in a state of 25,000,000 were by no means in error—but from genuine Italian fellow-feeling for their less happy compatriots beyond their confines.

At last, when the armistice concluded on the morrow of Novara had been prolonged for five months, the treaty of peace was signed. Prince Schwarzenberg offered to further reduce the indemnity, 75,000,000 to 71,000,000, but D'Azeglio having agreed to the former figure, preferred to abide by his agreement. He thought, probably, that he would thus gain some concession as to the amnesty, and, in fact, Austria finally consented to pardon all but a small number of the persons compromised in the late events. D'Azeglio still stood out, but finding that there was no shadow of a chance of obtaining more than this, he reluctantly accepted it. The great mass, the hundred thousand and more fugitives who had left their homes in Lombardy and Venetia, were, at any rate, promised a safe return. The city of Venice, as yet undominated, though on the brink of her fall, was totally excluded. The list of those whose banishment from Lombardy was confirmed, comprises the noblest names in the province; with the exception of a few who were excluded from the amnesty on the score that, before the revolution, they were Austrian functionaries, nearly every unpardoned Lombard was noble: Casati, Arese, Borromeo, Litta, Greppi, Pallavicini, and the Princess Cristina Belgiojoso of Milan, the two Camozzis of Bergamo, and G. Martinengo Cesaresco of Brescia.

It must not be imagined that this amnesty ushered in a reign of oblivion and mildness. It seemed, rather, that Austria, afraid of the moral consequences of the return of so many unloving subjects, redoubled her severity. The day following the promulgation of the amnesty was the 18th of August, the Emperor of Austria's birthday. In the morning, placards dissuading the citizens from taking part in the official rejoicings were to be seen on the walls of Milan. The persons who put these up were not caught, but in the course of the day a crowd, consisting of all classes, made what the official report called 'a scandalous and antipolitic demonstration,' raising revolutionary cries, and even saying uncomplimentary things of His Majesty, and worse still, of the Austrian soldiers. During this 'shameful scene,' of which the above is the Austrian and hence the most highly-coloured description, the military arrested at hazard some of the crowd, who, by a superior order,' were condemned to the following pains and penalties :—

1. Angelo Negroni, of Padua, aged thirty, proprietor, forty strokes;
2. Carlo Bossi, watchmaker, aged twenty-two, forty strokes;
3. Paolo Lodi, of Monza, student, aged twenty-one, thirty strokes;
4. Giovanni Mazzuchetti, Milanese, barrister, aged twenty-four, thirty strokes;
5. Bonnetti, Milanese, lithographer, aged thirty-one, fifty strokes;
6. Moretti, Milanese, domestic servant, aged twenty-six, fifty strokes;
7. Cesana, artist, aged thirty-two, forty strokes;
8. Scotti, shopkeeper, of Monza, fifty strokes;
9. Vigorelli, Milanese, proprietor, fifty strokes;
10. Garavaglia, of Novara, aged thirty-nine, thirty strokes;
11. Giuseppe Tandea, Milanese, aged forty, twenty-five strokes;
12. Rossi, Milanese, student, thirty strokes;
13. Carabelli, workman, forty strokes;
14. Giuseppe Berlusconi, fifty strokes;
15. Ferrandi, bookseller, thirty strokes;
16. Ernestina Galli, of Cremona, operatic singer, aged twenty, forty strokes;
17. Maria Conti, of Florence, operatic singer, aged eighteen, thirty strokes.

There were other sentences of imprisonment in

irons and on bread and water, but the roll of the bastinado, extracted from the official *Gazzetta di Milano* may be left to speak for all the rest, and to tell, with a laconicism more eloquent than the finest rhetoric, what the Austrian yoke in Italy really meant.

A few days after, the military commandant sent the Milanese Municipality a bill for thirty-nine florins, the cost of rods broken or worn-out, and of ice used to prevent gangrene, in the punishment administered to the persons arrested on the 18th of August. Sixty strokes with the Austrian stick were generally enough to prove fatal. Women were flogged half-naked, together with the men, and in the presence of the Austrian officers, who came to see the spectacle.

When the treaty of peace with Austria was signed, there arose a new difficulty; the Sardinian Chamber of Deputies refused to approve it. Some of the deputies asked why they should be called upon either to accept or reject it, on which they were reminded of the 75,000,000 francs indemnity, funds for the discharge of which could not be legally raised without a parliamentary vote. The reluctance to share in an odious though necessary responsibility made these novices in representative government anxious to throw away the greatest, if not the sole guarantee of constitutional freedom. Brofferio, by far the ablest man of the extreme radical party, who had opposed all peace proposals as long as Rome and Venice still resisted, now advised his friends to bow before the inevitable. But they did not comply, and the ministers had no other alternative than to resort to a fresh appeal to the country.

The crisis was serious, because no amount of loyalty on the part of the head of the state can save liberty when the representatives of a nation, taking the bit between their teeth, set themselves deliberately to work to make government impossible. People are too fond of talking of liberty as if it were something locked up in a box which remains safe as long as the guardian of the box does not steal it or sell it. Liberty is in the charge of all and at the mercy of all. There were not wanting persons who blamed the new dissolution as unconstitutional, and who called the proclamation of Moncalieri which announced it an act of despotism and of improper interference with the independence of the electors. It is hardly too much to say that it was this royal proclamation that saved Piedmont. The King appealed to Italy and to Europe for judgment on the conduct of the late Chamber. Having signed, he said, a 'not ruinous' treaty with Austria, which the honour of the country and the sanctity of his word required to be faithfully executed, the majority sought to make that execution legally impracticable. He continued: 'I have promised to save the nation from the tyranny of parties, whatever be the name, scope and position of the men who constitute them. These promises I fulfil by dissolving a Chamber which had become impossible, and by convoking the immediate assemblage of another parliament; but if the electors of the country deny me their help, not on me will fall henceforth the responsibility of the future; and if disorders follow, let them complain, not of me, but of themselves. Never, up till now, has the House of Savoy had recourse in vain to the faithfulness, wisdom and honour of its peoples. I have therefore the right to trust in them on the present occasion, and to hold for certain that, united together, we shall save the constitution and the country from the dangers by which they are menaced.'

The Proclamation produced a great effect, and the

parliament which met on the 20th of December contained a working majority of men who were not only patriotic, but who were also endowed with common sense. When the ratification of the peace came on for discussion, there was, indeed, one deputy who spoke in favour of immediate war, which, in a fortnight, was to effect the liberation, not only of Lombardy and Venetia, but also of Hungary, a speech worth recalling, as it shows how far madness will go. The debate concluded with a vote authorising the King's government to fully carry out the treaty of peace which was concluded at Milan on the 6th of August 1849, the ayes being 137 against 17 noes. Piedmont had learnt the bitter but useful lesson, that if you play and lose, you must pay the cost.

He who had played and lost his crown had already paid the last fee to fortune. Charles Albert was now a denizen of the Superga — of all kings' burial places, the most inspiring in its history, the most sublime in its situation. Here Victor Amadeus, as he looked down on the great French army which, for three months, had besieged his capital, vowed to erect a temple if it should please the Lord of Hosts to grant him and his people deliverance from the hands of the enemy. Five days later the French were in flight. All the Alps, from Mon Viso to the Simplon, all Piedmont, and beyond Piedmont, Italy to the Apennines, can be scanned from the church which fulfilled the royal vow.

To the Superga the body of Charles Albert was brought from the place of exile. Before the coffin, his sword was carried; after it, they led the war-horse he had ridden in all the battles. After the war-horse followed a great multitude. He had said truly that it was an opportune time for him to die. The pathos of his end rekindled the affections of the people for the dynasty.

As in the Mosque of dead Sultans in Stamboul, so in the Mausoleum of the Superga, each sovereign occupied the post of honour only till the next one came to join him. But the post of honour remains, and will remain, to Charles Albert. His son lies elsewhere.

CHAPTER X

THE REVIVAL OF PIEDMONT
1850-1856

Restoration of the Pope and Grand Duke of Tuscany—Misrule at Naples—The Struggle with the Church in Piedmont—The Crimean War.

THE decade from 1849 to 1859 may seem, at first sight, to resemble an interregnum, but it was an evolution. There is no pause in the life of nations any more than in the life of individuals: they go forward or they go backward. In these ten years Piedmont went forward; the other Italian governments did not stand still, they went backward. The diseases from which they suffered gained daily upon the whole body-politic, and even those clever foreign doctors who had been the most convinced that this or that remedy would set them on their feet, were in the end persuaded that there was only one place for them—the Hospital for Incurables. After the fall of Rome, Pius IX. issued a sort of canticle from Gaeta, in which he thanked the Lord at whose bidding the stormy ocean had been arrested, but he did not even so much as say thank you to the French, without whom, nevertheless, the stormy ocean would have proceeded on its way. To all suggestions from Paris that now that victory had been won by force the time was come for the Sovereign to give some guarantee that it would not be abused, the Pope turned a completely deaf ear.

'The Pope,' said M. Drouyn de Lhuys to the Nuncio in Paris, 'perfers to return to Rome upon the dead bodies of his subjects rather than amidst the applause which would have greeted him had he taken our advice.' That advice referred in particular to the secularisation of the public administration, and this was exactly what the Pope and the ex-Liberal Cardinal Antonelli, now and henceforth his most influential counsellor, were determined not to concede. They had grown wise in their generation, for a priest whose ministers are laymen is as much an anomaly as a layman whose ministers are priests. The French government desired that the Statute should be maintained, and demanded judicial reforms and an amnesty for political offenders. None of these points was accepted except the last, and that only nominally, as the amnesty of the 18th of September did not put a stop to proscriptions and vindictive measures. Count Mamiani, whose stainless character was venerated in all Italy, and who had devoted all his energies to the attempt to save the Papal government after the Pope's flight, was ruthlessly excluded, and so were many other persons who, though liberal-minded, had shown signal devotion to the Holy See. All sorts of means were used to serve the ends of vengeance; for instance, Alessandro Calandrelli, a Roman of high reputation, who held office under the republic, was condemned to death for high treason, and to twenty years at the galleys, on a trumped-up charge of theft, which was palpably absurd; but the Pope, while quashing the first sentence, confirmed the second, and Calandrelli would have remained in prison till the year of grace 1870, as many others did, but for the chance circumstance that his father had been a friend of the King of Prussia, who took up his cause so warmly that after two years he was let out and sent to Berlin, where the King and A. von Humboldt received him with open arms.

These were the auspices under which Pius IX. returned to Rome after seventeen months' absence. A four-fold invasion restored the Temporal Power, which Fénelon said was the root of all evil to the Church, but which, according to Pius IX., was necessary to the preservation of the Catholic religion. The re-established *régime* was characterised by Lord Clarendon at the Congress of Paris as 'the opprobrium of Europe.' The Pope tried to compensate for his real want of independence (for a prince who could not stand a day without foreign bayonets, whatever else he was, was not independent) by laughing at the entreaties of France to relieve that advanced nation from the annoyance of having set up a government fit for the Middle Ages. He rated at its correct value the support of Napoleon, and believing it to be purely interested, he believed in its permanence. The President had thought of nothing in the world but votes, and he thought of them still. The Roman Expedition secured him the services of M. de Falloux as minister, and won over to him the entire Clerical Party, including Montalembert and the so-called Liberal Catholics. Thus, and thus only, was the leap from the Presidental chair to the Imperial throne made possible. The result was flattering, but still there are reasons to think (apart from Prince Jérôme Napoleon's express statement to that effect) that Napoleon III. hated the whole business from the bottom of his soul, and that of his not few questionable acts, this was the only one of which he felt lastingly ashamed. Seeing that the communications of his ministers failed in their object, he tried the expedient of writing a private letter to his friend Edgar Ney, couched in the strongest terms of disapproval of the recalcitrant attitude of the Papal Government. This letter was published as it was intended to be, but in the Roman States, except that its circulation was forbidden, no notice was taken of it. Though the incident may be regarded as a stroke of facing-both-ways policy, the anger expressed was probably as sincere as any of Napoleon's sentiments could be, and the letter had the effect of awakening the idea in many minds that something of the former Italian conspirator still existed in the ruler of France. The question arose, What sort of pressure would be needed to turn that germ to account for Italy?

In the kingdom of Naples, where the laws, to look at them on paper, were incomparably better than those in force in the Roman States, the administration was such as would have disgraced a remote province of the Turkish Empire The King's naturally suspicious temperament was worked upon by his courtiers and priests till he came to detect in every Liberal a personal antagonist, whose immunity from harm was incompatible with his own, and in Liberalism a plague dangerous to society, which must be stamped out at all costs. Over 800 Liberals were sent to the galleys. The convictions were obtained, in a great proportion of cases, by false testimony. Bribes and secret protection in high quarters were the only means by which an innocent man could hope to escape; 50,000 persons were under police supervision, to be imprisoned at will. The police often refused to set at liberty those whom the judges had acquitted. The government had a Turkish or Russian fear of printed matter. A wretched barber was fined 1000 ducats for having in his possession a volume of Leopardi's poems, which was described as 'contrary to religion and morals.'

What was meant by being an inmate of a Neapolitan

prison was told by Mr. Gladstone in his two 'Letters to the Earl of Aberdeen,' which the latter sent to Prince Schwarzenberg, the Austrian Prime Minister, with a strong appeal to him to make known their contents to the King of the Two Sicilies, and to use his influence in procuring a mitigation of the abuses complained of. Prince Schwarzenberg did nothing, and it was then that the 'Letters' were published. The impression created on public opinion was almost without a parallel. The celebrated phrase, 'The negation of God erected into a system of government,' passing into currency as a short history of Bourbon rule at Naples, kept alive the wrathful feelings which the 'Letters' aroused, even when these ceased to be read. Some small errors of fact (such as that of stating that all the prisoners were chained, whereas an exception was made of those undergoing life sentences) were magnified by the partisans of Ferdinand II.; but the truth of the picture as a whole was amply confirmed from independent sources. Baron Carlo Poerio (condemned to nineteen years' imprisonment) *was* chained to a common malefactor, the chain never being undone, and producing in the end a disease of the bone from which he never recovered. His case was that of all the political prisoners in the same category with himself. Luigi Settembrini and the others on whom sentence of death had been passed, but commuted into one of life imprisonment, were not chained, but they were put to associate with the worst thieves and assassins, while their material surroundings accorded with the moral atmosphere they were forced to breathe.

The Neapolitan prisoners did more than suffer for freedom; they delivered the name of their country from being a reproach among the nations. They showed what men the South of Italy can produce. Those who wish to know what types of probity, honour and ideal patriotism may grow out of that soil, which is sometimes charged with yielding only the rank weeds planted by despotism, may read the letters and memoirs of the noble Poerios, of Settembrini, gentlest but most fearless of human souls, of the Calabrian Morellis, all patriots and martyrs; of the Duke of Castromediano, who lately, in his old age, has set down a few recollections of the years he spent at the Neapolitan galleys. He records in these notes what he calls the most perilous moment in his life. It was when he was summoned, with six fellow-prisoners who had asked for and obtained freedom, to hear, as he feared, his own pardon pronounced. For pardon was equivalent to dishonour; it was granted either in consequence of real submission and retraction, or in order to be able to blacken the character of the pardoned man by falsely asserting that such submission had been made. His fear was groundless. He had been led out, perhaps, in the hope that the example of the others would prove contagious. He was not pardoned. As he returned to his prison, he thanked Divine Providence for the chains which left him pure.

Strange to tell, Ferdinand II. rendered one considerable service to the national cause; not that he saw it in that light, but the service was none the less real because its motive was a narrow one. Austria proposed a defensive league between the Italian Sovereigns: defensive not only with the view to outward attack, but also and chiefly against 'internal disorder.' Piedmont was to be invited to join as soon as she had renounced her constitutional sins, which it was sanguinely expected she would do before very long. Meanwhile Parma, Modena, Tuscany and Rome embraced the idea with enthusiasm, but the King of the Two Sicilies, who dimly saw in it an opening for interference in his own peculiar governmental ways, boldly declined to have anything to do with it. And so, to Prince Schwarzenberg's serious disappointment, the scheme by which he had hoped to create an absolutist Italian federation, came to an untimely end.

The Grand Duke of Tuscany timidly inquired of the Austrian premier if he might renew the constitutional *régime* in his state. Schwarzenberg replied with the artful suggestion that he should hear what the Dukes of Modena and Parma, the Pope, and King Ferdinand had to say on the subject. Their advice was unanimously negative: Cardinal Antonelli going so far as to declare that Constitutionalism in Tuscany would be regarded as a constant menace and danger to the States of the Church. The different counsels of Piedmont, conveyed by Count Balbo, weighed little against so imposing an array of opinion, backed as it was by the Power which still stabled its horses in the Convent of San Marco. The Tuscan Statute was formally suspended in September 1850.

From that day forth, Tuscany sank lower and lower in the slough. To please the Pope, havoc was made of the Leopoldine laws—named after the son of Maria Theresa, the wise Grand Duke Leopold I.—laws by which a bridle was put on the power and extension of the Church. The prosecution and imprisonment of a Protestant couple who were accused of wishing to make proselytes, proclaimed the depth of intolerance into which what was once the freest and best-ordered government in Italy had descended.

The ecclesiastical question became the true test question in Piedmont as well as in Tuscany, but there it had another issue.

It had also a different basis. In Piedmont there were no Leopoldine laws to destroy; what was necessary was to create them. To privileges dating from the Middle Ages which in the kingdom of Sardinia almost alone had been restored without curtailment after the storm of the French Revolution, were added the favours, the vast wealth, the preponderating influence acquired during Charles Felix' reign, and the first seventeen years of that of Charles Albert. Theoretically, the Statute swept away all privileges of classes and sects, and made citizens equal before the law, but to put this theory into practice further legislation was needed, because, as a matter of fact, the clergy preserved their immunities untouched and showed not the slightest disposition to yield one jot of them. The Piedmontese clergy, more numerous in proportion to the population than in any state except Rome, were more intransigent than any ecclesiastical body in the world. The Italian priest of old days, whatever else might be said about him, was rarely a fanatic. The very nickname 'Ultramontane' given by Italians to the religious extremists north of the Alps, shows how foreign such excesses were to their own temperaments. But the Ultramontane spirit had already invaded Piedmont, and was embraced by its clergy with all the zeal of converts. There was still a *Foro Ecclesiastico* for the arraignment of religious offenders, and this was one of the first privileges against which Massimo d'Azeglio lifted his 'sacrilegious' hand. To go through all the list would be tedious, and would demand more explanation regarding the local modes of acquisition and tenure of religious property than would be interesting now. The object of the Siccardi laws, as they were named after the Minister of Grace and Justice who introduced them, and of the stronger measures to which they led up, was to make the priest amenable to the common law of the land in all except that which referred to his spiritual functions; to put a limit on the amassment of wealth by religious corporations; to check the multiplication of convents and the multiplication of feast days, both of which encouraged the people in sloth and idleness; to withdraw education from the sole control of ecclesiastics; and finally, to authorise civil marriage, but without making it compulsory. The programme was large, and it took years to carry it out. The Vatican contended that it was contrary to the Concordat which existed between the Holy See and the Court of Sardinia. Massimo d'Azeglio replied that the maintenance of the Concordat, in all its parts, meant the ruin of the state; that he had tried every means of conciliation, made every effort towards arriving at a compromise, and that since his endeavours had failed in consequence of the refusal of the Vatican to abate pretensions which it neither could nor did enforce in Austria, Naples or Spain, heaven and the world must judge between Rome and Piedmont, between Cardinal Antonelli and himself.

The struggle throughout was bitter in the extreme, but its most striking incident was the denial of the last Sacraments to a member of the Government, the Minister of Agriculture, Santa Rosa, who happened to die soon after the passing of the Act abolishing the *Foro Ecclesiastico*. Santa Rosa was a sincerely religious man, but he resisted all the attempts of the priest to extort a retractation, and died unabsolved rather than leave a dishonoured name to his children.

The popular indignation excited by this incident was in proportion with the importance attached to outward observances of religion in Catholic countries; the government had to protect the Archbishop of Turin from violence, while, at the same time, they sent him for a month to the Citadel for having forbidden his clergy to obey the law on the *Foro Ecclesiastico*. He and one or two of the other bishops were afterwards expelled from the kingdom. An unwelcome necessity, but whose was the fault? In other countries, where the privileges claimed by the Piedmontese clergy had been abolished for centuries, did the bishops dictate revolt against the law? If not, why should they do so in Piedmont?

The successor of Santa Rosa in the ministry was Count Cavour, who thus in 1850 for the first time became an official servant of the state. When D'Azeglio submitted the appointment to the King, Victor Emmanuel remarked that, though he did not object to it in the least, they had better take care, as this man would turn them all out before long. This man was, in fact, to stand at the helm of Piedmont, with short intervals, till he died, and was to carve out from the block of formless marble, not the Italy of sublime dreams, which, owing her deliverance to her sons alone, should arise immaculate from the grave a Messiah among the nations, but the actual Italy which has been accomplished; imperfect and peccable as human things mostly are, belonging rather to prose than to poetry, to matter than to spirit, but, for all that, an Italy which is one and is free.

Fifty years ago a great English writer pointed out what the real Italy would be, if it were to be; 'The prosperity of nations as of individuals,' wrote Mr Ruskin in one of his earliest papers, 'is cold and hard-hearted and forgetful. The dead lie, indeed, trampled down by the living; the place thereof shall know them no more, for that place is not in the hearts of the survivors, for whose interest they have made way. But adversity

Count Cavour.

and ruin point to the sepulchre, and it is not trodden on; to the chronicle, and it does not decay. Who would substitute the rush of a new nation, the struggle of an awakening power, for the dreamy sleep of Italy's desolation, for the sweet silence of melancholy thought, her twilight time of everlasting memories?'

There is the case, stated with beautiful lucidity, of the somewhat ghoulish dilettantism which, enjoying tombs, would condemn all mankind to breathe their atmosphere. It is not, however, in order to discuss that view that the passage is quoted, but because of its relevancy to what Cavour attempted and what he did. Never was there a mind which cherished fewer illusions. He believed that the pursuit of the unattainable was still more a political crime than a political blunder. He was, in this, what is now called an opportunist, and he was also an opportunist in believing that though in politics you can choose your aim, you can very rarely choose your means. He held (and this was the reason that he was so profoundly hated by men of very different parties) that to accomplish great changes you have to make sacrifices, not only of the higher sort, but, in a certain sense, also of the lower. As he thought that the Austrians could not be expelled from Italy for good and all without foreign help, he contemplated from the first securing that foreign help, though no one would have been more glad than he to do without it. He thought that Italian freedom could not be won without a closer alliance with the democratic party than politicians like D'Azeglio, who had the fear of the ermine, of tarnishing its whiteness, would have ever brought themselves to acquiesce in, and he therefore immediately took steps to establish that alliance. Cavour had no faith in the creation of ideally perfect states, such as the

Monarchy of Dante or the Republic of Mazzini, but he did think that a living land was better than a dead one, that the struggle of an awakening power, the rush of a new nation, was infinitely to be preferred to the desolation of dreamy sleeps, sweet silences, and everlasting memories that spelt regrets.

It may be possible now to see clearly that if no one had tried for the unattainable, Cavour would not have found the ground prepared for his work. The appreciation of his rank among Italian liberators rests on a different point, and it is this: without a man of his positive mould, of his practical genius, of his force of will and force of patience, would the era of splendid endeavours have passed into the era of accomplished facts? If the answer to this is 'No,' then nothing can take from Cavour the glory of having conferred an incalculable boon on the country which he loved with a love that was not the less strong because it lacked the divinising qualities of imagination.

An aristocrat by birth and the inheritor of considerable wealth, Cavour was singularly free from prejudices; his favourite study was political economy, and in quiet times he would probably have given all his energies to the interests of commerce and agriculture. He was an advocate of free trade, and was, perhaps, the only one of the many Italians who *fêted* Mr Cobden on his visit to Italy who cared in the least for the motive of his campaign. Cavour understood English politics better than they have ever been understood by a foreign statesman; his article on Ireland, written in 1843, may still be read with profit. Before parliamentary life existed in Piedmont, he took the only way open of influencing public opinion by founding a newspaper, the *Risorgimento*, in which he continued to write for several years. In the Chamber of Deputies he soon made his power felt —power is the word, for he was no orator in the ordinary sense; his speeches read well, as hard hitting and logical expositions, but they were not well delivered. Cavour never spoke Italian with true grace and ease though he selected it for his speeches, and not French, which was also allowed and which he spoke admirably. His presence, too, did not lend itself to oratory; short and thickset, and careless in his dress, he formed a contrast to the romantic figure of D'Azeglio. Yet his prosaic face, when animated, gave an impressive sense of that attribute which seemed to emanate from the whole man: power.

It needed a more wary hand than D'Azeglio's to steer out of the troubled waters caused by the ecclesiastical bills, and to put the final touches to the legislation which he, to his lasting honour be it said, had courageously and successfully initiated. In the autumn of 1852 D'Azeglio resigned, and Cavour was requested by the King to form a ministry. He was to remain, with short breaks, at the head of public affairs for the nine following years.

At this time the government of Lombardy and Venetia was vested in Field-Marshal Radetsky, with two lieutenant-governors under him, who only executed his orders. Radetsky resided at Verona. Politically and economically the two provinces were then undergoing an extremity of misery; the diseases of the vines and the silkworms had reached the point of causing absolute ruin to the great mass of proprietors who, reckoning on having always enough to live on, had not laid by. Many noble families sank to the condition of peasants. The taxation was heavier than in any other part of the Austrian Empire; in proof of which it may be mentioned that Lombardy paid 80,000,000 francs into the Austrian treasury, which, had the Empire been taxed equally, would have given an annual total of 1,100,000,000, whereas the revenue amounted to only 736,000,000. The landtax was almost double what it was in the German provinces. Italians, however, have a great capacity for supporting such burdens with patience, and it is doubtful whether the material aspect of the case did much to increase their hatred of foreign dominion. Its moral aspect grew daily worse; the terror became chronic. The possession of a sheet of printed paper issued by the revolutionary press at Capolago, on the lake of Lugano, was enough to send a man to the gallows. These old, badly printed leaflets, with no name of author or publisher attached, but chiefly written in the unmistakable style of Mazzini, can still be picked up in the little booksellers' shops in Canton Ticino, and it is difficult to look at them without emotion. What hopes were carried by them. What risks were run in passing them from hand to hand. Of what tragedies were they not the cause! In August 1851, Antonio Sciesa, of Milan, was shot for having one such leaflet on his person. The gendarmes led him past his own house, hoping that the sight of it would weaken his nerve, and make him accept the clemency which was eagerly proffered if he would reveal the names of others engaged in the patriotic propaganda. 'Tiremm innanz!' ('come along') he said, in his rough Milanese dialect, and marched incorruptible to death. On a similar charge, Dottesio and Grioli, the latter a priest, suffered in the same year, and early in 1852 the long trial was begun at Mantua of about fifty patriots whose names had been obtained by the aid of the bastinado from one or two unhappy wretches who had not the fortitude to endure. Of these fifty, nine were executed, among whom were the priests Grazioli and Tazzoli, Count Montanari of Verona, and Tito Speri, the young hero of the defence of Brescia. Speri had a trifling part in the propaganda, but the remembrance of his conduct in 1849 ensured his condemnation. He was deeply attached to the religion in which he was born, and his last letters show the fervour of a Christian joined to the calmness of a stoic. If he had a regret, it was that he had been unable to do more for his country; but here too his simple faith sustained him. Surely the Giver of all good would not refuse to listen to the prayers of the soul which passed to Him through martyrdom. 'To-morrow they lead me forth,' he wrote. 'I have done with this world, but, in the bosom of God, I promise you I will do what I can.' So did this clear and childlike spirit carry its cause from the Austrian Assizes to a higher tribunal.

In the spring of 1853 there was an attempt at a rising in Milan from which the mass of the citizens stood aloof, if they even knew of it till it was over; an attempt ill-considered and not easily justified from any point of view, the blame for which has been generally cast on Mazzini; but though he knew of it, he was unwilling that its authors should choose the time and mode of action which they chose. He was, moreover, misinformed as to the extent of the preparations, since no Milanese of any standing gave his support to the plan.

On the plea that the Lombard emigration was concerned in the abortive movement, which was by no means consistent with facts, the Austrian Government sequestered the landed property of the exiles and voluntary emigrants, reducing them and their families (which in most instances remained behind) to complete beggary. Nine hundred and seventy-eight estates were placed under sequestration. The Court of Sardinia held the measure to be a violation of the amnesty, which was one of the conditions of the peace of 1850. The Sardinian Minister was recalled from Vienna, and the relations between the two governments were once more on a footing of open rupture.

Not less important was the moral effect of the sequestrations in France and England, but particularly in England. They acted as the last straw, coming as they did on the top of the flogging system which had already enraged the English public mind to the highest degree. The Prince Consort wrote in March to his brother: 'To give you a conception of the maxims of justice and policy which Austria has been lately developing, I enclose an extract of a report from Turin which treats of the decrees of confiscation in Italy. People here will be very indignant.' He goes on to say (somewhat too broadly) that the English upper classes were till then thoroughly Austrian, but that she had succeeded in turning the whole of England against her, and there was now no one left to defend her.

Austria, through Count Buol, complained that she was dying of legality,' but England took the Sardinian view that the sequestrations directly violated the treaty between the two Powers. In the Austrian Note of the 9th of March, it was distinctly declared that Piedmont would be crushed if she did not perform the part of police-agent to Austria. Cavour's uncowed attitude at this crisis was what first fixed upon him the eyes of European diplomacy.

In the course of the summer, the Duke of Genoa, Victor Emmanuel's brother, paid a visit to the English Court, where the Duke of Saxe-Coburg was also staying, by whom he was described as 'one of the cleverest and most amiable men of our time.' Sunny Italy, adds Duke Ernest, seemed to have sent him to England so that by his mere presence alone, in the prime of his age, he might make propaganda for the cause of his country. The Queen presented her guest with a handsome riding-horse, and when he thanked her in warm and feeling terms, she spoke the memorable words, the effect of which spoken at that date by the Queen of England can hardly be imagined: 'I hope you will ride this horse when the battles are fought for the liberation of Italy.'

The battle-day was indeed to come, but when it came the sword which the young Duke wielded with such gallantry in the siege of Peschiera would be sheathed for ever. The Prince Charming of Casa Savoia died in February 1855, leaving a daughter to Italy, the beloved Queen Margaret.

In the space of a few weeks, Victor Emmanuel lost his brother, his mother, and his wife. The King, who felt keenly when he did feel, was driven distraught with grief; no circumstance was wanting which could sharpen the edge of his sorrow. The two Queens, both Austrian princesses, had never interfered in foreign politics; what they suffered they suffered in silence. But they were greatly influenced by the ministers of the religion which had been a comfort of their not too happy lives, and they had frequently told Victor Emmanuel that they would die of grief if the anti-papal policy of his government were persisted in. Now that they were dead, every partisan of the Church declared, without a shadow of reticence, that the mourning in which the House of Savoy was plunged was a clear manifestation of Divine wrath. Victor Emmanuel had been brought up in superstitious surroundings; it was hardly possible that he should listen to these things altogether unmoved. But on this as on the other occasions in his life when he was to be threatened with ghostly terrors, he did not belie the name of 'Re Galantuomo,' which he had written down as his profession when filling up the papers of the first census taken after his accession—a jest that gave him the title he will ever be known by. Harassed and tormented as the King was, when the law on religious corporations had been voted by the Senate and the Chamber, and was presented to him by Cavour for signature, he did his duty and signed it. The commentary which came from the Vatican was the decree of major excommunication promulgated in the Consistory of the 27th of July against all who had approved or sanctioned the measure, or who were concerned in putting it into execution.

The law was known as the 'Rattazziana,' from Urbano Rattazzi, whom Cavour appointed Minister of Grace and Justice, thereby effecting a coalition between the Right Centre, which he led himself, and the Left Centre, which was led by Rattazzi; an alliance not pleasing to the Pure Right or to the Advanced Left, but necessary to give the Prime Minister sufficient strength to command the respect, both at home and abroad, which can only be won by a statesman who is not afraid of being overturned by every whiff of the parliamentary wind. The 'Legge Rattazziana' certainly aimed at asserting the supremacy of the state, but in substance it was an arrangement for raising the stipend of the poorer clergy at the expense of the richer benefices and corporations, and save for the bitter animosity of Rome, it would not have excited the degree of anger that descended upon its promoters. In a country where the Church had a rental of 15,000,000 francs, there were many parish priests who had not an income of £20;

a state of things seen to be anomalous by the best ecclesiastics themselves, but their efforts at conciliation failed because the Holy See would not recognise the right of the civil authority to interfere in any question affecting the status or property of the clergy, and this right was the real point at issue.

In these days, Cavour came to an understanding with a friendly monk in order that when his last hour arrived, he should not, like Santa Rosa, go unshriven to his account. In 1861, Fra Giacomo performed his part in the agreement, and was duly punished for having saved his Church from a scandal which, from the position of the great minister, would have reached European dimensions.

Cavour's work of bringing into order the Sardinian finances, which, from the flourishing state they had attained prior to 1848, had fallen into what appeared the hopeless confusion of a large and steadily increasing deficit, is not to the ordinary observer his most brilliant achievement, but it is possibly the one for which he deserves most praise. It could not have been carried through except by a statesman who was completely indifferent to the applause of the hour. During all the earlier years that he held office, Cavour was extraordinarily unpopular. The nickname of 'la bestia neira' conferred on him by Victor Emmanuel referred to the opinion entertained of him by the Clerical party, but he was almost as much a 'bestia neira' to a large portion of the Liberals as to the Clericals or to the old Piedmontese party. His house was attacked by the mob in 1853, and had not his servants barred the entrance, something serious might have occurred. Happily the King and the majority in the Chamber and in the country had, if not much love for Cavour, a profound conviction that he could not be done without, and that, consequently, he must be allowed to do what he liked. Thus the large sacrifices he demanded of the taxpayers were regularly voted, and Cavour could afford to despise the abuse heaped upon himself since he saw his policy advancing to maturity along a steady line of success.

When, in 1854, Cavour resolved that Piedmont should join France and England in the coming war with Russia, it seemed to a large number of his countrymen that he had taken leave of his senses, but the firm support which in this instance he found in the King enabled him next year to equip and despatch the contingent, 15,000 strong, commanded by General La Marmora, which not only won the respect of friends and foes in the field, but offered an example of efficiency in all departments that compared favourably with the faulty organisation of the great armies beside which it fought. Its gallant conduct at the battle of the Tchernaja flattered the native pride, and when, in due time, 12,000 returned of the 15,000 that had gone forth, the increased credit of Piedmont in Europe was already felt to compensate for the heavy cost of the expedition.

Among the Italians living abroad, Cavour's motives in taking part in the Crimean War were, from the first, better understood than they were at home. Piedmont, by qualifying for the part of Italian advocate in the Councils of Europe, gave a guarantee of good faith which patriots like Daniel Manin and Giorgio Pallavicini accepted as a happy promise for the future. It was then that a large section of the republican party frankly embraced the programme of Italian unity under Victor Emmanuel. They foresaw that a repetition of the discordant action of 1848 would end in the same way. Manin wrote to Lorenzo Valerio in September 1855: 'I, who am a republican, plant the banner of unification; let all who desire that Italy should exist, rally round it, and Italy will exist.' The ex-dictator of Venice was eking out a scanty livelihood by giving lessons in Paris ; he had only three years left to live, and was not destined to see his words verified. But, poor and sick and obscure though he was, his support was worth legions.

It was not the first time that Italian republicans had said to the House of Savoy : If you will free Italy we are with you ; but the circumstances of the case were completely changed since Mazzini wrote in somewhat the same language to Charles Albert a quarter of a century before. Both times the proposal contained an ultimatum as well as an offer, but Manin made it without second thoughts in the strongest hope that the pact would be accepted and full of anticipatory joy at the prospect of its success; while by the Genoese republican it was made in mistrust and in the knowledge that were it accepted (which he did not believe), its acceptance, though bringing with it for Italy a state of things which he recognised as preferable to that which prevailed, would bring to him personally nothing but disappointment and the forfeiture of his dearest wishes.

It is difficult to say what were at this date Cavour's own private sentiments about Italian unity. Though he once confessed that as a young man he had fancied himself Prime Minister of Italy, whenever the subject was now discussed he disclaimed any belief in the feasibility of uniting all parts of the peninsula in one whole. He even called Manin 'a very good man, but mad about Italian unification.' It wanted, in truth, the prescience of the seer rather than the acumen of the politician to discern the unity of Italy in 1855. All outward facts seemed more adverse to its accomplishment than at any period since 1815. Yet it was for Italy that Cavour always pleaded; Italy, and not Piedmont or even Lombardy and Venetia. He invariably asserted the right of his King to uphold the cause of all the populations from the Alps to the Straits of Messina. If he adopted the proverb 'Chi va piano va sano,' he kept in view the end of it, 'Chi va sano va lontano.' In short, if he did not believe in Italian unity, he acted in the same way as he would have acted had he believed in it.

It is evident that one thing he could not do. Whatever was in his thoughts, unless he was prepared to retire into private life then and there, he could not proclaim from the house-tops that he espoused the artichoke theory attributed to Victor Amadeus. There were only too many old diplomatists as it was, who sought to cripple Cavour's resources by reviving that story. The time was not come when, without manifest damage to the cause, he could plead guilty to the charge of preparing an Italian crown for his Sovereign. 'The rule in politics,' Cavour once observed, 'is to be as moderate in language as you are resolute in act.'

At the end of 1855, Victor Emmanuel, with Cavour and Massimo d'Azeglio, paid a visit to the French and English Courts. He was received with more marked cordiality at the English Court than at the French. No Prince Charming, indeed, but the ideal of a bluff and burly Longobard chief, he managed to win the good graces of his entertainers, even if they thought him a trifle barbaric. The Duchess of Sutherland declared that of all the knights of St George whom she had ever seen, he was the only one who would have had the best of it in the fight with the dragon. The Queen rose at four o'clock in the morning to take leave of him. Cavour was so much struck by the interest which Her Majesty evinced in the efforts of Piedmont for constitutional freedom, that he did not hesitate to call her the best friend his country possessed in England.

It is not generally known, but it is quite true, that Victor Emmanuel wished to contract a matrimonial alliance with the English royal family. He did not take Cavour into his confidence, but a high English personage was sounded on the matter, a hint being given to him to say nothing about it to the Count. The lady who might have become Queen of Italy was the Princess Mary of Cambridge. The negotiations were broken off because the young Princess would not hear of any marriage which would have required her living out of England.

The Congress which met in Paris in February, 1856 for the conclusion of the peace between the Allies and Russia was to have far more momentous results for Italy than for the countries more immediately concerned in its discussions, but, contrary to the general impression, it does not appear that these results were anticipated by Cavour. He even said that it was idle for Sardinia to send delegates to a congress in which they would be treated like children. Cavour feared, perhaps, to lose the ground he had gained in the previous year with Napoleon III., when the Emperor's rather surprising question: 'Que peut-on faire pour l'Italie?' had suggested to the Piedmontese statesman that definite scheme of a French alliance, which henceforth he never let go. In any case, when D'Azeglio, who was appointed Sardinian representative, refused at the last moment to undertake a charge for which he knew he was not fitted, it was only at the urgent request of the King that Cavour consented to take his place. When once in Paris, however, he warmed to the work, finding an unexpectedly strong ally in Lord Clarendon. He won what was considered in all Europe a great diplomatic triumph, by getting a special sitting assigned to the examination of Italian affairs, which had as little to do with the natural work of the Congress as the affairs of China. The chief points discussed at the secret sitting of the 8th of April were the foreign occupations in Central Italy, and the state of the Roman and Neapolitan governments, which was stigmatised by Lord Clarendon in terms much more severe than Cavour himself thought it prudent to use. Count Buol, the chief Austrian representative, grew very angry, and his opposition was successful in reducing the sitting to a mere conversation; but what had been said had been said, and Cavour prepared the way for his future policy by remarking to everyone: 'You see that diplomacy can do nothing for us; the question needs another solution.' Lord Clarendon's vigorous support made him think for a moment that England might take an active part in that other solution, and with this idea in his mind he hurried over the Channel to see Lord Palmerston, but he left England convinced that nothing more than moral assistance was ever to be expected from that quarter. The Marquis Emmanuel d'Azeglio, who for many years represented Sardinia, and afterwards Italy, at the Court of St James, has placed it on record that the English Premier repeatedly assured him that an armed intervention on behalf of Italian freedom would have been much to his taste, but that the country would not have been with him. It is certain that Cavour would have preferred an English to a French alliance; as it was not to be had, he reposed his sole hopes in the Emperor Napoleon, who had not the French people really more with him in this matter than Lord Palmerston had the English—nay, he had them less with him, for in England there would have been a party of Italian sympathisers favourable to the war, and in France, there was no one except Prince Napoleon and the workmen of Paris. But the French Emperor was a despotic sovereign, and not the Prime Minister of a self-governing country. After all, some good may come out of despotism.

Upon Cavour's return to Turin, he received not only the approval of the King and Parliament, but also congratulations from all parts of Italy. His position had gained immensely in strength, both at home and abroad. Yet the power of the Clerical party in Piedmont was still such that, in the elections of 1857—the first that had taken place since the legislation affecting the Church—they obtained seventy seats out of a total of two hundred. Cavour did not conceal his alarm. What if eight years' labour were thrown away, and the movement of the State turned backward? 'Never,' he said, 'would he advise a *coup d'état*, nor would his master resort to one; but if the King abdicated, what then?' Victor Emmanuel said to his Prime Minister : 'Let us do our duty; stand firm, and we shall see!' He often declared that, sooner than beat a retreat from the path he had entered on, he would go to America and become plain *Monsù Savoia;* but he never lost faith in the predominating patriotism and good sense of his subjects; and at this time, as at others, he proved to be right. The crisis was surmounted. On the one hand, some elections were invalidated where the priests had exercised undue influence; and, on the other, Rattazzi, who was especially obnoxious to the Clerical party, retired from office. Cavour thus found himself still able to command the Chamber.

CHAPTER XI

PREMONITIONS OF THE STORM

1857-1858

Pisacane's Landing—Orsini's Attempt—The Compact of Plombières—Cavour's Triumph.

IN spite of the accusation of favouring political assassination which was frequently launched against the Italian secret societies, only one of the faithless Italian princes came to a violent death, and his murder had no connection with politics. Charles III., Duke of Parma, was mortally stabbed in March 1854; some said that the assassin was a groom whom he had struck with a riding-whip; others, that he was the father or brother of one of the victims of the Duke's dissolute habits. The Duchess, a daughter of the Duke de Berry, assumed the Regency on behalf of her son, who was a child. She began by initiating many reforms; but a street disturbance in July gave Austria the desired excuse for meddling in the government, when all progress was, of course, arrested.

In December 1856, a soldier named Ageslao Milano attempted to assassinate the King of the Two Sicilies at a review. He belonged to no sect, but he had long premeditated the act. A few days later an earthquake occurred in the kingdom of Naples, by which over ten thousand persons lost their lives. Ferdinand II. grew morose, and shut himself up in the royal palace of

Caserta. The constant lectures of France and England annoyed him without persuading him to take the means to put a stop to them. Not till 1859 did he open the doors of the prisons in which Poerio, Settembrini and their companions were confined. Many plans were made, meanwhile, for their liberation, and English friends even provided a ship by which they were to escape; but the ship foundered : perhaps fortunately, as Garibaldi, with characteristic disinterestedness, had agreed to direct the enterprise, which could not have been otherwise than perilous, and was not unlikely to end in the loss of all concerned.

Disaster attended Baron Bentivegna's attempt at a rising at Taormina in 1856, and Carlo Pisacane's landing at Sapri in the summer of the following year had no better result. Pisacane, a son of the Duke Gennaro di San Giovanni of Naples, had fought in the defence of Rome and was a firm adherent of Mazzini, in conjunction with whom he planned his unlucky venture. Pisacane watched the growing ascendency of Piedmont with sorrow; he was one of the few, if not the only one of his party to say that he would as soon have the dominion of Austria as that of the House of Savoy. But if he was an extremist in politics, none the less he was a patriot, who took his life in his hands and offered it up to his country in the spirit of the noblest devotion. He had the slenderest hope of success, but he believed that only by such failures could the people be roused from their apathy. 'For me,' he wrote, 'it will be victory even if I die on the scaffold. This is all I can do, and this I do; the rest depends on the country, not on me. I have only my affections and my life to give, and I give them without hesitation.'

With the young Baron Nicotera and twenty-three

others, Pisacane embarked on the *Cagliari*, a steamer belonging to a Sardinian mercantile line, which was bound for Tunis. When at sea, the captain was frightened into obedience, and the ship's course was directed to the isle of Ponza, where several hundred prisoners, mostly political, were undergoing their sentences. The guards made little resistance, and Pisacane opened the prisons, inviting who would to follow him. The first plan had been to make a descent on San Stefano, the island where Settembrini was imprisoned, but that good citizen had refused to admit the liberation of the non-political prisoners, which was an unavoidable feature in the scheme. With the addition of about three hundred men, Pisacane left Ponza for the mainland and disembarked near the village of Sapri, in the province of Salerno. From information received, he imagined that a revolutionary movement was on the point of breaking out in that district. Nothing could be further from the fact. The country people did all the harm they could to the band, which, after making a brave stand against the local militia, was cut to pieces by the royal troops. Pisacane fell fighting; those who were not killed were taken, and amongst these was Nicotera, who was kept in prison till set free by Garibaldi.

The *Cagliari* was captured and detained with its crew. As two of the seamen were British subjects, the English Government joined Sardinia in demanding its restitution, which, after long delays, was conceded.

In 1857, the Emperor of Austria relieved Field-Marshal Radetsky, then in his ninety-third year, of the burden of office. He was given the right of living in any of the royal palaces, even in the Emperor's own residence at Vienna, but he preferred to spend the one remaining year of his life in Italy. At the same time, the Archduke Maximilian was appointed Viceroy of Lombardy and Venetia. A more naturally amiable and cultivated Prince never had the evil fate forced upon him of attempting impossible tasks. Just married to the lovely Princess Charlotte of Belgium, he came to Italy radiant with happiness, and wishing to make everyone as happy as he was himself. Not even the chilling welcome he received damped his enthusiasm, for he thought the aversion of the population depended on undoubted wrongs, which it was his full intention to redress. He was to learn two things; firstly, that the day of reconciliation was past: there were too many ghosts between the Lombards and Venetians, and the House of Hapsburg. Secondly, that an unseen hand beyond the Brenner would diligently thwart each one of his benevolent designs. The system was, and was to remain, unchanged. It was not carried out quite as it was carried out in the first years after 1849. The exiles were allowed to return and the sequestrations were revoked. It should be said, because it shows the one white spot in Austrian despotism, its civil administration, that on resuming their rights of ownership the proprietors found that their estates had not been badly managed. But the depressing and deadening influence of an anti-national rule continued unabated. Lombardy and Venetia were governed not from Milan, but from Vienna. Very small were the crumbs which the Viceroy obtained, though he went on a journey to Austria expressly to plead for concessions. It is sad to think what an enlightened heir to the great Austrian empire was lost, when Napoleon III. and his own family sent Maximilian of Hapsburg to Queretaro.

While Cavour had come to the conclusion that the aid which he believed essential for the expulsion of the

Austrians could only come from the French Emperor, this sovereign was regarded by a not inconsiderable party of Italians as the greatest, if not the sole, obstacle to their liberation. All those, in particular, who came in contact with the French exiles, were impressed by them with the notion that France, the real France, was only waiting for the disappearance of the Man of December to throw herself into their arms. Among the Italians who held these opinions, there were a few with whom it became a fixed idea that the greatest service they could render their country was the removal of Napoleon from the political scene. They conceived and nourished the thought independently of one another; they belonged to no league, but for that reason they were the more dangerous; somewhere or other there was always someone planning to put an end to the Emperor's life. It is not worth while to pause to discuss the ethics of political assassination; civilisation has decided against it, and history proves its usual failure to promote the desired object. What benefit did the Confederate cause derive from the assassination of the good President Lincoln, or the cause of Russian liberty from that of Alexander II.? What will Anarchy gain by the murder of Carnot? It is certain, however, that never were men more convinced that they were executing a wild kind of justice than were the men who plotted against Napoleon III. They looked upon him as one of themselves who had turned traitor. There is a great probability that, in his early days when he was playing at conspiracy in Italy, he was actually enrolled as a Carbonaro. At all events, he had conspired for Italian freedom, and afterwards, to serve his own selfish interests, he extinguished it in Rome. The temporal power of the Pope was kept alive through him.

A true account of the attempts on Napoleon's life will never be written, because the only persons who were able and willing to throw light on the subject, ex-police agents and their kind, are authorities whose word is worth a very limited acceptance. It is pretty sure that there were more plots than the public ever knew of, and that in some cases the plotters were disposed of summarily. Most of them were poor, ignorant creatures, but in January 1858 an attempt was made by a man of an entirely different stamp, Felice Orsini.

Born at Meldola in Romagna in 1819, he was of the true Romagnol type in mind and body; daring, resourceful, intolerant of control. From his earliest youth all his actions had but one object, the liberation of his country. His youthful brain was enflamed by Alfieri and Foscolo, who remained his favourite authors. He hated Austria well, and he hated the Papal government as no one but one of its own subjects could hate it. 'When the French landed in Italy' (he told his judges) 'it was hoped that they were come as friends, but they proved the worst of enemies. For a time they were repulsed, then they resumed the cloak of friendship, but only to wait for reinforcements. When these arrived they returned to the assault, a thousand against ten, and we were judicially assassinated.' A succinct and true narrative.

During the republic Orsini was sent to Ancona, where anarchy had broken out; by vigorous measures he restored perfect order. In 1854 he was arrested in Hungary and condemned to death, but he escaped from Mantua under romantic circumstances and reached England, where the story of his audacious flight won for him many sympathisers. He was often seen in society. On one occasion he was asked to meet Prince Lucien Buonaparte. Orsini knew Mazzini, but he was impatient of his mystical leanings, and he disapproved of such enterprises as Pisacane's, by which, as he thought, twenty or thirty men were sacrificed here or there without anything coming of it. He finally repudiated Mazzini's leadership, and in March 1857 he wrote to Cavour, asking him for a passport to return to Italy, and placing at the disposal of the Sardinian government 'the courage and energy which it had pleased God to give him,' provided that government left wavering behind, and showed its unmistakable will to achieve the independence of Italy. Cavour sent no reply, 'because,' he said later, 'the letter was noble and energetic, and I should have had to pay Orsini compliments which I did not deem fitting. 'Unlike Victor Emmanuel, who in after years carried on regular negotiations with Mazzini, Cavour, while ready to make an alliance with the Radicals in the Chamber, was extremely loth to have anything to do with actual revolutionists. His not answering Orsini's letter certainly led up to the attempt of the 14th of January 1858.

Having quarrelled with Mazzini, and receiving no encouragement from Cavour, Orsini evolved the plan which on that day he endeavoured to put into execution. He would have preferred to act alone, but since that was impossible, he sought and found without much difficulty two or three accomplices. One of these, Pieri, a teacher of languages, was arrested by the police, who recognised him as an old conspirator, before he threw the bomb which he was carrying. The other bombs were thrown just as the carriage containing the Imperial party drove up to the opera house. A number of people in the street were killed or injured, but the Emperor and Empress escaped unhurt. When they entered the theatre the Rutli scene of the conspirators in *Guillaume Tell* was being performed. Not a breath of applause greeted them, though everyone knew what had happened. Napoleon III. had a striking proof of how little hold he possessed on the affections of his subjects.

When at his trial Orsini was asked what he expected would happen if he had succeeded in killing the Emperor he answered: 'We were convinced that the surest way of making a revolution in Italy was to excite one in France, and that the surest way of making a revolution in France was to kill the Emperor.' There is a good deal of curious evidence to show that very elaborate preparations had been made for a revolution in Paris. The French police had orders, however, to keep all this aspect of the affair out of sight. It was to be made to appear the isolated act of a misguided Italian patriot. 'The world possesses an Orsini legend,' writes the late Duke of Saxe-Coburg, who was present at the event, having been invited to join the Emperor at the opera, 'which is quite at variance with facts.' The duke clearly thinks that the conviction of the instability of his throne which was brought home to the Emperor on this occasion, was one of the causes which decided him to try the diversion of public opinion into other channels by means of a foreign war.

Everything was done to make Orsini a hero in the eyes of the French public, and to excite sympathy in his cause. Jules Favre by his eloquent defence in which he pleaded not for the life, but for the honour of his client, and still more Orsini's own letter to the Emperor, produced a powerful impression; there was a dramatic interest in the man who, disdaining to crave clemency for himself, tried a last supreme effort in the service of the country he had loved too well. 'Deliver my fatherland, and the blessings of twenty-five million citizens will be with you.' So concluded the letter in which Orsini told

Napoleon, that till Italy was free there would be no peace for Europe—nor for him. It was whispered that the Emperor had a secret interview with the condemned man at the Mazas prison; at any rate, when Orsini mounted the scaffold, he was borne up, not only by his invincible courage, but by the strongest hope, if not the certainty that his last prayer would have only a short time to wait for fulfilment.

Though persons who were able to read the signs of the times no longer doubted that Napoleon had resolved to solve the Italian question by force of arms, it suited his purpose to occupy the public mind for the moment with the furious agitation against England and Piedmont as 'dens of assassins,' which led to the fall of the Palmerston administration on the Conspiracy Bill, and seemed to almost place in jeopardy the throne of Victor Emmanuel. Napoleon sent the King of Sardinia demands so sweeping in language so threatening, that the old Savoy blood was fired, and Victor Emmanuel returned the answer: 'Tell the Emperor in whatever terms you think best that this is not the way to treat a faithful ally; that I have never tolerated violence from anyone; that I follow the path of unstained honour, and for that honour I am only answerable to God and to my people. That we have carried our head high for 850 years, and no one will make me lower it; and that, nevertheless, I desire nothing better than to remain his friend.' This reply was benevolently received; Cavour passed through the Chambers a bill which, though not corresponding to the extravagant pretensions of the French Government, gave reasonable security against the concoction of plots of a criminal nature; Napoleon expressed himself satisfied, and three months after, despatched Dr Conneau to Turin, to mention, quite by the way, to the Piedmontese minister, that he would be glad to have a conversation with him on Italian affairs. This was the preliminary of the interview of Plombières.

Plombières is a watering-place in the Vosges, which became famous on the 20th of July 1858, the day on which Napoleon III. and Cavour entered into the compact that laid down the conditions of the Italian war. The Emperor was to bring 200,000 men into Italy, and the King of Sardinia undertook to furnish 100,000. The Austrians were to be expelled from Italy. The kingdom of Upper Italy would embrace the Legations and the Marches then under the Pope. Savoy would be ceded to France. The marriage of the Emperor's cousin with the Princess Clotilde was not made a condition of the war, and only in case it had been made a condition, was Cavour empowered to agree to it. He, therefore, left it uncertain; but he came away from Plombières convinced that nearly everything depended upon its happening. Napoleon was beyond measure anxious for a marriage which would ally him with one of the oldest reigning families in Europe. It would be a fatal mistake, Cavour thought, to join the Emperor, and at the same time, to offend him in a way which he would never forget. Directly after the interview, he wrote a long letter to the King to persuade him to yield the point. After all, where would the Princess find a more promising match? Was it easy to provide husbands for princesses? Were not they generally extremely unhappy in marriage? What had happened to the King's four aunts, all charming princesses, who had married the Duke of Modena, the Duke of Lucca, the Emperor Ferdinand of Austria, and the King of Naples? Had they been happy? Prince Napoleon could not be so very bad, as he was known to have hurried to Cannes to pay a last visit to a woman whom he had loved, a great actress, then upon her deathbed.

This reminiscence was a singular one to evoke under the circumstances, but Cavour was not an Englishman, and he was not impressed by the propriety of drawing a veil over facts which everyone knew.

The King's instinct told him that his young daughter, pious and simple and destitute even of that seasoning of vanity which is so good and necessary a thing in a woman, but proud at heart like all her race, would derive no compensation from the outward brilliancy of the Imperial Court for the absence of domestic joy which would be her wedded lot unless a surprising change came over the bridegroom. When, however, he was persuaded of the importance, or rather, of the essential character of the concession, he said to Cavour: 'I am making a great sacrifice, but I yield to your arguments. Still my consent is subordinate to the freely given consent of my daughter.' The matter was referred to the Princess, who answered: 'It is the wish of my father; therefore this marriage will be useful to my family and my country, and I accept.' An answer worthy of one who, twelve years later, when the members of the Imperial House were flying, remained quietly in Paris, saying: 'Savoy and fear are not acquainted.'

The marriage was celebrated at Turin in January. The King made a present to Cavour, as a souvenir of the event, of a ring representing two heartseases. In thanking him, the minister said: 'Your Majesty knows that I shall never marry.' 'I know,' replied the King; 'your bride is the country.'

Though warlike rumours circulated off and on, the secret of the understanding arrived at in the Plombières interview was well preserved, and the words spoken by Napoleon to the Austrian Ambassador at the New Year's Day reception fell on Europe with the effect of a bombshell. Turning to Baron Hubner, he said: 'Je regrette que les relations entre nous soient si mauvaises; dites cependant à votre souverain que mes sentiments pour lui ne sont pas changés.'

Even Cavour was startled. Probably till that moment he had never felt sure that Napoleon would not after all throw the Italian cause to the winds. The Emperor's invariable method in dealing with men was to mystify them. He was pleased to pose as a faithful ally, but human intellect was insufficient to fathom what he meant. On this system, skilfully pursued, was reared the whole fabric of Louis Napoleon's reputation for being a profound politician. Bearing the fact in mind, we can easily see why that reputation crumbled away almost entirely when the present became the past. There are few cases in which there is more disagreement between the judgment of contemporaries and that of immediate posterity than the case of the French Emperor.

The least surprised, and, among Italians, the most dissatisfied at the New Year's Day pronouncement was Mazzini, who when he read it in the *Times* next morning felt that the Napoleonic war closed the heroic period of Italian Liberation. To men like Mazzini failure is apt to seem more heroic than success, and the war of 1859 did close the period of failure. The justification for calling in foreign arms could only be in necessity, and Mazzini denied the necessity. Charles Albert denied it in 1848 with no less confident a voice. Then, indeed, there did appear a chance of Italy making herself, but was there the slightest prospect, eleven years later, of that chance being repeated? Each student of history may answer for himself. What is plain is, that France and Sardinia *together* were to find it an exceedingly hard task even to drive the Austrians out of Lombardy.

The unconquerable dislike of men of principle, like Mazzini, to joining hands with the author of the *coup d'état* was perfectly explicable. There were doubtless some sincere Bulgarian patriots who disliked joining hands with the Autocrat of all the Russias. The gift of freedom from a despot means a long list of evils. Mazzini grasped the maleficent influence which Napoleon III. would be in a position to exercise over the young state; he knew, moreover, when only two or three other persons in Europe knew it, that the bargain of Plombières was on the principle of give-and-take. How Mazzini was for many years better informed than any cabinet in Europe, remains a secret. 'I know positively,' he wrote on the 4th of January 1859, 'that the idea of the war is only to hand over a zone of Lombardy to Piedmont, and the cession of Savoy and Nice to France: the peace, upon the offer of which they count, would abandon the whole of Venetia to Austria.' A month before this he had disclosed what was certainly true, namely, that Napoleon wanted to place a Murat on the throne of Naples, and to substitute Prince Napoleon for the Grand Duke of Tuscany. The point that is doubtful in the above revelation is the statement that the Emperor never meant to emancipate Venetia. The probabilities are against this. He may, however, have questioned all along whether his troops, with those of the King of Sardinia, would display a superiority over the Austrian forces sufficiently incontestable for him to risk taking them into the mouse-trap of the Quadrilateral. In this one thing Napoleon was amply justified—in having no sort of desire to take a beaten army back to Paris.

Mazzini, with the more extreme members of the Party of Action (including Crispi), issued a protest against the Napoleonic war, with the advice to have nothing to do with it or its authors. But Italy thought otherwise, and Garibaldi, the man who of all others most nearly represented the heart of Italy, rejoiced and was glad. He did not believe a word about the proposed cession of Savoy and Nice; no one did, except Mazzini and his few disciples. What he saw was, that a great step towards independence was about to be taken. In 1856, he not only adhered to Manin's call to all Italians to rally round the house of Savoy, but went further than Manin in accepting unconditionally what he called the 'Savoy Dictatorship,' to which he left full liberty of choice in the matter of ways and means. He did justice then to Cavour's patriotism: it was only after the sacrifice of Nice that a feeling of bitter antagonism grew up in him for the man who he thought had deceived Italy and himself. In December 1858, on a summons from Cavour, he left Caprera (the island which he had bought with a little inheritance falling to him on the death of his brother) and proceeded to Turin, where he was informed of a plan for a rising in Massa and Carrara, which was originally intended to be the signal of the war. The plan was given up, but in March 1859, Garibaldi was told by Victor Emmanuel in person of the imminence of war, and was invited to take part in it as commander of an auxiliary corps of volunteers which took the name of 'Cacciatori delle Alpi.' In this way, all his own followers, not only those in arms, but the great mass of the people which was obedient to his lead, became enrolled in the service of the Sardinian monarchy; a fact of capital importance in the future development of affairs. Without it, the Italian kingdom could not have been formed. And this fact was due to Cavour, who had to fight the arrayed strength of the old, narrow, military caste at Turin, which had succeeded in getting Garibaldi's sword refused in 1848, and wished for nothing in the world more than to get it refused in 1859. Near the end of his life, Cavour said in the Chamber that the difficulties he encountered in inducing the Sardinian War Office to sanction the appointment were all but insurmountable. Unfortunately, the jealousy of the heads of the regular army for the revolutionary captain never ceased. As for Cavour, even when he opposed Garibaldi politically, he always strove to have the highest personal honour paid to the man of whom he once wrote 'that he had rendered Italy the greatest service it was possible to render her.'

True to his *rôle* of mystification, one week after the shot fired on the 1st of January, Napoleon inserted an official statement in the *Moniteur* to the effect that, although public opinion had been agitated by alarming rumours, there was nothing in the foreign relations of France to justify the fears these rumours tended to create. He continued on this tack, with more or less consistency, to the very verge of the outbreak of hostilities. 'The Empire was peace,' as it was always announced to be in the intervals when it was not war; there was no more harmless dove in Europe than the person enthroned in the Tuileries. These assurances were given more credence than they deserved by the Conservative Cabinet then in power in England, and the British ministers believed to the last that war would be averted, to which end they strained every nerve. Besides the wish felt by every English government to preserve European peace, there was at this juncture, not only in the Cabinet, but in the country, so much fear of Napoleon's ambition and restlessness, that for the time being, sympathy with Italy was relegated to a second place.

Meanwhile there was no want of plainness in the language employed in Piedmont. In opening the second session of the sixth Sardinian Parliament, Victor Emmanuel pronounced, on 10th January, the historic phrase declaring that he could not remain insensible to the cry of grief, *il grido di dolore*, that reached him from all parts of Italy. Every corner of the fair country where the *Si* sounds was electrified. The words, as has since become known, were introduced into the speech by the King himself. As Cavour had foreseen, Austria played—into his hands. To Lord Malmesbury's appeal to evacuate the Roman Legations, and to use Austrian influence with the Italian princes in procuring the concession of necessary reforms, Count Buol replied in terms that were the reverse of obliging: 'We do not mean to abdicate our right of intervention, and if we are called upon to help the Italian sovereigns with our arms, we shall do so. We shall not recommend their governments to undertake any reforms. France plays the part of protectress of nationalities; we are, and shall be, protectors of dynastic rights.' Finally, England proposed a congress with a view to general disarmament. Piedmont, counting on the madness of her adversary, risked agreement with this plan. Austria gave a peremptory refusal to have anything to do with it.

Cavour now asked Parliament to vote a war loan of £2,000,000, which was passed by a majority of 81 out of 151 votes. No foreign banker would undertake to negotiate the loan, but it was twice covered by Italian buyers, nearly all small capitalists, who put their money into it as a patriotic duty. Amongst the few deputies who opposed the loan was the old apostle of retrogression, Count Solaro della Margherita, who raised his solitary voice against the tide of revolution; and the Savoyard

Marquis Costa de Beauregard, whose speech was pathetic from the melancholy foreboding which pervaded it that the making of Italy meant the unmaking of Savoy. Speaking in the name of his fellow-countrymen, the Marquis reconfirmed the profound love of Savoy for her Royal House and her total lack of solidarity with the aspirations of Italy. With time the Savoyards might have learnt to be Italians as their king had learnt to be an Italian king. Or they might not. Possibly the best solution would have been to join Savoy to the Swiss Confederation, though the martial instincts of the race were not favourable to their conversion into peaceful Helvetic citizens. From one point of view, that of military defence, the retention of the province was of infinitely more moment to the future Italy than to little Piedmont. Sardinia could keep the peace with France for an indefinite period; Italy cannot. What is true of Savoy is far more true of Nice. To have it in foreign keeping is to have a very partially reformed burglar inside your house.

'Notre roi,' said an old ragged fisherman of the Lac de Bourget to the writer of this book,—'Notre roi nous a vendus.' Not willingly did Victor Emmanuel incur that charge, in which the rebound from love to hate was so clearly heard; not willingly did he give up Maurienne, cradle of his race, Hautecombe, grave of his fathers. It was the greatest sacrifice, he said, that Italy could have asked of him. Nor is there any reason to doubt his word. But it is incorrect to suppose, as many have supposed, that Cavour promised at Plombières to give up Savoy (Nice he did not promise) without the King's knowledge. Before he went there, he had brought Victor Emmanuel over to his own belief, justified or not, that without a bait Napoleon could not be got to move. Directly after the interview, he wrote a full account of it to the King, in which he said: 'When the future fate of Italy was arranged, the Emperor asked me what France would have, and if your Majesty would cede Savoy and the county of Nice?' To which Cavour answered 'Yes' as to Savoy, but objected that Nice was essentially Italian. The Emperor twirled his moustache several times, and only said that these were secondary questions, about which there would be time to think later.

Austria was always appealing to the right of treaties and the right of nations; not, as it happened, with much reason, for she had ridden or tried to ride rough-shod through as many treaties and through quite as many rights as most European Powers. In 1816 she was so determined to possess herself of Alessandria and the Upper Novarese that Lord Castlereagh advised Piedmont to join the Austrian Confederation, as then and only then the Emperor might withdraw his pretensions to this large slice of territory of a Prince with whom he was at peace. If he did withdraw them, it was not from respect for the treaties which, a year before, had confirmed the King of Sardinia's rights as an independent sovereign, but from respect for the untoward results to himself which he was afraid, on reflection, might arise from enforcing his claims with the bayonet. But people forget; and it was of vital consequence that virtuous Austria should figure in the coming conflict not as the victim of aggression but as the aggressor. On all sides it was said that the Austrian Government would never commit an error of such magnitude; only Cavour thought the contrary. 'I shall *force* her to declare war against us,' he told Mr Odo Russell in December 1858. When asked by the incredulous diplomatist at what date he expected to perform so great a feat, Cavour quietly answered: 'In

P

the first week of May.' War was actually declared a few days sooner.

For months Austria had been pouring troops into Italy, a large portion of which were massed on the frontier line of the Ticino. Who shall count the number of the men brought to fight and die in the Italian plains between 1848 and 1866 to sustain 'for that short time the weight of a condemned despotism'? The supply was inexhaustible; they came from the Hungarian steppes, from the green valleys of Styria, from the mountains of Tyrol, from the woodlands of the Banat and of Bohemia; a blind million battling for a chimera. They came, and how many did not return?

Austria's final refusal to adhere to the Congress scheme meant, of course, war, and Cavour called the Chamber and demanded a vote conferring upon Government the power to take such prompt measures as the situation required. 'We trust,' he said, 'that the Chamber will not hesitate to sanction the proposal to invest the King with plenary powers. Who could be a better guardian of our liberty? Who more worthy of the faith of the nation? He it is whose name a ten years' reign had made synonymous with honour and loyalty; who has always held high the tricolor standard of Italy, who now prepares to unsheath his sword for freedom and independence.'

When Cavour walked out of the Chamber after the vote had been taken, he said: 'I am leaving the last sitting of the Piedmontese Parliament, the next will be that of the Kingdom of Italy.' At that moment, if ever in his career, the great minister who had fought so long a fight against incalculable obstacles learnt what it is to taste the sweetness of triumph.

CHAPTER XII

THE WAR FOR LOMBARDY

1859

Austria declares War—Montebello—Garibaldi's Campaign—Palestro—Magenta—The Allies enter Milan—Ricasoli saves Italian Unity—Accession of Francis II.—Solferino—The Armistice of Villafranca.

BARON VON KELLERSPERG reached Turin on the 23rd of April, bringing with him the Austrian ultimatum : 'Disarmament within three days, or war.' Cavour read the document, and then drew his watch out of his pocket. It was half-past five in the afternoon. At the same hour on the 26th, he gave Baron von Kellersperg the answer : 'Sardinia having accepted the principle of a general disarmament, as formulated by England, with the adhesion of France, Prussia and Russia, the Sardinian Government has no other explanation to make.' The retort was justified. Austria, which now required Sardinia to disarm, had refused to disarm herself. She must take the consequences.

The British Government made a last desperate effort to maintain peace, and the Austrians always said that this was their ruin, as it delayed the invasion of Piedmont for a week. On the 29th appeared the Emperor Francis Joseph's Declaration of War, and on the same day the first Austrian columns crossed the Ticino. The Austrian commander-in-chief was Count Gyulai, who was in high favour with the aristocratic party, by which his appointment was suggested to, if not forced upon, the Emperor. The latter, not altogether easy in his mind about Gyulai's capabilities, commissioned General Hess, in whom he placed full confidence, to keep his eye on him. Hess could not, however, do much more than take notes of one of the most remarkable and providential series of blunders ever committed by the commander of an army.

In spite of the delay which the Austrians ascribed to the English peace negotiations, there was time for them to destroy the Sardinian army before the French came up. Gyulai had 100,000 men in the theatre of war, a number increased up to 200,000 during the campaign. Both Sardinia and her ally mustered much fewer men than were spoken of at Plombières. The Piedmontese could dispose of 56,000 infantry, formed in five divisions, one division of cavalry numbering 4,000, and one brigade of volunteers, to which the name was given of 'Cacciatori delle Alpi.' The enrolment of these was stopped when it had reached the small figure of 4,500 men, a figure that looks out of all proportion with the brilliant part they played. The same influences which cut short the enrolment prevented Cavour from keeping his distinct promise to give Garibaldi, now invested with the official rank of major-general, 10,000 regulars, with a battery and a troop of horse.

The French army consisted of 128,000 men, including about 10,000 cavalry. The Emperor's Government had notified beforehand to Vienna that the passage of the Ticino by the Austrian troops would be considered equivalent to a declaration of war, and accordingly, on the 29th of April, diplomatic relations between the two Powers were broken off. The French forces had been really on the move for more than a week—ever since, in fact, by what the Marquis of Normanby called 'an unpardonable breach of confidence,' the intention of Austria to invade Sardinia was communicated to Paris. The mobilisation was conducted with rapidity; in spite of the snow, which lay deep on the Mont Cenis, the first corps, under Marshal Baraguay d'Hilliers, made a swift march over the Alps, and the foremost division entered Turin on the 30th of April. The troops of Canrobert and Niel, who commanded the third and fourth corps, were sent by Toulon and Marseilles, while the generals themselves went on to Turin in advance. MacMahon's corps, which was the second, was on its way from Algiers. The fifth corps, under the command of Prince Napoleon, was despatched at a later date to Tuscany, where it was kept in a state of inactivity, which suggested rather a political than a military mission. General Regnault de Saint-Jean d'Angély commanded the Imperial Guard. Napoleon III. assumed the supreme command of the allied armies, with General Vaillant as head of the staff.

The condition of neither French nor Austrian army was satisfactory. The former had more modern arms and a greater proportion of old soldiers, but it was generally thought that the French cavalry, so far superior to the Prussian in the war of 1870, was inferior to the Austrian in 1859. The commissariat and ambulance arrangements of the French were disgraceful, though they had this advantage, that when there was food to be had the soldiers were allowed to eat it, while the Austrians were limited to half-a-pound of beef a day, and were only allowed to cook once in the twenty-four hours, which led to their having constantly to fight fasting. In point of discipline, they were probably superior to the French, who fought, however, and this should always be remembered of them in Italy, with the best will in the world. They carried about their pet monkeys and dogs, and were always good-humoured and in good spirits, even when wounded. What would have been the effect on them of even a single defeat is a question which it is useless to discuss.

In Napoleon's proclamation to the French people it was stated that the scope of the war was to give Italy to herself, not to make her change masters; the recompense of France would be to have upon her frontiers a friendly people which owed its independence to her. As things stood there were but two alternatives: Austria supreme as far as the Alps, or Italy free to the Adriatic. On the 12th of May, the Imperial yacht, the *Reine Hortense*, steamed into the harbour of Genoa with the Emperor on board. A splendid reception awaited him, and amongst the first to greet him was Cavour. 'You may well rejoice,' said Napoleon, as he embraced the Sardinian statesman, 'for your plans are being realised.'

Gyulai, who had insisted on invading Piedmont, contrary to the opinion of Hess (who counselled waiting for reinforcements on the left bank of the Mincio), wasted his time after crossing the Ticino in making plans and changing them while he could unquestionably have thrown himself on Turin had he possessed more resolution, and this was the only operation that could have justified the initial folly of the invasion. The taking of the capital might not have altered the fortunes of the war, but it would have had all the appearance of a triumph, and would have raised the *moral* of the Austrian soldiers. The allies had time to concentrate their forces near Tortona, and it was left to them to assume the offensive. The Austrians retired towards the Apennines, but made a forward movement on the 20th of May with the object of seizing the heights of Casteggio which command the road to Piacenza; they were met by the allies at the village of Montebello where Marshal Lannes obtained a victory in 1800. The allies were completely successful in this first battle, the honours of the day falling to the Sardinian cavalry, which showed great gallantry. The Austrian forces were considerably superior in strength.

Almost at the same time as the engagement of Montebello, Garibaldi with his diminutive army (which through the weeding-out of men unfit for service was reduced to about 3,500 before it took the field), crossed the Lago Maggiore, and advanced boldly into the heart of the enemy's country. The volunteers had no artillery, and by way of cavalry only some forty or fifty were mounted on their own horses and dignified with the name of 'guides.' They were badly armed and worse equipped; the only good thing they had was an excellent ambulance organised by Dr Bertani, Garibaldi's surgeon-general from Roman days downwards. But they formed a picturesque sight as they marched along gaily to the everlasting song, 'Addio, mia bella, addio'; and a physiognomist would have been struck by their intelligent and often distinguished faces: nobles and poets, budding doctors and lawyers, bristled in the ranks, while the officers were the still young veterans of 1848-1849: Cosenz, hero of Venice; Medici, the defender of the Vascello; Bixio, Sirtori, Cairoli—all the Knights of the Legend.

Moving swiftly from place to place, and appearing where and when he was least expected, Garibaldi took the entire country of the Lombard lakes. Gyulai, who at first looked upon the Garibaldian march as a simple diversion intended to draw off his attention, now became concerned, and dispatched Urban with 10,000 men to destroy the volunteers, and stem the insurrection which everywhere followed in their wake. On the 27th of May Garibaldi drove Urban from his position near San Fermo, and that commander had his mission still unfulfilled when he received the order to retreat after the battle of Magenta. The volunteers were free to pursue their way to Brescia and the Valtellina, where they performed many feats in the latter period of the war, winning the admiration of Hayn, the Austrian general opposed to them, which he was generous enough to express in no measured terms.

The great war was meanwhile approaching its climax. After Montebello the whole French army executed a secret flank movement, changing its position from Voghera, where Gyulai believed it to be, and whence he expected it to move on to Piacenza, to the line of the Sesia, between Cameriano and Casale. To mask the main operations, the Sardinian forces were sent to Palestro, on the other side of the Sesia. On the 30th of May, they drove in the outposts of the enemy, and on the 31st fought the important engagement by which the Austrian attempt to retake Palestro was repelled, and great damage caused to Zobel's corps, which was obliged to leave eight guns sticking in the mud. The French Zouaves of the 3rd regiment fought with the Piedmontese, and made the battle famous by the reckless valour of their bayonet charges. Victor Emmanuel, deaf to all remonstrances, placed himself at their head, in consequence of which they elected him their corporal, an honour once paid to the first Napoleon.

There is reason to think that after Palestro, Gyulai, having at last realised what Napoleon was about, wished to evacuate Lombardy, but was prevented from doing so by strong protests sent by the Emperor Francis Joseph, who was at Verona. The Austrian army was in full retreat when it was pulled up near Magenta, with the object of checking the advance of the French, who had already begun to cross the Ticino by the bridges of San Martino and Buffalora, which the Austrians had tried to blow up, but had not succeeded from want of proper powder. In the great battle of the 4th of June, Austrians and French numbered respectively about 60,000 men; no Piedmontese were engaged till the evening, when a battalion of Bersaglieri arrived. The Imperial Guard, with which was Napoleon, had to bear the brunt of the fight for four hours, and ran a good chance of being annihilated; not a brilliant proof of French generalship, but happily the Austrians also committed grave mistakes. MacMahon's arrival at five in the afternoon prevented a catastrophe, and the fighting, which continued far into the night, was from this moment attended by results on the whole advantageous to the French. Not much more can be said. Magenta was very like a drawn battle. The Austrians are calculated to have lost 10,000 men, the French between 4,000 and 5,000. It was expected that the Austrians would renew the attack, but on the 5th, Gyulai ordered the retreat, which was the last order he had the opportunity of giving, as he was deprived of his command immediately after.

At mid-day on the 5th, Milan, which was trembling on the verge of revolution, made the pleasurable discovery that there were no Austrians left in the town. The municipality sent out delegates with the keys of the city to Victor Emmanuel. At ten a.m. on the 7th, MacMahon's corps began to file down the streets. Words cannot describe the welcome given to them. How MacMahon lifted to his saddle-bow a child that was in danger of being crushed by the crowd will be remembered from the pretty incident having passed into English poetry. On the 8th, the King and the Emperor made their entry amidst a new paroxysm of enthusiasm. Napoleon is reported to have exclaimed: 'How this people must have suffered!' In his proclamation 'to the Italian people,' which bears the same date as his entry into Milan, he renewed the assurance of the disinterested motives which had brought him to Italy: 'Your enemies, who are also mine, have endeavoured to diminish the universal sympathy felt in Europe for your cause, by causing it to be believed that I am making war for personal ambition, or to increase French territory. If there are men who fail to comprehend their epoch, I am not one of them. In the enlightened state of public opinion now prevailing, true greatness lies in the moral influence which we exercise rather than in sterile conquests.' The proclamation ended with the words: 'To-morrow you will be the citizens of a great country.' Not the least effusive demonstrations were reserved for Cavour, who joined his Sovereign a few days after the battle of Magenta.

Leaving the Milanese to put their faith in princes while yet there was time, a glance must be taken at what had been going on in the rest of Italy, which was becoming a great nation far more rapidly, and in a much fuller sense than Napoleon III. expected or wished. When Austria sent her ultimatum to Turin, the Sardinian minister at the Court of Tuscany invited the Grand Duke's Government to take part in the war of liberation. This they refused to do. On perceiving, however, that he could not depend on his troops, the Grand Duke promised to co-operate with Piedmont, but his advisers did not now think it possible to save the grand ducal throne, unless Leopold II. abdicated in favour of his son, who was not burdened with the fatal associations of the reaction of ten years before. Leopold probably thought that even his abdication would not keep out the deluge, and he took the more dignified course of declining to yield to force. On the 27th of April, accompanied by the Corps Diplomatique as far as the frontier, he left Tuscany. A Provisional Government was formed with Peruzzi at its head, which hastily raised 8000 men for immediate service under the command of General Ulloa. Before long Prince Napoleon, with the fifth corps of the French army, landed, for no reason that could be avowed, at Leghorn. The real motive was to prepare the way for the fabrication of a new kingdom of Etruria, which existed already in Napoleon's brain. This masterpiece of folly had but a lukewarm supporter in Prince Napoleon, who was the only Napoleon and about the only Frenchman (if he could be called one) who grasped the idea of the unity of Italy and sincerely applauded it. Had Jérôme Napoleon been born with the least comprehension of self-respect and personal dignity, his strong political intelligence and clear logical discernment must have produced something better than the most ineffectual career of the century.

On the 8th of May, Baron Ricasoli took office under the Provisional Government as Minister of the Interior, and for nearly twelve months he was the real ruler of Tuscany. He had an ally of great strength, though of humble origin, in Giuseppe Dolfi, the baker, of whom it was currently said that any day he could summon 10,000 men to the Piazza della Signoria, who would obey him to the death. To Dolfi it was due that there were no disorders after the Grand Duke left. What Italy owes to the Lord of Brolio, history will never adequately state, because it is well-nigh impossible fully to realise how critical was her position during all that year, from causes external and internal, and how disastrous would have been the slightest mistake or wavering in the direction of Tuscan affairs, which formed the central hinge of the whole complicated situation. Fortunate, indeed, was it that there was a man like the Iron Baron, who, by simple force of will, outwitted the enemies of Italy more thoroughly than even Cavour could do with all his astuteness. Austere, aristocratic, immovable from his purpose, indifferent to praise or blame, Ricasoli aimed at one point—the unity of the whole country; and neither Cavour's impatience for annexation to Piedmont, nor the scheme of Farini and Minghetti for averting the wrath of the French Emperor by a temporary and preparatory union of the central states, drew him one inch from the straight road, which was the only one he had ever learnt to walk in.

In June, the Duke of Modena and the Duchess-Regent of Parma found it impossible to remain in their states, now that Austrian protection was withdrawn. The latter had done what she could to preserve the duchy for her young son, but the tide was too strong. These revolutions were accomplished quietly; but, some months after, on the incautious return to Parma of a man deeply implicated in the abuses of Charles III.'s government—Colonel Anviti—he was cruelly murdered; an act of vengeance which happily remained alone.

After the battle of Magenta, when the Austrian troops were recalled from the Marches and Romagna, those districts rose and demanded the dictatorship of Piedmont. Napoleon foresaw that this would happen as far back as the Plombières interview, and at that date it did not appear that he meant to oppose it. But now, in Paris, the Clerical party were seized with panic, and the Empress-Regent, then, as always, completely under their control, did all in her power to arouse the Emperor's opposition.

The Pope, on his part, knowing that he was secure in Rome—thanks to the French garrison, which, though it hated its office, as the French writer Ampère and others bore witness, was sure to perform it faithfully—had the idea of sending his Swiss troops to put down the growing revolution. With these, and a few Roman troops of the line, Colonel Schmidt marched against Perugia, where, in restoring the Papal authority, he used a ferocity which, though denied by clerical writers, was attested by all contemporary accounts, and was called 'atrocious' by Sir James Hudson in a despatch to Lord John Russell. The significance of such facts, wrote the English minister at Turin, could only be the coming fall of the Pope's Temporal Power.

L. C. Farini was sent by Victor Emmanuel to administer the provinces of Modena and Parma, and Massimo d'Azeglio was charged with the same mission in Romagna. The Marches of Ancona had been recovered by the Papal troops, which were concentrated in the district called La Cattolica, near Rimini. A volunteer corps, under the Piedmontese General Mezzacapo, was entrusted with the task of preventing them from crossing into the Legations.

In the month of May, when the allies were reaping their first successes, an event occurred at Caserta which precipitated crisis in the South Italy. Ferdinand II. died at forty-eight years of age of a terrible complaint which had attacked him a few months earlier, when he went to meet his son's bride, the Princess Maria Sofia of Bavaria, sister of the Empress of Austria. The news from Upper Italy hastened his end; he is said to have exclaimed not long before he died: 'They have won the cause!'

The accession of a youth, of whom nothing bad was known, to a throne that had been occupied by a sovereign so out of place in modern civilisation as Ferdinand, would appear at first sight a fortunate circumstance for the chances of the dynasty; but it was not so. In an eastern country it matters little whether the best of the inhabitants loathe and detest their ruler; but it matters much whether he knows how to cajole and frighten the masses, and especially the army, into obedience. Naples, more Oriental than western, possessed in Ferdinand a monarch consummately expert in this side of the art of government. Though without the higher military virtues, his army was his favourite plaything; he always wore uniform, never forgot a face he had once seen, and treated the officers with a rather vulgar familiarity, guessing at their weaknesses and making use of them on occasion. The rank and file regarded him as a sort of supernatural being. Francis II., who succeeded him, could scarcely appear in this light even to the most ignorant. Popular opinion considered him not quite sound in his mind. Probably his timorous, awkward ways and his seeming stupidity were simply the result of an education conducted by bigoted priests in a home that was no home: populated as it was by the offspring of a stepmother who hated him. His own mother, the charming Princess Cristina of Savoy, died while the city was rejoicing at his birth. The story is well known of how, shortly after the marriage, Ferdinand thought it diverting to draw a music-stool from under his wife, causing her to fall heavily. It gives a sample of the sufferings of her brief married life. An inheritance of sorrow descended from her to her child.

If Francis II. was not popular, neither was the new queen. Far more virile in character and in tastes than her husband, her high spirit was not what the Neapolitans admire in women, and those who were devoted to the late King accused her of having shown impatience during his illness for the moment when the crown would fall to Francis. Malicious gossip of this kind, however false, serves its end. Thus, from one cause or another, the young King exercised a power sensibly weaker than that of his father, while, besides other enemies, he had an inveterate one in his stepmother, who began weaving a conspiracy to oust him from the throne and place on it the eldest of his half-brothers. This plot received, however, very little popular support.

The Sardinian Government sought to persuade Francis to join in the war against Austria; disinterested counsel, as in taking it lay his only hope, but it was opposed by England, Russia and France. In July two of the Swiss regiments at Naples mutinied. The Swiss Government, becoming alive to the discredit cast on the country by mercenary service, had decided that Swiss subjects serving abroad should lose their rights as citizens of the Confederation whilst so employed, and that they should no longer introduce the arms of their respective cantons into their regimental colours. This was the immediate cause of their insubordination. The mutineers, most of whom were unarmed, were ruthlessly shot down in the Campo di Marte to the terror of the population, and the two Swiss regiments which remained quiet were dissolved; by which the monarchy lôst the troops that were chiefly to be depended on in emergencies. The Austrians and Bavarians imported in their stead did not form separate regiments, but were incorporated among the native troops, though the regiments that contained them were commonly called 'Bavarian.' They only partially filled the place of the Swiss.

Between the 4th and the 24th of June, no engagement of any magnitude was fought in Lombardy except the attack on Benedek at Melegnano, a battle in which the French lost most men, and gained no strategical advantage. It was supposed to have been fought because Napoleon I. had gained a victory in the same neighbourhood. The Austrians retreated to the Mincio, destroying the bridges over the Adda, Serio, Oglio and Mella as they went; these rivers the allies had to make repassable, which is the excuse given for the dilatory nature of their pursuit of the enemy. The Emperor Francis Joseph had now assumed the command, with Hess as his principle adviser, and Wimpffen and Schlick, famous as the 'One-eyed,' as heads of the two great corps into which the army was divided.

On the 22nd of June, the Austrians were ranged along the left bank of the Mincio from Peschiera to Mantua, and the French were massed near Montechiaro, on the Brescia road, which Napoleon had made his headquarters. In withdrawing all their men from the right bank of the river, the Austrians desired to create the impression that they had finally abandoned it. It was their plan, which did not lack boldness, to throw the whole army back upon the right bank, and to perform a concentric movement on Montechiaro, where they hoped to fall unawares on the French and destroy them. They were confident of success, for they knew what a good stand they had made at Magenta, and now that Gyulai was got rid of, and the young Emperor had taken the field, they did not doubt that fortune would turn her wheel. To these men of many nations, the presence of their Emperor was the one inspiration that could rouse them, for if they were fighting for anything, it was for him in the most personal sense; it was to secure his mastery of the splendid land over which he looked from the castle of

Valleggio, on the 23rd of June, whilst his brilliant staff stood round, waiting for the signal to mount and clatter down the steep road to the Mincio bridge.. The army now advanced along all its line.

Even the soberest writers have not resisted making some reference to the magnificent scene of to-morrow's battle. On one side, the mountain bulwarks rising tier on tier, gorgeous with the trancendent beauty of colour and light of the Italian summer; on the other, the vine-clad hillocks which fall gently away from the blue lake of Garda till they are lost in the

> . . . . . harvest shining plain
> Where the peasant heaps his grain
> In the garner of his foe.

The 24th of June was to decide how much longer the Lombard peasant should labour to fill a stranger's treasury.

The calculations of the Austrians were founded on the slowness which had hitherto characterised Napoleon's movements. Hess thought that two days might be safely allowed for the Austrian advance, and that the enemy would remain passive on the west bank of the river Chiese, waiting to be attacked on the 25th. If the operation could have been performed in one day, and it is thought that it could, there would have been more prospect of success. But even then, the original plan of attacking the allies west of the Chiese could not have been carried out, as on the 23rd the whole allied army moved forward, the French occupying Castiglione and Lonato, and the Sardinians Rezzato and Desenzano, on the lake of Garda. It is not clear how far the allies believed in the Austrian advance; that they had warning of it from several quarters is certain. For instance, a gentleman living at Desenzano heard from the country people, who, for marketing or other purposes, constantly go to and fro between that place and Peschiera, that the Austrians had ordered a quantity of country carts and transport waggons to be in readiness on the 23rd, and he hastened with the intelligence to the Piedmontese General Della Rocca, who, in a fine spirit of red-tapism, pooh-poohed the information. The French encountered several Austrian patrols in the course of the day, but they were inclined to think that the Austrians were only executing a reconnaissance. On the whole, it seems that the conflict came as a surprise to both sides.

The Emperor of Austria, after accompanying the advance for a short distance, returned with Hess to Valleggio for the night. Napoleon slept at Montechiaro. The Austrian forces bivouacked on the little hills between Solferino and Cavriana. They rested well, still confident that no fighting would be done next day. At two in the morning, the French began to move in the direction of Solferino, and the Sardinians in that of Peschiera. There is a legend, that in the grey mists of dawn an advance party of French cavalry espied a huge and gaunt hussar standing by the roadside. For a moment the figure was lost sight of, but it reappeared, and after running across the road in front of the French, it turned and dealt the officer who led the party so tremendous a blow that he fell off his horse. Then the adventurous Austrian fled, followed by a volley from the French troopers; the sound vibrating through the dawn stillness gave the call to arms to the contrasted hosts. The battle of Solferino had begun.

The news flew to Montechiaro and to Valleggio. Napoleon started for the scene of action with the

Imperial Guard; Francis Joseph's staff was sent forward at six a.m., but the Emperor and Hess did not start till later. At near nine, the staff was looking for the Emperor, and the Emperor was looking for the staff in the open country about Volta; the sixty or seventy staff-officers dashed across ploughed fields and over hedges and ditches, in a style which would have done credit to an English fox-hunt. This remarkable incident was in keeping with the general management of the battle on the part of the Austrians, who had been fighting for many hours before the commander-in-chief arrived. After his arrival, they continued fighting without any visible plan, according to the expedients of the divisional generals. The particular expedient adopted by General Zedwitz was to withdraw 15,000 men, including six regiments of cavalry, from the field. At a critical moment, Count Clam Gallas had the misfortune to lose his artillery reserve, and sent everywhere to ask if anyone had seen it. The Prince of Hesse, acting without orders, or against orders, separated his division from Schwarzenberg's and brought it up at the nick of time to save the Austrians, when they were threatened with actual destruction, at two o'clock in the afternoon.

At that hour the French were in possession of the Spia d'Italia, and of all the heights of Solferino. They had been engaged in attacking them since eight in the morning, Napoleon having seen at once that they were the key to the position, and must be taken, cost what it might. The cost was great; if there is any episode in French military history in which soldiers and officers earned all the praise that can be given to brave men, it is the taking of these Solferino hills. Again and again Forey's division and Bazaine's brigade returned to the charge; the cemetery and streets of Solferino were piled up with their dead, mingled with the dead of the defenders, who contested every inch of ground. The individual valour of the French soldiers in that six hours' struggle made it possible to win the battle.

The Austrians, however, after their desperate straits at two o'clock recovered to so great an extent that, had Zedwitz returned with his cavalry, as the Emperor was hoping that he would, the day might still have been theirs. Even as it was, MacMahon's corps swerved under Zobel's repulse of his attack on San Cassiano, and Niel, in the plain, was dangerously hard pressed by Schwarzenberg. But, by degrees, the French recommenced gaining and the Austrians losing ground, and at six p.m., the latter were retreating in good order, defending each step before they yielded it.

In the last stage of the battle the French limbered up their guns in the belief that a vast reserve of Austrian cavalry was galloping into action. What made them think so was a dense yellowish wall advancing through the air. Had they been natives, they would have recognised the approach of one of those frightful storms which bring devastation in their train, and which, as they move forward in what appears a solid mass, look to the inexperienced eye exactly like the clouds of dust raised by innumerable horsemen. The bursting of the storm hastened the end of the fight.

All the day another fight, separate from this, had been going on between Benedek and the Sardinian army near the knoll of San Martino, overlooking the lake of Garda. The battle, which began in the early morning among the cypresses that crown the hillock, raged till seven p.m. with a fury which cost the Piedmontese over

4,000 in dead and wounded. It consisted largely in hand-to-hand fighting, which now gave an advantage to the Austrians, now to the Italians; many of the positions were lost and re-taken more than half-a-dozen times; the issue seemed long doubtful, and when Benedek, who commanded his side with unquestionable ability, received orders from the field of Solferino to begin a retreat, each combatant was firmly convinced that he was getting the best of it. Austrian writers allege that this order saved the Sardinians from defeat, while in both Italian and French narratives, the Piedmontese are represented as having been already sure of success. The courage shown alike by Piedmontese and Austrians could not be surpassed. Victor Emmanuel, as usual, set an example to his men.

An incident in the battle brings into striking relief what it was this bloody strife was meant to end. An Austrian corporal fell, mortally wounded by a Bersagliere whom he conjured, in Italian, to listen to what he had got to say. It was this: Forced into the Austrian army, he had been obliged to serve through the war, but had never fired his rifle on his fellow-countrymen; now he preferred to die rather than defend himself. So he yielded up his breath with his hand clasped in the hand which had slain him.

The Austrians lost, on the 24th of June, 13,000 men in killed and wounded; the French, 10,000. It was said that the frightful scene of carnage on the battlefield after Solferino influenced Napoleon III. in his desire to stop the war. Had that scene vanished from his recollection in June 1870?

Even a field of battle, with its unburied dead, speaks only of a small part of the miseries of a great war. Those who were at that time at Brescia, to which town the greater portion of the French wounded and all the worst cases were brought, still shudder as they recall the dreadful human suffering which no skill or devotion could do more than a very little to assuage. The noble Brescian ladies who had once nursed Bayard, turned, with one accord, into sisters of charity; every house, every church, became a hospital, all that gratitude and pity could do was done; but many were to leave their bones in Italy, and how many more to go home maimed for life, or bearing with them the seeds of death.

Other reasons than those of sentiment in reality decided Napoleon's course. Though these can only be guessed at, the guess, at the present date, amounts to certainty. In the first place, the skin-deep rejoicings in Paris at the news of the victories did not hide the fact that French public opinion, never genuinely favourable to the war, was becoming more and more hostile to it. Then there was the military question. It is true that the Fifth Corps, estimated at 30,000 men, had, at last, emerged from its crepuscular doings in Tuscany, and was available for future operations. Moreover, Kossuth paid a visit to the Imperial headquarters, and held out hopes of a revolution in Hungary which would oblige the Austrian Emperor to remove part of his troops from the scene of the war. Nevertheless, Napoleon was by no means convinced that his army was sufficient to take the Quadrilateral. He realised the bad organisation and numerous shortcomings of the forces under him so vividly that it seems incredible that, in the eleven following years, he should have done nothing to remedy them. He attributed his success mainly to chance, though in a less degree to a certain lack of energy in the Austrians, joined with the exaggerated fear of responsibility felt by their leaders. He never could thoroughly understand why the Austrians had not won Solferino. Naturally, he did not express these opinions to his marshals, but there is ample proof that he held them; and if the fact stood alone, it ought not to be difficult to explain why he was not anxious for a continuance of the war.

But it does not stand alone. Napoleon feared being defeated on the Rhine as well as in the Quadrilateral. Prussia had six army corps ready, and she was about to move them. That, after her long hesitations, she resolved to intervene was long doubted, but it cannot be so after the evidence which recent years have produced.

At the time things wore a different complexion. Europe was never more amazed than when, on the 6th of July, Napoleon the victor sent General Fleury to Francis Joseph the vanquished with a request for an armistice. One point only was plain; an armistice meant peace without Venetia, and never did profound sorrow so quickly succeed national joy than when this, to contemporaries astonishing intelligence, went forth. But the blow fell on no Italian with such tremendous force as on Cavour.

There are natives of Italy who appear to be more cool, more calculating, more completely masters of themselves, than the men of any other nationality. Cavour was one of these. But there comes, sooner or later, the assertion of southern blood, the explosion of feeling the more violent because long contained, and the cool, quiet Italian of yesterday is not to be recognised except by those who know the race intimately well, and who know the volcano that underlies its ice and snow as well as its luxuriant vegetation.

On Wednesday, the 6th of June, the French army was spread out in battle array along the left bank of the

Mincio, and everything led to the supposition that a new and immediate battle was in contemplation. The Piedmontese were engaged in making preparations to invest Peschiera. Napoleon's headquarters were at Valleggio, those of the King at Monzambano. By the evening a very few persons had picked up the information that Napoleon had sent a messenger to Verona. Victor Emmanuel knew nothing of it, nor did any of the French generals except Marshal Vaillant, but such things leak out, and two or three individuals were aware of the journey to Verona, and spent that night in racking their brains as to what it might mean. Next day at eleven o'clock General Fleury returned; the Austrian Emperor had accepted the armistice. Further secrecy was impossible, and like lightning the news flashed through the world.

Cavour rushed from Turin to Desenzano, where he arrived the day before the final meeting between Napoleon and Francis Joseph. He waited for a carriage in the little *café* in the piazza; no one guessed who it was, and conversation went on undisturbed: it was full of curses on the French Emperor. Mazzini, someone said, was right; this is the way the war was sure to end. When a shabby conveyance had at length been found, the great statesman drove to Monzambano. There, of course, his arrival did not escape notice, and all who saw him were horrified by the change that had come over his face. Instead of the jovial, witty smile, there was a look of frantic rage and desperation. What passed between him and his Sovereign is partly a matter of conjecture; the exact sense of the violent words into which his grief betrayed him is lost, in spite of the categorical versions of the interview which have been printed. Even in a fit of madness he can hardly have spoken some of the words attributed to him. That he advised the King to withdraw his army or to abdicate rather than agree to the peace which was being plotted behind his back, seems past doubting. It is said that after attempting in vain to calm him, Victor Emmanuel brought the interview to a sudden close. Cavour came out of the house flushed and exhausted, and drove back to Desenzano. He had resigned office.

The King showed extraordinary self-control. Bitter as the draught was, he saw that it must be drunk, and he was determined to drink it with dignity. Probably no other Italian grasped as clearly as he did the real reason which actuated Napoleon; at any rate his chivalrous appreciation of the benefits already received, closed his lips to reproaches. 'Whatever may be the decision of your Majesty,' he said to the Emperor on the eve of Villafranca, 'I shall feel an eternal gratitude for what you have done for the independence of Italy, and I beg you to believe that under all circumstances you may reckon on my complete fidelity.'

If there was sadness in the Sardinian camp, so there was in that of Austria. The Austrians by no means thought that the game was up for them. It would be interesting to know by what arguments Napoleon persuaded the young Emperor to renounce the hope of retrieving his disasters, whilst he slowly pulled to pieces some flowers which were on the table before which he and Francis Joseph sat. When they left the house, the heir to all the Hapsburgs looked pale and sad. Did he remember the dying counsels of 'Father' Radetsky—not to yield if he was beaten on the Mincio, on the Tagliamento, on the Isonzo, before the gates of Vienna.

When, on the evening of the same day, the Emperor of Austria signed the preliminaries of peace, he said to Prince Napoleon, who took the document to Verona for his signature: 'I pray God that if you are ever a sovereign He may spare you the hour of grief I have just passed.' Yet the defeat of Solferino and the loss of Lombardy were the first steps in the transformation of Radetsky's pupil from a despot, who hourly feared revolution in every land under his sceptre, to a wise and constitutional monarch ruling over a contented Empire. To some individuals and to some states, misfortune is fortune.

CHAPTER XIII

WHAT UNITY COST

1859-1860

Napoleon III. and Cavour—The Cession of Savoy and Nice—
Annexations in Central Italy.

NAPOLEON'S hurried journey to Turin on his way back to France was almost a flight. Everywhere his reception was cold in the extreme. He was surprised, he said, at the ingratitude of the Italians. It was still possible to ask for gratitude, as the services rendered had not been paid for; no one spoke yet of the barter of Savoy and Nice. But Napoleon, when he said these words to the Governor of Milan, forgot how the Lombards, in June 1848, absolutely refused to take their freedom at the cost of resigning Venice to Austria. And if Venice was dear to them and to Italy then, how much dearer had she not become since the heroic struggle in which she was the last to yield. The bones of Manin cried aloud for Venetian liberty from his grave of exile.

Venice was the one absorbing thought of the moment; yet there were clauses in the brief preliminaries of peace more fraught with insidious danger than the abandonment of Venice. If the rest of Italy became one and free, it needed no prophet to tell that not the might of twenty Austrias could keep Venetia permanently outside the fold. But if Italy was to remain divided and enslaved, then, indeed, the indignant question went up to heaven, To what end had so much blood been shed?

When he resolved to cut short the war, Napoleon still had it in his power to go down to history as the supreme benefactor of Italy. He chose instead to become her worst and by far her most dangerous enemy. The preliminaries of peace opened with the words: 'The Emperor of Austria and the Emperor of the French will favour the creation of an Italian Confederation under the honorary presidency of the Holy Father.' Further, it was stated that the Grand Duke of Tuscany and the Duke of Modena would return to their states. Though Napoleon proposed at first to add, 'without foreign armed intervention,' he waived the point (Rome was in his mind) and no such guarantee was inserted. Here, then, was the federative programme which all the personal influence and ingenuity of the French Emperor, all the arts of French diplomacy, were concentrated on maintaining, and which was only defeated by the true patriotism and strong good sense of the Italian populations, and of the men who led them through this, the most critical period in their history.

In England Lord Derby's administration had fallen and the Liberals were again in power. Napoleon was so strangely deluded as to expect to find support in that quarter for his anti-unionist conspiracy. His earliest scheme was that the federative plan should be presented to Europe by Great Britain. Lord John Russell answered: 'We are asked to propose a partition (*morcellement*) of the peoples of Italy, as if we had the right to dispose of them.' It was a happy circumstance for Italy that her unity had no better friends than in the English Government during those difficult years. Cavour's words soon after Villafranca, 'It is England's turn now,' were not belied.

One thing should have made Napoleon uneasy; a man like Cavour, when his blood is roused, when his nature is fired by the strongest passions that move the human heart, is an awkward adversary. If there was an instant in which the great statesman thought that all was lost, it was but an instant. With the quick rebound of virile characters he recovered his balance and understood his part. It was to fight and conquer.

'Your Emperor has dishonoured me,' he said to M. Pietri in the presence of Kossuth (the interview taking place at Turin on the 15th of July). 'Yes, sir, he has dishonoured me,' and he set forth how, after promising to hunt the last Austrian out of Italy, after secretly exacting the price of his assistance to which Cavour had induced his good and honest King to consent, he now left them solemnly in the lurch; Lombardy might suffice! And, for nothing to be wanting, the King was to be forced into a confederation with Austria and the Italian princes under the presidency of the Pope. After painting the situation with all the irony and scorn of which he was master, he gave his note of warning: 'If needs be, I will become a conspirator, I will become a revolutionist, but this treaty shall never be executed; a thousand times no—never!'

The routine business of the Prime Minister still fell to Cavour, as Rattazzi, who succeeded him, had not yet formed his cabinet. He was obliged, therefore, to write officially to the Royal Commissioners at Modena, Bologna and Florence to abandon their posts. But in the character of Cavour, the private citizen, he telegraphed to them at the same time to remain and do their duty. And they remained.

On one point there was a temporary lull of anxiety. Almost the last words spoken by Napoleon to Victor Emmanuel before he left Turin were: 'We shall think no more about Nice and Savoy.' The mention of Nice shows that though it had not been promised, Napoleon was all along set upon its acquisition. It is impossible to say how far, at the moment, he was sincere in the renunciation. That, very soon after his return to Paris, he was diligently weaving plans for getting both provinces into his net, is evident from the tenor of the articles and notes published in the 'inspired' French newspapers.

Two chief motives can be divined for Napoleon's determined opposition to Italian unity which never ceased till Sédan. The first was his wish, shared by all French politicians, that Italy should be weak. The second was his regard for the Temporal Power which proceeded from his still being convinced that he could not reign without the Clerical vote. The French prelates were perpetually giving him reminders that this vote depended on his keeping the Pope on his throne. For instance, Cardinal Donnet told him at Bordeaux in October 1859, that he could not choose a better way of showing his appreciation of the Blessed Virgin than 'en ménageant un triomphe à son Fils dans la personne de son Vicaire.' It would be a triumph which the Catholic world would salute with transport. Hints of this sort, the sense of which was not hard to read, in spite of their recondite phraseology, reached him from every quarter. He feared to set them aside. The origins of his power were too much tainted for him to advance boldly on an independent policy. Thus it was that bit by bit he deliberately forfeited all title to the help of Italy when the same whirlwind that dashed him to earth, cleared the way for the final accomplishment of her national destinies.

Whilst Victor Emmanuel was more alive than Cavour to the military arguments in favour of stopping hostilities when the tide of success was at its height, he was not one whit more disposed to stultify his past by becoming the vassal at once of Paris and Vienna. In a letter written to the Emperor of the French in October, in answer to a very long one in which Napoleon sought to convert him to the plan of an Austro-Italian Confederation, he wound up by saying: 'For the considerations above stated, and for many others, I cannot, Sire, second your Majesty's policy in Italy. If your Majesty is bound by treaties and cannot revoke your engagements in the (proposed) congress, I, Sire, am bound on my side, by honour in the face of Europe, by right and duty, by the interests of my house, of my people and of Italy. My fate is joined to that of the Italian people. We can succumb, but never betray. Solferino and San Martino may sometimes redeem Novara and Waterloo, but the apostasies of princes are always irreparable. I am moved to the bottom of my soul by the faith and love which this noble and unfortunate people has reposed in me, and rather than be unworthy of it, I will break my sword and throw the crown away as did my august father. Personal interest does not guide me in defending the annexations; the Sword and Time have borne my house from the summit of the Alps to the banks of the Mincio, and those two guardian angels of the Savoy race will bear it further still, when it pleases God.'

The events in Central Italy to which the King alludes were of the highest importance. L. C. Farini, the Sardinian Royal Commissioner at Modena, when relieved of his office, assumed the dictatorship by the will of the people. L. Cipriani became Governor of Romagna, and at Florence Ricasoli continued at the head of affairs, undismayed and unshaken in his resolve to defeat the combined machinations of France and Austria. In August the populations of Modena, Reggio, Parma and

Piacenza declared their union with Piedmont by an all but unanimous popular vote, the two last provinces placing themselves for temporary convenience under the Dictator Farini. A few days later, Tuscany and Romagna voted a like act of union through their Constituent Assemblies. The representatives of the four States, Modena, Parma, Romagna and Tuscany, formally announced to the great Powers their choice of Victor Emmanuel, in whose rule they recognised the sole hope of preserving their liberties and avoiding disorder. Delegates were sent to Turin with the offer of the crown.

Peace, of which the preliminaries only were signed at Villafranca, was not yet definitely concluded, and a large French army was still in Italy. The King's government feared therefore to adopt the bold course of accepting the annexations outright, and facing the responsibilities which might arise. Victor Emmanuel thanked the delegates, expressing his confidence that Europe would not undo the great work that had been done in Central Italy. The state of things, however, in these provinces, whose elected King could not yet govern them, was anomalous, most of all in what related to defence; they being menaced on the Austrian side by the Duke of Modena, and on the South by the Papal troops in the Cattolica. An armed force of 25,000 men was organised, of which the Tuscan contingent was under the command of Garibaldi, and the rest under that of the Sardinian General Fanti, 'lent' for the purpose. Garibaldi hoped not merely to defend the provinces already emancipated, but to carry war into the enemy's camp and make revolution possible throughout the States of the Church. To the Party of Action the chance seemed an unique one of hastening the progress of events. Unaccustomed as they were to weigh diplomatic difficulties, they saw the advantages but not the perils of a daring course. Meanwhile Napoleon threatened to occupy Piacenza with 30,000 men on the first forward step of Garibaldi, who, on his side, seemed by no means inclined to yield either to the orders of the Dictator Farini, or to the somewhat violent measures taken to stop him by General Fanti, who instructed the officers under his command to disobey him. It was then that Victor Emmanuel tried his personal influence, rarely tried without success, over the revolutionary chief, who reposed absolute faith in the King's patriotism, and who was therefore amenable to his arguments when all others failed. The general was summoned to Turin, and in an audience given on the 16th of November, Victor Emmanuel persuaded him that the proposed enterprise would retard rather than advance the cause of Italian freedom. Garibaldi left for Caprera, only insisting that his 'weak services' should be called into requisition whenever there was an opportunity to act.

Before quitting the Adriatic coast the hero of Rome went one evening with his two children, Menotti and Teresita, to the Chapel in the Pine Forest, where their mother was buried. Within a mile was the farmhouse where he had embraced her lifeless form before undertaking his perilous flight from sea to sea. In 1850, at Staten Island, when he was earning his bread as a factory hand, he wrote the prophetic words: 'Anita, a land of slavery holds your precious dust; Italy will make your grave free, but what can restore to your children their incomparable mother?' Garibaldi's visit to Anita's grave closes the story of the brave and tender woman who sacrificed all to the love she bore him.

After sitting for three months, the Conference which met at Zurich to establish the definite treaty of peace finished its labours on the 10th of November. The compact was substantially the same as that arranged at Villafranca. Victor Emmanuel, who had signed the Preliminaries with the reservation implied in the note: 'In so far as I am concerned,' preserved the same liberty of action in the Treaty of Zurich. He still hesitated, however, in assuming the government of the central provinces, and even the plan of sending the Prince of Carignano as governor fell through in consequence of Napoleon's opposition. His hesitations sprang from the general apprehension that a hint from Paris might any day be followed by a new eruption of Austrians in Modena and Tuscany for the purpose of replacing the former rulers of those states on their thrones. Such a fear existed at the time, and Rattazzi's timid policy was the result; it is impossible not to ask now whether it was not exaggerated? 'What statesman,' wrote the Prince Consort in June 1859, 'could adopt measures to force Austrian rule again upon delighted, free Italy?' If this was true in June was it less true in November? For the rest, would not the supreme ridicule that would have fallen on the French Emperor if he encouraged the Austrians to return to Central Italy after driving them out of Lombardy, have obliged him to support the principle of non-intervention, whether he wished it or not? England was prepared to back up the government of Piedmont, in which lay a great moral force. It is plain that the long wavering about what ought to be done with the central provinces is what cost the country Savoy and Nice, or at any rate, Nice. Napoleon did all in his power to prevent and to retard the annexations, especially that of Tuscany, which, as he said, 'would make Italian unity a mere question of time,' but when he found that neither threats nor blandishments could move the population from their resolve to have Victor Emmanuel for their king, he decided to sell his adhesion for a good price. Compelled for the sake of appearances to withdraw his claim after the abrupt termination of the war, he now saw an excellent excuse for reviving it, and he was not likely to let the opportunity slip.

At this period there was continual talk, which may or may not have been intended to end in talk, of a Congress to which the affairs of Italy were to be referred. It gave an opening to Napoleon for publishing one of the anonymous pamphlets by means of which he was in the habit of throwing out tentative ideas, and watching their effect. The chief idea broached in *Le Pape et le Congrès* was the voluntary renunciation by the Pope of all but a small zone of territory round Rome; it being pointed out that his position as an independent sovereign would remain unaffected by such an act, which would smooth the way to his assuming the hegemony of the Italian Confederation. The Pope, however, let it be clearly known that he had no intention of ceding a rood of his possessions, or of recognising the separation of the part which had already escaped from him. Anyone acquainted with the long strife and millennial manœuvres by which the Church had acquired the States called by her name, will understand the unwillingness there was to yield them. To do Pius IX. justice, an objection which merits more respect weighed then and always upon his mind. He thought that he was personally debarred by the oath taken on assuming the tiara from giving up the smallest part of the territory he received from his predecessor. The Ultramontane party knew that they had only to remind him of this oath to provoke a fresh assertion of *Non possumus*. The attitude of the Pope was one reason why the Congress was abandoned; but there was a deeper reason. A

European Congress would certainly not have approved the cession of Nice and Savoy, and to that object the French Emperor was now turning all his attention.

At Turin there was an ignoble cabal, supported not so much, perhaps, by Rattazzi himself as by followers, the design of which was to prevent Cavour from returning to power. Abroad, the Empress Eugénie, who looked on Cavour as the Pope's worst foe, did what she could to further the scheme, and its promoters counted much on the soreness left in Victor Emmanuel's mind by the scene after Villafranca. That soreness did, in fact, still exist; but when in January the Rattazzi ministry fell, the King saw that it was his duty to recall Cavour to his counsels, and he at once charged him to form a cabinet.

That Cavour accepted the task is the highest proof of his abnegation as a statesman. He was on the point of getting into his carriage to catch the train for Leri when the messenger reached the Palazzo Cavour with the royal command to go to the castle. If he had refused office and returned to the congenial activity of his life as a country gentleman, his name would not be attached to the melancholy sacrifice which Napoleon was now determined to exact from Italy. The French envoy, Baron de Talleyrand, whose business it was to communicate the unwelcome intelligence, arrived at Turin before the collapse of Rattazzi; but, on finding that a ministerial crisis was imminent, he deferred carrying out his mission till a more opportune moment.

On the 18th of January 1860, the Emperor admitted to Lord Cowley that, though there was as yet no arrangement between himself and Victor Emmanuel on the subject, he intended to have Savoy. After the long series of denials of any such design, the admission caused the most indignant feeling in the English ministers and in the

Queen, who wrote to Lord John Russell: 'We have been made regular dupes.' She went on to say that the revival of the English Alliance, and the hymns of universal peace chanted in Paris on the occasion of the Commercial Treaty, had been simply so many blinds, 'to hide from Europe a policy of spoliation.' Cavour came in for a part of the blame, as, during the war, he denied cognisance of the proposal to give up Savoy. The best that can be said of that denial is, that it was diplomatically impracticable for one party in the understanding of Plombières to make a clean breast of the truth, whilst the other party was assuring the whole universe that he was fighting for an idea.

When the war was broken off, Cavour fully expected that Napoleon, of whom he had the worst opinion, would then and there demand whole pay for his half service; and this had much to do with his furious anger at Villafranca; but later, in common with the best-informed persons, he believed that the claim was finally withdrawn. When, however, Napoleon asked again for the provinces—not as the price of the war, but of the annexations in Central Italy—Cavour instantly came to the conclusion that, cost what it might (and he thought that, amongst other things, it would cost his own reputation and popularity), the demand must be granted. Otherwise Italian unity would never be accomplished.

In considering whether he was mistaken, it must not be forgotten that the French troops were still in Italy. Not to speak of those in Rome, Marshal Vaillant had five divisions of infantry and two brigades of cavalry in Lombardy up to the 20th of March 1860. The engagement had been to send this army home as soon as the definite peace was concluded; why, then, was it still south of the Alps four months after?

In spite of this, however, and in spite of the difficulty of judging an act, all the reasons for which may not, even now, be in possession of the world, it is very hard indeed to pardon Cavour for having yielded Nice as well as Savoy to France. The Nizzards were Italians as the lower class of the population is Italian still; they had always shown warm sympathy with the hopes of Italy, which could not be said of the Savoyards; and Nice was the birthplace of Garibaldi!

England would have supported and applauded resistance to the claim for Nice on general grounds, though her particular interest was in Savoy, or rather in that part of the Savoy Alps which was neutralised by treaty in 1814. It was the refusal of Napoleon to adopt the compromise of ceding this district to Switzerland which caused the breach between him and the British ministry. From that moment, also, Prussia began to increase her army, and resolved, when she was ready, to check the imperial ambition by force of arms. 'The loss of Alsace and Lorraine,' writes an able publicist, M. E. Tallichet, 'was the direct consequence of the annexation of Nice and Savoy.'

If anything could have rendered more galling to Italy the deprivation of these two provinces, it was the tone adopted in France when speaking of the transaction. What were Savoy and Nice? A barren rock and an insignificant strip of coast! The French of thirty-four years ago travelled so little that they may have believed in the description. The vast military importance of the ceded districts has been already referred to. Some scraps on the Nice frontier were saved in a curious way: They were spots which formed part of the favourite playground of the Royal Hunter of the Alps, and it was pointed out to Napoleon that it would be a graceful act to leave these particular 'barren rocks' to his Sardinian Majesty. The zig-zags in the line of demarcation which were thus introduced are said to be of great strategic advantage to Italy. So far, so good; but it remains true that France is *inside* the Italian front-door.

At the elections for the new Chamber in March 1860, the Nizzards chose Garibaldi; and this was their real plebiscite—not that which followed at a short interval, and presented the phenomenon of a population which appeared to change its mind as to its nationality in the course of a few weeks. In voting for Garibaldi, they voted for Italy.

The Nizzard hero made some desperate efforts on behalf of his fellow-citizens in the Chamber, not his natural sphere, and was on the brink of making other efforts in a sphere in which he might have succeeded better. He had the idea of going to Nice with about 200 followers, and exciting just enough of a revolution to let the real will of the people be known, and to frustrate the wiles of French emissaries and the pressure of government in the official plebiscite of the 15th of April. The story of the conspiracy, which is unknown in Italy, has been told by one of the conspirators, the late Lawrence Oliphant. The English writer, who reached Turin full of wrath at the proposed cession, was introduced to Garibaldi, from whom he received the news of the proposed enterprise. Oliphant offered his services, which were accepted, and he accompanied the general to Genoa, where he engaged a diligence which was to carry the vanguard to Nice. But, on going to Garibaldi for the last orders, he found him supping with twenty or thirty young men; 'All Sicilians!' said the chief. 'We must give up the Nice programme; the general opinion is that we shall lose all if we try for too much.' He added that he had hoped to carry out the Nice plan first, but now everything must be sacrificed to freeing Sicily. And he asked Oliphant to join the Thousand, an offer which the adventurous Englishman never ceased to regret that he did not accept. As it was, he elected to go all the same to Nice, where he was the spectator and became the historian of the arts which brought about the semblance of an unanimous vote in favour of annexation to France.

The ratification of the treaty—which, by straining the constitution, was concluded without consulting Parliament—was reluctantly given by the Piedmontese Chambers, the majority of members fearing the responsibility of upsetting an accomplished fact. Cavour, when he laid down the pen after signing the deed of cession, turned to Baron de Talleyrand with the remark: 'Now we are accomplices!' His face, which had been depressed, resumed its cheerful air. In fact, though Napoleon's dislike of the central annexations was unabated, he could no longer oppose them. Victor Emmanuel accepted the four crowns of Central Italy, the people of which, during the long months of waiting, and under circumstances that applied the most crucial test to their resolution, had never swerved from the desire to form part of the Italian monarchy under the sceptre of the *Re Galantuomo*. The King of Sardinia, as he was still called, had eleven million subjects, and on his head rested one excommunication the more. The Bull fulminated against all who had, directly or indirectly, participated in the events which caused Romagna to change hands, was published a day or two before the opening of the new Parliament at Turin.

Addressing for the first time the representatives of his widened realm, Victor Emmanuel said: 'True to the creed of my fathers, and, like them, constant in my homage to the Supreme Head of the Church, whenever it happens that the ecclesiastical authority employs spiritual arms in support of temporal interests, I shall find in my steadfast conscience and in the very traditions of my ancestors, the power to maintain civil liberty in its integrity, and my own authority, for which I hold myself accountable to God alone and to my people.'

The words: 'Della quale debbo ragione a Dio solo ed ai miei popoli,' were added by the King to the speech prepared by his ministers; it was noticed that he pronounced them with remarkable energy. The speech concluded: 'Our country is no more the Italy of the Romans, nor the Italy of the Middle Ages; no longer the field for every foreign ambition, it becomes, henceforth, the Italy of the Italians.'

CHAPTER XIV

THE MARCH OF THE THOUSAND
1860

Origin of the Expedition—Garibaldi at Marsala—Calatafimi—The Taking of Palermo—Milazzo—The Bourbons evacuate Sicily.

DURING the journey from Turin to Genoa, Garibaldi was occupied in opening, reading and tearing up into small pieces an enormous mass of letters, while his English companion spent the time in vainly speculating as to what this vast correspondence was about. When they approached Genoa, the floor of the railway carriage resembled a gigantic wastepaper basket. It was only afterwards that Lawrence Oliphant guessed the letters to be responses to a call for volunteers for Sicily.

The origin of the Sicilian expedition has been related in various ways; there is the version which attributes it entirely to Cavour, and the version which attributes it to not irresponsible personages in England. The former was the French and Clerical official account; the latter has always obtained credence in Germany and Russia. For instance, the late Duke Ernest of Saxe-Coburg said that 'the mystery of how 150,000 men were vanquished by a thousand Red-shirts was wrapped in English bank-notes!' Of this theory, it need only be said that the notion of Lord Palmerston (for it comes to that) supporting a foreign revolution out of the British exchequer is not one that commends itself to the belief of the average Englishman. With regard to the other theory—namely, that Cavour 'got up' the Sicilian expedition, it has been favoured to a certain degree, both by his friends and foes; but it will not bear careful examination. As far as Sicily goes (Naples is another thing), the most that can be brought home to Cavour is a complicity of toleration; and even this statement should be qualified by the addition, 'after the act.' It is true that, in the early days after Villafranca, he had exclaimed: 'They have cut me off from making Italy from the north, by diplomacy; very well, I will make her from the south, by revolution!' True, also, that earlier still, in 1856, he expressed the opinion, shared by every man of common sense, that while the Bourbons ruled over the Two Sicilies there would be no real peace for Italy. Nevertheless, in April 1860, he neither thought the time ripe for the venture nor the means employed adequate for its accomplishment. He was afraid that Garibaldi would meet with the death of the Bandieras and Pisacane. No one was more convinced than Cavour of the importance of Garibaldi's life to Italy; and it is a sign of his true superiority of mind that this conviction was never entertained more strongly than at the moment when the general was passionately inveighing against him for the cession of Nice. To Cavour such invectives seemed natural, and even justified from one point of view; they excited in him no bitterness, and he was only too happy that they fell upon himself and not upon the King, since it was his fixed idea that, without the maintenance of a good understanding between Victor Emmanuel and Garibaldi, Italy would not be made. Few men under the sting of personal attacks have shown such complete self-control.

As has been stated, when Francis II. ascended the

Neapolitan throne, he was invited to join in the war with Austria, and he refused. Since then, the same negative result had attended the reiterated counsels of reform which the Piedmontese Government sent to that of Naples—the young King showing, by repeated acts, that not Sardinia but Rome was his monitress and chosen ally in Italy. The Pope had lately induced the French General Lamoricière to take the command of the Pontifical troops, and he and the King of Naples were organising their armies, with a view to co-operating at an early date against the common enemy at Turin. In January 1860, Lord Russell wrote to Mr Elliot, the English Minister at Naples: 'You will tell the King and his Ministers that the Government of her Majesty the Queen does not intend to accept any part in the responsibility nor to guarantee the certain consequences of a misgovernment which has scarcely a parallel in Europe.' Mr Elliot replied, early in March: 'I have used all imaginable arguments to convince this Government of the necessity of stopping short on the fatal path which it has entered. I finished by saying that I was persuaded of the inevitable fall of his Majesty and the dynasty if wiser counsels did not obtain a hearing, and requested an audience with the King; since, when the catastrophe occurs, I do not wish my conscience to reproach me with not having tried all means of saving an inexperienced Sovereign from the ruin which threatens him. The Ministers of France and Spain have spoken to the same effect.' Even Russia advised Francis to make common cause with Piedmont. In April, Victor Emmanuel wrote to his cousin, 'as a near relative and an Italian Prince,' urging him to listen while there was yet time to save something, if not everything. 'If you will not hear me,' he said, 'the day may come when I shall be obliged to be the instrument of your ruin!'

It has been said that the Sardinian Government, in tendering similar advice, hoped for its refusal and contemplated the eventuality hinted at with the reverse of apprehension. Of course this is true. Yet the responsibility of declining to take the only course which might by any possibility have saved him must rest with the King of Naples and not with Victor Emmanuel and his Ministers. The attempt to make Francis appear the innocent victim of a diabolical conspiracy will never succeed, however ingenious are the writers who devote their abilities to so unfruitful a task.

To trace the real beginning of the expedition we must go back to the summer of 1859. When the war ended in the manner which he alone had foreseen, Mazzini projected a revolutionary enterprise in the south which should restore to the Italian movement its purely national character and defeat in advance Napoleon's plans for gathering the Bourbon succession for his cousin, Prince Murat. He sent agents to Sicily, and notably Francesco Crispi, who, as a native of the island and a man of resource and quick intelligence, was well qualified to execute the work of propaganda and to elude the Bourbon police. Crispi travelled in all parts of Sicily for several months, and in September he was able to report to Mazzini that the insurrection might be expected in a few weeks—which proved incorrect, but only as to date. Mazzini forbade his agents to agitate in favour of a republic; unity was the sole object to be aimed at; unity in whatever form and at whatever cost.

In March 1860 he had an interview in London with the man who was to become the actual initiator of the revolutionary movement in South Italy. This was

Rosalino Pilo, son of the Count di Capaci, and descended through his mother from the royal house of Anjou, whose name, Italianised into Gioeni, is still borne by several noble families in Sicily. Rosalino Pilo, who was now in his fortieth year, had devoted all his life to his country's liberties. After 1849, when he was obliged to leave Sicily, he sold his ancestral acres to supply the wants of his fellow exiles, and help the work of revolutionary propaganda. Handsome in person, cultivated in mind, ready to give his life, as he had already given most of what makes life tolerable, to the Italian cause, he won the affection of all with whom he was brought in contact, and especially of Mazzini, from whom he parted after that last interview radiant with hope, and yet with a touch of sadness in his smile, as if in prevision that the place allotted to him in the ranks of men was among the sowers, not among the reapers.

Rosalino Pilo believed, as Mazzini believed, that Sicily was ripe for revolution, but he realised the fact that under existing circumstances there was an exceeding probability of a Sicilian revolution being rapidly crushed. It was the tendency of Mazzini's mind to think the contrary; to put more faith in the people themselves than in any leader or leaders; to imagine that the blast of the trumpet of an angered population was sufficient to bring down the walls of all the citadels of despotism, however well furnished with heavy artillery. Pilo saw that there was only one man who could give a real chance of success to a rising in his native island, and that man was Garibaldi. As early as February he began to write to Caprera, urging the general to give his co-operation to the projected movement. It is notorious that the scheme, until almost the last moment, did not find favour with Garibaldi. In spite of his perilous enterprises, the chief had never been a courtier of failure, and he understood more clearly than his correspondent what failure at that particular juncture would have meant. The ventures of the Bandieras and of Pisacane, similar in their general plan to the one now in view (though on a smaller scale), ended in disasters, but disasters that were useful to Italy. A disaster now would have been ruinous to Italy. Garibaldi's hesitations do not, as some writers of the extreme party have foolishly assumed, detract from his merit as victorious leader of the expedition; they only show him to have been more amenable to political prudence than most people have supposed.

Rosalino Pilo wrote, finally, that in any case he was determined to go to Sicily himself to complete the preparations, and he added: 'The insurrection in Sicily, consider it well, will carry with it that of the whole south of the peninsula,' by which means not only would the Muratist plots be frustrated, but also a new army and fleet would become available for the conquest of independence and the liberation of Venetia. The writer concluded by wishing the general 'new glories in Sicily in the accomplishment of our country's redemption.'

True to his word Rosalino Pilo embarked at Genoa on the 24th of March, on a crazy old coasting vessel, manned by five friendly sailors. He had with him a single companion, and carried such arms and ammunition as he had been able to get together. Terrible weather and the deplorable condition of their craft kept them at sea for fifteen days, during which time something of great importance happened at Palermo. On the 4th of April the authorities became aware that arms and conspirators were concealed in the convent of La Gancia, which was to have been the focus of the revolution. Troops were sent to besiege the convent, which they only succeeded in taking after four hours' resistance; its fall was the signal for a general slaughter of the inmates, both monks and laymen. The insurrection was thus stifled in its birth in the capital, but from this time it began to spread in the country, and when, at last, Rosalino Pilo landed near Messina on the 10th of April, he found that several armed bands were already roving the mountains, as yet almost unperceived by the Government, which had gone to sleep again after its exhibition of energy on the 4th. Events were, however, to awake it from its slumbers, and to cause it to renew its vigilance. It required all Rosalino Pilo's skill and courage to sustain the revolution of which he became henceforth the responsible head, till the fated deliverer arrived.

Pilo's letters, brought back to Genoa by the pilot who guided him to Sicilian waters, were what decided Garibaldi to go to the rescue. Some, like Bixio and Bertani, warmly and persistently urged him to accept the charge; others, like Sirtori, were convinced that the undertaking was foredoomed, and that its only result would be the death of their beloved captain; but this conviction did not lessen their eagerness to share his perils when once he was resolved to go.

Like all born men of action, Garibaldi did not know what doubt was after he came to a decision. From that moment his mental atmosphere cleared; he saw the goal and went straight for it. In a surprisingly short time the expedition was organised and ready to leave. 'Few and good,' had been the rule laid down by Garibaldi for the enrolments; if he had chosen he could have taken with him a much more numerous host. When it was the day to start few they were (according to the most recent computation the exact number was 1072 men), and they were certainly good. The force was divided into seven companies, the first entrusted to the ardent Nino Bixio, who acted in a general way as second-in-command through both the Sicilian and Neapolitan campaigns, and the seventh to Benedetto Cairoli, whose mother contributed a large sum of money as well as three of her sons to the freeing of Southern Italy. Sirtori, about whom there always clung something of the priestly vocation for which he had been designed, was the head of the staff; Türr (the Hungarian) was adjutant-general. The organisation was identical with that of the Italian army 'to which we belong,' said Garibaldi in his first order of the day.

One name is missing, that of Medici, who was left behind to take the command of a projected movement in the Papal States. By whom this plan was invented is not clear, but simultaneous operations in different parts of the peninsula had been always a favourite design of the more extreme members of the Party of Action, and Garibaldi probably yielded to their advice. All that came of it was the entry into Umbria of Zambianchi's small band of volunteers, which was promptly repulsed over the frontier. Medici, therefore, remained inactive till after the fall of Palermo; he headed the second expedition of 4,000 volunteers which arrived in time to take part in the final Sicilian battles.

Garibaldi's political programme was the cry of the Hunters of the Alps in 1859: *Italy and Victor Emmanuel.* Those who were strict republicans at heart, while abstaining from preaching the republic till the struggle was over, would have stopped short at the first word *Italy.* But Garibaldi told Rosalino Pilo, who was of this way of thinking, that either he marched in the King's name or he did not march at all. This was the condition of his acceptance, because he esteemed it the condition on which

S

hung the success of the enterprise, nay more, the existence of an united Italy.

The Thousand embarked at Quarto, near Genoa, during the night of the 5th of May on the two merchant vessels, the *Piemonte* and *Lombardo*, which, with the complicity of their patriotic owner, R. Rubattino, had been sequestered for the use of the expedition. On hearing of Garibaldi's departure, Cavour ordered Admiral Persano, whose squadron lay in the gulf of Cagliari, to arrest the expedition if the steamers entered any Sardinian port, but to let it go free if they were encountered on the high seas. Persano asked Cavour what he was to do if by stress of storms Garibaldi were forced to come into port? The answer was that 'the Ministry' decided for his arrest, which Persano rightly interpreted to mean that Cavour had decided the contrary. He resolved, therefore, not to stop him under any circumstances, but the case did not occur, for the fairest of May weather favoured the voyage, and six days after the start the men were quietly landed at Marsala without let or hindrance from the two Neapolitan warships which arrived almost at the same time as the *Piemonte* and *Lombardo*, an inconceivable stroke of good fortune which, like the eventful march that was to follow, seems to belong far more to romance than to history.

On the day before, the British gunboat *Intrepid* (Captain Marryat), and the steam vessel *Argus*, had cast anchor in the harbour of Marsala. Their presence was again and again spoken of by Garibaldi as the key to the mystery of why he was not attacked. No matter how it was done —it may have been a mere accident—but it can hardly be doubted that the English men-of-war did practically cover the landing of the Thousand. Lord John Russell denied emphatically to the House of Commons that they were sent there for the purpose, as to this day is believed by some grateful Italians, and by every Clerical writer who handles the subject. The British Government had early information of Italian revolutionary doings, just then, through Sir James Hudson, who was in communication with men of all shades of opinion, and it is credible that orders which must necessarily have been secret, were given to afford a refuge on board English ships to the flying patriots in the anticipated catastrophe. More than this is not credible, but the energy shown by Captain Marryat in safeguarding the interests of the British residents at Marsala caused the Neapolitan ships to delay opening fire till the very last Red-shirt was out of harm's way on dry land. Then and then only did they direct their guns on the *Piemonte* and *Lombardo*, and fire a few shots into the city, which caused no other damage than the destruction of two casks of wine.

On the 12th, Garibaldi left Marsala for Salemi, a mountain city approached by a steep, winding ascent, where he was sure of a warm reception, as it had already taken arms against the Bourbon king. Hence he promulgated the decree by which he assumed the dictatorship of Sicily in the name of Victor Emmanuel.

The Neapolitan army numbered from 120,000 to 130,000 men; of these 30,000 were actually in Sicily at the time the Thousand landed at Marsala, 18,000 being in and about Palermo, and the rest distributed over the island. At Salemi, Garibaldi reviewed his united forces: he had been joined by 200 fresh volunteers, and by a fluctuating mass of Sicilian irregulars, which might be estimated to consist of 2,000 men, but it increased or decreased along the road, because it was formed of peasants of the districts traversed, who did not go far from their homes. These undisciplined bands were not useless, as they gave the Bourbon generals the idea that Garibaldi had more men than he could ever really count upon, and also the peasants knew the country well. When they came under fire they behaved better than anyone would have expected. The first batch joined the Thousand half-way between Marsala and Salemi. There might have been fifty of them, dressed in goat-skins, and armed with the old flint muskets and rusty pistols dear to the Sicilian heart, which he would not for the world leave behind were he going no farther than to buy a lamb at the fair. The feudal lord marched at the head of his uncouth retainers—a company of bandits in an opera—yet, to Garibaldi, they seemed the blessed assurance that this people whom he was come to save was ready and willing to be saved. He received the poor little band with as much rapture as if it had been a powerful army, and, in their turn, the impressionable islanders were enraptured by the affability of the man whom the population of Sicily soon came seriously to consider as a new Messiah. It is a fact that the people of Southern Italy did believe that Garibaldi had in him something superhuman, only the Bourbon troops looked rather below than above for the source of it. The picturesque incidents of the historic march were many; one other may be mentioned. While the chief watered his horse at a spring a Franciscan friar threw himself on his knees, and implored to be allowed to follow him. Some of the volunteers thought the friar a traitor in disguise, but larger in faith, Garibaldi said: 'Come with us, you will be our Ugo Bassi.' Fra Pantaleo proved of no small use to the expedition.

A glance at the map makes clear the military situation. Garibaldi's objective was Palermo, and if anything shows his genius as a Condottiere it is this immediate determination to make straight for the capital where the largest number of the enemy's troops was massed, instead of seeking an illusionary safety for his weak army in the open country. As the crow flies the distance from Marsala to Palermo is not more than sixty or seventy miles, but the routes being mountainous, the actual ground to be covered is much longer. About midway lies Calatafimi, where all the roads leading from the eastern coast to Palermo converge, and above it towers the immensely strong position called Pianto dei Romani, from a battle in which the Romans were defeated. These heights command a vast prospect, and here General Landi, with 3,000 men and four pieces of artillery, prepared to intercept the Garibaldians with every probability of driving them back into the sea.

The royal troops took the offensive towards ten o'clock on the 15th of May. They met the Red-shirts half way down the mountain, but were driven up it again, inch by inch, till, at about three o'clock, they were back at Pianto dei Romani. A final vigorous assault dislodged them from this position, and they retreated in disorder to Calatafimi. Not wishing to tempt fortune further for that day, Garibaldi bivouacqued on the field of battle. In a letter written to Bertani, on the spur of the moment, he bore witness with a sort of fatherly pride to the courage displayed by the Neapolitans: 'It was the old misfortune,' he said, 'a fight between Italians; but it proved to me what can be done with this family when united. The Neapolitan soldiers, when their cartridges were exhausted, threw stones at us in desperation.' How then, with much superior numbers and a seemingly impregnable position, did they end in ignominious flight? The answer may be found in the reply given to Bixio, bravest of the brave, who yet feared, at one hotly-contested point, that retreat was inevitable. 'Here,' retorted the chief, 'we *die*.' Men who really mean to conquer or die can do miracles.

The moral effect of the victory was tremendous. The world at large had made absolutely sure of the destruction of the expedition. 'Garibaldi has chosen to go his own way,' said Victor Emmanuel; 'but if you only knew the fright I was in about him and the brave lads with him!' In Sicily, where the insurrectionary activity of April was almost totally spent, the news sent an electric shock of revolution through the whole island. In the mountains Rosalino Pilo still resisted, weary of waiting for the help that came not, discouraged or hopeless, but unyielding. Food and ammunition were almost gone; his ragged band, held together only by the magnetism of his personal influence, began to feel the pangs of hunger. A price was set on his head, and he was harassed on all sides by the Neapolitan troops, whose attacks became more frequent now that the Government realised that there was danger. He knew nothing of Garibaldi's movements; but he was resolved to keep his promise as long as he could: to hold out till the chief came. At the hour when everything looked most desperate, a messenger arrived in his camp with a letter in Garibaldi's handwriting, which bore the date of the 16th of May. 'Yesterday,' it ran, we fought and conquered.' Never was unexpected news more welcome. Filled with a joy such as few men have tasted, Rosalino read the glad tidings to his men. 'The cause is won,' he said. 'In a few days, if the enemy's balls respect me, we shall be in Palermo.'

Meanwhile Garibaldi had occupied Calatafimi, and was proceeding towards Monreale, from which side he contemplated a descent on the capital. On the high tableland of Renda he met Rosalino Pilo with his reanimated band. That day the Garibaldian army, all told, amounted to 5,000 men. On the 21st of May, Rosalino was ordered to make a reconnaissance in the direction of Monreale; while carrying out this order a Neapolitan bullet struck his forehead, causing almost instantaneous death. 'I am happy to be able to give my blood to Italy, but may heaven be propitious once for all,' he had written when he first landed, words realised to the letter.

The Neapolitans were put in high spirits by Rosalino Pilo's death; the discomfiture of Calatafimi was forgotten; they represented Garibaldi as a mouse that was obligingly walking into a well-laid trap. In fact, his position could not have been more critical, but he had recourse to a stratagem which saved him. He succeeded in placing the enemy upon a completely false scent. Abandoning the idea of reaching Palermo from the east (Monreale), he decided to attempt the assault from the south (Piana de' Greci and Misilimeri), but, all the while, he continued to throw the Sicilian *Picciotti* on the Monreale route, and gave them orders to fire stray shots in every direction and to light innumerable camp-fires. These troops frequently came in contact with the Neapolitans in trifling skirmishes, and kept their attention so well occupied that General Colonna, in command of the force sent in search of the 'Filibuster,' did not doubt that the whole Garibaldian army was concentrated over Monreale. Garibaldi rapidly moved his own column by night to its new base of operations. The ground was steep and difficult, and a storm raged all the night; fifteen years later he declared that none of his marches in the virgin forests of America was so arduous as this. While the Neapolitans remained in ignorance of these changes, three English naval officers, guided by a sort of sporting dog's instinct, happened to be driving through the village of Misilmeri just after

Garibaldi established his headquarters in that neighbourhood. Of course it was by chance; still, Misilmeri is an odd place to go for an afternoon drive, and the escapade ended in the issue of a severe warning to Her Majesty's officers and marines to keep in future 'within the bounds of the sentinels of the royal troops.' Luckily record exists of the experiences of Lieutenant Wilmot and his two companions at Misilmeri. Garibaldi, on hearing that three English naval officers were in the village, sent to invite them to the vineyard where he was taking his dinner. They found him standing in a large enclosure in the midst of a group of followers who all, like himself, wore the legendary red flannel shirt and grey trousers. Fra Pantaleo's brown habit formed the only exception. Several Hungarian officers were present, and by his father stood Menotti, then a stout youth of nineteen, with his arm in a sling from the severe wound he received at Calatafimi. Around were soldiers who looked like mere boys. They gazed with delight on the English uniforms. Garibaldi requested his guests to be seated and to partake of some freshly-gathered strawberries. He spoke of his affection and respect for England, and said it was his hope soon to make the acquaintance of the British admiral. He mentioned how he had seen and admired from the heights the beautiful effect of the salutes fired in honour of the Queen's birthday, two days before. He then retired into his tent, made of an old blanket stretched over pikes; a child, under the name of a sentry, paced before it to keep off the crowd.

To complete the deception of the enemy the Garibaldian artillery, under Colonel Orsini, was ordered to make a retrograde march on Corleone previous to joining the main force at Misilmeri. Orsini narrowly escaped getting caught while executing this movement, and for the sake of celerity was obliged to throw his five cannon (including one taken at Calatafimi) down deep water courses. He returned to pull them out again when the immediate danger was past. General Colonna, who followed him closely, was convinced that the whole of the Garibaldians were in disorderly retreat as witnessed by the mules and waggons purposely abandoned by Orsini along the route. For four days Colonna believed that he had Garibaldi flying before him, and sent intelligence to that effect to Naples, whence it was published through the world. On the fifth day he was immeasurably surprised by hearing that Garibaldi had entered Palermo!

It was at early dawn on Whitsunday, the 27th of May, that Garibaldi reached the threshold of the capital, and after overcoming the guard at Ponte dell' Ammiraglio, pushed on to Porta Termini, the strategic key to the city. The royalists, though taken by surprise in the first instance, had time to dispose a strong force behind walls and barricades before Garibaldi could reach the gate, and it required two hours of severe fighting to take the position. Many Red-shirts were killed, and Benedetto Cairoli received the severe wound from which he never wholly recovered. Success, however, was complete, and the Palermitans got up to find, to their frantic joy, the Liberator within their gates. According to the old usage their first impulse was to run to the belfries in order to sound the tocsin, but they found that the royalists had removed the clappers of the bells. Nothing daunted, they beat the bells all day with hammers and other implements, and so produced an indescribable noise which had a material influence on the nerves of the terrified Neapolitan troops. Being disarmed, the only other help which the inhabitants could render to their deliverers was the erection of barricades.

Even after Garibaldi's entry, it is thought that General Lanza could have crushed him in the streets by sheer force of superiority in numbers and artillery had he made proper use of his means. However, at about three p.m., he chose the less heroic plan of ordering the castle and the Neapolitan fleet to bombard the city. Most of his staff opposed the decision, and one officer broke his sword, but Lanza was inexorable. The measure so exasperated the Palermitans that even had it achieved its end for the moment, never after would they have proved governable from Naples. Thirteen hundred shells were thrown into the city. Lord Palmerston denounced the bombardment and its attendant horrors as 'unworthy of our time and of our civilisation.' The soldiers helped the work by setting fire to some quarters of the city. Among the spots where the shells fell in most abundance was the convent of the Sette Angeli. The Garibaldians escorted the nuns to a place of safety and carried their more valuable possessions after them. The good sisters were charmed by the courtesy with which the young Italians performed these duties.

Fighting in the streets went on more or less continuously, and the liberators kept their ground, but every hour brought fresh perils. A Bavarian regiment arrived to reinforce General Lanza, and the return of the Neapolitan column from Corleone was momentarily expected. The Garibaldians, and this was the gravest fact of all, had used almost their last cartridge. The issue of the struggle was awaited with varying sentiments on board the English, French, Austrian, Spanish and Sardinian warships at anchor in the bay. Admiral Mundy had placed his squadron so close to the land that the ships were in danger of suffering from the bombardment, a course attributed to the humane desire to afford a refuge for non-combatants, and in fact, the officers were soon engaged in entertaining a frightened crowd of ladies and children. The *Intrepid* in particular, was so near the Marina that a fair swimmer could have reached it in a few minutes; nobody guessed, least of all Garibaldi, that her mission in the mind of the British admiral was to save the chief's own life in what seemed the likely case of its being placed in peril.

Admiral Mundy begged the authorities to stop the bombardment before the city was destroyed, but Lanza appeared to have no intention of yielding to his counsels, and it is still uncertain what at last induced him on the 30th of May to sue the Filibuster, hastily transformed into his Excellency, for an armistice of twenty-four hours. 'God knows,' writes Garibaldi, 'if we had want of it!' The royalists had lost nearly the whole city except the palace and its surroundings, and, cut off from the sea, they began to feel a scarcity of food, but not to a severe extent. It seems most probable that with his men panic-stricken and constantly driven back in spite of the bombardment, Lanza looked upon the game as lost, when had he known the straits to which the Garibaldians were reduced for ammunition, he might have considered it as won.

An unforeseen incident now occurred; the royalist column, recalled from Corleone, which was largely composed of Bavarians, reached Porta Termini and opened a furious fire on the weak Garibaldian detachment stationed there. Was it ignorance or bad faith? Lieutenant Wilmot, who happened to be passing by, energetically waved his handkerchief and shouted that a truce was concluded; the assailants continued the attack till an officer of the Neapolitan staff who was in conference with Garibaldi at the time hurried to the spot, at his indignant request, and ordered them to desist. A few minutes later, Garibaldi himself rode up in a wrathful mood, and while he was renewing his protests, a shell fell close by him, thrown from a ship which re-opened the bombardment on its own account. Lieutenant Wilmot, who witnessed the whole affair, was convinced that there was a deliberate plan to surprise and capture the Italian chief after he had granted the armistice.

At a quarter past two on this eventful day, the 30th of May 1860, Garibaldi and the Neapolitan generals, Letizia and Chretien, stepped on board the flag-ship *Hannibal* which Admiral Mundy offered as neutral ground for their meeting. Curiously enough, both parties, reaching the mole simultaneously, were rowed out in the same ship's boat, which was waiting in readiness. The Neapolitans insisted that Garibaldi should go on board first, either from courtesy or, as the admiral suspected, out of desire to find out whether he would be received with military honours. With instinctive tact he had donned his old and rather shabby uniform of a major-general in the Sardinian army; the admiral's course was, therefore, marked out, and Garibaldi received the same salute as the two generals who followed him. After a foolish attempt on the part of the Neapolitan officers to make themselves disagreeable, which was repressed with dignified decision by Admiral Mundy, business began, and things went smoothly till the fifth article of the proposed convention came under discussion : ' That the municipality should direct a humble petition to his Majesty the King expressing the real wants of the city.' ' No,' cried Garibaldi, starting to his feet, ' the time for humble petitions to the King, or to anyone else, is past ; I am the municipality, and I refuse.' General Letizia grew excited at this declaration, but afterwards he agreed to submit the question of quashing the fifth article to his chief, General Lanza. The armistice was prolonged till nine the next morning.

As soon as he was back on shore, Garibaldi issued a manifesto, in which he announced that he had refused a proposal dishonouring the city, and that to-morrow, at the close of the armistice, he should renew hostilities. There was a splendid audacity in the threat; his powder was literally exhausted; nothing was left for him to do but to die with all his men, and to do this he and they were unquestionably ready. The conduct of the citizens was on a level with the occasion. As soon as the manifesto came to be known, the inhabitants rushed to the Palazzo Pretorio, where the man who had so proudly answered in their name, addressed them in these terms: 'People of Palermo; the enemy has made me propositions which I judged humiliating to you, and knowing that you are ready to bury yourselves under the ruins of your city, I refused.' Those who were present say that never did Garibaldi seem so great as at that moment. The answer was one deafening shout, in which the women and children joined, of 'War! war!' In the evening the city was illuminated as on a feast-day.

Once more in history, the game of greatly daring succeeded. Appalled by the reports of the dreadful threats emanating from a population without arms, and a handful of volunteers without powder, distrustful henceforth of the courage of his soldiers, and, if the truth must be told, of the fidelity of his fleet, Lanza sent General Letizia to Garibaldi betimes, on the 31st of May, with an unconditional demand for the continuance of the armistice. A convention was drawn up, which conceded the fullest liberty to the royalists to supply their material wants, succour the wounded, and, if they desired, embark them on board ships with their families for Naples. Garibaldi, always humane, had a special tenderness for the victims of that civil strife which his soul abhorred, and he never forgot that the enemy was his fellow-countryman. His influence sufficed to secure to the royal troops an immunity from reprisals which was the more creditable because some horrid crimes had been done by miscreants in their ranks when they found that they were getting the worst of it in the street-fighting. Unfortunately the same mercy was not extended to some of the secret agents of Maniscalco, head of the Sicilian police, who, discovered in hiding-places by the mob, were murdered before any protection could be given them. At the time the act of barbarity was judged, even by English observers, with more leniency than it deserved (because cruelty can have *no* excuse), so great was the disgust excited by the most odious system of espionage ever put in practice.

The convention bore the signatures of 'Ferdinando Lanza, General-in-Chief,' and of 'Francesco Crispi, Secretary of State to the Provisional Government of Sicily.' One article provided for the consignment of the Royal Mint to the victors; a large sum was stored in its coffers, and Garibaldi found himself in the novel position of being able to pay his men and the Silician *squadre*, and to send large orders for arms and ammunition to the Continent.

General Letizia made two journeys to Naples, and on his return from the second he came invested with full powers to treat with Garibaldi for the evacuation of the city. On the 7th of June, 15,000 royal troops marched down to the Marina to the ships that were to take them away. At the entrance of the Toledo, the great main street of Palermo, Menotti Garibaldi was on guard, on a prancing black charger, with a few other Red-shirts of his own age around him, and before this group of boys defiled the might and pomp of the disciplined army to which King Bomba had given the thoughtful care of a life-time.

The closing formalities which wound up these events at Palermo formed a fitting ending to the dramatic scenes which have been briefly narrated. On the 19th, General Lanza went on board the *Hannibal* to take leave of the British admiral. He was covered with decorations and attended by his brilliant personal staff. There, in the beautiful bay, lay the ship on board which he was to sail at sunset, and twenty-four steam transports were also there, each filled with Neapolitan troops. The defeated general was deeply moved as he walked on to the quarter-deck. 'We have been unfortunate,' he said—words never spoken by one officer of unquestioned personal courage to another without striking a responsive chord. When he quitted the *Hannibal*, the English admiral ordered the White Flag of the King of the Two Sicilies to be hoisted at the foretop-gallant masthead for the last time in Sicilian waters; and a salute of nineteen guns, the salute due to the direct representative or *alter ego* of a sovereign, speeded the the parting guest. Thus, wrapped in the dignity of misfortune, vanished the last semblance of the graceless and treacherous thraldom of the Spanish Bourbons in the capital of Sicily. The flag of Italy was run up on the tower of the Semaphore. Everywhere the revolution triumphed except at Messina, Milazzo and Syracuse. Even Catania, where a rising had been put down after a sanguinary struggle, was now evacuated and left to itself.

So the 20th of June dawned, and the Queen's ships in the harbour put forth all their bravery of flags in commemoration of her accession, which display was naturally interpreted by the Palermitans as a compliment to the

Dictator, who had fixed that day for calling on the British, French and Sardinian admirals and on the captain of the United States frigate *Iroquois*. With what honours the American captain received him is not recorded; for certain it was with cordial goodwill; of the others, Admiral Mundy treated him as on the previous occasion; the French admiral affected to consider him a 'simple monsieur' who had unexpectedly come to call, whilst Admiral Persano, on board the *Maria Adelaide*, gave him a salute of nineteen guns, which formed a virtual recognition on the part of Piedmont of his assumption of the dictatorship. Cavour had ordered Persano to act on his own responsibility as the exigencies of the hour demanded, and the admiral knew that these vague instructions assigned him a more vigorous policy than the other ministers would have agreed to officially. His bold initiative was therefore justified. As some severe words will have to be said of Persano in a later chapter, it is well to remark here that during his Sicilian command he behaved like a thorough patriot, although it was not in his power to render such great moral services to freedom as were undoubtedly rendered by Admiral Mundy, who at the same time acted with so much tact that his neutrality was not impugned, and he even won the equal personal gratitude of both parties. On the other hand, the Austrian commodore, Baron von Wüllersdorf, succeeded in pleasing no one and no one pleased him. He did not expect that the Garibaldians would lose much love to him, but he took it unkindly that the royalists fired at his boat with himself in it, and the Austrian flag at the stern. In high dudgeon he related this grievance to his British colleague, who gently suggested that since Austria had always supported the Bourbon system of Government, it was hardly strange if the royalists were hurt at receiving neither assistance nor even sympathy from the Austrian squadron which witnessed their destruction. The remark was acute; even Austria was, in fact, tired of the Bourbons of Naples; a portent of their not distant doom. But it was not likely that the royalists should appreciate the phlegmatic attitude of their erewhile protectors.

The concluding military operations in Sicily presented a more arduous task than, in the first flush of success, might have been anticipated. In the general panic, one, if one only, royalist officer, Colonel Del Bosco, turned round and stood at bay. His spirited course was not far from undoing all that had been done. Fortunately Garibaldi had received important reinforcements. General Medici touched the Sicilian shores three days after the evacuation of Palermo with 3500 volunteers, well-armed and equipped out of the so-called 'Million Rifle Fund,' which was formed by popular subscription in the north of Italy. The Dictator went as far as Alcamo to meet the hero of the last glorious fight of Rome, whom he greeted with delight and affection. Later, arrived the third and last expedition, consisting of 1500 men under Cosenz, till recently commander-in-chief of the Italian army. The Sicilian *squadre* had been brought into something like military organisation; and an Englishman, Colonel Dunne, had raised a picked corps of 400 Palermitans which contained, besides its commander, between thirty and forty of his countrymen, and was hence called the English Regiment. This battalion was ready to do anything and go anywhere; it performed excellent work both in Sicily and on the mainland.[1]

[1] Of Garibaldi's foreign officers, Colonel (afterwards General) Dunne was one of the most marked personalities. When quite a young man he sold his commission in the English army and took to fighting under many flags. In the Crimean War he commanded a company of Bashi Bazouks. He had in

Garibaldi arranged his forces in three divisions; one, under Türr, was sent to Catania; the second, under Bixio, to Girgenti; the third, under Medici, was to follow the northern sea-coast towards Messina, the strongest position still in the enemy's hands. All three were ultimately to converge with a view to the grand object of crossing over to the mainland. Medici had 2500 men; the royalists in and about Messina could dispose of 15,000. The Garibaldians did not expect much opposition till they got near Messina, but when they reached Barcelona they heard that the garrison of Milazzo had been reinforced by Del Bosco with 4000 men, with the evident design of cutting off their passage to Messina. It is said that this move was made in consequence of direct communications between that officer and Francis II., whose ministers had already decided to abandon the whole island. But Del Bosco secretly assured his King that such a measure was not necessary, and that he would undertake not only to bar Medici's advance, but to march over the dead bodies of the Garibaldians to Palermo. Milazzo is a small hilly peninsula, on which stands a fort and a little walled city. The spot was well chosen. On the 17th of July, Del

him more than a dash of Gordon, of Burton, and like them he could do what he chose with untamed natures. If he was not obeyed fast enough he adopted rather strong measures. A Sicilian company, under fire for the first time, failed to show sufficient promptitude in executing an order to escalade a wall and jump into a garden, from which the enemy was keeping up a brisk fire. Dunne caught up half-a-dozen of the men into his saddle and pitched them bodily over the wall. The effect was singular, for seeing the Garibaldians falling from the clouds, the Neapolitans took to their heels, exclaiming: 'They can fly! they can fly!' Generally, however, he infused his own courage into all who served under him with a touch, perhaps, of his own fatalistic mysticism. It was a strange experience to hear this courteous mild-mannered gentleman lament that Rome had not been burnt down; the disappearance of the scene of so many awful crimes he regarded necessary as a moral sanitary measure.

Bosco attacked the Garibaldian right, and it was not without difficulty that Medici retained his positions. Some further reinforcements were sent to Del Bosco from Messina, though not so numerous as they ought to have been, but they would have almost ensured him the victory had not Medici also received help; Cosenz' column, and, yet more important, Garibaldi himself with the 1000 men he had kept in Palermo, hastening at full speed to the rescue. The belligerents were, for once, about equally balanced in numbers when on the 20th of July Garibaldi attacked Del Bosco with the purpose of driving him on to the tongue of the peninsula, thus cutting him off from Messina and leaving the road open. A desperate engagement followed. The Neapolitans showed that they could fight if they were properly led, and inflicted a loss of 800 in killed and wounded (heavy out of a total of 5000) on their gallant opponents. Garibaldi's own life was nearly sacrificed. He was standing in a field of prickly pears in conversation with Major Missori when a party of the enemy's cavalry rode up, the captain of which dealt a violent blow at him with his sword, without knowing who it was. Garibaldi coolly parried the blow, and struck down his assailant, while Missori shot the three nearest dragoons with his revolver. Hearing the noise, other Garibaldians hurried up, and the chief was saved. For a long time the issue of the battle remained uncertain, and it was only after hours of severe fighting that Del Bosco was compelled to recognise his defeat, and to take refuge on the projecting strip of land as Garibaldi had meant that he should do.

A few days later, four transports arrived in the bay of Milazzo to carry Del Bosco and his men to Naples. The ministry had prevailed, and the complete abandonment of the island was decreed. General Clary, commandant of Messina, informed Garibaldi that he had orders to evacuate the town and its outlying forts; the citadel would be also handed over if the Dictator would engage not to cross to the mainland, but this conditional offer was declined. The citadel of Messina therefore remained in the power of the royalists, but on agreement that it should not resume hostilities unless attacked. It only capitulated in March 1861. Garibaldi reigned over the rest of the island. The convention was signed on the 28th of July by Marshal Tommaso de Clary for the King of Naples, and Major-General Giacomo Medici for the Dictator.

Before following Garibaldi across the Straits, some allusion is called for to the general political situation both in Sicily and in Italy. And first as regards Sicily. When a government is pulled down another must be set up, and the last task is often not the easiest. Garibaldi appointed a ministry in which the ruling spirit was Francesco Crispi. A Sicilian patriot from his youth, and one of the Thousand, he has been judged the man best fitted to direct the helm of United Italy in days of unexampled difficulty. This is enough to prove that he was not the first-come ignoramus or madman that some people then liked to think him. But Crispi had the art of making enemies, nor has he lost it. Though volumes have been written on the civil administration under the dictatorship, the writers' judgments are so warped by their political leanings that it is not easy to get at the truth. It would have been strange had no confusion existed, had no false steps been made; yet some of the old English residents in Sicily say that the island made more real progress during the few months of Garibaldi's reign than in all the years that have followed. Towards the end of June, Garibaldi appointed Agostino Depretis as Pro-Dictator. Of the many decrees formulated and measures adopted at this period, Garibaldi, who had many other things to think of, was personally responsible only for those of a philanthropic nature. Busy as he was, he found time to inquire minutely into the state of the population of Palermo, and he was horrified at the ignorance and misery in which the poorer classes were plunged. Forthwith, out came a bushel-basket of edicts and appeals on behalf of these poor children of the sun. He visited the orphan asylum and found that eighty per cent. of the inmates died of starvation. One nurse had to provide for the wants of four infants. Garibaldi wrote off an address to the ladies of Palermo, in which he implored them to interest themselves in the wretched little beings created in the image of God, at the sight of whose wasted and puny bodies he, an old soldier, had wept. He had money and food distributed every morning to the most destitute, at the gates of the royal palace, where he lived with a frugality that scandalised the aged servants of royalty, whom he kept, out of kindness, at their posts. Theoretically, he disapproved of indiscriminate almsgiving, but in the misery caused by the recent bombardment, such theories could not be strictly applied, or, at any rate, Garibaldi was not the man to so apply them; whence it happened that though, as *de facto* head of the State, he allowed himself a civil list of eight francs a day, the morning had never far advanced before his pockets were empty, and he had to borrow small sums from his friends, which next morning were faithfully repaid.

When he walked about the town, the women pressed forward to touch the hem of his *poncho*, and made their children kneel to receive his blessing. On one occasion a convent of nuns, from the youngest novice to the elderly abbess, insisted on giving him the kiss of peace. An idolatry which would have made anyone else ridiculous; but Garibaldi, being altogether simple and unselfconscious, was above ridicule. One of the good works that he initiated was the transformation of the Foundling Hospital, of which the large funds were turned to little account, into a Military School under the direction of his best officers. In less than a month the school could turn out two smart battalions, and there were few mornings that the Dictator did not go to watch the boys at their drill. He encouraged them with the promise that before long he would lead them himself to the wars.

Such actions smell sweeter from the dust, than the old story of the antagonism that sprang up in those days between Garibaldi and Cavour, between Crispi and La Farina. This dualism, as it was called, was the fruit of a mutual distrust, which, however much to be deplored, was not to be avoided. Although Cavour had a far juster idea of Garibaldi than that entertained by his *entourage*, he was nevertheless haunted by the fear that the general's revolutionary friends would persuade him to depart from his programme of 'Italy and Victor Emmanuel,' and embark upon some adventure of a republican complexion. He was also afraid that the Government of the Dictator would, by its unconventional methods, discredit the Italian cause in the eyes of European statesmen. These reasons caused him to desire and to endeavour to bring about the immediate annexation of Sicily to the Sardinian kingdom. On the other hand, Garibaldi's faith in Cavour had ceased with the cession of Nice, and he believed him to be even now contemplating the cession of the island of Sardinia as a further sop to Cerberus — a project which, if it existed nowhere else, did exist in the mind of Napoleon III. With regard to immediate annexation, he had no intention of agreeing to it, and for one sufficing reason: had he consented he could not have carried the war of liberation across the Straits of Messina. His Sicilian army must have laid down their arms at a command from Turin were it given. And it would have been given.

La Farina, like Crispi, a Sicilian by birth, arrived suddenly at Palermo, representing Cavour, as everyone thought, but in reality he represented himself. Strong-willed and prejudiced, he was, in his own way, a perfectly good patriot, and he had done all that was in his power (though not quite so much as in later years he fancied that he had done) to aid and further the expedition of the Thousand. But he tried to force the annexation scheme by means so openly hostile to the government of the day, that Garibaldi at length sent him on board Persano's flag-ship with a request that the admiral would forward him to Turin.

After the evacuation of Messina by the royal troops, Garibaldi received persuasions of all sorts to let the kingdom of Naples alone. On the part of King Francis an offer was made to him of 50,000,000 francs and the Neapolitan navy in aid of a war for the liberation of Venice. Almost simultaneously he received a letter from Victor Emmanuel sent by the hand of Count Giulio Litta, in which the writer said that in the event of the King of Naples giving up Sicily 'I think that our most reasonable course would be to renounce all ulterior undertakings against the Neapolitan kingdom.' This was the first direct communication between the King and

Garibaldi since the latter's landing at Marsala; it is to be surmised that of indirect communications there had been several, and that they took the form of substantial assistance, sent, probably without Cavour being aware of it, for Victor Emmanuel carried on his own little conspiracies with a remarkable amount of secrecy. What induced him now to address words of restraint to Garibaldi in the midway of his work, was the arrival of a letter from Napoleon III. in which the Emperor urged him in the strongest manner to use his well-known personal influence with the general to hold him back. It was not easy for Victor Emmanel to refuse point blank to make the last effort on behalf of his cousin. Francis had appointed a constitutional ministry, promised a statute, granted an amnesty and engaged to place himself in accord with the King of Sardinia, adopted even the tricolor flag with the royal arms of Bourbon in the centre. Concessions idle as desperate on the 25th of June 1860, the date which they bore. Their only consequence then was to facilitate the fall of the dynasty, the usual result of similar inspirations of the eleventh hour. Had all this been done on the day of the King's accession it might have imperilled Italian unity—not now. But the fatal words, 'Too late,' would have fallen with ill grace from Victor Emmanuel's lips. Garibaldi answered his royal correspondent that when he had made him King of Italy he would be only too happy to obey him for the rest of his life.

The King's letter, though delivered after the battle of Milazzo, was written before it. That event convinced Cavour, and doubtless the King with him, that it was utterly impossible to arrest the tide at Cape Faro. It convinced him of a great deal more. He saw that if Piedmont continued much longer a passive spectator of the march of events, she would lose the lead forever. And he prepared to act.

Meanwhile counsels reached Garibaldi from quite a different quarter not to abandon Naples, but to go there from Rome instead of by Calabria. This daring scheme was favoured by Mazzini, Nicotera, Bertani; indeed, by all the republicans. A corps of about 8000 volunteers was ready to start for a descent on the coast of the Papal States. At present it was in the island of Sardinia, awaiting the arrival of Garibaldi to assume the command. And now occurred Garibaldi's mysterious disappearance from Cape Faro, which at the time excited endless curiosity. The truth was, that he actually went to Sardinia, but instead of taking command of the volunteers bound for Rome, he induced them to alter their plans and to join his Sicilian army in the arduous undertaking before it of overthrowing the Bourbons in the Neapolitan kingdom. Thus he gained a reinforcement of which he knew the enormous need, for though he was willing to face difficulties, he was not blind to them, as were many men of the extreme party. He also prevented what would have been a step of exceeding danger to the national cause, as it would have obliged the Sardinian Government to break off all relations with Garibaldi and to use force against the patriots in suppressing a movement which, if successful, would have brought a hostile French army into Italy.

CHAPTER XV

THE MEETING OF THE WATERS

1860

Garibaldi's March on Naples—The Piedmontese in Umbria and the Marches—The Volturno—Victor Emmanuel enters Naples.

THE Italian kingdom is the fruit of the alliance between the strong monarchical principles of Piedmont and the dissolvent forces of revolution. Whenever either one side or the other, yielding to the influence of its individual sympathies or prejudices, failed to recognise that thus only, by the essential logic of events, could the unity of the country be achieved, the entire edifice was placed in danger of falling to the ground before it was completed.

When Garibaldi stood on Cape Faro, conqueror and liberator, clothed in a glory not that of Wellington or Moltke, but that of Arthur or Roland or the Cid Campeador; the subject of the gossip of the Arabs in their tents, of the wild horsemen of the Pampas, of the fishers in ice-bound seas; a solar myth, nevertheless certified to be alive in the nineteenth century—Cavour understood that if he were left much longer single occupant of the field, either he would rush to disaster, which would be fatal to Italy, or he would become so powerful that, in the event of his being plunged, willingly or unwillingly, by the more ardent apostles of revolution into opposition with the King of Sardinia, the issue of the contest would be by no means sure. To guard against both possibilities, Cavour decided to act, and to act at once. He said of the conjuncture in which he was placed that it was not one of the most difficult, but the most difficult of his political life. But he proved equal to the task, which does the more honour to his statesmanship because his first plan failed completely. This plan was, that the Neapolitan population should overthrow Francis II., and proclaim Victor Emmanuel their King before Garibaldi crossed the Straits. But the Neapolitans would not move hand or foot till Garibaldi was among them. The fact that when Cavour was convinced that the Bourbon dynasty at Naples was about to fall, he tried to hasten its collapse by a few weeks or days, was made the most of by his enemies as an example of base duplicity. At this distance of time, it need only be said that whether his conduct of affairs was scrupulous or unscrupulous, it deceived no one, for the Neapolitan King and his friends were well convinced that the Filibuster of Caprera was their less deadly foe than the Prime Minister of Piedmont.

But of all the foes of Franceschiello, to use the diminutive by which, half in pity, half in contempt, the people of Naples remember him, the most irrevocably fatal was himself. Two courses were open to him when, after losing Sicily, he saw the loss of his other kingdom and of his throne staring him in the face. One was to go forth like a man at the head of his troops to meet the storm. There had been such a thing as loyalty in the Kingdom of Naples; not loyalty of the highest sort, but still the sentiment had existed. Who knows what might not have been the effect of the presence of their young Sovereign on the broken *moral* of the Neapolitan soldiers? 'Sire, place yourself at the head of the 40,000 who remain, and risk a last stake, or, at least, fall gloriously after an honourable battle,' was the advice given him by his minister of war, Pianell. But his stepmother or somebody (certainly not his wife) said that the sacred life of a king ought to be kept in cotton wool, like other curiosities. Meanwhile his uncle, the Count of Syracuse, proposed the other course which, though not heroic, would have been intelligible and even patriotic. This was to absolve his subjects from their obedience, and embark on the first available ship for foreign parts. Fitting the action to the word, the Count himself started for Turin. Francis awaited the doom of those who only know how to take half measures.

The demoralisation, not only of the troops but of every branch of the public administration in the kingdom of Naples, was not yet a certified fact; and the enterprise which Garibaldi at Cape Faro had before him, of invading the dominions of a monarch who still had a large army, and whose subjects showed not the slightest visible sign of being disposed to strike a blow for their own freedom, looked rather fabulous than difficult. The only part of the *Regno* where the people were taking action was in the furthermost region of Calabria; a fortunate circumstance, since it was the first point to be attacked. Calabria, which had contributed its quota to the Thousand, contained more patriotic energy than the rest of the *Regno* put together. On the 8th of August, Garibaldi sent over a small vanguard of 200 men under a Calabrian officer, with the order to join the Calabrian band of insurgents which was hiding in the woods and gorges of Aspromonte, and to spread the news that his own coming would not be long delayed. The Neapolitan generals had acquired the idea that, instead of these few men, a large force had already disembarked, and so turned their attention to the mountains; while Garibaldi, after throwing the war-ships in the Straits on an equally false scent by various intentionally abortive operations, crossed in the night of the 19th and effected a landing not far from Reggio, of which, for both moral and strategic reasons, it was of vital importance to gain possession as soon as possible. He took with him 4500 men, and had between 14,000 and 15,000 more in readiness to follow. The royalist army in Calabria numbered about 27,000, including the garrison of Reggio, 2000 men, under the command of General Galotti. On the 20th, Bixio attacked the outposts; and on the 21st, Garibaldi fought his way into the city—not, however, without meeting a strong resistance on the part of the garrison, which might have been continued longer, and even with a different result, had not the Calabrian insurgents hurried down from Aspromonte on hearing the sound of guns, their sudden appearance making the Royalists think that they were being attacked on all sides. Next day the castle surrendered, and thus a quantity of valuable war material fell into Garibaldi's hands. His luck had not deserted him.

Cosenz and Medici landed their divisions in the night of the 21st of August, near Scilla, in the neighbourhood of which General Briganti had massed his Neapolitans, 7000 strong. On the 23rd, Briganti found himself attacked on the south and north—from Scilla by Cosenz, and from Reggio by Garibaldi. His position was critical but not desperate had he been able to depend upon his men, who were more numerous than their combined opponents; but he saw at once that fighting was the last thing they meant to do, and he had no choice but to surrender at discretion, almost without firing a shot. Unfortunately, Garibaldi had no power to keep prisoners of war, even if he wished to do so. Who was to feed and guard them? Now, as subsequently, he bade the disbanded troops go where they listed, undertaking to send to Naples by sea as many as desired to go there. About a thousand accepted; the rest dispersed, forming the first nucleus of the semi-political and wholly dastardly brigandage which was later to become the scourge of Southern Italy. Their earliest exploit was the savage murder of General Briganti, whom they called a traitor, after the fashion of cowards. This happened at Mileto on the 25th of August, when Briganti was on his way to join General Ghio, who had concentrated 12,000 men on the town of Monteleone. Garibaldi, whose sound principle it was to dispose of his enemies one by one as they cropped up, prepared to attack Ghio with his whole available forces, but he was spared the trouble. He came, he saw, and he had no need of conquering, for the soldiers of that bad thing that had been Bourbon despotism in the Italian south vanished before his path more quickly than the mists of the morning before the sun. No grounds that will bear scrutiny have ever been adduced for the reactionary explanation of the marvel: to wit, that the Neapolitan generals were bribed. By Cavour? The game would have been too risky. By 'English bank-notes,' that useful factor in European politics that has every pleasing quality except reality? It is not apparent how the corruptibility of the generals gives a better complexion to the matter, but the writers on the subject who are favourable to Francis II. seem to think that it does. Panic-stricken these helpless Neapolitan officers may deserve to be called, but they were not bought. And they had cause for panic with troops of whose untrustworthiness they held the clearest proofs, and with the country up in arms against them; for a few days after the taking of Reggio this was the case, and this was by far the greatest miracle operated by Garibaldi. The populations shook off their apathy, and not in Calabria only but in the Puglie, the Basilicata, the Abruzzi, there was a sudden awakening as from a too long sleep. When Garibaldi got to Monteleone he found that Ghio had evacuated the town. He pursued him to Soveria, where, on the 30th of August, the 12,000 men laid down their arms. A few days later, another officer, General Caldarelli, capitulated with 4000 men. Garibaldi's onward march was a perpetual *fête;* everywhere he was received with frantic demonstrations of delight. Still there was one point between himself and the capital which might reasonably cause him some anxiety. There were 30,000 men massed near Salerno, in positions of immense natural strength, where they ought to have been able to stop the advance of an army twice the size of Garibaldi's. How this obstacle was removed is far more suggestive of a scene in a comic opera than of a page in history. Colonel Peard, 'Garibaldi's Englishman,' went in advance of the army to Eboli, where he was mistaken, as commonly happened, for his chief. He was past middle age; very tall, with a magnificent beard and a stern, dictatorial air, which answered admirably to the popular idea of what the conqueror of Sicily ought to be like, although there was no resemblance to the real person. It happened that Eboli was a royalist town and beyond the pale of declared revolution—a placid and antiquated little city with a forgotten air, where life had been probably too easy for its inhabitants to wish for a change. But the supposed arrival of the Terrible Man turned everything upside-down. Peard, with Commander Forbes, who was following the campaign as a non-combatant, rode up to the house of the old Syndic, who instantly became their devoted servant. Like wildfire spread the news—the whole population besieged the house, brass bands resounded, chinese lanterns were hung out; the Church, led by the bishop, hurried to the spot, the Law, headed by a judge, closely following, while the wives of the local officials appeared in perfectly new bonnets. They all craved an audience, and the same answer was given to all: that General Garibaldi was much fatigued and was asleep—so he was, but ninety miles away. He would be pleased to receive the deputations if they would return punctually at half-past three a.m. In the meantime, Peard was in an inner room, engaged in cannonading Naples with telegrams. He had sent for the telegraph master, who came trembling like an aspen, and from whom it was elicited that he had already telegraphed to the Home Office at Naples, and to the general commanding at Salerno, that Garibaldi was in the town. Peard remarked casually that he supposed he knew his life was in jeopardy, and then handed him the following message: 'Eboli, 11.30 p.m.—Garibaldi has arrived with 5000 of his own men, and 5000 Calabrese are momentarily expected. Disembarkations are expected in the bay of Naples and the gulf of Salerno to-night. I strongly advise your withdrawing the garrison from the latter place without delay, or they will be cut off.' This was despatched to General Ulloa, whom rumour reported to have been just made minister of war, and was signed in the name of one of his personal friends. The rumour was false; but the telegram, of course, reached the desired quarter, and the name attached removed all doubt of its genuineness. It was hardly sent off when a despatch came from the real war minister, asking the telegraph clerk if news had been received of the division Caldarelli? To this Peard answered that General Caldarelli and his division had gone over to Garibaldi yesterday, and now formed part of the national army. Similar information was sent to General Scotti at Salerno. Finally, the Syndic of Salerno was asked if he had seen anything of the Garibaldian expeditions by sea?

Satisfied with his work, Colonel Peard, who knew that there were Neapolitan troops within four miles of Eboli, and who did not think that things looked entirely reassuring, decided to beat a somewhat precipitous retreat. He told the Syndic that he was going to reconnoitre in the direction of Salerno, and that his departure must be kept a dead secret, but as soon as he was out of the town he turned the horses' heads backwards towards the Garibaldian lines. He was still accompanied by Commander Forbes, to whom, during their midnight drive, he related his performance on the telegraph wires. 'What on earth is the good of all this?' said Forbes; 'you don't imagine they will be fools enough to believe it?' 'You will see,' answered the colonel, 'it will frighten them to death, and to-morrow they will evacuate Salerno.' And, in fact, at four o'clock in the morning the evacuation was begun in obedience to telegraphic orders from Naples.

The 30,000 men recalled from Salerno and the adjacent districts marched towards Capua. The river Volturno, which runs by that fortified town, was now chosen as the line of defence of the Bourbon monarchy.

On the 5th of September the King and Queen with the Austrian, Prussian, Bavarian and Spanish ministers, left Naples for Gaeta on board a Spanish man-of-war.

The King issued a proclamation of which the language was dignified and even pathetic: it is believed to have been written by Liborio Romano, the Prime Minister, who was at the same moment betraying his master. Be that as it may, the King's farewell to his subjects and fellow-citizens might have touched hearts of stone could they but have forgotten the record of the hundred and twenty-six years of rule to which he fondly alluded. As it was, in the vast crowds that watched him go, there was not found a man who said, 'God bless him;' not a woman who shed a tear. Had any one of the bullets aimed at Ferdinand II. taken fatal effect, it would have been a less striking punishment for his political sins than this leaden weight of indifference which descended on his son.

In the Royal Proclamation Francis II. stated that he had adhered to the great principles of Italian nationality, and had irrevocably surrounded his throne with free institutions; nevertheless it is alleged on what seems good authority that in those last days he veered round to the party of the Queen Dowager, who was doing all she could to provoke the lazzaroni to reaction. It was also believed at Naples that he left orders for Castel Sant' Elmo to bombard the town if Garibaldi entered.

The Dictator was so much pleased with Colonel Peard's telegraphic feats at Eboli, that he sent him on to Salerno to repeat the farce. Peard's despatches determined the departure of the Court, and it was to him (in the belief that he was Garibaldi) that Liborio Romano, three hours before the King embarked, addressed the celebrated telegram invoking the 'most desired presence' of the Dictator in Naples. With this document in his hand, Peard went out with the National Guard to meet the real Garibaldi who was on his way from Auletta. The Dictator hailed his double with the cry of 'Viva Garibaldi,' in which

Cosenz and the other officers cordially joined. The entry of the Liberator into Salerno was greeted with the wildest enthusiasm, the wonderful beauty of the surroundings seeming a fitting setting for a scene like the vision of some freedom-loving poet.

Next morning at half-past nine, Garibaldi, with thirteen of his staff, started by special train for the capital.

It must be remembered that though the army of Salerno was recalled to the Volturno, no troops had been withdrawn from Naples. The sentries still paced before the palaces and public offices, the barracks held their full complement, Castel Sant' Elmo had all its guns in position. These troops quartered in the capital, where everything contributed to stimulate their fidelity, were of different stuff from Ghio's or Caldarelli's frightened sheep; a White Terror, a repetition of the 15th of May 1848, would have been much to their mind. There had been no actual revolution; nothing officially proved that Naples had thrown off the royal allegiance. Such were the strange circumstances under which Garibaldi, without a single battalion, came to take possession of a city of 300,000 inhabitants.

Courage of this sort either does not exist, or it is supremely unconscious. It is likely, therefore, that the Dictator gave no thought to the enormous risk he ran, but his passage from the station to the palace of the Foresteria, where he descended, was a bad quarter-of-an-hour to the friends who followed him, and to whom his life seemed the point on which Italian regeneration yet hung. A chance shot fired by some Royalist fanatic, and who could measure the result? As he passed under the muzzle of the guns at the opening of the Toledo, he gave the order: 'Drive slower, slower—more slowly still.' And he rose and stood up for a moment in the carriage with his arms crossed. The artillerymen, who had begun to make a kind of hostile demonstration, changed their minds and saluted. The sullen looks of the royal soldiers was the only jarring note in the display of intoxicating joy with which the Neapolitans welcomed the bringer of their freedom; freedom all too easily had, for if anything could have purified the Neapolitans from the evil influences of servitude, it would have been the necessity of paying dearly for their liberties. The delirium in the streets lasted for several days and nights; what the consequences would have been of such a state of madness under a paler sky, it is not pleasant to reflect; here, at least, there were no robberies, no drunken person was seen; if there were some murders, a careful inquiry made by an Englishman showed that the number was the same as the average number of street-murders through the year. At night, when the word passed 'Il Dittatore dorme,' it was enough to clear the streets as if by magic near the palace (a private one) where in a sixth floor room the idol of the hour slept. The National Guard, who were the sole guardians of order, behaved admirably.

For a few days such of the townsfolk as had not completely lost their heads, underwent acute anxiety as they gazed at the frowning pile of Sant' Elmo; but finally the officers in command of the garrison decided to capitulate, contrary, in this instance, to the wishes of the soldiery. The royal troops marched out of the city towards Capua on the 11th of September.

Garibaldi's first act had been to hand over the Neapolitan fleet in the bay to Admiral Persano, a solemn reassertion of his loyalty to Victor Emmanuel, whom, in his every utterance, he held up to the people as the best of kings and the father of his country. He instructed his Neapolitan officer, Cosenz, to form a ministry, and wrote to the Marquis Pallavicini, the prisoner of Spielberg, inviting him to become Pro-Dictator. Had a man of authority like Pallavicini, who also entirely possessed the Dictator's confidence, at once assumed that office, much of the friction which followed might have been spared. But he did not enter into his functions till October, and in the meanwhile the 'dualism' of Sicily broke out in an exaggerated form, each side sincerely believing the other to be on the verge of ruining the country to which they were both sincerely attached. The appointment of Dr Bertani as Secretary of the Dictatorship gave rise to controversies which even now, when the grave has closed over the actors, are hardly at rest. It is time that they should be. Apart from the war about persons, some of them not very wise persons, and apart from the fears entertained at Turin, that the freeing of the Two Sicilies would drift into a republican movement: fears which were invincible, though, as far as they regarded Garibaldi, they were neither just nor generous, the question resolved itself, as was the case in Sicily, into whether the unification of Italy was to go on or whether it was to halt? Garibaldi refused to give up Sicily to the King's government because he intended making it the base for the liberation of Naples. Events had justified him. He now refused to hand over Naples because he intended making it the base for the liberation of Rome. It has been seen that he and he alone prevented an attempt at a landing in the Papal states from being made in the month of August. In deciding, however, that it was expedient to finish one enterprise before beginning another, he did not give up Rome: he merely chose what he thought a safer road to go there. And he now declared without the least concealment that he intended to proclaim Victor Emmanuel King of Italy from the Quirinal.

Would events have justified him again? There was a French garrison in Rome; this, to Cavour, seemed a conclusive answer.

Cavour was engaged on a series of measures, unscrupulous manœuvres as some have called them, masterpieces of statesmanship as they have been described by others, by which he got back the reins of the Italian team into his own hands. The plan of an annexionist revolution in Naples before Garibaldi arrived had failed. So much discontent was felt at the apparent indifference, or, at least, 'masterly inactivity' of the Sardinian government in presence of the great struggle in the south that Cavour began to be afraid of a revolution breaking out in quite a different quarter, in Victor Emmanuel's own kingdom. It was at this critical juncture that he resolved to invade the Papal states, and take possession of the Province of Umbria and the Marches of Ancona.

The decision was one of extreme boldness. For three months Cavour had been stormed at by all the Foreign Ministers in Turin, excepting Sir James Hudson, but, as he wrote to the Marquis E. D'Azeglio: 'I shall not draw back save before fleets and armies.'

Austria, France, Spain, Russia and Prussia now broke off diplomatic relations with Sardinia. What would be their next act? The danger of Austria intervening was smaller than it then appeared; Austria was too much embarrassed in her own house, and especially in Hungary, for her to covet adventures in Italy. But the French Government did, in the plainest terms, threaten to intervene, and this notwithstanding that the Emperor himself appeared to be convinced by Cavour's argument, that the proposed scheme was the only means of checking the march of revolution, which from Rome might spread to Paris. By announcing one line of policy in public and another in private, Napoleon left the door open to adopt either one or the other, according to the development of events. In the sequel, the Papal party had a right to say that he lured them to their destruction, as their plan of operations, and in particular the defence of Ancona, was undertaken in the distinct expectation of being supported by the French fleet.

As early as April 1860, the Pope invited the Orleanist General Lamoricière to organise and command the forces for the defence of the Temporal Power, which he had summoned from the four quarters of the Catholic world. 5000 men, more or less, answered the call; they came chiefly from France, Belgium and Ireland. Of his own subjects the Pope had 10,000 under arms. In a proclamation, issued on assuming the command, Lamoricière compared the Italian movement with Islamism, a comparison which aroused intense exasperation in Italy, where the rally of a foreign crusade against the object which was nearest to Italian hearts, and for which so many of the best Italians had suffered and died, could not but call up feelings which in their turn were expressed in no moderate language. It was a fresh illustration of the old truth—that the Papal throne existed only by force of foreign arms, foreign influence. Lamoricière's 'mercenaries' did much harm to the Pope's cause by bringing home this truth once more to the minds of all. That the corps contained some of the bluest blood of France, that there were good young men in it, who thought heaven the sure reward for death in defence of dominions painfully added in the course of centuries by devices not heavenly to the original patrimony of Peter, did not and could not reconcile the Italians to the defiance thrown down to them by a band of strangers in their own country.

Before the opening of hostilities, Victor Emmanuel offered Pius IX. to assume the administration of the Papal states (barring Rome) while leaving the nominal sovereignty to the Pope. Nothing came of the proposal, which was followed by a formal demand for the dissolution of Lamoricière's army, and an intimation that the Sardinian troops would intervene were force used to put down risings within the Papal border. On the 11th of September, symptoms of revolution having meanwhile broken out in the Marches, General Fanti in command of 35,000 men crossed the frontier. Half these forces under Fanti himself were directed on Perugia; the other half under Cialdini marched towards Ancona. The garrisons of Perugia and Spoleto were compelled to surrender, and Lamoricière found his communications cut off, so that he could only reach the last fortress in the power of the Papal troops, Ancona, by fighting his way through Cialdini's division, which by rapid marches had reached the heights of Castelfidardo. His men passed the day of the 17th in religious exercises, and in going to confession; the vicinity of the Holy House of Loreto, brought hither by angels from Bethlehem, filled the young Breton soldiers with transports of religious fervour. Lamoricière had taken from the Santa Casa some of the flags of the victors of Lepanto to wave over his columns. In the battle of the next day the French fought with the gallantry of the Vendéans whose descendants they were, and the Irish behaved as Irishmen generally behave under fire, but the Swiss and Romans mostly fought ill or not at all. Lamoricière excused the conduct of the latter on the ground that they were young troops; it is likely that they had but little eagerness to fire on their fellow-countrymen. Being Italians, and above all being Romans, they assuredly were not sustained by one scrap of the mystical enthusiasm of the French: such a state of mind would have been incomprehensible to them. They knew that so far as dogmas went Victor Emmanuel was as good a Catholic as the Pope. It is surprising that with part of his force demoralised Lamoricière was still able to hold his own for three or four hours. General Pimodan and many of the French officers were killed; Lamoricière could say truly: 'All the best names of France are left on the battlefield.'

After the victory of Castelfidardo, the Sardinian attack was concentrated on Ancona. Admiral Persano brought the squadron from Naples to co-operate with Fanti's land forces, and the fortress capitulated on the 29th of September. The campaign had lasted eighteen days. The Piedmontese held Umbria and the Marches, and a road was thus opened for the army of Victor Emmanuel to march to Naples. During the progress of these events Garibaldi was preparing for the final struggle on the Volturno. He had not yet given up the hope of carrying his victorious arms to the Capitol, and from the Capitol to the Square of St Mark. The whole republican party, and Mazzini himself, who had arrived in Naples, ardently adhered to this programme. Their argument was not without force, risk or no risk, when would there be another opportunity as good as the present? It was very well for Cavour to look forward, as he did to the day of his death, to a pacific solution of the Roman question; Mazzini saw—in which he was far more clear-sighted than Cavour—that such a solution would never take place. His arrival at Naples caused alarm at Turin, both on account of his presumed influence over Garibaldi, the extent of which was much exaggerated, and from the terror his name spread among European diplomatists. The

Dictator was asked to proscribe the man whose latest act had been to give the last 30,000 francs he possessed in the world to the expenses of the Calabrian campaign. He refused to do this. 'How could I have insisted upon sending Mazzini into exile when he has done so much for Italian unity?' he said afterwards to Victor Emmanuel, who agreed that he was right. However, he allowed the Pro-Dictator Pallavicini to write a letter to Mazzini, inviting him to show his generosity by spontaneously leaving Naples in order to remove the unjust fears occasioned by his presence. Mazzini replied, as he had a perfect right to do, that every citizen is entitled to remain in a free country as long as he does not break the laws. And so the incident closed.

While the Party of Action urged Garibaldi not to give up Rome, other influences were brought to bear on him in the opposite sense, and especially that of the English Government, which instructed Admiral Mundy to arrange a 'chance' meeting between the Dictator and the English Minister at Naples, Mr Elliot, on board the flagship *Hannibal*. Mr Elliot pointed out the likelihood of a European war arising from an attack on Venice, and the certainty of French intervention in case of a revolutionary dash on Rome. Garibaldi replied that Rome was an Italian city, and that neither the Emperor nor anyone else had a right to keep him out of it. 'He was evidently,' writes Admiral Mundy in reporting the interview, 'not to be swayed by any dictates of prudence.'

In Sicily, the rival factions were bringing about a state approaching anarchy, but a flying visit from Garibaldi in the middle of September averted the storm. At this time, Garibaldi's headquarters were at Caserta, in the vast palace where Ferdinand II. breathed his last. The Garibaldian and the Royal armies lay

The Meeting of the Waters

face to face with one another, and each was engaged in completing its preparations. It might have been expected, and for a moment it seems that Garibaldi did expect, that after the solemn collapse of the Neapolitan army south of Naples, the comedy was now only awaiting its final act and the fall of the curtain. But it soon became apparent that, instead of the last act of a comedy, the next might be the first of a tragedy. The troops concentrated on the right bank of the Volturno amounted to 35,000, with 6000 garrisoning Capua. About 15,000 more formed the reserves and the garrison of Gaeta. The position on the Volturno was favourable to the Royalists; the fortress of Capua on the left bank gave them a free passage to and fro, while the Volturno, which is rather wide and very deep, formed a grave impediment to the advance of their opponents. But the chief reason why there was a serious possibility of the fortunes of war being reversed, lay in the fact that the *moral* of these troops was good. All the picked regiments of the army were here, including 2500 cavalry. The men were ashamed of the stampede from the south, and were sincerely anxious to take their revenge. Thus the Neapolitan plan of a pitched battle and a victorious march on Naples was by no means foredoomed, on the face of things, to failure.

In Garibaldi's short absence at Palermo, the Southern Army (as he now called his forces) was left under the command of the Hungarian General Türr, as brave an officer as ever lived, and a fast friend to Italy, but his merits do not undo the fact that as soon as the Dictator's back was turned, everything got into a muddle. Pontoon bridges had been thrown across the river at four points; availing himself of one of these, Türr crossed the Volturno with a view to taking up a position on the right bank at a place called Caiazzo, a step which, if attempted at all, ought to have been supported by a very strong force. On the 19th of September, Caiazzo was actually taken, but on the 21st the Royalists came out of Capua with 3000 men and defeated with great loss the thousand or fewer Garibaldians charged with its defence, only a small number of whom were able to recross the bridges and join their companions. The saddest part of this adventure was the slaughter of nearly the whole of the boys' company—lads under fifteen, who had run away from home or school to fight with Garibaldi. Fight they did for five mortal hours, with the heroism of veterans or of children. Only about twenty were left.

When Garibaldi returned from Sicily, this was the first news he heard, and it was not cheering. The Royalists, who thought they had won another Waterloo, were in the wildest spirits, and the march on Naples was talked of in their camp as being as good as accomplished.

Garibaldi's lines were spread in the shape of a semicircle, of which the two ends started from Santa Maria on the left, and Maddaloni on the right, with Castel Morone at the apex. The country is hilly, and this fact, together with the great distance covered, divided the 20,000 men into a number of practically distinct bodies, each of which, in the decisive battle, had to fight its own fight. Here and there improvised fortifications were thrown up. Garibaldi was aware that his line of battle was perilously extended, but the necessity of blocking all the roads and by-ways which led to Naples, dictated tactics which he was the last to defend.

The best policy for the Royalists would have been

to bring overwhelming numbers to bear on a single point, and, breaking the line, to march straight on the capital. They were doubtless afraid of an advance which would have left a portion of the Garibaldian army unbeaten in their rear. Nevertheless, of the chances that remained to them, this was the best. At Naples there were no Garibaldian troops to speak of, and the powers of reaction had been working night and day to procure for the rightful King the reception due to a saviour of society. Perhaps they would not have completely failed. There were nobles who were sulking, shopkeepers who were frightened, professional beggars with whom the Dictator had opened a fierce but unequal contest, for no blue-bottle fly is more difficult to tackle than a genuine Neapolitan mendicant; there were priests who, though not by any means all unpatriotic, were beginning to be scared by Garibaldi's gift of a piece of land for the erection of an English church, and by the sale of Diodati's Bible in the streets. And finally, there was the Carrozzella driver whom a Garibaldian officer had struck because he beat his horse. These individuals formed a nucleus respectably numerous, if not otherwise respectable, of anxious watchers for the Happy Return.

If anyone question the fairness of this catalogue of the partisans of the fallen dynasty, the answer is, that had their ranks contained worthier elements, they would not have carefully reserved the demonstration of their allegiance till the King should prove that he had the right of the strongest.

Towards five o'clock in the morning of the 1st of October, the royalists, who crossed the river in three columns, fired the first shots, and the fight soon became general. King Francis had come from Gaeta to Capua to witness what was meant to be an auspicious celebration of his birthday. General Ritucci held the chief command. Of the Garibaldians, Milbitz and Medici commanded the left wing (Santa Maria and Sant' Angelo), and Bixio the right (Maddaloni), while Castel Morone, through which a road led to Caserta, was entrusted to Colonel Pilade Bronzetti and three hundred picked volunteers. Garibaldi's own headquarters was with the reserves at Caserta, but he appeared, as if by magic, at all parts of the line during the day, sometimes bringing up reinforcements, sometimes almost alone, always arriving at the nick of time whenever things looked serious, to help, direct and reanimate the men. A dozen times in these journeys by the rugged mountain paths he narrowly escaped falling into the enemy's hands. No trace of uneasiness was visible on his placid face; there was, however, more than enough to make a man uneasy. In the early part of the battle, both Medici and Bixio were pushed back from their positions. Only Pilade Bronzetti with his handful of Lombard Bersaglieri never swerved, and held in check an entire Neapolitan column, whose commander (Perrone) has been blamed for wasting so much time in trying to take that position instead of joining his 2000 men to the troops attacking Bixio, but his object was to march on Caserta, where his appearance might have caused very serious embarrassment.

Up to midday the Royalists advanced, not fast, indeed, but surely. They fired all the buildings on their path, and amongst others one in which there were thirty wounded Garibaldians who were burned to death. It was said to be an accident, but such accidents had better not happen. Victory seemed assured to them. It is not disputed that on this occasion they fought well, and they had all the advantages of ground, numbers and artillery. But the volunteers, also, were at their best; they surpassed themselves. If every man of them had not shown the best military qualities, skill, resource, the power of recovery, Francis II. would have slept that night at Naples.

Medici acted with splendid firmness, but at the most critical moment he had Garibaldi by his side. Bixio was left to fight his separate battle unaided (so great was the chief's confidence in him), and consummately well he fought it. After the middle of the day, the Garibaldians began to retake their positions, and at some points to assume the offensive; still it was five o'clock before Garibaldi could send his famous despatch to Naples: 'Victory along all the line.' The battle had lasted ten hours.

The Sicilians and Calabrese under Dunne, who stemmed the first onset at Casa Brucciata, and under Eber, whose desperate charge at Porta Capua ushered in the changing fortunes of the day, rivalled the North Italians in steadiness and in dash. The French company and the Hungarian Legion covered themselves with glory; it was a pity there was not the English brigade, 600 strong, which mismanaged to arrive at Naples the day after the fair. Had they been in time for the fight, they would doubtless have left a brighter record than the only one which they did leave: that of being out of place in a country where wine was cheap.

Putting aside Dunne and a few other English officers, England was represented on the Volturno by three or four Royal Marines who had slipped away from their ship, the *Renown*, and were come over to see the 'fun.' It seems that they did ask for rifles, but they did not get them, their martial deeds consisting in the help they gave in dragging off two captured field-pieces. Never did an exploit cause so much discussion in proportion with its importance; the Neapolitan Minister in London informed Lord John Russell that a body of armed men from the British fleet had been sent by Admiral Mundy to serve pieces of Garibaldian artillery.

Of all the striking incidents of the day, that which should be remembered while Italy endures, was the defence of the hillock of Castel Morone by Bronzetti and his Lombards. Their invincible courage contributed in no small degree to the final result. One man to eight, they held their own for ten hours; when summoned to yield by the Neapolitan officer, who could not help admiring his courage, Pilade Bronzetti replied: 'Soldiers of liberty never surrender!' It was only in the moment of victory that Perrone passed over their dead bodies and uselessly advanced — which cost him dear on the morrow.

The Garibaldian losses were 2000 killed and wounded and 150 prisoners; the Neapolitans had the same number placed *hors de combat*, and lost 3000 prisoners.

Garibaldi had none but his own men; the report that the battle had been won by soldiers of the Sardinian army who arrived in the afternoon was false, because they did not arrive till next day, when a battalion of Piedmontese Bersaglieri took part in defeating Perrone's column, which (it is hard to say with what idea) descended nearly to Caserta, as its commander wished to do on the first. Did Perrone not know of the defeat of yesterday? His column was surrounded and all the men were taken prisoners.

After the battle of the Volturno the belligerents reoccupied the positions on the right and left banks of that river which they held before. Military critics speculate as to why Garibaldi did not follow up his advantage, and the opinion seems general that he did not feel himself strong enough to do so. The fortress of Capua was a serious obstacle, but Garibaldi was not accustomed to attach much weight to obstacles whatever they were, and it is pretty certain that he would have gone in pursuit had he not received a letter from Victor Emmanuel, who bade him wait till he came.

By this time he had abandoned all thoughts of marching on Rome. From the moment that the King's army started for Naples he understood that persistence in the Roman programme would lead to something graver than a war of words with the authorities at Turin. Always positive, he gathered some consolation from the gain to Italy of two Roman provinces, Umbria and the Marches, and trusted the future with the larger hope.

Constitutional government triumphed over the old absolutism and over the new dictatorship. And here it may be noted, which Constitutional government, which never had a more sincere and faithful votary than Cavour, found no favour with Garibaldi at any period of his life. Its hampering restrictions, its slow processes, irritated his mind, intolerant of constraint, and he failed to see that this cumbersome mechanism still gives the best, if not the only, guarantee for the maintenance of freedom. The sudden transition of Southern Italy from a corrupt despotism to free institutions brought with it a train of evils, but there was no alternative. If Italy was to be one, all parts of it must be placed under the same laws, and that at once.

On the 11th of October the Sardinian parliament sitting at Turin passed all but unanimously the motion authorising the King's Government to accept the annexation of those Italian provinces which manifested, by

X

universal suffrage, their desire to form part of the Constitutional Monarchy. Cavour's speech on this occasion was memorable: 'Rome,' he said, 'would inevitably become the splendid capital of the Italian kingdom, but that great result would be reached by means of moral force; it was impossible that enlightened Catholics should not end by recognising that the Head of Catholicism would exercise his high office with truer freedom and independence guarded by the love and respect of 22,000,000 Italians than entrenched behind 25,000 bayonets.' Of Venice, the martyr-city, he said 'that public opinion was rapidly turning against its retention by Austria, and that when the great majority of Germans refused to be any longer accomplices in its subjection, that subjection would be brought to a close either by force of arms or by pacific negotiations.'

The words were strangely prescient at a time when the Prince Regent of Prussia was making most melancholy wails over the fall of the Neapolitan King. The Prussian Government issued a formal protest, which Cavour met by observing that Prussia, of all Powers, had the least reason to object, as Piedmont was simply setting her an example which she ought to follow and would follow, the mission of the two nations being identical. He already thought of Prussia as an ally: 'Never more French alliances,' he was once heard to say.

On the same day, the 11th of October, Victor Emmanuel crossed the Neapolitan frontier at the head of the army which Cialdini led to victory at Castelfidardo. The King published a proclamation, in which he said that he closed the era of revolution in Italy. Other bodies of Piedmontese troops had been despatched by sea to Naples and Manfredonia. The passage of the

Piedmontese troops over the Abruzzi mountains was opposed both by a division of the Bourbon army and by armed peasants, who burnt a man alive at a place called Isernia; but their advance was not long delayed.

The Neapolitans now began to retire from the right bank of the Volturno, and retreat towards the Garigliano, their last line of defence. Garibaldi crossed the river with 5000 men, and moved in the direction by which the vanguard of the Piedmontese was expected to arrive. At daybreak on the 26th of October, near Teano, the Piedmontese came in sight. Garibaldi, who had dismounted, walked up to Victor Emmanuel and said: 'Hail, King of Italy!'

Once before the title was given to a prince of the House of Savoy—to Charles Albert, in the bitterest irony by the Austrian officers who saw him flying from his friends and country by order of his implacable uncle. A change had come since then.

Victor Emmanuel answered simply: 'Thanks,' and remained talking for a quarter of an hour in the particularly kind and affectionate manner he used with Garibaldi, but at the end of the interview, when the leader of the volunteers asked that in the imminent battle on the Garigliano they might have the honour of occupying the front line, he received the reply: 'Your troops are tired, mine are fresh, it is my turn now.'

Garibaldi said sadly that evening to an English friend: 'They have sent us to the rear.' It was the first sign of the ungenerous treatment meted out to the Garibaldian army to which the King lent himself more than he ought to have done. He promised to be present on the 6th of November, when Garibaldi reviewed his volunteers, but after keeping them waiting, sent a message to say that he could not come. The last meeting of all between the chief and his faithful followers was at Naples, on the occasion of the distribution of medals to as many as were left of the Thousand—less than half. In all his farewell addresses the same note sounded: 'We have done much in a short time. . . . I thank you in the name of our country. . . . We shall meet again.'

The plebiscites in Umbria and the Marches and in the kingdoms of Naples and Sicily took place in October. The formula adopted at Naples was more broadly framed than in the previous plebiscites; it ran: 'The people desire an united Italy under the sceptre of the House of Savoy.' The vote was almost unanimous.

On the 7th of November, Victor Emmanuel made his entry into Naples, with Garibaldi at his side. Next day, in the great throne-room of the palace, the king-maker delivered to the King the plebiscites of the Two Sicilies.

Garibaldi had nothing more to do except to pay a last visit to Admiral Mundy, whose flagship still lay at anchor in the bay. This duty was performed in the grey dawn of the 9th of November. 'There is the ship which is to carry me away to my island home,' he said, pointing to an American merchant vessel, 'but, Admiral, I could not depart without paying you a farewell visit. Your conduct to me since our first meeting at Palermo has been so kind, so generous, that it can never be erased from my memory; it is engraven there indelibly—it will last my life.'

On leaving the flagship he rowed straight to the American vessel, which soon afterwards steamed out of the bay. The parting salute fired by the guns of the *Hannibal* was all the pomp that attended his departure. Several hours later the people of Naples knew that their liberator had gone to dig up the potatoes which he had planted in the spring.

By Cavour's advice, Victor Emmanuel offered Garibaldi a dukedom and the Collar of the Annunziata, which confers the rank of cousin to the King, besides riches to support these honours. He refused everything, and returned to Caprera poorer than when he left it.

CHAPTER XVI

BEGINNINGS OF THE ITALIAN KINGDOM

1860-1861

Beginnings of the Italian Kingdom—The Fall of Gaeta—Political Brigandage—The Proclamation of the Italian Kingdom—Cavour's Death.

THE Neapolitan army retreated, as has been already stated, beyond the Garigliano. Capua, isolated and surrounded, could render no material service to the royal cause; it capitulated on the 2nd of November, though not until the town had been bombarded for forty-eight hours. The siege was witnessed by Victor Emmanuel, who said to General Della Rocca: 'It breaks my heart to think that we are sending death and destruction into an Italian town.' Two days after the surrender of Capua, Cialdini threw a bridge over the Garigliano near its mouth, an operation covered by the guns of Admiral Persano's squadron. His first attempt on the 29th of October had met with a decided repulse, another proof that this last remnant of the Neapolitan army was not an enemy to be despised. The second attempt, however, was successful; part of the Neapolitans fell back upon Gaeta, and the other part fled over the Papal frontier.

Gaeta, the refuge of the Pope and the fugitive Princes in 1848, now became the ultimate rock of defence of the Bourbon dynasty. The position of the fortress is extremely strong and not unlike Gibraltar in its main features. A headland running out into the sea and rising to a height of three or four hundred feet, it is divided by a strip of sand from the shore-line. The principal defences were then composed of a triple semi-circle of ditches and ramparts one higher than the other. Had the country been flat the difficulties of the siege would have been much increased; its hilly character allowed Cialdini to fix his batteries on heights which commanded the top of the Gaeta hill. But to profit by this, the Piedmontese were obliged to make fourteen miles of roads by which to bring up their artillery. For a month, 10,000 out of the 20,000 besiegers were at work with the spade. The defending force amounted to 11,000 men, and was commanded by General Ritucci. From the first, it was certain that the obstinate stand made at Gaeta could only result in what Lord John Russell called a useless effusion of blood; nevertheless it seems to have been prompted by a real belief that Francis would still recover his kingdom. The precedent of his father's return from Gaeta may have strengthened the King's illusion; every day he received highly-coloured reports of a gathering reaction, and as the French fleet in the bay prevented Admiral Persano from attacking from the sea, he believed that the time which he could hold out was indefinite. This policy of the French Government need not have greatly cheered him, as its motive was less to help Francis than to prepare the way, by hampering the Piedmontese, for a little fishing in troubled waters. Prince Murat, descendant of the *Beau Sabreur*, was busy writing proclamations to remind the world that if Francis were impossible and Victor Emmanuel 'wanted finish,' there was an elegible young man ready to sacrifice the charms of the Boulevards for the cares of kingship.

On the representations of the British Government the Emperor withdrew his fleet in January, advising Francis II.

to renounce a hopeless resistance. But at this eleventh hour the King had adopted the principle of 'no surrender,' and he meant to stick to it. It is difficult to blame him; at anyrate, much more serious is the blame due to the methods of warfare which he was to adopt or to approve thereafter. His young Queen, who was frequently seen on the ramparts encouraging the artillerymen at their guns, had probably much to do with his virile resolution. The fortress was now attacked by land and by sea, and the bursting of a powder-magazine inside the walls hastened its doom. On the 15th of January the Neapolitans laid down their arms, the King having left his dominions by sea. The first act of the conquerors in the half-ruined town was to attend a mass for the repose of the souls of the brave men, friends and foes, who had fallen during the siege. Noisy rejoicings would have been unseemly, for the vanquished were fellow-countrymen.

The telegram announcing the fall of Gaeta went to Caprera; Garibaldi read it, and a weight was taken off his mind. 'Civil war is at an end,' he announced to the little party round the supper-table; 'Cialdini with our army is in Gaeta; now the Italians will not cut one another's throats any more.' Later in the evening he seemed so depressed that they thought him ill; Colonel Vecchj went to his bedside to discover what was the matter. He found him reading the *Times*, and inquired why he had become so suddenly sad. After a pause, Garibaldi said : 'Poor boy! Born at the foot of a throne and perhaps not by his own fault, hurled from it. He too will have to feel the bitterness of exile without preparation.' 'Is that all?' asked Vecchj. 'Do you think it nothing?' was the answer. 'Why then,' persisted Vecchj, half in jest, 'did you go to Marsala?' 'It was the duty of us all to go,' Garibaldi said quickly, 'else how could there have been one Italy?'

Francis II. would have been happy had he found counsellors to persuade him to keep pure such titles to sympathy as he then possessed. Decorum, if not humanity, should have urged him to retire, surrounded by the solitary flash of glory cast on his fallen cause by the brave defence of Gaeta. But the revolution, the new Islam, if it could not be conquered must be made to suffer for its triumph. Hence the exiled King was advised to call in murder, pillage and rapine as accomplices. The political brigandage which followed the downfall of the King of the Two Sicilies began after the battle of the Volturno and extended over five years. Its effect on the general situation was nil; it harassed and distracted the Italian Government and created the odious necessity of using severe repressive measures, but it never placed the crown in danger. One effect it did have, and that was to raise all over Italy a feeling of reprobation for the late dynasty, which not all the crimes and follies of the two Ferdinands and the first Francis had succeeded in evoking. How many bright lives, full of promise, were lost in that warfare which even the sacred name of duty could not save from being ungrateful and inglorious! Italians who have lost their children in their country's battles have never been heard to complain; nowhere was the seemliness of death for native land better understood than it has been in the Italy of this century, but to lose son or brother in a brigand ambush by the hand of an escaped galley-slave—this was hard. The thrust was sharpened by the knowledge that the fomenter of the mischief was dwelling securely in the heart of Italy, the guest of the Head of the Church. From Rome came money and instructions; from Rome, whether with or without the cognizance of the authorities, came recruits. The Roman frontier afforded a means of escape for all who could reach it, however red their hands were with blood. What further evidence was needed of the impossibility of an indefinite duration of this state within a state?

King Francis held back at first, but his uncle, the Count of Trapani, who openly abetted the brigand partisans, drew him more and more into collusion with them and their works. The Belgian ecclesiastic, Mgr. de Mérode, who had then an influence at the Vatican not possessed even by Antonelli, looked, unless he was much belied, with a very kind eye upon the new defenders of throne and altar. Efforts have been made to represent the war as one carried on by loyal peasants. No one denies that every peasants' war must assume, more or less, an aspect of brigandage; nevertheless there have been righteous and patriotic peasants' wars, such as that of the Klephts in Greece. The question is, Whether the political brigandage in South Italy had any real affinity with the wars of the Klephts, or even of the Carlists? And the answer must be a negative.

The partisan chiefs in the kingdom of Naples were brigands, pure and simple, most of whom had either been long wanted by the police, or had already suffered in prison for their crimes. They organised their troops on the strict principles of brigand bands, and proposed to them the same object: pillage. 'Lieut.-General' Chiavone who had a mania for imitating Garibaldi, was the least bad among them; unlike his prototype, he did not like being under fire, but neither did he care to spill innocent blood. What, however, can be said for Pilone, 'commander of His Majesty's forces' on Vesuvius; for Ninco Nanco, Bianco dei Bianchi, Tardio, Palma; for

Carusso, who cut the throats of thirteen out of fourteen labourers and told the one left to go and tell the tale; for the brothers La Gala, who roasted and ate a priest? It was said that no horror committed during the Indian Mutiny was here without a parallel.

Of respectable Neapolitans who held responsible posts under the late *régime* not one joined the bands, but they contained French, Austrian and Belgian officers, and one Prussian. A nephew of Mgr. de Mérode, the young Marquis de Trazégnies, was with Chiavone; the Carlist, Josè Borjès, was with a scoundrel named Crocco. Borjès' case is a hard one. He had been made to believe in the genuine character of the insurrection and thought that he was giving his sword to an honourable cause. The melancholy disillusion can be traced in the pages of a note-book which he kept from day to day, and which fell into the hands of the Italians when he was captured. The brief entries show a poetic mind; he observes the fertile soil, deploring, only, that it is not better cultivated; he admires the smiling valleys and the magnificent woods whose kings of the forest show no mark of the centuries that passed over their fresh verdure. At first Borjès was pleased with the peasants who came to him, but as they were few, he was obliged to join Crocco's large band, and he now began to see, with horror, what kind of associates he had fallen amongst. He had no authority; the brigands laughed at his rebukes; never in his life, he writes, had he come across such thieves. Before the enemy they ran away like a flock of sheep, but when it was safe to do so, they murdered both men and women. In desperation, Borjès resolved to try and get to Rome, that he might lay the whole truth before the King, but after suffering many hardships, he was taken with a few others close to the Papal frontier and was immediately shot. He died bravely, chanting a Spanish litany.

Borjès' journal notes the opposition of all classes, except the very poorest and most ignorant. Was it to be believed, therefore, that this mountain warfare, however long drawn out, could alter one iota the course of events? If Francis II. supposed the insurrection to be the work of a virtuous peasantry, why did he allow them to rush to their destruction?

The task of restoring order was assigned to General Cialdini. He found the whole country, from the Abruzzi to Calabria, terrorised by the league of native assassins and foreign noblemen. The Modenese general was a severe officer who had learnt war in Spain, not a gentle school. If he exceeded the bounds of dire necessity he merits blame; but no one then hoped in the efficacy of half measures.

One element in the epidemic of brigandage, and looking forward; the most serious of all, was an unconscious but profoundly real socialism. If half-a-dozen socialistic emissaries had assumed the office of guides and instructors, it is even odds that the red flag of communism would have displaced the white one of Bourbon. This feature became more accentuated as the struggle wore on, and after experience had been made of the new political state. The economic condition of a great part of the southern population was deplorable, but liberty, so many thought, would exercise an instantaneous effect, filling the mouths of the hungry, clothing the naked, providing firing in winter, sending rain or sunshine as it was wanted. But liberty does none of these things. The disappointment of the discovery did not count for nothing in the difficulties of that period; it counts for everything in the difficulties of this.

Beginnings of the Italian Kingdom   333

The reorganisation of the southern provinces proceeded very slowly. The post of Lieutenant-Governor was successively conferred on L. C. Farini, Prince Eugene of Carignano, and Count Ponza di San Martino; for a short time Cialdini was invested with the supreme civil as well as military power. None of these changes met with entire success. The government was sometimes too weak, sometimes too arbitrary; of the great number of Piedmontese officials distributed through the south, a few won general approval, but the majority betrayed want of knowledge and tact, and were judged accordingly. It was a misfortune for the new administration that it was not assisted by the steam power of moral enthusiasm which appeared and disappeared with Garibaldi. There is a great amount of certainty that the vast bulk of the population desired union with Italy; but it is equally certain that the new Government, though not without good intentions, began by failing to please anybody, and the seeds of much future trouble were planted.

On the 18th of February 1861, the first Italian legislature assembled at Turin in the old Chamber, where, by long years of patient work and self-sacrificing fidelity to principle, the possibility of establishing an Italian constitutional monarchy had been laboriously tested and established. Only the deputies of Rome and Venice were still missing. The first act of the new parliament was to pass an unanimous vote to the effect that Victor Emmanuel and his heirs should assume the title of King of Italy. The Italian kingdom thus constituted was recognised by England in a fortnight, by France in three months, by Prussia in a year, by Spain in four years, by the Pope never.

After the merging of Naples in the Italian body-politic, one of the thorniest questions that arose was the disposal of the Garibaldian forces. The chief implored Victor Emmanuel to receive his comrades into his own army, a prayer which the King had not the power, even if he had the will, to grant, as in the constitutional course of things the decision was referred to the ministers, who, again, were crippled in their action by the military authorities at Turin. Though it is natural to sympathise with Garibaldi in his eagerness to obtain generous terms for his old companions-in-arms, it may be true that his demand was not one that could be satisfied in its full extent. The volunteers were not inferior to the ordinary soldier; about half of them were decidedly his superior, but they were a political body improvised for a special purpose, and it is easy to see how many were the reasons against their forming a division of a conventional army like that of Piedmont. Nevertheless, the means ought to have been found of convincing them that their King and country were proud of them, that their great, their incalculable services were appreciated. That such means were not found was supposed to be the fault of Cavour. It was only in 1885, on the publication of the fourth volume of the Count's letters, that it became known how strenuously he had fought for justice. Military prejudice was what was really to blame; General Fanti, the Minister of War, even provoked Cavour into telling him 'that they were not in Spain, and that in Italy the army obeyed.' 'A cry of reprobation would be raised,' he wrote, 'if, while the Bourbon officers who ran away disgracefully were confirmed in their rank, the Garibaldians who beat them were coolly sent about their business. Rather than bear the responsibility of such an act of black ingratitude, I would go and bury myself at Leri. I despise the ungrateful to the point of not feeling angered by them, and I forgive their abuse. But, by Heaven, I could not bear the merited blot of having failed to recognise services such as the conquest of a kingdom of 9,000,000 inhabitants.'

Cavour, in fact, did obtain something; much more than the army authorities wished to give, but much less than Garibaldi asked or than the Count would doubtless have given had not his hands been tied. And, doubtless, he would have given it with more grace.

As it was, the volunteers were deeply offended and sent their griefs by every post to Caprera. Garibaldi, who refused every favour and honour for himself, was worked up into a state of fury by what he deemed the wrongs of his faithful followers, and in April he arrived unexpectedly at Turin to plead their cause before the Chamber of Deputies. Perhaps by a wise presentiment he had refused to stand for any constituency; but when Naples elected him her representative, almost without opposition, he submitted to the popular will. At Turin he fell ill with rheumatic fever, but on the day of the debate on the Southern Army he rose from his bed to take his seat in the Chamber. The case for the volunteers was opened, and this is worthy of note, by Baron Ricasoli, aristocrat and conservative. Afterwards Garibaldi got up —at first he tried to make out the statistics and particulars which he had on paper, but blinded by passion and by fever, he threw down his notes and launched into a fierce invective against 'the man who had made him a foreigner in his own birthplace and the government which was driving the country straight into civil war.' At the words 'civil war' Cavour sprang to his feet, unwontedly moved, and uttered some expressions of protest, which were lost in the general uproar. When this was quieted, Garibaldi finished his speech in a moderate tone, and then

General Bixio rose to make that noble appeal to concord which, had he done nothing else for Italy, should be a lasting title to her gratitude. 'I am one of those,' he said, 'who believe in the sacredness of the thoughts which have guided General Garibaldi, but I am also one of those who have faith in the patriotism of Count Cavour. In God's holy name let us make an Italy superior to the strife of parties.' He might not be making a parliamentary speech, he added, but he would give his children and his life to see peace established — words flowing so plainly from his honest heart that savage indeed would have been the enmity which, for the time, at least, was not quelled. Cavour grasped the olive branch at once; all his momentary ire vanished. He made excuses for his adversary; from the grief which he had felt himself when he advised the King to cede Savoy and Nice, he could understand the general's resentment. He had always been, he said in general terms, a friend to the volunteers. What he did not even remotely suggest was the dissension which existed between himself and his military colleague on the subject of the Garibaldians. The least hint would have gained for Cavour any amount of applause and popularity; but he preferred to bear all the blame rather than bring the national army into disfavour. Garibaldi replied 'that he had never doubted the Count's patriotism;' but at the end of the three days' debate he declared himself dissatisfied with the Ministerial assurances touching the volunteers in particular and the country's armaments as a whole. As Cavour left the Chamber after the final night's sitting, he remarked to a friend—all his fine equanimity returned: 'And yet, and yet, when the time comes for war, I shall take General Garibaldi under my arm and say: "Let's go and see what they are about inside Verona!"'

Cialdini tried to stir up the quarrel anew by a letter full of foolish personalities; but to this sort of attack Garibaldi was impervious. It mattered nothing to him that a man should make rude remarks about his wearing a red shirt. He admired the victor of Castelfidardo as one of Italy's best soldiers. He was, therefore, perfectly ready to embrace Cialdini at the King's request before he left Turin for Caprera. It cost him more to consent to an interview of reconciliation with the Prime Minister in the royal presence, because his disagreement with Cavour was purely political and impersonal, and was rooted more deeply in his heart than any private irritation could be; but he did consent, and the interview took place on the 23rd of April. Probably Victor Emmanuel in after days was never gladder of anything he had done than of having caused his two great subjects—both his subjects born—to part for the last time in this mortal life in peace.

On one other memorable occasion the man who, at twenty-two, said that he meant to be Prime Minister of Italy, and who now, at fifty-one, was keeping his word, filled with his presence the Chamber of which he seemed to incarnate the life and history—which may be said to have been his only home, for Cavour hardly had a private life. Very soon the familiar figure was to vacate the accustomed place for ever.

An obscure deputy put a question on the 25th of May, which gave Cavour the opportunity of expounding his views about Rome still more explicitly than in the previous autumn. It was impossible, he said, to conceive Italian unity without Rome as capital. Were there any other solution to the problem he would be willing to give it due consideration, but there was not. The position of a capital was not decided by climatic or topographical reasons: a glance at capitals of Europe was sufficient to certify the fact; it was decided by moral reasons. Now Rome, alone out of the Italian cities, had an undisputed moral claim to primacy. 'As far as I am personally concerned,' he said, 'I shall go to Rome with sorrow; not caring for art, I am sure that among the most splendid monuments of ancient and modern Rome I shall regret the sedate and unpoetic streets of my native town.' It grieved him to think that Turin must resign her most cherished privilege, but he knew his fellow-citizens, and he knew them to be ready to make this last sacrifice to their country. Might Italy not forget the cradle of her liberties when her seat of government was firmly established in the Eternal City!

He went on to say that he had not lost the hope that France and the Head of the Church would yield to the inexorable logic of the situation, and that the same generation which had resuscitated Italy would accomplish the still grander task of concluding a peace between the State and the Church, liberty and religion. These were no formal words; Cavour's whole heart was set on their realisation. He did not doubt that the knot, if not untied, would be cut by the sword sooner or later. He felt as sure as Mazzini felt that this would happen; but more than any man of any party he had reckoned the cost of ranging the Church with its vast potential powers for good, for order, for public morality, among the implacable enemies of the nascent kingdom. And, therefore, his last public utterance was a cry for religious peace.

Always an immense worker, in these latter months Cavour had been possessed by a feverish activity. 'I must make haste to finish my work,' he said; 'I feel that this miserable body of mine is giving way beneath the mind and will which still urge it on. Some fine day you will see me break down upon the road.' On the 6th of June, after two or three days of so-called sudden illness, he broke down upon the road.

Fra Giacomo, faithful to his old promise, administered the sacraments to the dying minister, who told Farini 'to tell the good people of Turin that he died a Christian.' After this his mind rambled, but always upon the themes that had so completely absorbed it: Rome, Venice, Naples—'no state of siege,' was one of his broken sayings that referred to Naples. It was his farewell protest against brute force in which he had never believed. 'Cleanse them, cleanse them,' he repeated; cleanse the people of the South of their moral contagion; that, not force, was the remedy. He was able to recognise the King, but unable to collect the ideas which he wished to express to him.

Cavour's death caused a profound sensation in Europe, and in Italy and in England awakened great sorrow. Hardly any public man has received so splendid a tribute as that rendered to his memory in the British Houses of Parliament. The same words were on the lips of all: What would Italy do without him? Death is commonly the great reminder that no man is necessary. Nations fulfil their destinies even though their greatest sons be laid under the turf. And Italy has fulfilled her destinies, but there are Italians who believe that had Cavour lived to complete his task, although his dream of an Eirenicon might never have been realised, their country would not have passed through the *selva selvaggia* of mistakes and humiliations into which she now entered.

CHAPTER XVII

ROME OR DEATH

1861-1864

Cavour's Successors—Aspromonte—The September Convention—Garibaldi's Visit to England.

THERE were two possible successors to Cavour, the Tuscan, Bettino Ricasoli, and Urban Rattazzi, a Piedmontese barrister. The first belonged to the right, the second to the left centre in the Parliamentary combinations. Cavour had no very close personal relations with either, but he knew their characters. Rattazzi formerly held ministerial office under him, and the long Tuscan crisis of 1859, looked at, as he looked at it, from the inside, gave him opportunities of judging the Iron Baron who opposed even his own will on more than one occasion in that great emergency. Ricasoli was rigid, frigid, a frequenter of the straightest possible roads; Rattazzi, supple, accommodating, with an incorrigible partiality for umbrageous by-ways. He was already an 'old parliamentary hand,' and in the future, through a series of ministerial lapses, any one of which would have condemned most men to seclusion, he preserved his talent for manufacturing majorities and holding his party together. Choosing between these two candidates, Cavour before he died gave his preference to Ricasoli, who was charged by the King with the formation of a ministry in which he took the Treasury and the Foreign Office.

Ricasoli was without ambition, and he rather under than over-rated his abilities, but he went to work with considerable confidence in his power of setting everything right. A perfectly open and honest statesman ought to be able, he imagined, to solve the most difficult problems. Why not, except that the world is not what it ought to be? In home politics he offended the Party of Action by telling them plainly that if they broke the law they would have to pay the cost, and he offended his own party by refusing to interfere with the right of meeting or any other constitutional right of citizens, whether they were followers of Mazzini or of anybody else, as long as they kept within legal bounds. He wrote an elaborate letter to Pius IX., in which he sought to persuade the Pontiff of the sweet reasonableness of renouncing claims which, for a very long spell, had cast nothing but discredit on religion. Ricasoli's attitude towards the Temporal Power was unique in this century. Like Dante's, his hatred of it was religious. He was a Catholic, not because he had never thought or studied, but because, having thought and studied, he assented, and from this standpoint he ascribed most of the wounds of the Church to her subordination of her spiritual mission to material interests. He encouraged Padre Passaglia to collect the signatures of priests for a petition praying the Pope to cease opposing the desires of all Italy; 8943 names were affixed in a short time. The only result of these transactions was that Cardinal Antonelli remarked to the French Government that the Holy See would never come to terms with robbers, and that, although at war with the Turin Cabinet, 'the Pope's relations with Italy were excellent.' More harmful to Ricasoli than the fulminations of the Vatican was the veiled but determined hostility of Napoleon III. Cavour succeeded in more or less keeping the Emperor in ignorance of the degree to which their long partnership resembled a duel. He made him think that he was leading while he was being led. With Ricasoli there could be no such illusions. Napoleon understood him to be a man whom he might break, not bend. He thought it desirable to break him, and Imperial desires had many channels, at that time, towards fulfilment.

The Ricasoli ministry fell in February 1862, and, as a matter of course, Rattazzi was called to power. The new premier soon ingratiated himself with the King, who found him easier to get on with than the Florentine *grand seigneur;* with Garibaldi, whom he persuaded that some great step in the national redemption was on the eve of accomplishment; with Napoleon, who divined in him an instrument. Meanwhile, in his own mind, he proposed to eclipse Cavour, out-manœuvre all parties, and make his name immortal. This remains the most probable, as it is the most lenient interpretation to which his strange policy is open.

Garibaldi was encouraged to visit the principal towns of North Italy in order to institute the *Tiro Nazionale* or Rifle Association, which was said to be meant to form the basis of a permanent volunteer force on the English pattern. For many reasons, such a scheme was not likely to succeed in Italy, but most people supposed the object to be different—namely, the preparation of the youth of the nation for an immediate war. The idea was strengthened when it was observed that Trescorre, in the province of Bergamo, where Garibaldi stopped to take a course of sulphur baths, became the centre of a gathering which included the greater part of his old Sicilian staff. There was no concealment in what was done, and the Government manifested no alarm. The air was full of rumours, and in particular much was said about a Garibaldian expedition to Greece, for which, it was stated and re-stated, Rattazzi had promised £40,000. That Garibaldi meant to cast his lot in any struggle not bearing directly on Italian affairs, as long as the questions of Rome and Venice still hung in the balance, is not to be believed. A little earlier than this date, President Lincoln invited him to take the supreme command of the Federal army in the war for the Union, and he declined the offer, attractive though it must have been to him, both as a soldier and an abhorrer of slavery, because he did not think that Italy could spare him. But the 'Greek Expedition,' though a misleading name, was not altogether a blind. Before Cavour's death, there had been frequent discussion of a project for revolutionising the east of Europe on a grand scale; Hungary and the southern provinces of the Austrian Empire were to co-operate with the Slavs and other populations under Turkey in a movement which, even if only partially successful, would go far to facilitate the liberation of Venice. It cannot be doubted that Rattazzi's brain was at work on something of this sort, but the mobilisation, so to speak, of the Garibaldians suggested proceedings nearer home. Trescorre was very far from the sea, very near the Austrian frontier.

In spite of contradictions, a plan for invading the Trentino, or South Tyrol, almost certainly did exist. Whether Garibaldi was alone answerable for it cannot be determined. The Government became suddenly alive to the enormous peril such an attack would involve, and arrested several of the Garibaldian officers at Sarnico. They were conveyed to Brescia, where a popular attempt was made to liberate them; the troops fired on the crowd, and some blood was shed. Garibaldi wrote an indignant protest and retired, first to the villa of Signora Cairoli at Belgirate, and then to Caprera. He did not, however, remain there long.

After this point, the thread of events becomes tangled beyond the hope of unravelment. What were the causes which led Garibaldi into the desperate venture that ended at Aspromonte? Recollecting his hesitation before assuming the leadership of the Sicilian expedition, it seemed the more unintelligible that he should now undertake an enterprise which, unless he could rely on the complicity of Government, had not a single possibility of success. His own old comrades were opposed to it, and it was notorious that Mazzini, to whom the counsels of despair were generally either rightly or wrongly attributed, had nothing to do with inspiring this attempt. In justice to Rattazzi, it must be allowed that, after the arrests at Sarnico, Garibaldi went into open opposition to the ministry, which he denounced as subservient to Napoleon. Nevertheless, with the remembrance of past circumstances in his mind, he may have felt convinced that the Prime Minister did not mean or that he would not dare to oppose him by force. One thing is certain; from beginning to end he never contemplated civil war. His disobedience to the King of Italy had only one purpose — to give him Rome. He was no more a rebel to Victor Emmanuel than when he marched through Sicily in 1860.

The earlier stages of the affair were not calculated to weaken a belief in the effective non-intervention of Government. Garibaldi went to Palermo, where he arrived in the evening of the 28th of June. The young Princes Umberto and Amedeo were on a visit to the Prefect, the Marquis Pallavicini, and happened to be that night at the opera. All at once they perceived the spectators leave the house in a body, and they were left alone; on asking the reason, they heard that Garibaldi had just landed—all were gone to greet him! Before the departure of the Princes next day, the chief and his future King had an affectionate meeting, while the population renewed the scenes of wild enthusiasm of two years ago. Some of Garibaldi's intimate friends assert that when he reached Palermo he had still no intention of taking up arms. He soon began, however, to speak in a warlike tone, and at a review of the National Guard in presence of the Prefect, the Syndic, and all the authorities, he told the 'People of the Vespers' that if another Vespers were wanted to do it, Napoleon III., head of the brigands, must be ejected from Rome. The epithet was not bestowed at random; Lord Palmerston confirmed it when he said from his place in the House of Commons: 'In Rome there is a French garrison; under its shelter there exists a committee of 200, whose practice is to organise a band of murderers, the scum and dross of every nation, and send them into the Neapolitan territory to commit every atrocity!' As a criticism the words are not less strong; but the public defiance of Napoleon, and the threat with which it was accompanied, dictated one plain duty to the Italian Government if they meant to keep the peace—the arrest of Garibaldi and his embarkation for Caprera.

This they did not do; confining themselves to the recall of the Marquis Pallavicini. Garibaldi went over the ground made glorious by his former exploits—past Calatafimi to Marsala. It was at Marsala that, while he harangued his followers in a church, a voice in the crowd raised a cry of '*Rome or death!*' 'Yes; Rome or death!'

repeated Garibaldi; and thus the watchword originated which will endure written in blood on the Bitter Mount and on the Plain of Nomentum. Who raised it first? Perhaps some humble Sicilian fisherman. Its haunting music coming he knew not whence, sounding in his ear like an omen, was what wedded Garibaldi irrevocably to the undertaking. It was the casting interposition of chance, or, shall it be said, of Providence? Like all men of his mould, Garibaldi was governed by poetry, by romance. Besides the general patriotic sentiment, he had a peculiar personal feeling about Rome, 'which for me,' he once wrote, 'is Italy.' In 1849, the Assembly in its last moments invested him with plenary powers for the defence of the Eternal City, and this vote, never revoked, imposed on his imagination a permanent mandate. 'Rome or death' suggested an idea to him which he had never before entertained, prodigal though he had been of his person in a hundred fights: What if his own death were the one thing needful to precipitate the solution of the problem?

From Marsala he returned to Palermo, where, in the broad light of day, he summoned the Faithful, who came, as usual, at his bidding, without asking why or where?—the happy few who followed him in 1859 and 1860; who would follow him in 1867, and even in 1870, when they gave their lives for a people that did not thank them, because he willed it so. He sent out also a call to the Sicilian *Picciotti*, the *Squadre* of last year; and it is much to their credit that they too who cared possibly remarkably little for *Roma Capitale*, obeyed the man who had freed them. And Rattazzi knew of all this, and did nothing.

On the 1st of August, Garibaldi took command of 3000 volunteers in the woods of Ficuzza. Then, indeed, the Government wasted much paper on proclamations, and closed the door of the stable when the horse was gone. General Cugia was sent to Palermo to repress the movement. Nevertheless Garibaldi, with his constantly increasing band, made a triumphant progress across the island, and a more than royal entry into Catania. At Mezzojuso he was present at a *Te Deum* chanted in his honour. On the 22nd, when the royal troops were, it seems, really ordered to march on Catania, Garibaldi took possession of a couple of merchant vessels that had just reached the port, and sailed away by night for the Calabrian coast with about 1000 of his men.

By this time the Italian Government, whether by spontaneous conviction or by pressure from without, had resolved that the band should never get as far as the Papal frontier. If Garibaldi knew or realised their resolution, it is a mystery why he did not attempt to effect a landing nearer that frontier, if not actually within it. The deserted shore of the Pontine marshes would, one would think, have offered attractions to men who were as little afraid of fever as of bullets. A sort of superstition may have ruled the choice of the path, which was that which led to victory in 1860. It was not practicable, however, to follow it exactly. The tactics were different. Then the desire was to meet the enemy anywhere and everywhere; now the pursuer had to be eluded, because Garibaldi was determined not to fight him. Thus, instead of marching straight on Reggio, the volunteers sought concealment in the great mountain mass which forms the southernmost bulwark of the Apennines. The dense and trackless forests could have given cover for a long while to a native brigand troop, with intimate knowledge of the country and ways and means of obtaining provisions — not to a band like this of Garibaldi. They wandered about for three days, suffering from almost total want of food, and from the great fatigue of climbing the dried-up watercourses which serve as paths. On the 28th of August they reached the heights of Aspromonte—a strong position, from which only a large force could have dislodged them had they defended it.

General La Marmora, then Prefect of Naples, and commander-in-chief of the army in the south, reinforced the troops in Calabria to prevent Garibaldi's advance, but the direction of the decisive operation fell by accident to Cialdini, whom the Government despatched to Sicily when they tardily made up their minds to take energetic measures. On his voyage to Messina, Cialdini heard that the volunteers had already crossed the Straits; he therefore changed his course, and hastening to Reggio, invested himself with the command on the mainland. At Reggio he met Colonel Pallavicini, whom he ordered in terms that might have been more suitable had he been engaged in hunting brigands, 'to crush Garibaldi completely, and only accept from him unconditional surrender.' Pallavicini started with six or seven battalions of Bersaglieri. It was the 29th of August. Garibaldi saw them coming when they were still three miles off. He could have dispersed his men in the forest and himself escaped, for the time, and perhaps altogether, for the sea which had so often befriended him was not far off. But although he did not mean to resist, a dogged instinct drove away the thought of flight. In the official account it was stated that an officer was sent in advance of the royal troops to demand surrender. No such officer was seen in the Garibaldian encampment till after the attack. The troops rapidly ascended an eminence, facing that on which the Garibaldians were posted, and opened a violent fusillade. which, to Garibaldi's dismay, was returned for a few minutes by his right, consisting of young Sicilians who were not sufficiently disciplined to stand being made targets of without replying. The contention, however, that they were the first to fire, has the testimony of every eye-witness on the side of the volunteers against it. All the Garibaldian bugles sounded 'Cease firing,' and Garibaldi walked down in front of the ranks conjuring the men to obey. While he was thus employed, a spent ball struck his thigh, and a bullet entered his right foot. At first he remained standing, and repeated, 'Do not fire,' but he was obliged to sit down, and some of his officers carried him under a tree. The whole 'feat of arms,' as General Cialdini described it, did not last more than a quarter of an hour.

Pallavicini approached the wounded hero bareheaded, and said that he made his acquaintance on the most unfortunate day of his own life. He was received with nothing but kind praise for doing his duty. The first night was passed by the prisoner in a shepherd's hut. The few devoted followers who were with him were strangely impressed by that midnight watch; the moon shining on the forest, the shepherds' dogs howling in the mountain silence, and their chief lying wounded, it might be to death, in the name of the King to whom he had given this land.

Next day, in a litter sheltered from the sun with branches of wild laurel, Garibaldi was carried down the steep rocks to Scilla, whence he was conveyed by sea to the fort of Varignano. It was not till after months of acute suffering, borne with a gentleness that made the doctors say: 'This man is not a soldier, but a saint,' that, through the skill of the French surgeon, Nélaton, the position of the ball was determined, and its extraction rendered possible.

A general amnesty issued on the occasion of the marriage of the King's second daughter with the King of Portugal relieved the Government of having to decide whether Garibaldi was to be tried, and if so, what for ; but the unpopularity into which the ministry had fallen could not be so easily dissipated. The Minister of Foreign Affairs (Durando) published a note in which it was stated that Garibaldi had only attempted to realise, in an irregular way, the desire of the whole nation, and that, although he had been checked, the tension of the situation was such that it could not be indefinitely prolonged. This was true, but it hardly improved the case for the Government. In Latin countries, ministers do not cling to power; as soon as the wind blows against them, they resign to give the public time to forget their faults, and to become dissatisfied with their political rivals. Usually a very short time is required. Therefore, forestalling a vote of censure in the Chambers, where he had never yet had a real majority, Rattazzi resigned office with a parting homily in which he claimed to have saved the national institutions.

The administration which followed contained the well-known names of Farini, Minghetti, Pasolini, Peruzzi, Della Rovere, Menabrea. When Farini's fatal illness set in, Minghetti replaced him as Prime Minister, and Visconti Venosta took the Foreign Office. They found the country in a lamentable state, embittered by Aspromonte, still infected with brigandage, and suffering from an increasing deficit, coupled with a diminishing revenue. The administrative and financial unification of Italy, still far from complete, presented the gravest difficulties. The political aspect of affairs, and especially the presence of the French in Rome, provoked a general sense of instability which was contrary to the organisation of the new state and the development of its resources. The ministers sought remedies or palliatives for these several evils, and to meet the last they opened negotiations with France, which resulted in the compromise known as the September Convention. It was long before the treaty was concluded, as for more than a year the French Government refused to remove the garrison on any terms ; but in the autumn of 1864 the following arrangement was signed by both parties : that Italy should protect the Papal frontier from all attack from the outside ; that France should gradually withdraw her troops, the complete evacuation to take place within two years ; that Italy should waive the right of protest against the internal organisation of the Papal army unless its proportions became such as to be a manifest threat to the Italian kingdom ; that the Italian capital should be moved to Florence within six months of the approval of the Convention by Parliament.

These terms were in part the same as those proposed by Prince Napoleon to Cavour shortly before the death of that statesman, who had promised to support them as a temporary makeshift, and in order to get the French out of Italy. But they were in part different, and they contained two new provisions which it is morally certain that Cavour would never have agreed to—the prolongation of the French occupation for two years (Cavour had insisted that it should cease in a fortnight), and the transfer of the capital, which was now made a *sine quâ non* by Napoleon, for evident reasons. While it was clear that Turin could not be the permanent capital of a kingdom that stretched to Ætna, if once the seat of government were removed to Florence a thousand arguments and interests would spring up in favour of keeping it there. So, at least, it was sure to seem to a foreigner. As a matter of fact, the solution was no solution ; the Italians could not be reconciled to the loss of Rome either by the beauty and historic splendour of the city on the Arno, or by its immunity from malaria, which was then feared as a serious drawback, though Rome has become, under its present rulers, the healthiest capital in Europe. But Napoleon thought that he was playing a trump card when he dictated the sacrifice of Turin.

The patriotic Turinese were unprepared for the blow. They had been told again and again that till the seat of government was established on the Tiber, it should abide under the shadow of the Alps—white guardian angels of Italy—in the custody of the hardy population which had shown itself so well worthy of the trust. The ministry foresaw the effect which the convention would have on the minds of the Turinese, and they resorted to the weak subterfuge of keeping its terms secret as long as they could. Rumours, however, leaked out, and these, as usual, exaggerated the evil. It was said that Rome was categorically abandoned. On the 20th of September crowds began to fill the streets, crying : ' Rome or Turin !' and on the two following days there were encounters between the populace and the military, in which the latter resorted to unnecessary and almost provocative violence. Amidst the chorus of censure aroused by these events, the Minghetti cabinet resigned, and General La Marmora, who, as a Piedmontese, was fitted to soothe the excited feelings of his fellow-citizens, was called upon to form a ministry.

The change of capital received the sanction of Parliament on the 19th of November. Outside Piedmont it was not unpopular ; people felt that, after all, it rested with themselves to make Florence no final halting-place, but a step towards Rome. The Papal Government, which had been a stranger to the late negotiations, expressed a supreme indifference to the whole affair, even to the contemplated departure of the French troops, 'which concerned the Imperial Government, not the Pope,' said Cardinal Antonelli, 'since the occupation had been determined by French interests.' It cannot be asserted that the Pope ever assumed a gratitude which he did not feel towards the monarch who kept him on his throne for twenty years.

This year, 1864, was marked by an incident which, though not a political event, should never be forgotten in the history of Italian liberation—Garibaldi's visit to England. He came, the prisoner of Aspromonte, not the conqueror of Sicily: a distinction that might have made a difference elsewhere, but the English sometimes worship misfortune as other peoples worship success. No sovereign from oversea was ever received by them as they received the Italian hero; a reception showing the sympathies of a century rather than the caprice or curiosity of an hour. Half a million throats shouted London's welcome; the soldier of two worlds knew the roar of battle, and the roar of the sea was familiar to the Nizzard sailor, but it is said that when Garibaldi heard the stupendous and almost awful British roar which greeted him as he came out of the Nine Elms station, and took his seat in the carriage that was to convey him to Stafford House, he looked completely disconcerted. From the heir to the throne to the crossing-sweeper, all combined to do him honour; where Garibaldi was not, through the breadth of the land the very poor bought his portrait and pasted it on their whitewashed cottage walls. London made him its citizen. The greatest living English poet invited him to plant a tree in his garden: a memory he recalled nearly at the close of his own honoured life:—

> Or watch the waving pine which here
>   The warrior of Caprera set,
> A name that earth shall not forget
> Till earth has rolled her latest year.

Garibaldi showed himself mindful of old friends; at the opera he recognised Admiral Mundy in a box, and immediately rose and went to offer him his respects. At Portsmouth, he not only went to see the mother of Signora White-Mario (the providence of his wounded in many a campaign), but also paid an unrecorded visit to two maiden sisters in humble circumstances, who had shown him kindness when he was an exile in England; they related ever afterwards the sensation caused by his appearance in their narrow courtyard, where it was difficult to turn the big carriage which the authorities had placed at his disposal. He twice met the great Italian whom he addressed as Master: transferring, as it were, to Mazzini's brows the crown of glory that surrounded his own. Another exile, Louis Blanc, used to tell how, when he went to call on Garibaldi, he found him seated on a sofa, receiving the homage of the fairest and most illustrious members of the English aristocracy; when the Friend of the People was announced (a title deserved by Louis Blanc, if not for his possibly fallacious theories, still for the rare sincerity of his life), the hero started to his feet and most earnestly begged him to sit beside him. 'Which I could not do!' the narrator of the scene would add with a look of comical alarm for his threatened modesty.

These friendly passages with the proscripts in London as well as the stirring appeal spoken by Garibaldi on behalf of the Poles, did not please foreign Powers. The Austrian ambassador shut himself up in his house; was remarked that the only members of the diplomati body who were seen at the Garibaldi *fêtes* were the representatives of the United States and of the Sublime Porte. The Emperor Napoleon was said to be angry. Lord Palmerston assured the House of Commons that no remonstrance had been received from France or from any foreign government, and that if it had been received, it would not have been heeded. Yet the English Government took the course of hinting to the guest of England that his visit had lasted long enough. In some quarters it was reported that they feared disturbances among the Irish operatives in the manufacturing towns, had he gone, as he intended, to the north. Whatever were the motives that inspired it, their action in the matter cannot be remembered with complacency, but it was powerless to undo the significance of the great current of enthusiasm which had passed through the English land.

CHAPTER XVIII

THE WAR FOR VENICE

1864-1866

The Prussian Alliance—Custoza—Lissa—The Volunteers—
Acquisition of Venetia.

THE change of capital was carried out in 1865, and the lull which followed gave an appearance of correctness to the surmise that if the September Convention had not solved the Roman question, it had, anyhow, reduced it to a state of quiescence. But there were other reasons why Rome was kept, for the moment, not indeed out of mind, but out of sight. The opinion grew that the emancipation of Venice, too long delayed, ought to take precedence of every other political object. On this point there was no disagreement among the 22,000,000 free Italians, who felt the servitude of Venice to be an hourly disgrace and reproach; no one even ventured to preach patience. A curious chapter might be written on the schemes woven between the Peace of Villafranca and the year 1866, for the realisation of the unfulfilled promise of freedom from Alps to sea. Foremost among the schemers was Victor Emmanuel, and if some persons may be shocked by the idea of a royal conspirator, more will admire the patriotism which made the King hold out his hand to Mazzini, whose sentiments about monarchy, and especially about the Savoy dynasty, were a secret to no one, least of all to him. But as Mazzini placed those sentiments on second rank to the grand end of Italian unity, so the King, to serve the same end, showed himself superior to prejudices which in most men would have proved insuperable. The fact that Victor Emmanuel opened negotiations with Mazzini, and maintained them, off and on, for years, proves amongst other things, that he knew the exiled patriot better than the world yet knew him. He may have understood that by turning republican sympathies into the groove of unity (not their necessary or even their most natural groove), Mazzini made an Italian kingdom possible. There is reason to think that the King's ministers were kept entirely ignorant of his correspondence with the Agitator. The letters were impersonal drafts carried to and fro by means of trusted emissaries; each party freely expounded his views, and stated the terms on which his support could be given. Victor Emmanuel's favourite idea was a revolution in Galicia. When Garibaldi returned from England he was nearly commissioned to start for Constantinople, whence he was to lead an expedition through Roumania into Galicia. It seems to have been due to Garibaldi's own good sense that so extremely unpromising a project was abandoned. General Klapka was another of Victor Emmanuel's secret revolutionary correspondents. The very wildness of the plans that floated in the air betokened the feverish anxiety to do something which had taken hold of all minds.

In 1865 a scheme of a different sort, and of momentous consequences, grew into shape. It was a scheme of which Cavour first guessed the possibility, as well as the far-reaching results. In August 1865 Count Bismarck asked General La Marmora whether Italy would join Prussia in the contingency of a war with Austria? Only a year before he was still thinking of carrying out his policy with the aid of Austria, and he had offered to help her to wrench Lombardy from Italy (and from France if she intervened), in payment for her consent to his designs. But now, though the Austrians did not even remotely suspect it, his thoughts were resolutely turned to the Italian alliance. Without this alliance Italy might, indeed, have acquired Venice, but would the German Empire have been founded?

For a time the proposal was suspended, owing to the temporary understanding concluded between Prussia and Austria at Gastein; and in the interim, General La Marmora urged the Viennese Government to cede Venetia in return for a compensation of five hundred million francs. But those whom the gods would destroy they make mad. Austria preserved her infatuated sense of security almost till the rude awakening caused by the rifle-shots that ushered in the campaign of Sadowa.

One thing which contributed to keeping Europe in the dark as to the impending cataclysm was the character and known tendencies of King William I. of Prussia, whose conservative, not to say retrograde sentiments made it difficult to picture him at the head of what was really a great revolutionary movement, in spite of the militarism that surrounded it. With consummate art, Count Bismarck little by little concentrated all his master's ideas about royal divinity in general into one overwhelming belief in his own divine right to be German Emperor, and so transformed an obstacle into the corner-stone of the edifice he wished to build. But this could hardly be foreseen. At the New Year's Day reception of 1866, Napoleon announced an era of universal peace; henceforth all nations were to arrange their differences amicably, as had been done at Gastein

If the illusion was complete, it was destined to be of short duration.

In the spring the Prussian proposal to Italy was formally renewed, and this time it was accepted. The secret treaty of an offensive and defensive alliance for three months was signed on the 8th of April. Less than three weeks later, Austria, which was slowly beginning to feel some uneasiness, proposed to Napoleon the cession of Venetia, while exacting from Italy only a simple promise of neutrality in case of war. General La Marmora held the honour of the country and his own to compel fidelity to the prior arrangement with Prussia, and he refused the tempting offer. His choice has been variously characterised as one of common honesty and of uncommon magnanimity; at all events, it was of incalculable advantage to Prussia, which already gave signs of not being a particularly delicate-minded ally. When La Marmora asked Bismarck whether, in case Austria took the initiative of attacking Italy, Prussia would intervene, the answer was 'No.'

The three countries now pushed on their war preparations: Austria with less ardour than the others, as she still failed to more than faintly realise her danger. The Italian army, which the opening of the year found in a deplorably unserviceable condition, was rapidly placed on a war-footing, and, considering the shortness of the time allowed for the work, and the secrecy with which, at the outset, it had to be conducted, it is generally agreed that La Marmora produced surprising results. As was natural in an army which, except for the old Piedmontese nucleus, might almost be called improvised, the weakest points were the cavalry and the artillery. The infantry was good; not only the picked corps of Bersaglieri, but also the line regiments were equal to any troops likely to be opposed to them. No one can see the fine appearance of a line regiment marching down the streets of an Italian town without receiving the impression that, however much the other branches of the service may have improved since the Sixties, the fondest hopes of Italy in case of war still lie in that common soldier who best supported the rigours of the Russian snows.

Unfortunately, the attention paid to the army was not extended to the fleet, which continued totally unready; nor was the organisation of the volunteers carried out in an efficient manner. The excuse afterwards advanced was that not more than 15,000 enrolments were expected, while the actual figure reached 35,000. Besides being from its very bulk less manageable than the 'few and good' of 1859, this mass of men was ill-provided with officers who could inspire and keep discipline. Garibaldi's own generals, Bixio, Medici, Cosenz and Sirtori, were now all in the regular army, and therefore not free to join him. He begged for the loan of a few regular officers, indicating amongst other names that of Colonel Pallavicini, who commanded against him at Aspromonte: a trait characteristic of the man. But this assistance, though promised, was not granted, and the same was the case with the guns which were vainly asked for. Without charging La Marmora with a deliberate intention of neglecting the volunteers, it must be owned that under the influence of the prejudice which holds irregular troops in small esteem, he did not do for them what ought to have been done if their services were accepted at all.

The Austrian Southern Army, excellent in discipline and equipment though weak in numbers, was commanded up to the outbreak of the war by Field-Marshal Benedek, but he was called to Vienna to take command of the unfortunate army of operation against Prussia, and was succeeded in Italy by the Archduke Albrecht, with General Von John, an officer of the first capacity, as chief of the staff.

The numerical strength of the forces which could be put in the field has been stated with startling divergence by different military writers on the war, but every calculation gives the Italian side (exclusive of the volunteers) a superiority of not less than two to one. The Austrian mobilised army has been reckoned at as low a figure as 63,000, certainly an understatement, as it appears that the Archduke mustered not less than 70,000 at the battle of Custoza. That he mustered on that day every man he could produce is probably a fact. Had the Italian generals followed the same rule, however enormous their other errors might have been, they would have won. Of all conceivable faults in a military commander that which is the least pardonable is the neglect to crush his antagonist by force of superior numbers when he has them at his disposal. How many great military reputations have been built up, and justly built up, on the care never to meet an enemy without the odds being largely in your favour!

For obvious political reasons the King of Italy assumed the supreme command of the army, with General La Marmora as chief of the staff. Cialdini had been offered the latter post, but he declined it, objecting, it is said, to the arrangement by which the real head of the army has no guarantee against the possible interference of its nominal head. When La Marmora went to the front, Baron Ricasoli took his place as Prime Minister; Visconti-Venosta became Minister of Foreign Affairs; and the Ministry of the Marine was offered to Quintino Sella, who refused it on the ground that he knew nothing of naval matters. It was then offered to and accepted by a man who knew still less, because he did not even know his own ignorance, Agostino Depretis, a Piedmontese advocate.

Before the commencement of hostilities a secret treaty was concluded between Napoleon III. and the Austrian Government, according to which Venetia was to be ceded to the Emperor for Italy, even if Austrian arms were victorious both on the Mincio and on the Maine. Napoleon's real purpose in this singular transaction is not perfectly clear; but he was probably acting under a semi-romantic desire to have the appearance of completing his programme of freeing Italy from the Alps to the Adriatic which had been interrupted at Villafranca. In spite of his enmity towards Italian unity, there is no reason to doubt that he was in very few things as sincere as in the wish to see the Austrians out of Italy. His reckonings at this time were all founded on the assumption that Prussia would be defeated; he even seems to have had some hopes of getting the Rhine bank in return for his good offices on behalf of that Power with triumphant Austria. Be this as it may, he inspired the Italian Government (or rather La Marmora, for there were then two Italian Governments, and the real one was on the Mincio) with his own expectation of Prussian disasters, and it is possible that this expectation had a material and unfavourable influence on the manner of conducting the war in Italy.

Through the Prussian Minister at Florence, General La Marmora received the draft of a plan of campaign which is known to have been prepared by Count Moltke; in it the great feature was a descent on the Dalmatian coast. From an independent quarter he received another plan in which a descent on the east coast of the Adriatic was contemplated, the main difference being that Istria, instead of Dalmatia, was proposed for the landing-point.

This second plan was modestly submitted to him by Garibaldi, who was thus in substantial accord with the Prussian strategist. The prospect which either of these plans opened was one of great fascination. What Italian can look across the sea to where the sun rises and forget that along that horizon lies a land colonised by Rome and guarded for four hundred years by Venice?

Istria was marked out by Dante as the frontier province of Italy:

> Si come a Pola presso del Quarnero
> Che Italia chiude e i suoi termini bagna.

It forms, with the Trentino, what is called *Italia Irredenta*. Although the feeling of Italians for unredeemed Italy is not what their feeling was for Lombardy or Venetia, it is a mistake to imagine that they have renounced all aspirations in that direction. Only fanatics of the worst kind would be disposed to attempt, in the present situation, to win those provinces by force, but that has nothing to do with the matter. The aspiration exists and cannot help existing. It has always been shared by patriots of all denominations. An English statesman who called on Pius IX. was somewhat surprised by the Pope saying that Italian unity was very well, but it was a pity it did not include Trento and Trieste.

The case of Dalmatia is different; there the mass of the population is unquestionably of a non-Italian race, though that race is one which, whenever left to itself, seems created to amalgamate with the Italian. Slav and Teuton are racially antagonistic, but the Slav falls into Italian ways, speaks the Italian language and mixes his blood with Italian blood: with what results Venice can tell. For more than two thousand years the civilisation of Dalmatia has been exclusively Latin; the Roman column points to the Venetian Campanile; all the proudest memories are gathered round the Lion of St Mark, which in every town, almost in every village, recalls the splendid though not blameless suzerainty of the Serene Republic. The sky, the olive-groves, the wild pomegranates make us think of Salerno; by the spoken tongue we are often reminded of Tuscany, for few Italian dialects are so pure. The political subjection of the country to Italy dates from Augustus; its political subjection to Austria dates from Napoleon. Dalmatia, with the glorious little commonwealth of Ragusa, and the free city of Cattaro, was bartered away with Venice at Campo Formio; and as with Venice, so with Dalmatia, the Holy Alliance violated its own principle of restoring the prœ-Napoleonic state of things and confirmed the sale.

At the beginning of the war, Austria did not ignore that her loss of territory might exceed Venetia. The Archduke Albrecht, in his proclamation to his soldiers, appealed to them to protect their mothers, wives and sisters from being ruled by a foreign race.

Even a successful raid upon Dalmatia or Istria need not have given those districts to Italy, but it would have brought such an event within the range of a moderately strong political telescope. The Slavs (erected since into a party hostile to their Italian fellow-citizens by a fostering of Panslavism which may not, in the long run, prove sound policy for Austria) were then ready to make friends with anyone opposed to their actual rulers. They would not have been easy to govern after an Italian invasion; still less easy to govern would the Latin element have been, which was and is *Italianissimo*. Since Prussia became the German Empire, she has set her face against Italian extension eastward, but in 1866, had her advice been intelligently acted upon, it might have generated facts the logic of which none would have had the power to stay.

Moltke's plan more than hinted at a march on Vienna by the Semmering, and this is what is supposed to have induced La Marmora to treat it with scorn. With the bogey of Prussia vanquished before his eyes, he doubtless asked what the Italians would do at Vienna if they got there? He put the plan in his pocket, and showed it neither to his staff nor to the King, who would certainly have been attracted by it, as he had set his heart on the volunteers, at least, crossing the Adriatic. With regard to the campaign at home, both Moltke and Garibaldi counselled turning the Quadrilateral in preference to a direct attack upon fortresses which had been proved impregnable except with the assistance of hunger, and at present they were better provisioned than in 1848. The turning of the Quadrilateral meant the adoption of a route into Venetia across the Po below Mantua. An objection not without gravity to that route was the unfavourable nature of the ground which, being marshy, is liable after heavy rains to become impassable. But against this disadvantage had to be weighed the advantage of keeping out of the mouse-trap, the fatality of which needed no new demonstration.

In Italy it is common to hear it said that it was necessary to station a large army on the Mincio to bar the Archduke's path to Milan. But apart from the rumoured existence of a promise to the French Emperor not to invade Lombardy, it was unlikely that so good a general as the Archduke would have taken his small army far from the security it enjoyed among the four fortresses which, if the worst came to the worst, assured him a safe line of retreat.

The plan adopted by La Marmora is vaguely said to have been that which was prepared by the French and Sardinian staffs for use in 1859, had the war been continued. But in what it really consisted is not to this day placed beyond dispute. The army, roughly speaking, was divided into halves; one (the larger) half under the King and La Marmora was to operate on the Mincio; the other, under Cialdini, was to operate on the lower Po. It is supposed that one of these portions was intended to act as a blind to deceive the enemy as to the movements of the other portion; the undecided question is, which was meant to be the principal and which the accessory?

The volunteers were thrown against the precipices of the Tridentine mountains, where a detachment of the regular army, well-armed and properly supplied with artillery, would have been better suited for the work. The Garibaldian headquarters was at Salò on the Lake of Garda. Less than half of the 35,000 volunteers who appear upon paper, were ever ready to be sent to the front. It was widely said that only patriotism prevented Garibaldi from throwing up his command, so dissatisfied was he with the conduct of affairs.

Prussia invaded Hanover and Saxony on the 16th of June, and declared war with Austria on the 21st, one day after the Italian declaration of war had been delivered to the Archduke Albrecht. On the 23rd La Marmora's army began to cross the Mincio. It consisted of three *corps d'armée* under the command of Generals Durando, Cucchiari and Della Rocca, each corps containing four divisions. The force under Cialdini was composed of eight divisions forming one *corps d'armée*. An Italian military writer rates the numbers at 133,000 and 82,000 respectively. La Marmora acquired the belief that the Archduke's attention was absorbed by Cialdini's movements on the Po, and that his own operations on the Mincio would pass unobserved.

While the Italian commander had no information of what was going on in the enemy's camp, the Archduke's intelligence department was so efficient that he knew quite well the disposition of both Italian armies. Cialdini's advance, if he meant to advance, was checked by floods. On the night of the 23rd most of La Marmora's force bivouacked on the left (Venetian) bank of the Mincio. No reconnaissances were made; everyone supposed that the Austrians were still beyond the Adige, and that they intended to stay there. The King slept at Goito.

Before the early dawn next morning the whole Italian army of the Mincio had orders to advance. The soldiers marched with heavy knapsacks and empty stomachs, and with no more precautions than in time of peace. The Austrian Archduke was in the saddle at four a.m., and watched from an eminence the moving clouds of dust which announced the approach of his unsuspecting foe.

La Marmora's intention had been to occupy the heights of Santa Giustina, Sona and Somma Campagna, but the Archduke anticipated his design, and while the Italians were moving from the Mincio, the Austrians were ranging themselves in those positions. At half-past five on the midsummer Sunday morning, the Austrian advance guard led by Colonel Pulz came up with Prince Humbert's division near Villafranca. The battle began dramatically, with a charge of the splendid Polish and Hungarian Hussars, who dashed their horses against the Italian squares, in one of which, opportunely formed for his shelter, was the gallant heir to the throne. Bixio's division was also engaged in this prelude, which augured not ill for the Italians, since at about eight o'clock Pulz received the Archduke's orders to retire.

The first hours of the battle were spent in fortuitous encounters along the extensive chain of hillocks which La Marmora had intended to occupy. As the Italians approached each position they found it in the possession of a strong force of the enemy. On the right, however, Custoza and the heights between it and Somma Campagna had not been occupied by the Austrians. Here La Marmora placed the flower of his army, the Sardinian and Lombard Grenadiers, the latter commanded by Prince Amedeo. The fighting continued through the day over very widely distributed ground, but from about nine in the morning the supreme interest was concentrated at and near Custoza, in which the Archduke promptly detected the turning-point of the battle. To wrest Custoza from the hold of the Italians was to the Austrians on the 24th of June 1866, what the taking of the crest of Solferino had been to the French on the 24th of June 1859. La Marmora in person led the Grenadiers into action; they proved worthy of their reputation, but after losing a great many men, Prince Amedeo being among the wounded, they were obliged to retreat. At about midday, however, the Italian prospects improved so much that in the opinion of Austrian military writers, with moderate reinforcements they would have had a strong probability of winning the battle. La Marmora saw the importance of getting fresh troops into the field, but, instead of sending for the divisions under Bixio and Prince Humbert, which since eight a.m. had been fretting in inaction close by, at Villafranca, he rode himself to Goito, a great distance away, to look after the reserves belonging to the 2nd *corps d'armée;* a task which any staff officer could have performed as well. This inexplicable proceeding left the army without a commander-in-chief. The generals of division followed their individual inspirations, Govone,

Pianel and Cugia especially distinguishing themselves: it is sad to think that death has removed these three officers from the Italian ranks. But the Austrians fatally gained ground, and as the afternoon closed in the Archduke began to feel sure that the Italian reinforcements whose arrival he had so much feared, were never coming. He therefore prepared for the final effort which was to give him the well-deserved honours of the day. Towards seven o'clock in the evening, his soldiers succeeded in storming the heights of Custoza, and Austria could write a second battle of that name among her victories.

The Italians lost 720 killed, 3112 wounded and 3608 prisoners. The Austrian loss was 960 killed, 3690 wounded and 1000 prisoners. Both sides were much tried by the scorching midsummer sun, but the Italians laboured under the additional drawback of having to fight fasting. In his report, the Archduke Albrecht mentioned that the prisoners said they had not tasted food for twenty-four hours. In the same report, he did ample justice to the courage of the Italian soldiers.

As has been stated, the Archduke fought Custoza with not less, probably with rather more, than 70,000 men. The force which La Marmora placed in the field was actually inferior in number. The divisions of Bixio and Prince Humbert were kept doing nothing all day at a stone's throw from the scene of action. Of the whole 2nd *corps d'armée* only a trifling detachment ever reached the ground. Inexplicably little use was made of the Italian cavalry.

This bungling had lost the battle, but the fact that on the morrow, six divisions of the army of the Mincio were practically fresh, might have suggested to a general of enterprise to try again, since it was known that the Archduke had not a single new man to fall back on.

And there was Cialdini on the Po with his eight divisions that had not been engaged at all. But, instead of adopting a spirited course, the Italian authorities gave way to unreasoning panic. It appears, unfortunately, that the King was the first to be overcome by this moral vertigo. The long and fiercely discussed question of who telegraphed to Cialdini: 'Irreparable disaster; cover the capital,' seems to have been settled since that general's death in 1892. It is now alleged that the telegram, the authorship of which was disowned by La Marmora, was signed by the King's adjutant, Count Verasio di Castiglione. Cialdini obeyed the order and fell back on Modena. Whether he was bound to obey an almost anonymous communication signed by an irresponsible officer is a moot point; it is reported that he repented having done so to the last day of his life.

A great event now happened across the Alps; one of the decisive battles of the world was lost and won on the 5th of July at Sadowa near Königgrätz in Bohemia. The fate of Europe was shaped on that day for decades, if not for centuries. Of the immediate results, the first was the scattering to the wind of all calculations based upon a long continuance of the war, the issue of which, as far as Prussia was concerned, could not be regarded as doubtful. In respect to Italy, Austria's first thought was to prevent her from taking a revenge for Custoza. She attempted to compass this by ceding Venetia to Napoleon two days after Sadowa. It was making a virtue of necessity, as she was bound in any case to cede it at the conclusion of the war; but as the secret of the treaty had been well kept, the step caused great surprise, and in Italy, where the public mind had leapt from profound discouragement to buoyant hope, the impression was one of embarrassment and mortification. Italy was distinctly precluded by her engagement with Prussia from accepting Napoleon's invitation to conclude a separate peace. Meanwhile, Austria gained by the move, as it set her at liberty to recall the larger part of her troops from Venetia for the defence of Vienna. Her honour did not require her to contest the ground in a province which she had already given away. When Cialdini, at the head of the reorganised Italian army of which he now held the chief command, advanced across the Po to Padua, he found the path practically open.

It was still possible for Italy to accomplish two things which would have in a great measure retrieved her *prestige*. The first was to occupy the Trentino; the second was to destroy the Austrian fleet. With the means at her disposal she ought to have been able to do both.

In the earlier phases of Italian liberation, no one disputed that if Lombardy and Venetia were lost to the Empire the Tridentine province, wedged in as it is between them, would follow suit. When, in 1848, Lord Palmerston offered his services as mediator between Austria and revolted Italy, it was on a minimum basis of a frontier north of Trento. The arguments for the retention of Trieste—that Austria had made it what it was; that Germany needed it as a seaport, etc.—were inapplicable here; and even after the defeat of Custoza, an occupation of the Trentino, had it happened in conjunction with a naval victory, would have opened a fair prospect to possession. But there was no time to lose, and much time was lost by ordering Garibaldi to descend to the southern extremity of the lake of Garda to 'cover Brescia' from an imaginary attack. When the fear of an Austrian invasion subsided, and Garibaldi returned to the mountains, he endeavoured to re-take the position of Monte Suello which he had previously held, but the attempt failed. The volunteers were forced to retire with great loss, and the chief himself was wounded. On the 16th of July the volunteers renewed their advance up the mountain ravines, and, after taking Fort Ampola, reached the village of Bezzecca, where they were attacked by the Austrians early on the 21st. Each side claimed that sanguinary day as a victory; the Garibaldians remained masters of the ground, but the Austrians, in retiring, took with them a large number of prisoners. The losses of the volunteers on this and other occasions when they were engaged were disproportionately heavy. They were spendthrift of their lives, but in war, and especially in mountain warfare, caution is as needful as courage, and in caution they were so deficient that they were always being surprised. General Kuhn's numerically inferior force of tried marksmen, supported by good artillery and favoured by ground which may be described as one great natural fortification, had succeeded up till now in holding the Trentino, but his position was becoming critical, because while Garibaldi sought to approach Trento from the west, Medici with 10,000 men detached from the main army at Padua, was ascending the Venetian valleys that lead to the same destination from the east. Kuhn was therefore on the point of being taken between two fires when the armistice saved him.

These operations on the Tridentine frontier, though not without a real importance, passed almost unnoticed in the excitement which attended the first calamitous appearance of United Italy as a naval power.

When invited to assume the command of the Italian fleet, Admiral Persano twice refused; it was only when the King pressed upon him a third invitation that he weakly accepted a charge to which he felt himself unequal. He had been living in retirement for some years, and neither knew nor was known by most of the officers and men whom he was now to command. The fleet under his orders comprised thirty-three vessels, of which twelve were ironclads. The Austrian fleet numbered twenty-seven ships, including seven ironclads. When the war broke out, both fleets were far from ready for active service; but, while the Austrian Admiral Tegethoff said nothing, but worked night and day at Pola to make his ships and his men serviceable, Persano despatched hourly lamentable reports to the Minister of Marine, without finding the way to bring about a change for the better. He wasted time in minutiæ, and took into his head to paint all the Italian ships a light grey, which was of the greatest use to the Austrians in the battle of Lissa, as it enabled them to distinguish between them and their own dark-coloured ships.

After long delaying at Taranto, Persano brought his fleet to Ancona; and, two days later, Tegethoff appeared in front of that town—not knowing, it seems, that the Italian squadrons had arrived. Tegethoff was bound on a simple reconnaissance, and, after firing a few shots, he sailed away. On this occasion, Persano issued orders so hesitating and confused that the Austrian admiral must have correctly gauged the capacity of the man opposed to him, while the superior officers of the Italian fleet were filled with little less than dismay. A strong effort was made to induce Depretis to supersede Persano then and there; he promised to do so, but it is said that the fear of offending the King prevented him. Instead, he set about showering instructions on the admiral, the worth of which may be easily imagined. The mistrust felt by the fleet in its commander invaded all ranks; and if it did not break out in open insubordination, it deprived officers and men of all confidence in the issue of the campaign.

Left to himself, Persano would have stayed quietly at Ancona, but the imperative orders of a cabinet council, presided over by the King, forced him to take some action. Against the advice of Admiral Albini, but in agreement with another admiral, Vacca, Persano decided to attack the fortified island of Lissa, on the Dalmatian coast. Though Lissa is a strong position, the usual comparison of it with Gibraltar is exaggerated. It ought to have been possible to land the Italian troops which Persano had with him under cover of his guns, and to take the island before Tegethoff came up. The surf caused by the rough weather, to which he chiefly attributed his failure, would not have proved an insuperable obstacle had the ships' crews been exercised in landing troops under similar circumstances.

Persano reached Lissa on the morning of the 18th of July, and began a tremendous bombardment of the forts, which, though answered with the highest spirit by the Austrians, did most deadly damage to their batteries. In fact, by the evening, except one or two at a high elevation, they were practically silenced. At six o'clock Captain Saint Bon took the *Formidabile* into the narrow harbour to silence the inner works: a murderous fire rained on the corvette from Fort Wellington, which was too high for the Italian guns to get it into range. Though Saint Bon's attempt was not successful, the Italians had effected most of what they aimed at, and might have effected the rest had they continued the bombardment through the night, and so given the Austrians no time to repair their batteries, but at sunset Persano withdrew his fleet to a distance of eight miles. The Austrians worked all night at mending the batteries that could still be used, and hoped in the coming of Tegethoff.

The telegraph cable connecting the neighbouring island of Lesina with the coast, and so with Pola, had been cut by Persano's orders; but either (as the writer was told on the spot last year) there was another line that was not noticed, or before the cable was destroyed the official in charge got off a message to Tegethoff, informing him of the arrival of the Italian fleet. An answer, to the effect that Tegethoff would come to the rescue as soon as possible, fell into the hands of the Italians, but Persano appears not to have believed in it.

The 19th was spent in attempts at landing, which the surf and the energetic play of the repaired batteries rendered fruitless. The bombardment was renewed, but it was not well conducted. Saint Bon, who made another plucky entry into the harbour, was unsupported, and, after an hour's fighting, he was obliged to retire, his ship having suffered severely.

Next morning there was a blinding summer storm, but at about eight o'clock the *Esploratore* distinguished the forms of ironclads through the rain, and signalled to Persano: 'Suspicious vessels in sight.' Persano answered: 'No doubt they are fishing-boats.' When obliged to admit the truth he gave the order to unite, his ships being scattered in all directions with everything on board at sixes and sevens. The troops which had again been attempting to land, were in boats, tossed about by the heavy sea. The surprise was complete.

Persano fought the battle of Lissa with nine ironclads, most of which had received some injuries during the bombardment. He ordered his wooden ships to keep out of the action altogether. Tegethoff had seven ironclads and fourteen wooden vessels, all of which he turned to the best account.

Just before the battle Persano left his flagship, the *Re*

d'Italia, and went on board the *Affondatore*. By somebody's mistake it was a long time before the *Affondatore* hoisted the admiral's flag, and the fleet continued to look to the *Re d'Italia* for signals when he was no longer on board.

Contrary to a well-known rule in naval science, Persano formed his squadron in single file, and quite at the beginning of the battle Tegethoff managed to break the line by dashing in between the first and second division whilst they were going at full speed, and under a furious cannonade from their guns. This daring operation placed him in the middle of the Italian ironclads, which, well directed, could have closed round him and destroyed him, but they were not directed either well nor ill—they were not directed at all. Persano put up contradictory signals, most of which were not seen, and those which were seen meant nothing. The plan followed by Admiral Tegethoff may be best described in his own words: 'It was hard to make out friend from foe, so I just rammed away at anything I saw painted grey.' Two Italian vessels had been already damaged, but not vitally injured, by the *Ferdinand Max*, when in the dense smoke a vast wall of grey appeared close to the bows of the Austrian flagship, which, to the cry of 'Ram her!' put on full steam and crashed into the enemy's flank. The shock was so great that the crew of the *Max* were thrown about in indescribable confusion. The Italian ship was the *Re d'Italia*, the flagship which did not carry the admiral. She quivered for one, two, some say for three minutes in her death agony, and then went down in two hundred fathoms of water.

After the *Re d'Italia* was struck, one of her seamen, thinking to assert a claim to pity, began to lower her flag, but a young officer pushed him aside and hoisted it again; so the great ship sank with her colours flying. The incident was noticed by the Austrians, who spoke of it in feeling terms. Willing enough were they to help, for after the first cheer of triumph they felt sick with horror at their own work, the fearful work of modern naval warfare. There were 550 men on board the doomed ship. Tegethoff shouted for the boats to be lowered, and signalled to the despatch boat *Elizabeth* to pick up all she could, but two Italian ironclads were bearing down upon him, and little could be done to save the drowning multitude either by the Austrians or by their own people. Persano did not know of the disaster till some hours after it happened.

The sea had scarcely closed over the *Re d'Italia* when another misfortune occurred; the gunboat *Palestro* took fire. Her captain, Alfredo Cappellini, disembarked the sick and wounded, but remained himself with the rest of the crew, endeavouring to put out the fire. The ship blew up at 2.30 p.m., and over two hundred perished with her.

Persano, still on the *Affondatore*, now led his fleet out of action, and it was the first time he had led it during the day. Tegethoff gazed after the vanishing squadron with anxiety, as had Persano turned and renewed the battle from a distance, he could have revenged his defeat at close quarters without receiving a shot, owing to the longer range of his guns. But for such an operation skilful manœuvring was wanted, and also, perhaps, more precision in firing than the Italian gunners possessed. At any rate, Persano had no mind for new adventures. He took what remained of his fleet straight back to Ancona, where the *Affondatore* sank in the harbour from injuries received during the battle. For three days the Italian people were told that they had won a victory, then the bitter truth was known. The admiral, tried before the Senate, was deprived of his rank and command in the Italian navy. The politician who, when convinced of his unfitness, yet had not the nerve to remove him from his post, died, full of years and honours, Prime Minister of Italy.

Lissa was fought on the 20th of July. On the 25th, Prussia signed the preliminaries of peace with Austria without consulting her ally, who, if unfortunate, had been eminently loyal to her. Thus the whole forces of the Empire, not less than 350,000 men, were let loose to fall upon Italy. Such was the wrathful disappointment of the Italians at their defeats by land and sea, that if a vote had been taken they would possibly have decided for a renewal of the struggle. Ricasoli was inclined to risk war rather than bow to the Austrian demand that the evacuation of the Trentino should precede the conclusion of an armistice. At this crisis, La Marmora acted as a true patriot in forcing the hand of the Ministry by ordering the recall of the troops and sending General Petitti to treat directly with the Austrian military authorities. 'They will say that we have betrayed the country,' said the King in the interview in which these measures were concerted; to which La Marmora answered: 'Come what may, I take the whole responsibility upon myself.' 'This is too much,' replied Victor Emmanuel with tears in his eyes; 'I, also, will have my part in it.' In which brief dialogue the character of the two men stands revealed; men who might fall short in talent or in judgment, not in honour.

The volunteers, so many of whose comrades lay dead along the mountain gorges—who believed, too, that they were in sight of the reward of their sacrifices—were thrown into a ferment, almost into a revolt by the order to retreat. They had expected in a day or two to shake hands with Medici, who, after some hard fighting, was within a march of Trento. The order was explicit: instant evacuation of the enemy's territory. Garibaldi, to whom from first to last had fallen an ungrateful part, took up his pen and wrote the laconic telegram: 'Obbedisco.' 'I have obeyed,' he said to the would-be mutineers, 'do you obey likewise.' Someone murmured 'Rome.' 'Yes,' said the chief, 'we will march on Rome.'

The armistice was signed at Cormons on the 12th of August, and the treaty of peace on the 3rd of October at Vienna. Italy received Venice from the hands of the French Emperor, whose interference since the beginning of the campaign had incensed Prussia against her ally without benefiting the Power which he affected and, perhaps, really meant to serve. Italy would have received Venetia without his interposition, for besides the Prussian obligation to claim it for her, Austria had no further wish to keep it. Despite the fact that Italian populations still remained under the rule of the Empire, the melancholy book of Austrian dominion in Italy might be fairly said to be closed forever. A new era was dawning for the House of Hapsburg, which was to show that, unlike the Bourbons, it could learn and unlearn.

The comedy of the cession of Venice to Napoleon was enacted between General Le Bœuf and General Alemann, the Austrian military commandant. Among other formalities, the French delegate went the round of the museums and galleries to see that everything was in its place. Suddenly he came upon a most suspicious blank. 'A picture is missing here,' he said. 'It is, blandly assented the Austrian officer. 'Well, but it must be sent back immediately—where is it?' 'In the Louvre.'

At last Austrians and French departed, and Italy shook off her mourning, for however it had come about, the great object which had cost so much blood, so many tears, was attained; the stranger was gone!

Out of 642,000 votes, only 69 were recorded against the union of Venetia with the Italian kingdom. When the plebiscite was presented to the King, he said: 'This is the greatest day of my life: Italy is made, though not complete.' On the 7th of November he entered Venice, and of all the pageants that greeted him in the hundred cities of Italy, the welcome of the Bride of the Adriatic was, if not the most imposing, certainly the fairest to see. More touching, however, than the glorious beauty of the Piazza San Marco and the Grand Canal in their rich adornment, was the universal decoration of the poorest quarters, which were all flagged and festooned so thickly that little could be seen of the stones of Venice. One poor cobbler, however, living at the end of a blind alley, had no flag, no garland to deck his abode: he had therefore pasted three strips of coloured paper, red, white and green, over his door, inscribing on the middle strip these words, which in their sublime simplicity merit to be rescued from oblivion: 'O mia cara Italia, voglio ma non posso fare più per te.'

The Iron Crown of the Lombard Kings of Italy, which the Austrians had taken away in 1859, was brought back and restored to the Cathedral of Monza. Less presumptuous than Napoleon, Victor Emmanuel never placed the mystical fillet upon his head, but it was carried after his coffin to the Pantheon.

CHAPTER XIX

THE LAST CRUSADE
1867

The French leave Rome—Garibaldi's Arrest and Escape—The Second French Intervention—Monte Rotondo—Mentana.

THE words of Victor Emmanuel to the Venetian Deputation contained a riddle easy to solve: what was meant by the 'completion' of Italy was the establishment of her capital on the Tiber. In most minds there was an intense belief in the inevitability of the union of Rome with the rest of Italy, but no one saw how it was to be brought about. What soothsayer foretold Sédan?

In the first period after the war, domestic difficulties fixed the attention of the Italian Government on the present rather than on the future. An insurrection at Palermo assumed threatening proportions owing to the smallness of the garrison, and might have had still more serious consequences but for the courage and presence of mind shown by the Syndic, the young Marquis di Rudinì. Crime and poverty, republican hankerings, the irritation of the priesthood at recent legislation, and most of all, the feeling that little had been done since 1860 to realise the millennium then promised, contributed to the outbreak which was quelled when troops arrived from the mainland, but the ministers were blamed for not having taken better precautions against its occurrence. Another stumbling-block lay in the path of Ricasoli, namely, the application of the law for the suppression of religious houses, and the expropriation of ecclesiastical property. After an unsuccessful endeavour to cope with it, he dissolved the Chamber, but the new Parliament proved no more willing to support his measures, which were of the nature of a compromise, than the old one, and he finally resigned office. He was succeeded by Urban Rattazzi, under whose administration a measure was passed which, though drastic in appearance, has not prevented the re-establishment of a great many convents of which the property was bought in under the name of private individuals. Every Catholic country has seen the necessity sooner or later of putting a check to the increase of monasticism, but it may be a matter of regret that in Italy, the toleration granted to the learned community of Monte Cassino was not extended to more of the historic monasteries. The abstention of the Clerical party from the voting urns deprived them of an influence which, on such points as these, they might have exercised legitimately and perhaps beneficially. To that abstention, the disequilibrium of Italian political life, from first to last, is largely due.

The time allowed to the French under the September Convention for the evacuation of Rome expired in December 1866, and at the opening of the new year, for the first time since 1849, the Eternal City was without a garrison in the service of a foreign Power. While executing their engagement, the French Government took occasion to say that they kept their hands perfectly free as concerned future action. The anomalous obligations of the September Convention now came into force, and it was not long before their inconvenience was felt. Had Ricasoli remained at the head of affairs the *status quo* might have lasted for a time; because, although he was an unflinching opponent of the Temporal Power, he would have made it clear that since the Convention existed he meant to respect it, and to make others respect it. He had shown that he could dare, but that was when he bore himself the whole responsibility of his daring. He was not the man to tolerate heroic imprudence in others with the mental reservation of owning or disowning the results, as might prove convenient. Rattazzi, on the other hand, was believed to answer very closely to this description; and patriots who were willing to bear all the blame in case of failure and yield all the praise in case of success, began once more to speculate on the profit to the national cause which might be extracted from the peculiarities of his character. Aspromonte, that should have placed them on their guard, had the contrary effect, for it was supposed that the Prime Minister was very anxious to wipe that stain from his reputation.

Nevertheless, the Party of Action considered that, for the present, the wisest course was to wait and watch the development of events. This was Mazzini's personal view, but Garibaldi, almost alone in his dissent, did not share it. Impelled partly, no doubt, by the impatience of a man who sees the years going by and his own life ebbing away without the realisation of its dearest dream, but partly also by the deliberate belief that the political situation offered some favourable features which might not soon be repeated, Garibaldi decided to take the field in the autumn of 1867. His friends, who one and all tried to dissuade him, found him immovable. It is too much to say that he expected assistance from the Government, but that he hoped to draw Rattazzi after him is scarcely doubtful, and he had good reason for the hope.

In Rattazzi's own version and defence of his policy, it is set forth that before the die was cast he did all that was humanly possible to prevent the expedition, but that having failed, he intended sending the Italian army over the frontier in the wake of the broken-loose condottiere. Though this gives a colour of consistency to his conduct, it is not satisfactory as an explanation, and still less as an apology.

General La Marmora, who had always opposed the Convention, though he belonged to the party which made it, once declared that 200,000 men would not be sufficient to hold the Papal frontier against a guerilla invasion. True as this may be, it is impossible to resist the conclusion that a minister who had resolutely made up his mind to prevent any attempt from being made would not have acted as Rattazzi acted. The Prime Minister thought that he was imitating Cavour, but in reality he simply imitated the pendulum of a clock.

Rattazzi's taste was for intrigue rather than for adventure in the grand sense. An adventurous minister would have accelerated the enterprise to the utmost, in secret or not in secret, and would then have preceded Garibaldi to Rome before the Clerical party in France had time to force Napoleon to act. The rest could have been left to the Roman· people. What they did in 1870 they would have done in 1867; they were ready to acclaim any conquering liberator; they were not ready to make a revolution on their own account, and with all their leaders in prison or in exile, they are hardly to be blamed for it. For such a policy Italy might have pleaded that necessity which knows no law. Everybody allowed that if Garibaldi went to Rome the Italians must go there too: the very security of the Pope demanded it—at least, he said so. As to the first part of the programme, complicity in the preparation of the movement, it would have been an infringement of the Convention, but had France kept the Convention? French bishops recruited soldiers for the Pope in every province of France, and the Antibes Legion was drawn, officers and men, from the French army. When some of the men deserted, the French War Office sent General Dumont to Rome to look to the discipline of the regiment. Those who argued that the spirit, if not the letter, of the agreement had been already evaded, could make out a good case for their position.

It has been suggested that this is what Rattazzi's policy would have been, but for the opposition of the King. Were it so, the minister ought to have resigned at the beginning of the proceedings instead of at the end. That in the ultimate crisis it was the King who prevented the troops from moving is a fact, but the propitious moment was then past and gone. 'Do as you like, but do it quickly,' Napoleon said to Cavour when Cialdini was to be sent to the Cattolica. And it was done quickly.

After letting Garibaldi make what arrangements and issue what manifestoes he chose for six weeks, Rattazzi suddenly had him arrested at Sinalunga on the 23rd of September. The only consequence was fatal delay; not knowing what to do with their prisoner, the Government shipped him to Caprera. Personally he was perfectly free; no conditions were imposed; but nine men-of-war were despatched to the island to sweep the seas of erratic heroes. In spite of which, Garibaldi escaped in a canoe on the 14th of October.

That night, between sundown and moonrise, there was only one hour's dark, but it sufficed the fugitive to make good his passage from Caprera to the island of Maddalena.

A strong south-east breeze was blowing; the waves, however, were rather favourable to the venture, as they hid the frail bark from any eyes that might be peering through the night. Garibaldi did not fear; he had often put out on this terrible sea when lashed to fury to succour sailors in their peril. On reaching Maddalena he scrambled over the rocks to the house of an English lady who was delighted to give him hospitality. Next evening he proceeded to Sardinia, from which, after several adventures, he sailed for the Tuscan coast in a boat held in readiness by his son-in-law, Canzio. And so, to the amazement of friends and foes, he arrived in Florence, where, before many hours were past, he was haranguing the enthusiastic crowd from a balcony.

Garibaldi had escaped, but the mischief done to the movement by the loss of nearly a month could not be remedied. Although large armed bands under Acerbi, Nicotera and Menotti Garibaldi were gathered near Viterbo, as usually happened in the absence of the chief, nothing effectual was done. But it was in Paris that the delay brought the most ruinous results.

The history of the second French expedition to Rome will never be satisfactorily told, because, while the outward circumstances point one way, the inward probabilities point another. Napoleon had said that if the Convention were not observed he would intervene, and he did intervene; nothing could seem simpler. Yet it is not doubtful that, in his inmost heart, he was wishing day and night that something would turn up to extricate him from the Roman dilemma once for all. While he hesitated, the Clerical party in France did not hesitate. Not a moment was thrown away by them. Towards the middle of October, it was reported that 'half royalist and half Catholic France will be in Rome in the course of the week. Men with names belonging to the proudest French nobility—the De Lusignans, De Clissons, De Lumleys, De Bourbon-Chalens, etc., are chartering vessels, arriving in Rome by scores and hundreds, and hence hurrying to the front to take their places as privates in the Zouaves.' That, however, does not describe the most important sphere of their activity which was the ante-chamber, nay, the boudoir of St Cloud. In that palace, three years later to be rased to the ground by the Germans, the net was woven which every day closed tighter and tighter round Napoleon, till he was enveloped in its meshes past escape. Ever since De Morny's death, the influence nearest the throne had been increasing in strength; it is needless to say in which direction it was exercised. Napoleon was ill; Maximilian's ghost floated over him; he felt his power slipping from his hands in spite of the noise and show of the Exhibition, which was supposed to mark its zenith. The words of the old pact with the Royalists buzzed in his ears: 'Do you keep the Pope on his throne, and we will keep you on yours.' And he yielded.

The 'principle' of French intervention was adopted by the council of ministers on the 17th of October. Then, and not till then, Rattazzi decided to send the Italian troops over the frontier. On finding that neither the King nor several of his colleagues in the ministry would support him, he resigned office on the 19th of the month.

It was on the day after that Garibaldi appeared in Florence. As there was no ministry, no one thought it his business to interfere with him. Cialdini, whom the King had requested to form a cabinet, did go and ask him to keep quiet till there was some properly qualified person to arrest him; but this, not unnaturally, he declined to do. He left Florence by special train for Terni, whence he crossed the frontier and joined the insurgent bands near Rome.

From the 19th to the 26th, Napoleon again and again ordered and countermanded the departure of the transports from Toulon. On the last date the final order was given and the ships started. The news must have just reached Paris that the King had called upon General Menabrea to undertake the task which had been abandoned by Cialdini, whose name recalled Castelfidardo too strongly to have a sound welcome either in the Vatican or at St Cloud. When Napoleon heard that Menabrea was to be Rattazzi's successor, he knew that there was no fear that the new Government, carried away by the popular current which was manifestly having its effect on the King, should, after all, order the Italian army to the front. Menabrea, the Savoyard who in 1860 chose the Italian nationality which his son has lately cast away, was the old opponent of Cavour in the Turinese chamber, and of all Italian politicians he was the most lukewarm on the Roman question. All chance of a collision between the French and Italian armies was removed. Menabrea did occupy some positions over the Papal frontier, it would be hard to say with what intention, unless it were to appear to fulfil a sort of promise given by the King during the ministerial interregnum. The troops were ordered on no account to attack the French, and as soon as the Garibaldian campaign was at an end, they were brought home. It was not worth while to send them with their hands tied to almost within earshot of where other Italians were fighting and falling. Menabrea's attitude towards the volunteers was immediately revealed by the issue of a royal proclamation, in which they were declared rebels. The French were free to act.

All this time the revolution in Rome, which it was admitted on all sides would have gone far towards cutting the knot, did not begin. Besides the cause already assigned, the absence of the heads, there was another, the almost total lack of arms. To remedy this, Enrico and Giovanni Cairoli, with some seventy followers, tried to take a supply of arms up the Tiber to Rome. Only the immense importance of the object could have justified so desperate an attempt. Obliged to abandon their boats near Ponte Molle, they struck off into the Monti Parioli, where they were attacked, within sight of the promised land, at a spot called Villa Gloria. Their assailants were three times their number, and those who were not killed were carried prisoners to Rome. Among the killed was the captain of the band, who fell in the arms of his young brother. As Enrico Cairoli lay dying, the French Zouaves (was this the chivalry of France?) charged the two brothers with their bayonets, piercing Giovanni with ten wounds, from injuries arising from one of which he expired a year later, after long torments. 'Dastardly French!' cried Enrico with his last breath. They were the third and fourth sons of Adelaide Cairoli who died for their country. One only of her five children remained to stand by her own death-bed—Benedetto, the future Prime Minister, and saviour of King Humbert from the knife of an assassin.

The Papal army was composed of 13,000 men, General de Courten commanding the portion of it which could be spared out of Rome. The Breton, Colonel Charette, had charge of the Zouaves. Since the French garrison left, much trouble had been taken to make this force efficient. Under Garibaldi's own orders there were between 7000 and 8000 volunteers. Those who have made a higher estimate have included other bands which, either from the difficulty of provisioning a larger number, or from want of time for concentration, remained at a distance.

The chief's arrival soon infused new life into the camp. On the 24th he moved towards Monte Rotondo, one of the castellated heights near Rome, which commands the Nomentane and Tiburtine ways to the south, and the railway and Via Salara to the west. It was generally considered the most important military position in the Papal states. The garrison was small, but, perched as they were on a hill crest which looks inaccessible, the defenders might well hope to hold out till help came from Rome. They had artillery, of which the volunteers had none, and the old castle of the Orsini, where they made their principal stand, was well adapted for defence. From the morning of the 25th till midnight, the Garibaldians hurled themselves against the walls of the rock town without making much way; but at last the resistance grew weak, and when the morning light came, the white flag was seen flying. At four in the afternoon of the 26th a Papal column tardily arrived upon the scene, but they perceived that all was over at Monte Rotondo, and, after firing a few musket shots, they fled to Rome in disorder.

Garibaldi rode into the cathedral, where he fixed his quarters for the night. In Italy churches have ever been applied to such uses. After the reduction of Milan, Francesco Sforza rode into the Duomo, and when King Ladislaus of Naples conquered Rome, he rode into the basilica of St John Lateran. The guerilla chief bivouacked in a confessional, while his Red-shirts slept where they could on the cathedral floor. Four hundred of them had been killed or wounded in the assault.

The prisoners of war were brought before Garibaldi, who praised their valour and sent them under an escort to the Italian frontier. Two or three were retained for the following reason. Garibaldi had heard of the Cairolis' heroic failure, and after his victory his first thought was of them and of their sorrowing mother. He asked Signora Mario if there were any notabilities among the Papal prisoners. She mentioned Captain Quatrebras and others, and he sent her into Rome on a mission to the Papal commander with a view to exchanging these prisoners for the wounded Giovanni and for his brother's body. The proposal was accepted, and the compact kept after Mentana had changed the aspect of affairs.

'Garibaldi at the gates!' was the news that spread like wildfire through Rome on the evening of the 26th of October. Terror, real terror, and no less real joy filled all hearts; but the sides were soon to be reversed. Another piece of news was not long in coming: 'The French at Civita Vecchia!'

The French arrived on the 29th, and on the same day Garibaldi advanced almost to the walls of Rome, still hoping for a revolutionary movement to break out within the city; but the information which he then received deprived him finally of this hope, and he gave the order to return to Monte Rotondo. Volunteers have the defect of being soldiers who *think;* on this occasion they thought that the backward march was the beginning of the end—that, in short, the game was up. A third of the whole number deserted, and took the road towards the Italian frontier. Garibaldi himself seems to have had a first idea of crossing into the Abruzzi, and there waiting to see what turn events would take; but he did not long entertain it, and, when he again left Monte Rotondo, it was with the fixed design of fighting a battle. He expected, however, to fight the Papal troops alone, and not the French.

This was very nearly being the case. On the 1st of November, the Papal General Kanzler called on General De Failly at Civita Vecchia, and found him, to his concern, by no means anxious to rush into the fray. Even when sending the troops, Napoleon seems to have hoped to escape from being seriously compromised. He probably thought that the moral effect of their landing would cause Garibaldi to retire, and that thus the whole affair would collapse. But the Papal authorities did not want it to collapse; they wanted more bloodshed, and if the words which express the ungarnished truth as acknowledged by their own writers and apologists, sound indecent when describing the government of the Vicar of Christ, it only shows once more the irreconcilability of the offices of priest and king in the nineteenth century. Kanzler insisted that a crushing blow must be inflicted on the volunteers before they had time to retreat. He argued so long and so well that De Failly promised him a brigade under General Polhès to aid in the attack which he proposed to make on Monte Rotondo.

The Papal forces left Rome by Porta Pia, and took the Via Nomentana, which leads to Monte Rotondo by Mentana. They were on the march at four o'clock a.m. Garibaldi had ordered his men to be ready at dawn on the same day (it was the 3rd of November); but Menotti suggested that, before they started, there should be a distribution of shoes, a consignment of which had just reached the camp. Many of the volunteers were barefoot, which gives a notion of their general equipment. Garibaldi, who rarely took advice, yielded to his son. Had he not done so, before the Papal army reached Mentana, he would have been at Tivoli. One delay brings another, and it was midday when the march began. Garibaldi looked sad, and spoke to no one, but hummed some bars of Riego's hymn, the Spanish song of freedom, full of a wild, sweet pathos, to which his tanned-faced legionaries had marched under the Monte Videan sun. Could he but have had with him those strong warriors now! He mounted his horse, put it to a gallop, which he rarely did, and, riding down the ranks of the column, took his place at its head. When he arrived at the village of Mentana, he heard that the Pontificals were close by, and he waited to give them battle.

Mentana lies in a depression commanded by the neighbouring mounds, not a good configuration for defence. This village in the Roman Campagna sprang into history on a November day one thousand and sixty-seven years before, as the meeting-place of Charlemagne and Leo III. Here they shook hands over their bargain : that the Pope should crown the great Charles Emperor, and that the Emperor should assure to the Pope his temporal power. And now the ragged band of Italian youths was come to say that of bargains between Popes and Emperors there had been enough.

They numbered less than 5000. General De Failly reckoned the Papal troops engaged at 3000 and the French at 2000, but Italian authorities compute the former at a higher figure. The most experienced of the Garibaldian officers thought that the attackers were twice as numerous as they were. At the first onslaught great confusion prevailed among the volunteers. Mentana seemed lost, but the sound of the guns they had captured at Monte Rotondo restored their *moral*, and making a gallant rush forward they retook the principal positions with the bayonet. As they saw the Pontificals swerve back they uttered cries of joy. It was two o'clock. The enemy's fire slackened ; something was going on which the volunteers could not make out. All at once there was a sharp unfamiliar detonation, resembling the whirring sound of a machine. The French had come into action.

A hailstorm of bullets mowed down the Garibaldian ranks. Their two guns were useless, for the ammunition, seventy rounds in all, was exhausted. They fought till four o'clock—till nearly their last cartridge was gone; then they slowly retreated. Very few of them guessed what that peculiar sound meant, or imagined that they had been engaged with the French, but next morning Europe knew from General De Failly's report that 'the Chassepots had done wonders.'

Garibaldi left the field, haggard and aged, unable to reconcile himself to a defeat which he thought that more discipline, more steadiness in his rank and file, would have turned into a victory. He had always demanded the impossible of his men; till now they had given it to him. In time he judged more justly. Those miserably-armed lads who lately had been glad to eat the herbs of the field, if haply they found any, stood out for four hours against the pick of two regular armies, one of which was supposed to be the finest in the world. They had done well.

Mentana remained that night in the hands of 1500 Garibaldians, who still occupied the castle and most of the houses when the general retreat was ordered. In the morning the Garibaldian officer who held the castle capitulated, on condition that the volunteers 'shut up in Mentana' should be reconducted across the frontier; terms which the French and Papal generals interpreted to embrace only the defenders of the castle. Eight hundred of the others were taken in triumph to Rome. It would have been wiser to let them go. The Romans had been told that the Garibaldians were cut-throats, incendiaries, human bloodhounds waiting to fly at them. What did they behold? 'The beast is gentle,' as Euripides makes his captors say of Dionysius. The stalwart Romans saw a host of boys, with pale, wistful, very young-looking faces. If anything was wanting to seal the fate of the Temporal Power it was the sight of that procession of famished and wounded Italians brought to Rome by the foreigner.

The victors, however, were jubilant. Their inharmonious shouts of *Vive Pie Neuf* vexed the delicate Roman ears. It was the battle-cry of the day of Mentana. Begun by the masked, finished by the unmasked soldiers of France, Mentana was a French victory, and it was the last.

The Garibaldian retreat continued through the night to Passo Corese on the Italian frontier. The silence of the Campagna was only broken by little gusts of a chilly wind off the Tiber; it seemed as if a spectral army moved without sound. Garibaldi rode with his hat pressed down over his eyes; only once he spoke: 'It is the first time they make me turn my back like this,' he said to an old comrade, 'it would have been better . . .' He stopped, but it was easy to supply the words: 'to die.'

As he was getting into the train at Figline, with the intention of going straight to Caprera, he was placed under arrest by order of the Italian Government. His officers had their hands on their swords, but he forbade their using force. The arrest seemed an unnecessary slight on the beaten man, who had loved Italy too well. But General Menabrea, who ordered it, believes that he thereby saved Italian unity. According to an account given by him many years after to the correspondent of an English newspaper, Napoleon wrote at this juncture to King Victor Emmanuel, that as he was not strong enough to govern his kingdom, he, Napoleon, was about to help him by relieving him of all parts of it except Piedmont, Lombardy and Venetia. The arrest of Garibaldi, by showing that the King 'could govern,' averted the impending danger. In communicating it to Napoleon, the King is said to have added 'that Italians would lose their last drop of blood before consenting to disruption,' a warning which he was not unlikely to give, but the whole story lacks verisimilitude. It appears more credible that an old man's memory is at fault than that a letter, so colossally insolent, was actually written. Menabrea, and even the King, may have feared that something of the kind was in the mind of the Emperor.

As after Aspromonte so after Mentana; Garibaldi was confined in the fortress of Varignano, on the bay of Spezia. A few weeks later he was released and sent to Caprera. As he left the fortress-prison he wrote the words: 'Farewell, Rome; farewell, Capitol; who knows who will think of thee, and when?'

The last crusade was over; destiny would do the rest.

CHAPTER XX

ROME, THE CAPITAL
1867-1870

M. Rouher's 'Never'—Papal Infallibility—Sédan—The Breach in Porta Pia—The King of Italy in Rome.

MENTANA had its epilogue in the debate in the French Corps Législatif, which lasted from the 2nd to the 5th of December. Jules Favre proposed a vote of censure on the Ministry for their Roman policy. The most distinguished speaker who followed him was Thiers, who said that though in opposition, he would support the Government tooth and nail in their defence of French interests at Rome. The debate was wound up by the memorable declaration of the Prime Minister, Rouher, that 'never' should Italy get possession of Rome. 'Is that clear?' he asked. It was quite clear. The word escaped him, he afterwards said, in 'the heat of improvisation.' The French Chamber confirmed it by throwing out Favre's motion by 237 votes against 17.

Now, indeed, the Ultramontanes were jubilant throughout the world. Napoleon was compromised, enmeshed beyond extrication.

Of all these events, Prussia, or rather the great man who was the brain of Prussia, took attentive note. He was convinced that the wonders accomplished by the Chassepot at Mentana would soon lead France to try the effect of the new rifle on larger game. Among the measures which he took with a view to that contingency, his correspondence with Mazzini is not the least remarkable. It began in November 1867, and was continued for a year. The object of both Bismarck and Mazzini was to prevent Italy from taking sides with France. The negotiations were carried on partly through Count d'Usedom, Prussian Minister at Florence, and partly through other intermediaries. Mazzini began by saying, that although the Chancellor's methods of unification had not his sympathy, he admired his energy, tenacity and independence; that he believed in German unity and opposed the supremacy which France arrogated to herself in Europe. He engaged to use his influence in Italy to make it difficult for an Italian Government to take up arms for the victors of Mentana. Bismarck was well aware that in speaking of his influence the writer used no idle phrase, but possibly one of his reasons for continuing the correspondence was to find out what Mazzini knew of the hidden plots and counter plots then in manufacture both in Paris and at Florence, because the Italian was more conversant with diplomatic secrets than any man living, except, perhaps, Cardinal Antonelli. In April 1868, Mazzini received through the Prussian Embassy at Florence, a document which even now possesses real interest on the relative advantages to Italy of a French or German Alliance. The whole question turned, observed the Prussian Chancellor, on the mastery of the Mediterranean: here France and Italy must find themselves at variance whether they willed it or not. 'The configuration of the terrestial globe not being amenable to change, they will be always rivals and often enemies.' Nature has thrown between them an apple of discord, the possession of which they will not cease to contest. The Mediterranean ought to become an Italian lake. 'It is impossible for Italy to put up with the perpetual threats of France to obtain the mastery over Tunis, which would be for her the first stage to arriving in Sardinia.'

At the Berlin Congress eight years later, Prince Bismarck pressed the same views upon Count Corti, the Italian delegate. He would have been glad to see the Italians go to Tunis, but Count Corti ingenuously replied: 'You want to make us quarrel with France.' Meanwhile the Englishman who represented France and the Englishman who represented England were discussing the same subject, and out of their discussion arose the French occupation of Tunis. Disquieting rumours got about at once, but they were dispelled. 'No French Government would be so rash,' said Gambetta, 'as to make Italy the *irreconcilable* foe of France.' M. Waddington declared that he was personally opposed to the acquisition of Tunis, and gave his word of honour that nothing would be done without the full consent of Italy. What was done and how it was done is known to all. And so it happens that a great French naval station is in course of construction almost within sight of Sicily *and of Malta*.

In the document communicated by Bismarck to Mazzini, there is a curious inclusion of Trieste among Italian seaports which seems to indicate that he was still not averse from a rectification of the Italian north-east frontier. Whence it may be supposed that he expected to find Austria ranged on the part of France in the struggle for the Rhine bank. To explain how it was that this did not happen, we must leave the Chancellor and the Revolutionist, and see what at the same time was going on between Napoleon on the one side and Austria and Italy on the other.

The French Emperor was not so infatuated as to court

the risk of making war on Prussia single-handed if he could avoid it. He hoped for a triple alliance of France, Austria and Italy, or, if that could not be compassed, a dual alliance of France with either of these Powers. Now, wisely or unwisely, both the Italian and Austrian Governments were far from rejecting these proposals off-hand. The secret negotiations lasted from 1868 till June 1869. They took the shape of informal letters between the King of Italy and Napoleon, and of private communications with Count Beust through Prince Metternich, the Austrian Ambassador in Paris, who was the intimate friend and confidant of the Emperor and Empress. General Menabrea was not let into the secret till later. With regard to Victor Emmanuel, there is no doubt that he wished with all his heart to be able to do a good turn to his Imperial ally of 1859 if the occasion presented itself. Some men see their wives even to old age as they saw them when they were young and fair. The first print on the retina of the mental vision was so strong that no later impression can change or efface it. This hallucination is not confined to the marital relationship, and Victor Emmanuel never left off seeing Napoleon in one sole light: as the friend of Solferino. It may be that he perceived what the Italians did not perceive: that the obligation was owed to Napoleon alone, while all France had a part in the subsequent injuries. At any rate the idea of refusing the Emperor's appeal was repugnant in the extreme to the Italian King, who personally would have strained any point rather than give that refusal.

The King, however, and General Menabrea, who was finally admitted into the conspiracy, could not be blind to the fact that an unpopular war might create so great an agitation in the country that the dynasty itself would be in danger. A war for France while the French were in

Rome would have raised one storm of indignation from Palermo to Turin. So their ultimatum was this: Rome capital of Italy, or no alliance.

There remained Austria, but if Napoleon ever hoped to conclude a separate treaty with her, he was to discover his mistake. From the moment that Austria resigned the Iron Crown, the symbol of her Italian power, she acted towards Italy with a loyalty that has few parallels in history. And she, too, replied to Napoleon: Rome capital of Italy, or no alliance.

The Vatican has never forgiven this to Austria. At the present hour, while republican France with her open antagonism to all religion, is the favoured daughter of the Church, Austria, the only country in Europe except Spain where the Roman Catholic cultus retains all its original pomp and almost all its mediæval privileges, meets from the Vatican a studied plan of opposition, the object of which can only be to bring her Government to a deadlock. From France the Pope still hopes for aid in the recovery of his temporalities; from Austria he knows that he will never receive it. So much have politics and so little has religion to do now, as in all ages, with the motives that govern the Holy See.

> Ahi, Costantin, di quanto mal fu matre
> Non la tua conversion, ma quella dote
> Che da te prese il primo ricco patre!

The years 1868 and 1869 passed uneventfully for Italy. In the former year Prince Humbert married his cousin Margherita of Savoy. He was previously engaged to the Archduchess Matilda, the only daughter of the Victor of Custoza, but the young Princess met with a terrible death just when the betrothal was about to be announced. No one worthier to receive from Adelaide of Burgundy the lovely title of Queen of Italy could have been found than the Princess Margaret, who inherited the sunny charm which had endeared her father, the Duke of Genoa, to all who knew him.

In the autumn of 1869 another domestic event, the severe illness of Victor Emmanuel, gave rise to an incident which made a deep impression in Italy, and attached the nation by one link more to the King of its choice. The illness which seized Victor Emmanuel at his hunting-box of San Rossore, in a malarious part of Tuscany, proved so serious that his life was despaired of. A priest was called to hear the King's last confession, and to administer the Sacraments for the dying. After hearing the confession, the priest said he could not give absolution unless Victor Emmanuel signed a solemn retractation of all the acts performed during his reign that were contrary to the interests of the Church. The King answered, without a moment's hesitation, that he died a Christian and a Catholic, and that if he had wronged anyone he sincerely repented and asked pardon of God, but the signature demanded was a political act, and if the priest wished to talk politics his ministers were in the next room. Thither the ecclesiastic retired, but he very soon returned, and administered the rite without more ado. What had passed was this: General Menabrea, with a decision for which he cannot be too much praised, threatened the priest with instant arrest unless he surrendered his pretensions. Only those who know the extraordinary terror inspired in an Italian Catholic by the prospect of dying unshriven can appreciate the merit of the King, whose faith was childlike, in standing as firm in the presence of supernatural arms as he stood before the Austrian guns.

Menabrea's administration was then upon the eve of

falling. The cause was one of those financial crises that were symptomatic of a mischief which has been growing from then till now, when some critics think they see in it the fatal upas tree of Italy. The process of transforming a country where everything was wanting—roads, railways, lines of navigation, schools, water, lighting, sanitary provisions, and the other hundred thousand requirements of modern life—into the Italy of to-day, where all these things have made leaps almost incredible to those who knew her in her former state, has proved costly without example. During the whole period it has been necessary to spend in ever-increasing ratio on the army and navy, and this expenditure, though emphatically not the chief, has yet been a concomitant cause of financial trouble. The point cannot be inquired into here of how far greater wisdom and higher character in Italian public servants might have limited the evil and reconciled progress with economy; but it may be said that if the path entered upon by the man who took charge of the exchequer after Menabrea's fall, Quintino Sella, had been rigorously followed by his successors, the present situation would not be what it is.

Giovanni Lanza assumed the premiership in the government in which Sella was Minister of Finance. Both these politicians were Piedmontese, and both were known as men of conspicuous integrity, but Lanza's rigid conservatism made it seem unlikely that the Roman question would take a fresh turn under his administration. In politics, however, the unlikely is what generally happens; events are stronger than men.

On the 8th of December the twenty-first Ecumenical Council assembled in Rome. From the day of its meeting, in spite of the strenuous opposition of its most learned and illustrious members, there was no more doubt that the dogma under consideration would be voted by the partly astute and partly complaisant majority than that it would have been rejected in the twenty preceding Councils. On the 18th of July 1870, the Pope was proclaimed Infallible.

That was a moment of excitement such as has not often thrilled Europe, but the cause was not the Infallibility of Pius IX. On the 16th, Napoleon declared war with Prussia. War, like death, comes as a shock, however plainly it has been foreseen; besides, it was only the well-informed who knew how near the match had been to the powder-magazine for two years and more. Whether the explosion, at the last, was timed by Napoleon or by Bismarck is not of great importance; it could have been but little delayed. Napoleon was beset alike by the revolutionary spectre and by the gaunt King of Terrors; he knew the throw was desperate, but with the gambler's instinct, which had always been so strong in him, he was magnetised by it because it was desperate. Pitiful egotist though he was, history may forgive him sooner than it forgives the selfish Chauvinism of Thiers, who had been goading his countrymen to war ever since Sadowa, or the insane bigotry of the party which, having triumphed over revolution at Mentana, now sought to triumph over heresy in what the Empress called 'Ma guerre.'

Napoleon had the remaining sagacity to see the extreme danger of leaving a few thousand men isolated in Rome at a time when, happen what might, it would be impossible to reinforce them. Directly after declaring war, notwithstanding the cries of the Ultramontanes, he decided on recalling the French troops. He induced the Italian Government to resume the obligations of the September Convention, by which the inviolability of the Papal frontier was guaranteed. Lanza is open to grave criticism for entering into a contract which it was morally certain that he would not be able to keep. Perhaps he hoped that Napoleon would himself release Italy from her bond. But the 'Jamais' of Rouher stood in the way. Could the Emperor, after such boasting, coolly throw the Pope overboard the first time it suited his convenience? Moreover, his present Prime Minister, M. Emile Olivier, when the question was put to him, did not hesitate to renew the declaration that the Italians must not be allowed to go to Rome.

Napoleon made some last frantic efforts to get Austria and Italy to befriend him unconditionally. How far he knew the real state of his army before he declared war may be doubtful, but that he possessed overwhelming proof of it, even before the first defeats, cannot be doubted at all. His heart was not so light as his Prime Minister's. At the end of July he sent General Türr on a secret mission to try and obtain the help of Austria and Italy. The Hungarian general wrote from Florence, that unless something could be done to assure Italy that the national question would be settled in accordance with the wishes of her people, the Italian alliance was not possible. The Convention, he pointed out, was a bane instead of a boon to Italy. This letter was answered by a telegram through the French Ambassador at Vienna: 'Can't do anything for Rome; if Italy will not march, let her stand still.

As in the former negotiations, Austria took her stand on precisely the same ground as Italy. And thus it was that France plunged into the campaign of 1870 singlehanded.

After Wörth, and once more after Gravelotte, the endeavour to draw Italy into the struggle was renewed.

Napoleon was aware that Victor Emmanuel was wildly anxious to come to the rescue, and on this personal goodwill his last hope was built. Prince Napoleon was despatched from the camp at Châlons to see what he could do. At this eleventh hour (19th August) Napoleon was ready to yield about Rome. At the camp, the influence which guided him in Paris was less felt, or it is probable that he would not have yielded even now. Prince Napoleon carried a sheet of white paper with the Emperor's signature at the foot. He showed it to Lanza when he reached Florence, and told him to fill it up as he chose. Whatever he asked for was already granted. A month before, such terms would have won both Italy and Austria—not now.

The Prince found his father-in-law eager to give the 50,000 men that were asked for, but the ministers protested that the Italian army was unprepared for war. Still, to satisfy the King, who signified his irritation so clearly to Lanza that this good servant was on the point of resigning, they agreed to submit the case to Austria; if Austria would co-operate, they would re-consider their decision. Austria replied: 'Too late.'

When, in 1873, Victor Emmanuel paid a visit to Berlin, he caused some sensation at a grand State banquet by saying to his host: 'But for these gentlemen' (and he waved his hand towards the ministers who accompanied him) 'I should have gone to war with you.' Courtiers did not know which way to look, but the aged Emperor was not displeased by the soldierly bluntness of the avowal.

Prince Napoleon remained in Florence, throwing away his eloquence, till the 2nd of September cut short the argument. When he had left his cousin, the Emperor was resolved to fall back on Paris according to Mac-

Mahon's plan, but the ministers and the Empress Regent forced him to his doom. On the 2nd of September Sédan was lost; on the 4th the Empire fell.

'And to think,' exclaimed Victor Emmanuel when he heard the news, 'that this good man was always wanting to give me advice!'

From the date of the declaration of war, and still more since the evacuation of Rome by the French troops (begun on the 29th of July, ended on the 19th of August), Italy had been too deeply agitated for any sane person to suppose that the prescriptive right of the nation to seize the opportunity which offered itself of completing its unity could be resisted by the artificial dyke of a compromise which made the Government the instrument of France. Lanza was determined to maintain order; he had Mazzini arrested at Palermo, and suppressed disorders where they occurred, but the rising tide of the will of the people could not be suppressed, and had the ministry resisted it, something more than the ministry would have fallen.

In justification of Lanza's slowness to move, and of the apparent, if not real, unwillingness with which he took every forward step, it is contended that more precipitate action would have caused what most people will agree would have been a misfortune for Italy, the departure of the Pope from Rome. It was only on the 29th of August that the Minister of Foreign Affairs, Visconti-Venosta, sent a memorandum to the European Powers which announced that the Government had decided on occupying Rome at once. A week after, the fall of the Empire came as a godsend to the ministry which had possibly hardly deserved such a stroke of luck. They were no longer hampered by the September Convention, because the September Convention was dead.

This was amply admitted by Jules Favre, though he declined to denounce the treaty formally; even a French Radical, in the hour of setting up the Republic, was afraid to proclaim aloud that France renounced all claim to interfere in her neighbour's concerns.

Of the other Powers, Switzerland signified her approval, and the rest engaged to abstain from any opposition.

The King addressed a letter to the Pope, in which, with the affection of a son and the faith of a Catholic, he appealed to his spirit of benevolence and his Italian patriotism to speak the word of peace in the midst of the storm of war that was distracting Europe, and to accept the love and protection of the people of Italy in lieu of a sovereignty which could not stand without the support of foreign arms. Pius IX. merely answered by saying that the letter was not worthy of an affectionate son, and that he prayed God to bestow upon His Majesty the mercy of which he had much need. To the bearer of the royal appeal, Count Ponza di San Martino, he said that he might yield to violence, but would never sanction injustice.

This was about the time that the Pope, on his side, wrote an appeal not, be it observed, to any Catholic monarch, but to King William of Prussia, who would certainly not have read unmoved the complaint of one who, like himself, was crowned with white hairs, but Count Bismarck took the precaution of causing the letter not to reach his master's hands till the Italians were in Rome.

The day following the Pope's interview with Count Ponza, the 11th of September, the Italian troops received the order to enter the Papal states. For several weeks five divisions under General Cadorna had been in course of concentration along the frontier; this force now marched on Rome. Bixio was sent to Civita Vecchia where resistance was expected, and had been ordered by

Kanzler, but the native element prevailed over the foreign in the garrison, and the Spanish commandant, Colonel Serra, interpreting the wishes of the Roman troops, surrendered without firing a shot.

Great was the indignation of the French and Belgian Zouaves. They were resolved that the same thing should not happen in Rome. That there was a chance of avoiding bloodshed may be inferred, from Count Arnim's numerous journeys between the Vatican and General Cadorna's headquarters outside Porta Salara; the Prussian representative hoping till the last moment to arrange matters in a pacific sense. Cardinal Antonelli is said to have been nearly persuaded, when he received a message from Colonel Charette in these terms: 'You had better go and say mass while we look after defending you.' The war party so far carried the day that the Pope adhered to his plan of 'sufficient resistance to show that he yielded only to force.'

At half-past five on the morning of the 20th of September, all attempts at conciliation having failed, the Italian attack was opened upon five different points, Porta San Pancrazio, Porta San Giovanni Laterano, Porta San Lorenzo, Porta del Popolo and Porta Pia. General Mazé de la Roche's division attacked the latter gate, and the wall near it, in which a breach was rapidly effected by the steady fire of the Italian batteries, though it was not till past eight o'clock that it seemed large enough to admit of an assault. Then the 41st of the line, and the 12th and 34th Bersaglieri were ordered up, and dashed into the breach with the cry of 'Savoia! Savoia!' The challenge was returned by the Zouaves with their 'Vive Pie Neuf.' They had been already ordered to desist, as the Pope's instructions were clear, 'to stop when a breach was made;' but on the plea that the order was sent to them verbally they continued firing. When the written order came, they displayed a white handkerchief fastened to a bayonet, and at this point the fight was over. Hundreds of Roman exiles poured through the breach after the soldiers; 15,000 of them had arrived or were arriving at the gates of the city.

At the same time the white flag was hoisted on Porta Pia, but on the advance of the 40th Regiment and a battalion of Bersaglieri, shots were fired which killed and wounded several officers and men; when they saw their companions falling, the troops could not be restrained from scaling the barricade which had been formed to defend the gate, and surrounding and capturing the Zouaves who were behind it. The whole Diplomatic Corps now came out in full uniform to urge General Cadorna to effect the occupation as quickly as possible, that order might be maintained. By midday, the Italian troops had penetrated into most parts of the city left of the Tiber; as yet there was no formal capitulation on the part of the Zouaves, and their attitude was not exactly reassuring. This did not prevent the population, both men and women, from filling the streets and greeting the Italians with every sign of rejoicing. They cheered, they wept, they kissed the national flag, and the cry of *Roma Capitale* drowned all other cries, even as the fact it saluted closed the discords and the factions of ages.

In the afternoon all the Papal troops were persuaded to lay down their arms, which, in the case of the foreigners, were given back to them. Next day they were reviewed by General Cadorna. As the Italians presented arms to the retiring host, some of the Antibes Legion shouted at them : 'We are French, we shall meet you again.' The Roman troops were sent to their homes; the foreigners conducted to the frontier. Charette and other of the French officers went to the battlefields of their prostrate country, and thus it came to pass that the Pope's defenders were found fighting side by side with Garibaldi; they, indeed, only doing their simple duty, but he, acting on an impulse of Quixotic generosity which was repaid—the world knows how!

Cadorna received three pressing requests from the Pope to occupy the Leonine City, and the third he granted. The idea of leaving the part of Rome on which the Vatican stands under the Pope's jurisdiction had been long favoured by a certain class of politicians, and Lanza made a last effort to give it effect by excluding the Leonine City from the plebiscite which was ordered to take place in Rome and in the Roman province on the 2nd of October. It was in vain. The first voting urn to arrive at the Capitol on the appointed day was a glass receptacle borne by a huge Trasteverino, and preceded by a banner inscribed: 'Città Leonina Si.' As the Government had not supplied the inhabitants with an official urn, it occurred to them to provide themselves with an unofficial one in which they duly deposited their votes. The Roman plebiscite yielded the results of 133,681 affirmative and 1507 negative votes.

In December the Italian Parliament met for the last time in the Hall of the Five Hundred. 'Italy,' said the King in the speech from the throne, 'is free and united; it depends on us to make her great and happy.' Of this last session at Florence the principal labour was the Act embodying the Papal guarantees which was intended to safeguard the legitimate independence and decorum of the Holy See on the lines formerly advocated by Cavour. Neither extreme party was satisfied, but it seemed at first not unlikely that the Pope would tacitly acquiesce in the arrangement. The first monthly payment of the national dotation, calculated to correspond with his civil list, was accepted. But though the influence of Cardinal Antonelli and the Italian prelates had been sufficient to keep the Pope in Rome, the influence of those who wished him to leave was strong enough to establish at the Vatican the intransigent policy which has been pursued till now.

During the flood of the Tiber which devastated the city that winter, the King of Italy paid a first informal visit to his capital, accompanied only by a few attendants, and bent on bringing help to the suffering population. In July 1872, he made his solemn entry, and at the same time the seat of Government was transferred to the Eternal City.

Victor Emmanuel could say what few men have been able to say of so large a promise: 'I have kept my word.' He gathered up the Italian flag from the dust of Novara, and carried it to the Capitol. In spite of the grandeur of republican tradition in Italy, and the lofty character of the men who represented it during the struggle for unity, a study of these events leaves on the mind the conviction that, at least in our time, the country could neither have been freed from the stranger nor welded into a single body-politic without a symbol which appealed to the imagination, and a centre of gravity which kept the diverse elements together by giving the whole its proper balance. The Liberating Prince whom Machiavelli sought was found in the Savoyard King. 'Quali porte se gli serrerebbono? Quali popoli gli negherebbono la obbedienza? Quale invidia se gli opporrebbe? Quale Italiano gli negherebbe l'ossequio?' To fill the appointed part Victor Emmanuel possessed the supreme qualification, which was patriotism. Though he came of an ambitious race, not even his enemies could with any seriousness bring to his charge personal ambition, since every step which took him further from the Alps, his fathers' cradle, involved a sacrifice of tastes and habits, and of most that made life congenial. When his work was finished, though he was not old, he had the presentiment that he should not long survive its completion. And so it proved.

In the first days of January 1878, the King was seized with one of those attacks on the lungs which his vigorous constitution had hitherto enabled him to throw off. But in Rome this kind of illness is more fatal than elsewhere, and the doctors were soon obliged to tell him that there was no hope. 'Are we come to that?' he asked; and then directed that the chaplain should be summoned. There was no repetition of the scene at San Rossore; the highest authority had already sanctioned the adminstration of the Sacraments to the dying King, nay, it is said that the Pope's first impulse was to be himself the bearer of them. At that hour the man got the better of the priest; Francis drove out Dominic. The heart that had been made to pity and the lips that had been formed to bless returned to their natural functions. When the aged Pius heard that all was over, exclaimed: 'He died like a Christian, a Sovereign and an honest man (galantuomo).' Very soon the Pope followed the King to the grave, and so, almost together, these two historical figures disappear.

Six years before, solitary and unsatisfied, Mazzini died at Pisa, his heart gnawed with the desire of the extreme, as the hearts have been of all those who aspired less to change what men do, or even what they believe, than what they are. More deep than political regrets was the pain with which he watched the absorption of human energies in the race for wealth, for ease, for material happiness; he discerned that if the egotism of capital led to oppression, the egotism of labour would lead to anarchy. To the end he preached the moral law of which he had been the apostle through life. His last message to his countrymen, written when the pen was falling from his hand, was a warning to Italian workingmen to beware of the false gods of the new socialism. When others saw darkness he saw light; now, Cassandra-like, he saw darkness when others saw light; yet he did not doubt the ultimate triumph of the light, but he no longer thought that his eyes would see it, and he was glad to close them.

Less sad, notwithstanding his physical martyrdom, were Garibaldi's last years. Italy showed him an unforgetting love; when he came to the continent, the same multitudes waited for him as of old, but instead of cheers there was a not less impressive silence now, lest the invalid should be disturbed. Soon after the transfer of the capital he went to Rome to speak in favour of the works by which it was proposed to control the inundations of the Tiber, and it was curious to hear it said on all sides that, of course, the Tiber works must be taken in hand as Garibaldi wished it. Pius IX. summed up the situation wittily in the remark: 'Lately we were two here; now we are three.' The old hero invoked the day when bayonets might be turned into pruning-hooks, but he by no means thought that it had arrived, and in the meanwhile he urged the Italians to look to their defences, and above all, 'to be strong on the sea, like England.' In the matter of government he remained the impenitent advocate of the rule of one honest man—call him Dictator or what you please, so he be one! Garibaldi died at Caprera on the 2nd of June 1882.

Rome, the Capital

The play was ended, the actors vanished :

Δότε κρότον, καὶ πάντες ὑμεῖς μετὰ χαρᾶς κτυπήσατε.

A new epoch has begun which need not detain the chronicler of Italian Liberation. The prose of possession succeeds the poetry of desire. Nothing, however, can lessen the greatness of the achievement. With regard to the future, it may be allowable to recall the superstition which, like so many other seemingly meaningless beliefs, becomes full of meaning when read according to the spirit : that a house stands long if its foundations be watered with the blood of sacrifice. No work of man was ever watered with a purer blood than the restoration of Italy to the ranks of living nations. And the last word of this book shall be Hope.

THE END.

INDEX

ALBRECHT, Archduke, 364, 369.
Alessandria, 225.
Alfieri, 8, 18.
Alemann, General, 379.
Amedeo, Prince, 169, 344, 368.
Amadeus, Victor, 73.
Amadeus with the Tail, 172.
Ampère, 237.
Andreoli, Giuseppe, 51.
Antonelli, Cardinal, 101, 130, 184, 189, 191, 398, 409.
Anzani, Francesco, 124.
Appel, General, 140.
Arnim, Count, 409.
Aspre, d', General, 104, 139, 140.
Aspromonte, 300, 348, 350.
Austerlitz, 5.
Azeglio, Massimo d', 73, 74, 113, 175, 190, 195, 206.

BANDIERA, 67-69.
Bassi, Ugo, 154, 163.
Bastide, Jules, 117.
Bava, General, 106, 114.
Bazaine, Marshal, 243
Beauharnais, Eugène, 6-9.
Beauregard, Costa de, 224.
Bellegarde, Marshal, 9-11.
Benedek, 240, 244, 245.
Bentinck, Lord William, 7, 11, 13, 14.
Bentivegna, Count, 209..
Berlin, Congress of, 399.
Bertani, Dr, 231, 297, 309.
Beust, Count, 400.
Bianchi, B. dei, 330.
Bismarck, 358, 397-8, 408.
Bixio, 101, 272, 301, 318, 360, 368, 408.
Boccheciampi, 68.
Borjès, Josè, 331.
Brescia, Revolution at, 142, 232, 245, 343.
Briganti, General, 301, 302.
Brofferio, 179.
Bronzetta, Pilade, 318, 320.
Bubna, Count, 43.
Brunetti, Angelo, 82.
Buol, Count, 223
Buonaparte, Joseph, 6.
Buonaparte, Lucien, 213.

CADORNA, Gen., 408-9, 410-11.
Caiazzo, 316.
Cairoli, Benedetto, 281, 389, 391.
Calabria helps Garibaldi, 300.
Calandrelli, 184.
Calatafimi, 278.
Calderai del Contrapeso, 24.
Campo Formio, Treaty of, 4.
Canrobert, General, 229.
Capponi, 39, 135.
Caprera, 221, 325, 328, 337, 385, 396.
Capua, War around, 305, 318; capitulation, 326.
Carignano, Prince of, 30, 32, 37.
Carignano, Eugène de, 333.
Carlyle, Thomas, 69.
Caroline, Queen, 13.
Casati, 100.
Caserta, 314, 318.
Carusso, 331.
Castelfidardo, 322, 337.
Castelnuovo, burning of village, 107.
Castel Sant' Elmo, 306, 307.
Castiglione, Count, 370.
Castlereagh, Lord, 11, 12, 14, 27.
Cattaneo, 100; party of,
Cavour, Count, 85; becomes minister, 192; resolves Piedmont shall join Allies in Crimean War, 202; visits England, 204; meets Napoleon at Plombières, 247; resigns office, 249; recalled, 260; resolves to invade Papal States, 310; Garibaldi's veterans, 335; Rome to be capital, 337; death, 339.
Centurioni, Society of, 78.
Charette, General, 389.
Charles III., 208, 236.
Charles Albert, 30, 31, 34, 36, 38, 46; accession, 56; Re Tentenna, 74; promulgates Charter, 94; retreat to Milan, 114; abdicates, 141; burial, 181.
Charles Emmanuel, 19, 30.
Charles Felix, Duke of Genoa, 30, 31, 36, 56.
Charles Ludovico, 87.
Chiavone, General, 330.
Chretien, General, 284, 286.
Chrzanowski, 139, 140.
Cialdini, General, 322, 328, 332, 348, 366, 370, 337.
Cipriani, L., 255.

Index

Civita Vecchia, the French at, 391-408.
Clam Gallas, Count, 243.
Clarendon, Lord, 185, 206.
Clary, General, 292.
Clotilde, Princess, 217, 218.
Colonna, General, 281.
Commacchio, 16.
Confalonieri, Count, 39, 41, 42, 43, 45, 64.
Conneau, 216.
Corsini, Prince, 130, 135.
Corti, Count, 399.
Cosenz, 301, 308, 360.
Cowley, Lord, 260.
Crispi, Francesco, 269, 292, 294.
Cristina, Princess, 238.
Crocco, 331.
Custozza, 114, 370.

DALMATIA, sold with Venice, 364.
Dante, 1-3, 341, 363.
De Castillia, 42.
Del Bosco, 290, 291.
Depretis, Agostino, 293.
D'Este, Francis, 31, 51.
Dolfi, Giuseppe, 235.
Drouyn de Lhuys, 184.
Dunne, Colonel, 289, 319.
Durando, General, 102, 107, 112.

EBOLI, 303.
Elliot, Mr, 314.
Ernest, Duke of Saxe-Coburg, 199, 266.

FALLOUX, de, 185.
Fanti, General, 257, 312, 334.
Farini, L. C., 73, 127, 237, 255, 257, 333, 339.
Faro, Cape of, 297, 298, 300.
Favre, Jules, 215, 397.
Ferdinand II, 48, 90, 92, 93, 102, 188, 237.
Ferdinand III., 12, 26, 28.
Ferdinand, Emperor of Austria, 118.
Ferrara, Austrians in, 16.
Ferretti, Cardinal, 82.
Fleury, General, 247.
Florence, capital of Italy, 352-411.
Forbes, Commander, 304, 305.
Foscolo, Ugo, 17, 18.
Fra Giacomo, 201, 339.
Francis I., 47
Francis II., 238, 267, 295, 299, 306, 327, 330.
Francis Joseph, Emperor, 119, 160, 227, 240, 242, 249.

GAETA, Fall of, 317-326.
Gamba, Pietro, 24, 50.
Gambetta, 399.
Gaminara, Emmanuele, 9.
Garibaldi, Giuseppe, 64, 120; declared enemy of the State, 121; in South America, 123; marries Anita, 123; in Rome, 148; death of Anita, 158; leaves Caprera, 221, 256-263; Sicilian expedition, 256; march on Naples, 298; Battle of Solferino, 319; of Garigliano, 323; returns to Caprera, 325, 334, 347;

wounded, 349; arrested, 383; in Rome, 39 defeat at Mentana, 394; death, 414.
Garibaldi, Menotti, 257, 280, 286, 386, 392.
Garigliano, Battle of, 323.
Genoa, ceded to Sardinia, 13-15.
Genoa, Charles Felix, Duke of, 30-32.
Ghio, General, 302, 303.
Giacinta di Collegno, 38.
Gioberti, 78, 133.
Gladstone, W. E., 187.
Goito, Battle of, 112.
Gravelotte, Battle of, 405.
Gregory XVI., 50, 76, 77.
Guerrazzi, 135, 136.
Gyulai, Count, 227, 230, 231, 240.

HAYNAU, General, 145, 162.
Hess, General, 228, 230, 242.
Hilliers, Baraguay d', 229.
Hoche, 5.
Hortense, Queen, 55.
Humbert of the White Hands, 172.

IMMACULATE CONCEPTION, Doctrine of, 77.

JESUITS, 51, 75, 128, 379.

KANZLER, General, 392.
Kellersperg, Baron von, 227.
Klapka, General, 357.
Kohlen-Brenners, 22.
Kossuth, 246, 253.
Kuhn, General, 372.

LADERCHI, Count, 40.
La Farina, 295.
La Gala, 331.
Lamartine, 117.
La Marmora, General, 170, 171, 202, 348, 3! 357, 359, 361-366.
Lamoricière, General, 311, 313.
Lannes, Marshal, 231.
Lanza, General, 282, 283, 286, 403, 406, 407.
Le Bœuf, General, 379.
Leo XII., 49.
Leopardi, 186.
Leopold II., 89, 159, 234.
Lesseps, Ferdinand, 151, 154.
Letizia, General, 284, 286.
Liborio Romano, 306.
Lincoln, President, 343.
Lissa, Battle of, 374.
Lodi, 4.
Lombardy, trials in, 40; Revolution, 100, 1(
Louis Philippe, 128.
Lucca, 16.

MACHIAVELLI, 2, 3, 52, 412.
MacMahon, Marshal, 229, 233, 244, 406.
Magenta, Battle of, 232, 234, 236.
Malghella, 23.
Malmesbury, Lord, 223.
Mamelli, Goffredo, 154, 155.
Manin, Daniel, 99, 116, 160, 168, 203.

Index

Mantua, Prince Eugene in, 8-10; gallant defence, 105.
Manzoni, Alessandro, 19.
Margaret, Queen, 199, 401.
Maria Adelaide, Queen, 169.
Maria Teresa, Queen, 31.
Marie Louise, Empress, 12, 31; death, 88.
Marie Sofia, Princess, 237.
Mamiani, Terenzio, 126, 131.
Maroncelli, Pietro, 44.
Marryat, Captain, 274.
Marsala, 274, 276, 345.
Martinengo, Count, 145.
Mary, Princess, of Cambridge, 205
Mastai Ferretti, Cardinal, 77.
Matilda, Archduchess, 401.
Maximilian, Archduke, 211.
Mazzini, Giuseppe, 53, 57, 58; early life, 59; becomes a Carbonaro, 60; Association of Young Italy, 63; takes refuge in England, 66; writes 'Duties of Man,' 67; meets Garibaldi, 120; at Rome, 132, 157; letters from Orsini, 214; protests against Napoleonic war, 220; in Naples, 313. 354-357; corresponds with the king, 398; arrested, 407; death, 413.
Medici, Giacomo, 124, 125, 155, 231, 273, 289, 292, 301, 318, 360.
Melegnano, Battle of, 240.
Menabrea, General, 388-395, 400-402.
Menechini, 25.
Menotti, Ciro, 52, 55, 64.
Mentana, Battle of, 392-397, 404.
Merode, Marquis de, 330.
Messina, held by Royal troops, 290; evacuated, 295.
Metternich, Prince, 15, 32, 46, 56, 83, 84, 86, 95, 400.
Mezzacapo, 237.
Micca, Pietro, 36.
Milan, revolt, 8-10; fighting in the city, 95; Austrains depart, 233.
Milano, Ageslao, 208.
Milazzo, Battle of, 290.
Mincio, Battle of, 107, 241, 365, 366, 369.
Minghetti, Marco, 101, 129.
Minto, Lord, 87, 116
Misilmeri, 280.
Misley, Dr, 52.
Missori, Major. 291.
Modena, revolution in, 53.
Monreale, 278.
Montalembert, 185.
Montanelli, Giuseppe, 112, 135, 136.
Monti, 16.
Montebello, Battle of, 231.
Morelli, 25, 29.
Moro, Domenico, 68.
Moscow, retreat from, 8.
Mundy, Admiral, 282, 283, 287, 288, 314, 320, 324, 354.
Murat, Joachim, 6, 7, 10, 13, 23.

Napier, Lord, 90, 92.
Naples, 25-29, 101; massacre, 110; misrule in, 186-187; Galibaldi's march on, 299; King enters, 324.
Napoleon Buonaparte, 2-10, 240.
Napoleon III., 55; elected President of French Republic, 119, 149; letter to Ney, 185; attempt on his life, 212; compact at Plombières, 217, 253; demands Nice and Savoy, 260-262; era of peace, 358.
Napoleon, Prince, 185, 229, 235, 351, 406.
Nelaton, Dr, 349.
Ney, Edgar, 185.
Nice, cession of, 221, 224, 258, 262
Nicotera, 209, 297.
Niel, 229, 244.
Ninco-Nanco, 330.
Normanby, Lord, 117, 228.
Novara, 37-39; battle of, 141, 412.
Nugent, General, 107, 112, 113, 143.

O'Donnell, Count, 95.
Oliphant, Laurence, 263, 266.
Olivier, Emile, 405.
Orsini, Colonel, 280.
Orsini, Felice, 213, 216.
Oudinot, General, 150, 156.

Palermo, strange discovery, 92; Sicilian expedition, 271-290; insurrection, 381.
Pallavicini, Giorgio, 42, 137, 309, 314, 344, 348, 360.
Palma, 330.
Palmerston, Lord, 83, 111, 117, 161, 266, 282, 355, 371.
Panizzi, Anthony, 52.
Paris, Treaty of, 13; Congress of, 185.
Parma, 12-16.
Passaglia, 341.
Pastrengo, Battle of, 109.
Peard, Colonel, 303-306.
Pellico, Silvio, 40, 43.
Pepe, Guglielmo, 29, 111, 126.
Perier, Casimir, 53.
Persano, Admiral, 274, 288, 308, 372, 377.
Peschiera, 112, 240, 242, 248.
Petitti, General, 378.
Petre, 81, 82.
Piaceuza, garrisoned by Austrians, 16.
Piedmont, Revolution in, 33; struggle with the Church, 189-192.
Pietri, 253.
Pilone, 330.
Pilo, Rosalino, 270, 278.
Pisacane, Carlo, 209
Pius VII., 12, 49.
Pius VIII., 50
Pius IX., 78; election, 79, 93; grants constitution, 101; encyclical letter, 108; flight to Gaeta, 130; calls foreign aid to support temporal power, 132; thanksgiving, 183, 259; character, 311; calls to arms, 363, 408; death, 413.
Plombières, 217; meeting between Napoleon and Cavour.
Poerio, Carlo, 90, 126, 134.
Pralormo, Count, 176.

Prina, General, 8.
Prince Consort, 198, 258.

RADETSKY, 96, 104, 111, 139, 162, 167, 195, 249.
Raimondi, Captain, 35
Rattazzi, 138, 200, 207, 252, 260, 340, 342, 350, 382, 384.
Reggio, 301, 347.
Renzi, Pietro, 73.
Ricasoli, Baron, 135, 235, 236, 255, 335, 340, 361.
Rienzi, Cola di, 132.
Rimini, 9.
Risorgimento, 194.
Rolandis, de, 51.
Romagna, Carbonarism in the, 24, 50.
Rome, Entry of French, 157; French depart from, 382; declared capital, 412
Romeo, Domenico. 90.
Rossaroll, General, 29.
Rossetti, Gabriele, 49.
Rossi, 81, 128.
Rouher, 397, 405.
Ruffini, Jacobo, 65.
Ruskin, J., 192.
Russell, Lord John, 252, 268, 274, 327.
Russell, Odo, 225.

SADOWA, Battle of, 370.
Salemi, 275.
Salerno, 305.
San Bon, 374.
Sanfedesti, Secret Society of, 50.
San Marino, 13, 73.
San Martino, Count, 408.
Santa Rosa, 191.
Santorre di Santa Rosa, 38.
Sardinia—War with Austria, 137.
Savoy, 13; cession of, 221, 224, 258, 259, 262.
Schmidt, Colonel, 237.
Schwarzenberg, Prince, 176, 187, 243, 244.
Sella, Quintino, 361.
Settembrini, 209.
Sicily—Insurrection, 91; Sicilian expedition, 266.
Silvati, 25, 29.
Sirtori, 272, 360.
Speri, Tito, 144.
Spielberg, 44.
Solaro della Margherita, 223.
Solferino. Battle of, 243, 245.
Superga, the, 181.

TALLEYRAND, Prince, 32, 260, 264.
Tardio, 330.
Tchernaja, Battle of, 202.
Tegethoff, Admiral, 373-377.
Theobald de Brie, 22.
Theodolinda, Crown of, 6.
Thiers, 175, 397, 404.

Thurn, General, 140.
Ticino, 120, 139, 226, 228, 233.
Tolentino, Battle of, 10.
Torelli, Prince, 134.
Tortona, 230.
Trazegnies, Marquis de, 331.
Trentino, 343, 363, 371.
Trescorre, 342, 343.
Türr, General, 315, 405.

ULLOA, General, 304.
Ultramontanes, 190, 259, 397, 404.
Umberto, Prince, 169, 344, 367, 368, 401.
Urban, 231, 232.

VACCA, Admiral, 374.
Vaillant, General, 229, 261.
Vecchj, Colonel, 328.
Venice, 3-5; political trials in, 40-44; Austrian expelled, 99; re-occupied by Austria, 160-163 251, 322, 356, 371; united to Italy, 379.
Venosta, 350, 361, 407.
Verona, Congress of, 56.
Victor Amadeus, 181.
Victor Emmanuel I., at Turin, 12; King of Sardinia, 30; abdicates, 36; recommend mercy, 38.
Victor Emmanuel II.; accession, 141; unpopularity, 165-166; visits English and French courts, 204; invites Garibaldi to join his army, 221; enters Milan, 234; courage at Soferino, 245; peace with Austria, 249 letter to Napoleon, 255; hailed King of Italy, 323; entry into Naples, 324; in Venice, 380; illness, 402; visit to Berlin 406; death, 413.
Victoria, Queen, 261.
Vienna, Congress of, 13, 15, 32, 10; Treaty of 379.
Vimercati, Count, 168, 169.
Volturno, 307, 313, 315; Battle of, 319.

WADDINGTON, 399.
Welden, General, 127.
Wellesley, Admiral, 68.
Wellington, Duke of, 56.
William I., Emperor, 358, 408.
Wilmot, Lieutenant, 280, 284.
Wörth, Battle of, 405.
Wratislaw, 140.

YOUNG ITALY, Association of, founded by Mazzini, 63.

ZAMBONI, Luigi, 51.
Zedwitz, 243, 244.
Zobel, 232.
Zorzi, 126.
Zucchi, General, 54.
Zurich, Conference of, 257; Treaty of, 258.

www.ingramcontent.com/pod-product-compliance
Lightning Source LLC
Chambersburg PA
CBHW051724300426
44115CB00007B/455